CELTIC HERITAGE

CELTIC HERITAGE

Ancient Tradition in Ireland and Wales

ALWYN REES *and* BRINLEY REES

THAMES AND HUDSON

Copyright © 1961 by Alwyn and Brinley Rees

First published in Great Britain in 1961 by Thames and Hudson Ltd, London

Published in the United States of America in paperback in 1978 by Thames and Hudson Inc., 500 Fifth Avenue, New York, New York 10110

Reprinted 1998

Library of Congress Catalog Card Number 78-63038

British Library Cataloguing-in-Publication Data A catalogue record for this book is available from the British Library

ISBN 0-500-27039-2

Printed and bound in the United States of America

CONTENTS

6 Contents

PREFACE

THE BIBLIOGRAPHICAL REFERENCES AT THE END OF THE
book give some indication of what we owe both to the Celtic
scholars who have edited, translated and otherwise studied the
medieval texts in which Irish and Welsh traditions are enshrined, and to those scholars who have made the traditions
of other peoples accessible to us.

We are grateful to Professor Georges Dumézil, of the Collège
de France, for reading the typescript and particularly for the
encouragement he gave us after reading an early draft of
Chapters IV—IX. Dr Proinsias Mac Cana, of the University
College of Wales (and professor-elect in the Dublin Institute
for Advanced Studies), was also kind enough to read this
draft and the final typescript, and furthermore, both he and
Professor J. E. Caerwyn Williams, of the University College
of North Wales, read the proofs. We wish to thank them for
their advice and corrections and for the interest they have
taken in our work. None of these friends, of course, should be
held responsible for anything we have written.

We gratefully acknowledge the award of a research grant by
the Leverhulme Trustees, and we should like to thank Professor J. H. Delargy, Hon. Director of the Irish Folklore
Commission, for his kindness to us when we read at the
library of the Commission and also for allowing us to quote
so freely from his lecture on 'The Gaelic Story-teller'. Finally,
our thanks are due to Miss Phyllis Manning for typing our
manuscript and to the publishers for their patience.

7

Part One

THE TRADITION

CHAPTER I

Introduction

'. . . for as God uses the help of our reason to illuminate us, so should we likewise turn it every way, that we may be more capable of under-standing His mysteries; provided only that the mind be enlarged, according to its capacity, to the grandeur of the mysteries, and not the mysteries contracted to the narrowness of the mind.'

FRANCIS BACON

IN A CERTAIN PARISH in Galway there are more good storytellers than are to be found anywhere else in Western Europe. Such was the claim made recently by an Irish folklorist.[1] He was speaking of the art of telling traditional tales and it certainly seems as though the remoter parts of Ireland and the Western islands of Scotland will be the last refuge of this ancient art in Western Europe. Here it is still possible to come across an old man or woman who can relate scores or even hundreds of tales of 'long ago' and 'once upon a time', and in some districts people may even now foregather in a house where such tales are to be told. The storytellers are people who from early youth have availed themselves of every opportunity to add to their repertoire and to perfect their manner of delivery. Many of the listeners at the fireside gatherings will have heard the stories before. Some of them may even know them by heart, though they would never venture to recite them before an audience. But the lack of novelty seems in no way to detract from the delight they take in listening to them again.

A brief account of such a gathering in a crofter-storyteller's house was given by Alexander Carmichael at the close of the last century.[2] From his description of the scene, we will note that the peat fire was in the middle of the floor; that the house was full, with girls crouched between the knees of fathers, brothers, or friends, and boys perched wherever they could climb; that the host and his family and neighbours were engaged in crafts such as twisting heather twigs into ropes to hold down thatch, making baskets, spinning, carving, knitting, and sewing, and that there was no lack of general conversation. With 'that politeness native to the people,' the stranger was pressed to come forward and occupy the seat vacated for him beside the man of the house, and it was he who in due course asked his host to tell a story:

> 'First story from the host,
> Story till day from the guest.'

This tale was 'full of incident, action and pathos' and it was told 'simply yet graphically, and at times dramatically—compelling the undivided attention of the listener'.

Here in the memories and on the lips of these country people are the living survivals of the tradition which we shall try to present in this book. Let us look at them more closely before turning to the written texts of an earlier age. In the tiny mountain hamlet of Cíllrialaig in the south-western corner of Co. Kerry, J. H. Delargy, now Honorary Director of the Irish Folklore Commission, met in 1923 'the man in whose tales or traditions I found the inspiration to collect or have collected, in so far as in me lay, the unwritten traditions of the people of Ireland'. He was Seán Ó Conaill, a farmer-fisherman, then seventy years of age. It is worth quoting Professor Delargy's description of his background and his art at some length.[3]

> 'His family had lived in the same place for at least five generations. . . . He had never left his native district except on the memorable occasion when he had gone by train to the famous fair at Killorglin, and had walked home again! He had never been to school, was illiterate so far as unimaginative census-officials were concerned, and he could neither speak nor understand English. But he was

one of the best-read men in the unwritten literature of the people whom I have ever known, his mind a storehouse of tradition of all kinds, pithy anecdotes, and intricate hero-tales, proverbs and rimes and riddles, and other features of the rich orally preserved lore common to all Ireland three hundred years ago. He was a conscious literary artist. He took a deep pleasure in telling his tales; his language was clear and vigorous, and had in it the stuff of literature.

'It was my custom to visit him three nights a week during my holiday visits to the locality. His house was a two-roomed thatched cottage, one room a kitchen where all the indoor work was done, the other a bedroom. Over the bedroom was a loft which contained also a bed, fishing gear, a spinning-wheel, and the various lumber of an old farm-house.

'On the kitchen hearth was a turf fire, and on either side of the fire was a little stone seat from which one could look up the soot-covered chimney, and see the twinkling stars. To the right of the fire was a well-scoured deal table, and in the corner a bag of salt for salting fish. On this bag I used to sit, pulling in the table beside me, and there at various times I wrote down from the dictation of my friend nearly 200 pieces of prose narrative. Before we began work, I used to help Seán and his old wife to tidy up the house: I swept the floor, strewed clean sand on it, brought in an armful of turf, and lit the oil lamp. Part of my task was to chase the hens which hopped in over the half-door. From the door-way one gazed right down into the sea, and the distant roar of the waves crept into the kitchen and was the ever-present background of the folk-tale.

'While I wrote from Seán's dictation, the neighbours would drop in, one by one, or in small groups, and they would listen in patience until the last word of the tale was written. Then the old story-teller would take a burning ember from the fire, press it down with a horny thumb on the tobacco of his pipe, lean back in his straw-bottomed chair, and listen to the congratulations of the listeners, who, although they had probably often heard the tale before, found pleasure in hearing it again. Their plaudits merged into gossip, in which the events of the countryside would be discussed. Then after a while, someone might ask the "man of the house" to tell another story, and for perhaps an hour or so we would be transported by the wonder of the tale into the land where all one's dreams come true. Silently, the audience would listen, with a hearty laugh at the discomfiture of the villain, or at some humorous incident introduced into the tale; at times, too, they would applaud with appropriate remarks the valour of the hero fighting against impossible odds seven-headed giants or monsters from the sea, or the serried ranks of the armies of the King of the Eastern World.'

These stories were told around the fire to while away the long winter evenings. Old people speak of storytellers who could recite a different story every night the whole winter through, but it was unlucky to tell hero-tales during the day-time. Apart from this regular activity of the winter season, storytelling had a recognized place on certain ceremonial occasions: during night vigils at holy wells, after 'stations' and religious services held in private houses, and at wakes and christenings, while fishermen have often listened to tales being told at night as they waited for the haul. Stories are not the only traditional forms which came to life at these gatherings; there were also rhymes, riddles, songs, folk-prayers, proverbs, genealogical lore, and local traditions. But pride of place was given to the hero-tales and wonder-tales, many of which would take an hour to deliver, some of them as long as six hours or more.[4] It was not considered proper for a woman to tell the stories of traditional heroes. Furthermore, no man would tell a story in the presence of his father or of an elder brother, and it was young men in particular who on winter nights regularly frequented the houses where such stories were told.[5]

The storytellers do not claim to be the authors of their stories. Most of the longer tales they round off with the traditional tag: 'That is my story! If there be a lie in it, be it so! It is not I who made or invented it.' They have learned them through hearing them told by earlier practitioners of the art, be they members of their own families, neighbours, 'travelling men', or beggars, and individual stories can sometimes be traced back from one storyteller to another for several generations, in rare cases as far as the early eighteenth century.[6] The feats of memory of these unlettered folk are such as to amaze those of us who rely on the written and printed record. Of a Benbecula storyteller who died in 1954 it is said that if he heard a tale told once and then told it himself, he retained it all his life. Thus he would sometimes recite stories he had heard only once, fifty years before. A crofter-fisherman of Barra maintained that in his youth he went to listen to the same storyteller almost every winter's night for fifteen years and that he hardly ever heard the same story twice.[7]

An interesting feature of the storyteller's art, and a mark of its high antiquity, is the use made of stereotyped descriptive passages or rhetorical 'runs'. Archaic and obscure in diction, they are introduced when it is required to describe a hero setting out on his adventures, a battle being fought, or other recognized scenes. They serve to embellish the story and to impress the listeners while affording the narrator an opportunity to be ready with the next step in the story. How many of the tales themselves belong to ancient Celtic tradition no one can tell, but it can be said that as regards form, characters, and motifs, they have much in common with those tales from medieval manuscripts which are the pride and glory of Irish literature.

2

Traditional tales have not always been confined to the peasantry. On the contrary they were once a fundamental part of the culture of the aristocracy of the Celtic lands, and in Irish and Welsh tales from medieval manscripts there are references to the recitation of tales by poets of high rank. In a Welsh story[8] it is related how the magician Gwydion and his eleven companions arrive at a prince's court in the guise of poets. The guests are invited to tell a story. 'Lord,' said Gwydion, 'it is our custom that the first night after one comes to a nobleman, the master poet shall speak. I will tell a tale gladly.' Gwydion, the story goes on, was the best storyteller in the world. In an Irish story, the language of which shows it to have been written in the eighth century, the learned poet Forgoll recites a story to Mongán, an Ulster king, every night throughout a whole winter, 'from Samain to Beltaine (November 1st to May 1st)'— a phrase still to be heard in connection with storytelling.[9] The custom of telling the stories at night, and during the winter, is not to be dismissed as merely a matter of convenience. Reports concerning peoples from parts of native America, Europe, Africa, and Asia show them to be almost unanimous in prohibiting the telling of sacred stories in summer or in daylight, except on certain special occasions.[10] Similarly, the significance of telling the stories around the fire cannot be fully appreciated without reference to the central role of the hearth and the fire-altar in Indo-European and other traditions, while the recitation of tales by poets brings to mind that prose interspersed with speech poems was a narrative form known in ancient Egypt as in medieval Europe, in Vedic India as in modern Ireland.[11]

In medieval Ireland and Wales, poets were not regarded as eccentric individuals as they are in the modern world. They were members of a privileged order within the learned class. Though, in Ireland, their profession was largely hereditary, their apprenticeship was both long and arduous, and an essential part of it consisted in learning hundreds of tales, 'to narrate them to kings and lords and gentlemen'.[12] The learned class, comprising druids and poets, was comparable in many ways with the Brahman caste in India, and an account of the art, status, and conduct of Irish and Welsh court poets was described by an eminent orientalist as 'almost a chapter in the history of India under another name'.[13] These classes are survivals, in the East and in the West, from the social and religious hierarchy of the peoples who spoke the ancient Indo-European languages.

There is evidence from the Celtic countries and from India that the poets were also the official historians and the royal genealogists. The poet's praises confirmed and sustained the king in his kingship, while his satire could blast both the king and his kingdom. There was a tradition that the learned poets (*filid*) of Ireland were once judges. They were certainly the experts on the prerogatives and duties of the kings, and a master-poet (*ollam*) was himself equal to a king before the law. Such priestly functions as divination and prophecy also came within the province of these early Irish poets who, it may be added, wore cloaks of bird-feathers as do the shamans of Siberia when, through ritual and trance, they conduct their audiences on journeys to another world.[14] It was initiates with this power and authority who had the custody of the original tales, and they recited them on auspicious occasions, even as the priests of other religions recite the scriptures.

It is no wonder that the greatest care was taken to ensure the integrity of the tradition. In the Book of Leinster* a colophon to *Táin Bó Cuailnge*, the most famous of all Irish sagas, reminds one of the end of the Book of Revelation. 'A blessing on everyone who will memorize the *Táin* with fidelity in this form and will not put any other form on it.'[15] The rewards promised to those who listened to the recitation of the tales make it abundantly clear that they were no mere entertainment. One of the three wonders concerning the *Táin* was: 'a year's protection to him to whom it is recited'.[16] At the end of the tale called 'The Fosterage of the Houses of the Two Methers'[17] it is said that St Patrick ordered 'that there should not be sleep or conversation during this story, and not to tell it except to a

* A twelfth-century manuscript.

few good people so that it might be the better listened to, and Patrick ordained many other virtues for it . . .'

'I shall leave these virtues
for the story of Ethne from the fair Maigue.
Success in children, success in foster-sister or brother,
to those it may find sleeping with fair women.

'If you tell of the fosterage
before going in a ship or vessel,
you will come safe and prosperous
without danger from waves and billows.

'If you tell of the fosterage
(before going to a) judgement or a hunting,
your case will be (prosperous),
all will be submissive before you.

'To tell the story of Ethne
when bringing home a stately wife,
good the step you have decided on,
it will be a success of spouse and children.

'Tell the story of noble Ethne
before going into a new banqueting house,
(you will be) without bitter fight or folly,
without the drawing of valiant, pointed weapons.

'Tell to a king of many followers
the story of Ethne to a musical instrument,
he gets no cause to repent it,
provided he listen without conversation.

'If you tell this story
to the captives of Ireland,
it will be the same as if were opened
their locks and their bonds.'

As Professor Myles Dillon has pointed out,[18] all this bears a striking similarity to the power ascribed to traditional stories in India, where tale after tale is wound up with the assurance that 'he who knows this conquers all the quarters'.[19] Several stories in the epic *Mahābhārata* end with the claim that those who recite them or listen to them attentively shall be blessed with health, wealth, and progeny. The *Rāmāyaṇa* of Vālmīki promises long life to men, and to kings victory:

> 'He who listens to this wonderous tale of Ráma unwearied in action shall be absolved from all his sins. By listening to the deeds of Ráma he who wishes for sons shall obtain his heart's desire, and to him who longs for riches shall riches be given. The virgin who asks for a husband shall obtain a husband suited to her mind, and shall meet again her dear folk who are far away. They who hear the poem . . . shall obtain all their desires and all their prayers shall be fulfilled.'[20]

Another story ends with a promise of rewards in this life and entry into the heaven of Indra.[21] But the power of the tale is effective even while it is being narrated. Thus, in a folktale from Galway[22] it is said that the Devil could not enter a certain house because Fenian tales were being recited there, while the Indian 'Twenty-five stories of the Spectre in the Corpse' (*Vetālapañcaviṃśati*) end with the spectre's promise that 'neither ghosts nor demons shall have any power whenever and wherever those tales are told. And whosoever recites with devotion even a single one of them shall be free from sin.'[23]

When one inquires what kind of stories are these which have been credited with such extraordinary power, one finds that they tell of the adventures of heroes and heroines; enchantments and disenchantments; kings and queens, ogres and monsters and fairies; animals which speak and act as humans; journeys to another world, beyond the sea or under a lake, where time holds no sway; ghosts and revenants, prophecies and destinies; quests for magic vessels and weapons, and similar marvels. Such is the stuff of the stories told by all peoples whose traditional culture has not been upset by the teaching of modern history and modern science, and it is remarkable how the same

themes or motifs, and even series of motifs, recur in the traditions of peoples widely separated from one another in space and
in time. The very homogeneity of the material presents a considerable problem to the modernist. What is there in this fantastic heritage that from time immemorial it should have retained
the sympathy and excited the wonder of mankind?

This question is presented in a dramatic way by the strange
contrast that appears in the attitude of two successive generations
towards the tradition. The old storytellers believed in all the
marvels of the tales. Hector Maclean, writing in 1860, observed
that the adventures of heroes such as Ossian were as true and
real to the storytellers of Barra and those who listened to them
as were the latest exploits of the British Army to the readers of
newspapers.[24] Even in our own day Professor Delargy speaks of
the horrified dismay shown by a storyteller in Co. Kerry when
one of his audience ventured to cast doubt upon the story of
Oisín returning from the Land of Youth and to wonder
whether Oisín ever existed.[25] 'There was magic in old times',
but with the spread of elementary education and the amenities
and outlook of a materialistic civilization, these ancient wonders pass with remarkable rapidity into the realm of bygone
superstitions. They are out of harmony with the new-found
faith in historical and scientific explanations, and once the
horizons have been narrowed by this new *Weltanschauung*, the
old-world tales can no longer compete with the effusions of
popular novelists.

Thus what remains even in Ireland and the Islands is only
the last vestige of the tradition. Here as elsewhere the tales will
soon be regarded as suitable only for children's books, childish
things to be discarded as the child grows up to be an 'educated'
man of the modern world. The pathos of the situation is indicated by Professor Delargy:[26]

'In Seán Ó Conaill's youth story-tellers were quite common in the district, but as he grew older the old tales were
not so much heard as formerly. Finally, there came a time

when it was but rarely that he had an opportunity himself of practising his art in public. So, lest he should lose command over the tales he loved, he used to repeat them aloud when he thought no one was near, using the gesticulations and the emphasis, and all the other tricks of narration, as if he were once again the centre of a fireside story-telling. His son, Pats, told me that he had seen his father thus engaged, telling his tales to an unresponsive stone wall, while herding the grazing cattle. On returning from market, as he walked slowly up the hills behind his old grey mare, he could be heard declaiming his tales to the back of the cart!'

3

While the traditional tales have been losing their hold on the countryman, scholars have been finding a new interest in them. They have recorded them with elaborate care, classified their motifs, and tried to trace their history. But whereas the story-tellers and their unlettered listeners found no difficulty in believing the wonders of the tales, modern scholars, conditioned by a factual and rationalistic education, cannot accord them the same naive faith. For many, the tales are true only in the sense that, together with old customs and beliefs, they form a corpus of facts which are relevant to the study of human history. They have no intrinsic worth. A generation or two ago it was the fashion to explain them away as products of a 'disease of language' or as examples of 'primitive science', 'primitive philosophy', 'fertility magic', or 'the childhood of fiction'. But the scepticism of writers who never questioned the adequacy of the current evolutionistic theories was sometimes belied by their own life's work. At the age of sixty Sir James Frazer still found it impossible to justify even to himself his preoccupation with mythology: 'If we are taxed with wasting life in seeking to know what cannot be known, and what, if it were discovered, would not be worth knowing, what can we plead in our defence? I fear, very little.'[27] Yet he continued to be engrossed in this 'worthless' subject for the remaining twenty-seven years of his long life. When, at the end of *The Golden Bough*[28], he looks back at 'the melancholy record of human error and folly which has engaged our attention' and welcomes the displacement of religion by science, we again see the sceptic assuming absolute authority. The 'revels now are ended', and those magic themes—'The Perils of the Soul', 'The Scape-goat', 'The Marriage of the Gods', 'The Dying God'—become 'insubstantial pageants' which fade in the cold light of day. But mere scepticism would not have given us *The Golden Bough*.

The conflict between scientific rationalism and intuitive faith is seldom completely resolved in any of us, and it manifests itself in various prejudices and inconsistencies. There are some who would read the tales as if they were modern works of imaginative literature. They insist that they should be studied 'as tales'—which usually means that they are studied *in vacuo*, as though they had no relation to life, while their original meaning is disdainfully left to the anthropologist. But this deliberate superficiality, again, does not always accord with the values cherished by those who seek refuge in it. There are scholars who, though they refuse to regard the tales as anything more than fine things to pass the night away, nevertheless treasure the tradition of which the tales are an integral part as a priceless heritage which can be a source of inspiration even in our modern world.

Though the old rationalism dies hard, the intellectual outlook of our own day is profoundly different from that in which the tales were studied half a century ago. There is a growing awareness of the deep significance of realities that cannot be fully reconciled with the categories of reason, or explained by history and science. The study of social anthropology and of the history of religions has brought home to many scholars that for countless ages men have found in these stories a support for their material and spiritual life. Peoples throughout the world

accept their sacred tales, or 'myths', as 'a statement of a prime/
val, greater, and more relevant reality by which the present
life, fates and activities of mankind are determined, the know/
ledge of which supplies man with the motive for ritual and
moral actions, as well as with indications as to how to perform
them'.[29] Furthermore, fantastic as they are, such tales have
proved an inexhaustible fount of inspiration for poets and
artists throughout the ages. Only through blind arrogance can
all this testimony be dismissed as of little or no significance.
More recently psychologists have found that recourse to 'this
treasure/house of archetypal forms' is invaluable for the cure
of psychological illnesses[30]—a rediscovery within a limited
sphere of the 'life/giving' powers which the stories were
believed to possess in days of old. Other scholars discern in this
heritage a body of metaphysical doctrines and maintain that
although the modern folk storyteller may be unconscious and
unaware of the import of his tales, 'that of which he is uncon/
scious and unaware is itself far superior to the empirical science
and realistic art of the "educated" man'.[31] A crucifix would
still be a crucifix even if it were found being used as a child's
plaything, and to insist on considering only its function as a
toy, or its aesthetic qualities as an ornament, would be to dis/
regard its nature and its essential form. Theories and emphases
continue to vary, but it is true to say that increasing numbers of
modern scholars, including many who are not given to making
pronouncements on the ultimate nature of myths, are learning
to treat tradition with respect and to realize that 'wisdom did
not begin with us'.

As we have explained, traditional tales used to be trans/
mitted by a priestly order in the Celtic lands, and diverse bless/
ings accrued to those who heard them related. The prototypes
of these tales were clearly parts of the oral 'scriptures' of the pre/
Christian Celts. But there are many obstacles in the way of
reading the surviving versions as such to/day. None of them
is available in a manuscript dated earlier than the twelfth

century, though it is clear that some of them were already in writing centuries earlier. These remnants of ancient tradition have come down to us through the hands of Christian scribes, and while it is remarkable that those scribes recorded them at all, they have taken liberties which would not have been per, missible in the oral transmission of a sacred tradition the authority of which had not been challenged. We have already cited an Irish colophon to *Táin Bó Cuailnge* which invokes a blessing on all who memorize the tale in that form. But there is a Latin colophon, to the same version of the *Táin*, which ex, presses a point of view that must have been common among the monastic scribes:[32]

> 'But I who have written this history, or rather story, do not give faith to many of the things in this history or story. For some things therein are delusions of the demons, some things are poetic figments, some are like the truth and some are not, and some are for the amusement of fools!'

How far the tales found in medieval manuscripts may have been deliberately altered or rearranged we do not pretend to know. It cannot even be assumed that the earliest recorded ver, sions are more authentic than later ones. When faced with stories, and they are many, which defy our understanding, or which appear to be out of harmony with others of the same kind, it is tempting to accuse the writers of invention. In the words, though not perhaps in the meaning, of the colophon, some of the stories 'are like the truth and some are not'! But since the fault may lie in our own ignorance, we have left the problematic ones as they are rather than explain them away. Tales recorded in modern times from oral tradition may have been less subject to literary manipulation, but there has been no insurmountable barrier between the learned tradition and that of the people and, moreover, for well over a millennium the storytellers too have been Christians who have gone to Mass and believed in the heaven of the Trinity, the Virgin, the Angels, and the Saints. It is small wonder that the divinity of

Celtic gods is hardly ever recognized in these stories. The tradition has also probably lost many myths which, though they may have been of great importance in the living religion, did not make good stories when divorced from the rites.

A religious tradition consists of a ritual and an art as well as a mythology, and each of these components is intelligible in terms of the others. Symbols, whether they be myths or ceremonies or objects, reveal their full significance only within a particular tradition; one must be part and parcel of that tradition to experience fully the power and illumination of the myth. Such participation in the old Celtic tradition is no longer possible. For these reasons we do not consider it enough to re-tell the stories as they stand, without comment. In pondering upon these fragments of tradition it is not enough for modern man to disabuse his mind of the preconceptions of the historian, the prejudices of the scientist, and the aestheticism of those who read the Bible 'as literature'. He needs all the clues he can find. Although the full meaning can never be fathomed, we believe that a comparative study of the stories, combined with some acquaintance with the myths, rituals, and doctrines of other lands and other ages, may help us to obtain glimpses of the tradition of which the stories, even in their original form, were but one expression.

CHAPTER II

Branches of the Tradition

THE TRADITIONAL IRISH TALES which appear in medieval manuscripts comprise four groups or cycles, usually
referred to as

1 The Mythological Cycle
2 The Ulster Cycle
3 The Fenian Cycle
4 The Historical Cycle

In the so-called Mythological Cycle, the chief characters belong
to Tuatha Dé Danann, 'The Peoples of the Goddess Danann',
who are said to have occupied Ireland before the coming of the
Sons of Míl, the ancestors of the present inhabitants. The stories
of the Ulster Cycle are mainly about the warriors of King
Conchobar of Ulster, and especially about the exploits of the
foremost among them, CúChulainn. The Fenian stories are
about Finn mac Cumaill and his roving warbands (*fiana*).
This cycle is sometimes described as the Ossianic Cycle because
most of the poems which belong to it are attributed to Finn's
son Oisín, or Ossian as he is known through the work of
Macpherson. The so-called Historical Cycle is a more miscellaneous group of stories centred on various high-kings of Ireland and on a number of provincial or lesser kings. Each of
these four cycles[1] contains material which appears to belong to
a common Indo-European heritage and which presumably
was part of the tradition of the Celtic peoples before they ever
came to these islands. But in the works of early Irish historians,
the personages about whom the tales are told are arranged in a
chronological sequence extending from the time of the Deluge
to the time of the Viking raids in Ireland. The events of the

Mythological Cycle of traditions are synchronized with the main events in ancient world history; King Conchobar is said to have reigned in Ulster at the beginning of the Christian era; Finn and his *fiana* served Cormac mac Airt who is be-lieved to have been King of Ireland in the third century A.D., while the tales of the Historical Cycle are centred on kings who are ascribed dates ranging from the third century B.C. to the eighth century A.D.

A certain amount of supplementary information concern-ing the characters and events in these four groups of stories is supplied by various learned works compiled in the early Middle Ages,[2] in particular *Lebor Gabála Erenn*,* a 'history' of the Irish and of the peoples who occupied Ireland before them, with its accompanying List of Kings, the Glossary attributed to Cormac mac Cuilennáin, the king bishop of Cashel who was killed in the year 908, the *Dindšenchas*, lore associated with hills and other features in the Irish landscape, *Cóir Anmann*,** which gives brief stories in explanation of the origin of the names of traditional personages, and finally poems, triads, and genealogies, which record famous names.

Early Welsh traditions are found in the 'Four Branches of the Mabinogi',† comparable in some ways with the Irish Mythological Cycle, in the poems and stories of the Arthurian Cycle, which is also represented by extensive texts in many other languages, in some miscellaneous stories, and in poems which probably once formed parts of sagas.[3] Most of the latter poems are attributed to Llywarch Hen, Taliesin, and Myrddin, poets who are said to have been associated with kings of those regions of north Britain which, in the sixth century, were still Welsh. Wales too has her genealogies, triads, and stanzas of the graves of heroes, compilations that bear witness to traditions which perhaps were never embodied in extensive narratives,

---

* 'The Book of the Taking of Ireland' (*LG*).
** 'The Fitness of Names' (CA).
† (*PKM*)—*Mabinogi*: 'story of youth' or 'story'.

and to these may again be added two important Latin texts, both of them landmarks in the history of the Arthurian tradition: the *Historia Brittonum* of Nennius (early ninth century) and the more elaborate and presumably more fictional *Historia Regum Britanniae* of Geoffrey of Monmouth. In Wales and in Ireland, the lives of native saints, written either in Latin or in the vernacular, may perhaps be regarded as an extra cycle of stories. Like the saints' lives of other countries, they have many motifs in common with the 'secular' tales and they are by no means irrelevant to a study of the preChristian tradition.

2

Five successive groups of invaders are said to have occupied Ireland before the ancestors of the Gaels eventually settled there. Their significance will be discussed in a later chapter; here we will only give a brief indication of their several fates. The first three groups are known by the names of their respective leaders, the last two by group names, thus:

1 Cessair
2 Partholón
3 Nemed
4 Fir Bolg (*Fir*='Men')
5 Tuatha Dé Danann ('The Peoples of the Goddess Danann')

Cessair was a woman and her predominantly female expedition came before the Flood. The only member of the company to survive that catastrophe was Cessair's consort, Fintan, who after spending long periods in the shapes of a salmon, an eagle, and a hawk, and witnessing all the succeeding invasions, appears (in stories of Christian Ireland) as the supreme authority in matters of tradition. The country had been waste for several hundred years when Partholón and his followers settled in it.

They and all their progeny eventually perished in a plague, but a story similar to that of Fintan is told of Tuan son of Starn in this second group. Nemed, who came next, also died in Ireland, but his people, after suffering great tribulations, ultimately abandoned the country. They dispersed in three groups, two of which were the ancestors of the two peoples who next occupied Ireland. The first of these two were Fir Bolg, and they were still in occupation when the second, Tuatha Dé Danann, arrived there. According to some accounts, these last comers demanded either battle or the king⁄ship, and Fir Bolg were defeated in the First Battle of Mag Tuired and fled to the islands of Islay, Arran, Man and Rath⁄lin. They are said to have returned, as a subordinate people, to Ireland, about the beginning of the Christian era. According to another story,[4] it was half the realm that the Tuatha de⁄manded of Fir Bolg and this was refused them: when the First Battle of Mag Tuired was fought between the two peoples, it ended in a compact of peace, goodwill, and friend⁄ship.

Here we shall confine our attention to Tuatha Dé Danann. As we have noted, the chief characters in a whole group of independent stories belong to the Tuatha, who are thus dis⁄tinguished from all the four peoples who occupied Ireland before them. In contrast with all their predecessors and the Sons of Míl, their successors, they stand out too as a people of magic wonders, learned in all the arts and supreme masters of wizardry. Before coming to Ireland they had sojourned in the northern islands of the world, where they had acquired their incomparable esoteric knowledge and whence they brought with them four talismans: the Great Fál—the person under whom this stone shrieked was king of Ireland; the spear of Lug—no victory could be won against it nor against him who had it in his hand; the sword of Nuadu—no one escaped from it when it was drawn from its scabbard; and the cauldron of the Dagda, from which no company would go away unsatisfied. All the other groups reached Ireland by ship, but the Tuatha

came in dark clouds through the air and alighted on a moun/
tain of Conmaicne Réin, and for three days they cast a darkness
over the face of the sun. The late, rhetorical account of the First
Battle of Mag Tuired describes them as 'the most handsome
and delightful company, the fairest of form, the most distin/
guished in their equipment and apparel, and their skill in
music and playing, the most gifted in mind and temperament
that ever came to Ireland. That too was the company that was
bravest and inspired most horror and fear and dread, for the
Tuatha Dé excelled all the peoples of the world in their pro/
ficiency in every art.'[5]

The learned men who recorded the old Irish traditions in the
Middle Ages were embarrassed to know whether to regard the
Tuatha as men, as demons, or as fallen gods. In the story of
Tuan mac Cairill in the Book of the Dun Cow, written about
1100, it is said that the learned did not know whence Tuatha
Dé Danann had come, but that 'it seems likely to them that
they came from heaven on account of their intelligence and for
the excellence of their knowledge'. According to a text in a
fifteenth/century manuscript, they used to be worshipped,
while a poet writing about A.D. 1000 finds it necessary to say
that 'though he enumerates them, he does not worship them'.[6]

It is said of the Tuatha in general that the men of art were
gods, the labourers non/gods.[7] Danann is herself called 'mother
of the gods',[8] and several of her people are described, indivi/
dually, as gods. Thus, the name of the Dagda is interpreted
as meaning 'the good god', and this is upheld by modern
philologists. He is also called Aed (*aed*=fire), Eochaid Olla/
thair ('Eochaid All/father'), and Ruad Rofessa ('Lord of
Great Knowledge'), and described as the god of druidism or
magic (*draídecht*) of the Tuatha.[9] In Cormac's Glossary, Brigit,
daughter of the Dagda, is described as 'a poetess . . . a goddess
whom poets worshipped', and her two sisters, both of the same
name as herself, women of healing and of smith/work respec/
tively, are also described as goddesses. Dian Cécht, according
to the same text, was 'the sage of leechcraft of Ireland' and 'god

of health', Néit was 'the god of battle', and Manannán mac Lir, 'a renowned trader who dwelt in the Isle of Man . . . the best pilot in the west of Europe', was called 'god of the sea' and 'son of the sea' (*mac lir*) by both the Scots and the Britons, and the Isle of Man (*Inis Manann*) was named after him.[10] Furthermore, names corresponding to those of Nuadu, the king of the Tuatha when they came to Ireland, and of Brigit, mentioned above, occur as names of divinities in inscriptions of the Roman period in Britain. In Irish story, Nuadu's place as king is said to have been taken by Lug, and the name Lugoves, found in a few inscriptions on the Continent, may be a plural form of Lug(us). The same god is also possibly commemorated in place-names such as Lyons, Laon, Leyden (*Lug(u)dunum*), on the Continent, and Carlisle (*Luguvalium*) in Britain.[11]

We have already mentioned the First Battle of Mag Tuired, fought between the Tuatha and Fir Bolg whom they found in occupation of Ireland. The Second Battle of Mag Tuired is the subject of one of the greatest stories of the Mythological Cycle. The adversaries of the Tuatha in this battle were the Fomoire, the only mythological beings comparable in mystery and magic with the Tuatha themselves, and in this story the character of 'the Peoples of the Goddess' is revealed more fully than in any other text. The Fomoire had already made their presence known in the time of Partholón. *Lebor Gabála Érenn* describes them, in that context, as beings with single arms and single legs.[12] They were led by Cichol Gricenchos son of Goll ('One-eye') son of Garb ('Rough'). Each of their four ships' companies comprised fifty men and thrice fifty women, and their predominantly female character is further emphasized by the description of Cichol's monstrous mother, Lot. Her bloated lips were in her breast, she had four eyes in her back, and she equalled all her troop in strength. According to some versions the Fomoire were destroyed in their battle with Partholón; according to others, though the battle was fought for a week, 'not a man was slain there, for it was a magic battle!'[13] Nemed,

the leader of the next group of invaders, defeated and slew two
kings of the Fomoire, and later he again defeated the Fomoire
in three battles. However, after his death, his progeny suffered
oppression at the hands of these same enemies under Morc
and Conand. Every Samain (first of November) two-thirds of
their corn, of their milk, and of their offspring had to be sur-
rendered to them. Ultimately, Nemed's people assaulted the
sea-tower of Conand, but after they had secured his downfall,
Morc appeared with three-score ships, and only one ship with
thirty warriors of Nemed's people escaped from the slaughter
that ensued.

In the *First* Battle of Mag Tuired, the arm of Nuadu, King
of Tuatha Dé Danann, was severed, and thereafter[14] a contention arose between the Tuatha and their wives concerning
the sovereignty. As Nuadu was no longer suitable to be king,
their wives said it would be better to give the kingship to their
adopted son, Bres, or Eochaid Bres,* son of Elatha. Bres's
father, Elatha son of Delbaeth, was a king of the Fomoire,
and his mother, Ériu daughter of Delbaeth, belonged to
Tuatha Dé Danann. At first sight this proposal, which was
accepted by the Tuatha, seems strange in view of what has
been said of the Fomoire as the monstrous enemies who challenged Partholón and as the oppressors who caused the remnant of Nemed's people to abandon the country. Moreover, in
late stories the name of the Fomoire signifies giants, and in
ecclesiastical texts they are classed with elves, horseheads,
and other mis-shapen creatures as the race either of Cain or of
Ham, the accursed son of Noah.[15] Nevertheless, before coming
to Ireland, Tuatha Dé Danann had made an alliance with the
Fomoire, and Ethniu daughter of Balor, Fomorian king of the
Isles, had been given in marriage to Cian son of Dian Cécht.
From this union was born Lug, the dominant figure in this
story. When the wives of the Tuatha urged that Bres the Fomorian should be made king, they said this would bind the alliance between the Fomoire and the Tuatha.

* Eochaid the Handsome.

The kingdom was bestowed upon Bres on condition that
he would surrender the sovereignty if his misdeeds should give
cause. Nevertheless he proceeded to strip the Tuatha of their
jewels and their tribute, their cattle and their food. There was
no house in the country that was not under tribute to the
Fomorian kings, Indech mac Dé Domnann,* Elatha (father
of Bres), and Tethra. The Dagda, the 'god of druidism',
laboured at building a fort for Bres, while every day he sur-
rendered the best part of his food to a monstrous satirist who
tyrannized him. Ogma, the mighty champion of the Tuatha,
likewise suffering from lack of food, had to supply the host
every day with firewood from nearby islands, and the sea
would sweep away two-thirds of his bundle because of his
weakness. The niggardly Bres deprived the Tuatha of the
pleasure they might have enjoyed from the feats of their men of
skill and their champions and, moreover, 'their knives were
not greased by him and however often they visited him their
breath did not smell of ale'. At last he became the victim of the
first satire ever made in Ireland—'nought but decay was on
him from that hour'—and Tuatha Dé demanded the restitu-
tion of the realm. Even then he was allowed to remain to
the end of seven years and he proceeded to muster the champions
of the *Síd*,** that is the Fomoire, from Lochlann to the Western
Isles, to impose their rule by force. 'Never came to Ireland a
host more horrible or fearful' than that host led by Balor, the
champion, and Indech son of Dé Domnann.

The maimed Nuadu had long since been provided with a silver arm (*airgetlám*) by Dian Cécht—hence he was called Nuadu
Airgetlám—but later Dian Cécht's son, Miach, healed his
arm of flesh, and he was reinstated as King of Tuatha Dé
Danann. He was now holding a great feast for them at Tara,
when a strange company was seen approaching, headed by a
young warrior, fair and shapely, with a king's trappings. He

* Indech son of the Goddess Domnann.
** *síd*: magic dwelling-place.

was announced to the doorkeeper as 'Lug of the fierce combats, son of Cian son of Dian Cécht and of Ethniu daughter of Balor', and as 'the fosterson of Talann daughter of Magmór, king of Spain, and of Echaid the Rough son of Duí'. The doorkeeper asked him what art he practised, 'for no one with-out an art enters Tara'.[16] 'Question me,' he said, 'I am a wright.' The doorkeeper answered: 'We need thee not. We have a wright already, Luchta son of Lúachaid.' He said: 'Question me, doorkeeper: I am a smith.' The doorkeeper answered him: 'We have a smith already . . .' And so the dialogue goes on:

'Question me: I am a champion.'

'We need thee not. We have a champion already, Ogma son of Ethliu.'

'Question me: I am a harper.'

'We have a harper already, Abcán son of Bicelmos whom the Men of the Three Gods entertained in magic dwellings (*síde*).'

'Question me: I am a warrior.'

'We need thee not . . .'

'I am a poet and historian.'

'We need thee not . . .'

'I am a sorcerer.'

'We have sorcerers already: our wizards and men of power are many.'

'Question me: I am a leech.'

'We need thee not. We already have Dian Cécht as leech.'

'I am a cupbearer.'

'We already have cupbearers . . .'

'Question me: I am a good metal worker.'

'We need thee not: we already have a metal worker, Credne Cerd.'

He spoke again: 'Ask the king whether he has one man who possesses all these arts, and if he has I shall not enter Tara.'

The doorkeeper announced the arrival of the *Samildánach*, 'the man of each and every art', whereupon the king bade them bring the *fidchell* boards. Lug won all the stakes. 'Let him enter the garth, for his like has never before come to this fortress.' Lug entered and sat in the seat of the sage, 'for he was a sage in every art', and then Ogma gave his challenge. It would require four score yoke of oxen to move the great flag-stone which he hurled through the house so that it lay on the outside of Tara. Lug cast it back to the centre of the palace and made the building whole again. The host demanded that a harp be played for them. Lug played three magic strains which set them first sleeping and then lamenting and then rejoicing. Nuadu now considered whether Samildánach might release them from the bondage of the Fomoire and decided to change seats with him. 'So Samildánach went to the king's seat, and the king rose before him till thirteen days had ended.'

Lug conferred with the two brothers, the Dagda and Ogma, and then the brothers Goibniu and Dian Cécht were summoned to them. At the end of the year Nuadu enquired of his experts what each could do. The sorcerer Mathgen pro-mised to cast the mountains of Ireland on the Fomoire, the cupbearer that he would hide the lakes and rivers of Ireland from the Fomoire whereas the men of Ireland would not lack water though they should fight for seven years. Figol, the druid, said that he would cause three showers of fire to fall on the faces of the enemy host, 'and I will take out of them two-thirds of their valour and their bravery and their strength, and I will bind their urine in their own bodies and in the bodies of their horses. Every breath that the men of Ireland shall ex-hale will be an increase of valour and bravery and strength to them.' It became the turn of the Dagda to declare his powers: 'The power which ye boast,' said he, 'I shall wield it all my-self.' Upon which everyone said, 'Thou art indeed the Excel-lent God,' whence his name, the Dagda.

Lug, the Dagda and Ogma went to the three Gods of Danann, and for seven years they were preparing for the battle and making weapons. Then we are told of the Dagda, 'about the Samain (1st November) of the battle', having intercourse with the Morrígan.* She and Badb ('scald-crow') and Macha** were three sinister and destructive female beings who prophesied carnage and haunted battlefields.[17] She now said she would go and destroy Indech son of Dé Domnann and 'deprive him of the blood of his heart and the kidneys of his valour', and she gave two handfuls of that blood to the hosts. When Indech later appeared in the battle, he was already doomed.

Lug then sent the Dagda to the camp of the Fomoire, to spy on them and to delay the battle until the men of Ireland should be ready. The Fomoire granted his request for a truce, but in his relations with them he again appears as a figure of fun. Porridge was made for him, 'to mock him, for great was his love of porridge'. Goats and sheep and pigs, as well as meal and milk, were cast into the king's gigantic cauldron. The food was then spilt into a hole in the ground, and the Dagda was obliged to eat it all on pain of death, so that he might not reproach them with inhospitality. The ladle was big enough for a man and a woman to lie in but the Dagda finished by scraping the hole with his finger, and then he fell asleep. The Fomoire laughed at his huge belly and his uncouth apparel—a hood over his head, a cape reaching to his elbows, a tunic reaching only to his buttocks, and shoes of horsehide with the hair on the outside. The track made behind him by his enormous club was enough for the boundary ditch of a province. A Rabe-laisian passage follows which tells of his intercourse with Indech's daughter, who promised her magic assistance against the host of the Fomoire.

Then we hear how Lug inquired of the chiefs of the Tuatha what power they wielded. Goibniu, the smith, promised to provide a new weapon in place of every one that was broken —'no spearpoint which my hand shall forge shall make a missing cast. No one which it pierces shall taste life afterwards.' Dian Cécht undertook to heal the wounded overnight,

* Either 'Great Queen' or 'Queen of Phantoms'.
** The plural *morrígna* is used for the trio.

Credne to supply rivets for the spears, hilts for swords, and bosses and rims for shields, and Luchta to make all shields and spear-shafts. Ogma declared that he would repel the king and his friends and capture a large proportion of the enemy host, Carpre, the poet, that he would satirize the enemy, and the sorceresses, Bé Chuille and Danann (or Dianann), that trees and stones and sods of the earth, through their enchant-ment, would become an armed host and rout the enemy. The sorcerers, the druids, the cupbearers, the Morrígan, and the Dagda again declared their powers.

When the battle had begun, the Fomoire sent Ruadán, son of Bres and of Brígh (i.e. Brigit) daughter of the Dagda, to report on the fighting and also to kill Goibniu. He succeeded in wounding him with a spear but he himself was slain in revenge. Then Brígh came to bewail her son, and this was the first time crying and shrieking were heard in Ireland.[18] The Tuatha, fearing an early death for Lug 'owing to the multitude of his arts', tried to prevent him from entering the battle, but he escaped from his guardians and appeared in the forefront of the men of Ireland, heartening them to fight. Singing a chant he went round the host on one foot and with only one eye open. Eventually he met Balor, who had already slain Nuadu. Balor had an evil eye, never opened except on the battlefield, when it needed four men to lift the eyelid. If an army looked at that eye it was rendered powerless. He now bade the eyelid be lifted so that he might see 'the babbler' who was conversing with him, whereupon Lug cast a sling-stone which carried the eye through his head, and its destructive power fell on the Fomoire. According to some versions,[19] Lug cut off Balor's head, and though Balor had bidden him set it on his own head so that he should gain its power, he set it on a pillar-stone. Its venom split the stone into four pieces.

In the rout which followed, Lug spared the life of Loch Lethglas,* the Fomorian poet, on condition that he should be

* 'Half-green'.

granted three wishes, one of which was that till Doom Lug should ward off from Ireland all plundering by the Fomoire. Bres, seeking quarter, offered that the cattle of Ireland should always be in milk. Lug brought him the verdict of Maeltne of Great Judgements: 'That does not save thee: thou hast no power over their age and their offspring though thou canst milk them.' Bres then offered that the men of Ireland should reap a harvest in every quarter of the year. But that again did not save him, for they were satisfied with the normal yearly round. 'Less than that rescues thee,' said Lug. 'How shall the men of Ireland plough? How shall they sow? How shall they reap?' His answer to these questions was accepted, that their ploughing should be on a Tuesday, their sowing on a Tuesday, and their reaping on a Tuesday—a formula which recurs in modern folk charms used to ward off supernatural beings who would steal the produce of the farmer's labours.[20] According to the *dindsenchas*, the death of Bres was encompassed by Lug in a magic contest in which Bres, while seeking to deprive the men of Munster of the milk of their dun cows, was obliged to drink milk which was not real milk from cows which were not real cows.[21] After the Battle of Mag Tuired, Lug, the Dagda, and Ogma pursued the Fomoire and recovered the Dagda's harp. All the cattle of Ireland, recalled by the lowing of the black heifer which the Dagda had chosen as his modest reward for his labours as a builder, resumed their grazing. The Morrígan and Badb then proclaimed the victory and the return of prosperity, and also prophesied the end of the world and the return of chaos.

The world in which the Tuatha reigned supreme did eventually come to an end with the arrival of the Sons of Míl. After their defeat in battle, Amairgen, poet and judge of the newcomers, is said to have 'divided Ireland in two, and the half of Ireland that was underground he gave to Tuatha Dé Danann, and the other half to the Sons of Míl'. The Tuatha then 'went into hills and fairy regions (*sídbrugaib*), so that fairies (*sída*) under ground were subject to them. For each province in Ireland they left five of their number increasing battles, struggles, strife, and conflict among the Sons of Míl.'[22] One early text says that Tuatha Dé provided the Sons of Míl with wives; according to another, they destroyed the corn and milk round about the Sons of Míl until the latter made the friendship of the Dagda. Afterwards he saved their corn and milk.[23] In the same story the Dagda is said to have shared the magic mound-dwellings (*síde*) between Lug, Ogma, and himself, the three protagonists of the Tuatha in their battle with the Fomoire, but Oengus,* son of the Dagda, ousted his father from Bruig na Bóinne.**

In a later text, the king of Tuatha Dé Danann is Bodb, son of the Dagda, but it is Manannán mac Lir, described as over-king of the Tuatha, who distributes the *síde*, ten of them in all, among the nobles of the Tuatha, while he himself dwells be-yond the sea in Emain Ablach, 'Emain of the Apple-trees'. It is Manannán too who institutes the *Feth Fiada* 'through which the Tuatha lords were not seen', the Feast of Goibniu 'to ward off age and death from their high-kings', and the Pigs of Mannanán 'to be killed and yet continue to exist for the warriors'.[24] Under this new dispensation, therefore, the high-king of the Tuatha is the 'god of the sea', who dwells beyond the sea, even as the mysterious Tethra, king of the Fomoire, dwelt beyond the sea when the Fomorian Bres was king of Ireland. For both Manannán and Tethra the fish are cattle[25] and Tethra's name, like Manannán's patronymic, is synony-mous with 'sea'. Henceforth, the Tuatha occupy those hidden and external regions, the mound-dwellings and the islands, which were the portion of the Fomoire when the Tuatha possessed Ireland, and their role now becomes similar to that of the Fomoire: they provide wives, they promote strife and conflict, and they have power to destroy or to save for the rulers of Ireland the produce of the land. From now on, the

---

* He is also called Mac ind Óc, or In Mac Óc ('The Young Son').
** ' The Mansion of the Boyne.'

distinction between the Tuatha and the Fomoire is blurred. The opposition which divides them holds only while the Tuatha appear openly as the occupiers of Ireland. In the islands of the north before the Tuatha come to Ireland, and in the underground *síde* and the islands after the coming of the Sons of Míl, Tuatha Dé Danann are at one with the Fomoire. Originally and ultimately, or in the realm of the occult, there is no hostility between them; the opposition belongs to the realm of the manifest.

The Fomoire never appear as settlers in Ireland. Champions of the *Síd*, they remain in the background throughout, constantly associated with the sea and the islands. They are only vaguely depicted, and their chief features are their unformed or monstrous appearance, their single eyes, single arms, and single legs—the oneness which is split in the world of manifestation—and their hostility to the established order.[26] Nevertheless, they intermarry with the Tuatha, and in some respects they seem to represent the feminine principle. It will be recalled that as opponents of Partholón they were predominantly a female company, and that it was the wives of the Tuatha who urged that Bres of the Fomoire should be made king. Furthermore, the contests, lavish hospitality, obligatory over-eating, obscenity, and mockery which characterize the way in which the Tuatha and the Fomoire behave towards one another in certain episodes have their counterpart in the ritual hostility and disrespectful joking which is typical of the conduct of people in many human societies towards the kin groups from which they obtain their wives.[27]

From the point of view of the contingent world, the supernatural world, whether it be inhabited by the Fomoire, the Tuatha, or other beings, has an essentially feminine quality. Women are far more prominent than men in medieval accounts of the magic mound-dwellings and of the islands of immortality which lie beyond the sea. In the delectable Other World of 'The Adventure of Conle', 'There is no race there but women and maidens alone.' The fairies are known as 'The Mothers' or 'The Mothers' Blessing', in parts of Wales, and they are sometimes thought of as being exclusively female.[28] We shall revert to this subject in Chapter XV.

A primeval battle between the gods and their adversaries, such as we have described, occurs of course in other mytho/logies, and there are striking similarities between the stories told of these conflicts by the ancient Indians, Scandinavians, Greeks, and other peoples whose languages are derived from Indo/European.[29] At this point we will only notice the oppo/sition between the two Indian groups, the Devas ('gods') and the Asuras, which has been described as 'the basic theme of the Vedic tradition'.[30] The Asuras were malevolent beings, the regular adversaries of the gods, and yet the name *Asura*, which means 'possessor of occult power', may be used of the greatest gods.[31] According to A. K. Coomaraswamy, all the Devas are Asuras by birth, 'for the female principle is always an Asurī in the Rig Veda'. The Devas and Asuras are thus kinsmen. Distinct and opposite in operation, they are in essence consubstantial: 'the Darkness *in actu* is Light, the Light *in potentia* Darkness'.[32]

3

Both Tuatha Dé Danann and the Fomoire have their counter/parts in 'The Four Branches of the Mabinogi',[33] which may be said to constitute a Welsh 'mythological cycle'. These tales are full of marvellous happenings and feats of magic, but such is the storyteller's artistry that what is mysterious and wonderful is accepted as naturally and immediately as the realistic dia/logue and the familiar setting.

The tales are about three groups of personages: the First and Third Branches about the family of Pwyll, Lord of Dyfed, the Second Branch about the family of Llŷr, and the Fourth Branch about the family of Dôn. A son is born in each of these families, and the tales are mostly about the marriages of the mothers and the birth and destiny of the three sons: Pryderi the son of Pwyll and Rhiannon, Gwern the son of Branwen daughter of Llŷr, and Lleu Llaw Gyffes the son of Aranrhod daughter of Dôn. What follows here is a mere summary.

We are first told about the parents of Pryderi, the only person who figures in all four branches. Pwyll, Lord of Dyfed, sets out from Arberth, a chief court of his, to hunt in that part of his domain known as Glyn Cuch. He loses his companions and soon finds himself face to face with the king of a mysterious realm with whom he is obliged to come to terms. It happens in this way. When he sees a strange pack of hounds bringing down a stag, Pwyll drives the pack away and baits his own hounds on the stag. Thereupon the strange hunter appears. He rebukes Pwyll* for his discourtesy and reveals that he is Arawn, King of Annwfn.** To redeem his friendship, Pwyll is obliged to take his place in Annwfn for a year and a day, after Arawn has exchanged their forms, and at the end of the year to meet Arawn's enemy, Hafgan, king of another realm in Annwfn, in a contest at a ford. To defeat Hafgan he must refrain from giving him a second blow, for that would restore his power. During the year Pwyll observes strict chastity while sharing the bed of Arawn's queen, and in due course he defeats Hafgan and so becomes sole king of Annwfn. A firm friendship is thereby established between Pwyll and Arawn, and moreover, Pwyll, as a result of his stay in Annwfn and his success in uniting the two kingdoms, is known henceforth not as Pwyll the Lord of Dyfed but as Pwyll the Head of Annwfn.

The second episode begins with Pwyll holding a feast at Arberth. When, after the first part of the feast, he takes his seat on the throne-mound (*gorssed*) by the court, he knows that he will thereby either suffer wounds and blows or else see a marvel. Presently he sees a lady riding past on a majestic white horse. Three attempts to overtake her prove of no avail, though the

---

* *pwyll*: prudence, deliberation, wisdom.
** ? 'Great World', 'Non-world', 'Underworld'.

swiftest horses are used, while she does not change her leisurely pace. Yet, when Pwyll at last asks her to wait for him, she readily does so. She is Rhiannon and she declares she has come to offer to be his bride. At their marriage feast a year later, Pwyll, by thoughtlessly granting a boon to a suppliant, allows his bride to pass to Gwawl, the disappointed suitor who has the support of her family. Rhiannon however insists on a year's delay, and by means of a ruse, Gwawl too, at his wedding-feast, is obliged to give up his bride. Pwyll enters disguised in ragged garb and entices Gwawl into a magic bag provided before-hand by Rhiannon. Then Pwyll's men descend upon the court and each gives the bag a blow or a kick, thus making Gwawl the first victim ever in the game of 'Badger in the Bag'.

In the third year of Pwyll's marriage with Rhiannon, his subjects remonstrate with him on account of his wife's child-lessness, but he counsels patience. Before the end of another year she gives birth to a son, but the night he is born the women who are in attendance fall asleep, and the child disappears mysteriously. To save themselves, the women kill some pups, smear Rhiannon's face and hands with the blood, and cast the bones before her. As a result, she is cruelly punished for the alleged crime of destroying her child. Meanwhile, Teyrnon Lord of Gwent Is-coed, who always loses the colt his incom-parable mare foals on May Eve, at last decides to keep watch. After a big commotion, a great claw comes through the win-dow and seizes the new-born colt, but Teyrnon strikes off the claw at the elbow and rushes out. He fails to see anything, because of the dark, but at the door when he returns he finds a child in swaddling clothes. The child is brought up by Teyrnon and his wife as their own son, but when they realize who he is they restore him to Pwyll and Rhiannon. He is then named Pryderi ('Care'), because of his mother's words when she has news of him: 'I should be delivered of my care if that were true.'

The Third Branch takes up the story after Pryderi has married and has succeeded his father as Lord of Dyfed. He now gives his mother, Rhiannon, in marriage to Manawydan son of Llŷr, of whose family we shall speak presently. With their wives, Pryderi and Manawydan resort to Arberth. After the first part of their feast there, they sit on the throne-mound, whereupon a great peal of thunder is followed by a fall of mist, and when it lightens, all signs of human life have vanished. They can see 'neither house nor beast nor smoke nor fire nor man nor dwelling, but the houses of the court empty, desolate, without man or beast in them'. After remaining for two years in the deserted country, the four of them go to England, and Pryderi and Manawydan earn their living as saddlers, shield-makers, and shoemakers, successively, moving from town to town on account of the conspiracies of villein rivals. Eventually they return to Arberth and the two men set out to hunt. In spite of Manawydan's explicit counsel, the impulsive Pryderi allows himself to be enticed into a magic fortress where he sees, in the centre of the floor, a well with a finely wrought golden bowl hanging above a marble slab. On taking hold of the bowl, he is unable to remove his hands from it or his feet from the slab, and he loses all power of speech. Rhiannon, chiding her husband as a poor companion to Pryderi, straightway goes in search of her son, but the same fate befalls her too, and the fortress then vanishes. When the humble Manawydan turns again to shoemaking, he is once more faced with opposition, and returns to Arberth. There he sows corn, but two of his three crofts are plundered, and on keeping watch he sees a host of mice making off with the ears of corn from the third croft. He catches the only slow-moving mouse among them and, again on the throne-mound, he prepares to hang it as a thief. Three clerics who appear in succession offer to buy its freedom. The third, a bishop, ultimately reveals that the thief is his own wife, in the form of a mouse, and she is with child. He himself is Llwyd, captor of Pryderi and Rhiannon, author of the enchantment which has made the country desolate, and friend and avenger of Gwawl, Rhiannon's ill-treated suitor. To redeem his wife, Llwyd frees Rhiannon and Pryderi, removes the enchantment from Dyfed and promises that no spell shall ever again be cast upon the land.

Pwyll and the members of his family—including Rhiannon after her marriage—are not shown to be possessed of any magic power, though they have to contend at every turn with the hostility of mysterious enemies. But here, as in the Irish stories, there is ambiguity. Pwyll himself is called the Head of Annwfn. In this story, Annwfn is a country of elegant perfection; in other texts, it is a palace or realm located sometimes beyond the sea, sometimes underground—in a word, the equivalent of the Irish *Síd*.[34] Again, the manner in which Rhiannon makes her first appearance is magical enough, and the singing of 'the birds of Rhiannon', according to a reference in another story,[35] would give sleep to the living and awaken the dead. It may be added that originally her name may have meant 'Great Queen',* and she is repeatedly associated with horses. Wrongly deemed guilty of destroying her child, she is obliged to sit by the horseblock ready to carry visitors on her back to the court. After disappearing in Llwyd's magic fortress, her punishment is to have the collars of asses, after they have been carrying hay, about her neck. Furthermore, the loss and recovery of her son is linked with the birth of a colt which is later given to him when he shows a remarkable interest in horses, and (in the Fourth Branch) his acceptance of a gift of horses is the prelude to his death. This aspect of the story has been described as the myth of Epona,[36] whose name occurs in more inscriptions of the Roman period, and with a wider distribution, than any other Celtic name of god or goddess. Epona is sometimes styled Regina, and she is the only Celtic goddess known to have been honoured in Rome itself. Three of the inscriptions are associated with figures of the goddess, who is depicted with horses on either side of her. About two hundred other images, most of which show a mare ridden by a female, are also

---

* *Teyrnon* perhaps originally meant 'Great King'.

assumed to be representations of Epona. It has been argued that her concern was as much with the journey of the soul after death as with the welfare of horses and mules and their attend-ants.

The three plagues that befall Britain in the short tale called 'Lludd and Llefelys'[37] bear certain resemblances to the en-chantment of Dyfed and to the despoiling of Tuatha Dé Danann by the Fomoire. The first of these plagues was wrought by beings called Coraniaid (a name derived from *corr*, 'dwarf') —'so great was their knowledge that there was no discourse over the face of the Island, however low it might be spoken, that they did not know about if the wind met it'. The second was a terrifying scream which was raised every May Eve over every hearth in Britain and which left all animals and trees and the earth and the waters barren. It is found to be the scream of a dragon in conflict with a foreign dragon, and the contestants are revealed beneath the mid-point of the Island. The third plague was a giant who stole all the food prepared at the king's court, except what was consumed the very first night.

It will be remembered that Nuadu, King of Tuatha Dé Danann, yields his throne to Lug, the sage, in order to be delivered from the bondage of the Fomoire. In this Welsh story, Lludd the king of Britain, whose name is probably the equivalent of *Nuadu*,[38] rids the Island of the three plagues by fol-lowing the instructions of his wise brother Llefelys. The barren-ness caused on May Eve by the dragon's cry brings to mind the theft of Teyrnon's foals by the mysterious claw every May Eve and the precautions which in some districts are still considered necessary on this night of witchery.[39] After the dragons have been buried, they ensure that no plague shall enter the Island. This safeguard, together with the giant's promise that he will restore the losses he has inflicted and never repeat them, and that he himself will become the liegeman of Lludd, recalls the conditions which Manawydan demands of Llwyd and those which Lug, after the Battle of Mag Tuired, demands of Loch and of Bres.

The chief characters in the Second Branch of the Mabinogi belong to the family of Llŷr: two brothers, namely Brân the Blessed, a colossus who rules the Island of the Mighty,* and Manawydan, and a sister Branwen, 'one of the three matriarchs of the Island'. These three have two halfbrothers: Efnisien, who always creates hostility, and the peacemaker Nisien. The story begins with the marriage of Branwen to Matholwch, King of Ireland, who comes to Harlech to seek her hand. On the occasion of her marriage feast at Aberffraw, Efnisien, who has not been consulted in the matter, takes his revenge by mutilating the bridegroom's horses. As part of the compensation for this insult, Brân gives Matholwch a magic cauldron which originally was brought out of a lake in Ireland: slain men would be resuscitated in it overnight, but they would be bereft of speech.

For a year Branwen is held in high honour in Ireland. She gives birth to a son, Gwern. But afterwards Matholwch is constrained by his subjects to make her suffer for Efnisien's outrage. Driven from the king's room, she is compelled to work as a cook in the court, and every day the butcher comes and strikes her a blow. This goes on for three years. Meanwhile, Branwen rears a starling and teaches it to convey to her brother news of her woe. Thereupon the hosts of the Isle of the Mighty invade Ireland, the gigantic Brân striding through the channel and later lying down to form a bridge for his men to cross the Llinon.** Matholwch offers his submission and Branwen urges that it should be accepted 'lest the country be spoiled'; but when peace is in sight, Efnisien again takes offence and casts Branwen's son into the blazing fire. In the battle that follows, Brân is mortally wounded and Efnisien sacrifices himself in order to destroy the magic cauldron which has been giving new life to the slain Irish warriors. Only five pregnant women are left alive to repeople Ireland; only seven survivors, among them Manawydan and Pryderi, return to Britain,

* Britain.
** ? Shannon.

bringing with them the head of Brân for burial. When they come to land, Branwen—throughout a figure of great dignity and restraint—looks at the two countries, what can be seen of them, and, saying that two good islands have been laid waste because of her, she dies of a broken heart.

Soon, news is brought that the seven lords left in charge of the Island of the Mighty have been overpowered by their kinsman Caswallawn son of Beli, who wore a magic mantle to make himself invisible, and that Brân's own son has died of heartbreak 'at the sight of the sword slaying his men and he not knowing who slew them'. Following the instructions given them by Brân, the seven survivors then spend seven years in a feast at Harlech, with the three birds of Rhiannon singing over the sea to delight them, and another fourscore years in a royal hall at Gwales,* where they remain, oblivious of every sorrow and loss and unaware of the passage of time, until a forbidden door is opened and they are obliged to continue their sorrowful journey. The head of Brân, which has been as pleasant company as Brân himself was during his life, is then buried in London, and like the buried dragons mentioned above, it ensures that no invaders shall plague the Island.

The story of Branwen has some features in common with two Irish stories which have little or no connection with one another.[40] Inasmuch as it is an account of a marriage alliance between two peoples which is followed by a great battle ending in annihilation, it has affinities with the story of the Second Battle of Mag Tuired, which concludes with forebodings of chaos, the end of the world. In the Irish tale, the function of the magic cauldron is performed by a well which restores the dead warriors of the Tuatha to life. But while the evidence of two early Welsh poems might suggest that the Ireland of this Branch represents Annwfn or 'Caer Siddi',[41] no close comparison with the story of the Tuatha and the Fomoire seems possible.

* An island off the coast of south-west Wales (Grassholm).

Another Irish tale,[42] which we would mention, was written (in its present form) in the Early Modern Period. It is concerned with the tragic suffering inflicted on the daughter and the three sons of Lir—Manannán does not appear among them—through the spell cast upon them by their jealous stepmother. It will be recalled that the pathos of the Welsh story of the family of Llŷr is heightened by the account of the blissful interludes provided by the feasting at Harlech, during which the seven survivors are charmed by the singing of the birds of Rhiannon, and the untroubled timeless sojourn at Gwales. The Irish story provides the same contrast, for the singing of the Children of Lir, in the form of swans, above Lake Derry- varagh, holds Tuatha Dé Danann and the men of Ireland entranced for three hundred years. Their singing would give sleep even to the sick and the troubled, and make happy all who heard it. After spending equally long periods in two places off the coast of Ireland, the Children of Lir return home from their exile only to find desolation awaiting them, and as in the Welsh story, it is the daughter who gives voice to their grief.

The name of Manawydan son of Llŷr, who is closely linked with Brân in the story of Branwen, is clearly related to that of Manannán mac Lir.[43] In an early Irish story, a personage named Bran son of Febal, voyaging to a magic wonderland, meets Manannán riding over the waves, while according to the *dindsenchas* Manannán had a brother by the name of Bron.[41] It will be remembered that when Manannán distributes the *síde* among the lords of Tuatha Dé Danann, he himself takes none of them, but dwells beyond the sea in Emain Ablach. Similarly, Manawydan, who plays no part in the action of the Second Branch, is in the Third described as a humble lord who has never claimed land or territory, and though, by be- coming Rhiannon's second husband, he secures the use of the seven cantreds of Dyfed, this territory remains Pryderi's in name. Nevertheless, it is Manawydan who succeeds in com- pelling Llwyd, the hostile wizard, to remove the enchantment from Dyfed, to restore Pryderi and Rhiannon, and to promise that never again shall a spell be cast upon the country.

The Fourth Branch of the Mabinogi, like the Second, introduces a new group of characters. They may be broadly described as the family of Dôn. It is a peculiarity of Math son of Mathonwy, Lord of Gwynedd, that he can live only if his feet are held in a maiden's lap, unless the turmoil of war should make this impossible. He loses the services of one such maiden through the intrigue of his sister's sons, Gwydion son of Dôn and Gilfaethwy son of Dôn, an intrigue which also results in the death of Pryderi. Nevertheless it is Gwydion, the counsellor and schemer in each section of this Branch, who advises Math about seeking a new foot-holder. Gwydion's sister, Aranrhod daughter of Dôn, is fetched, and to prove her virginity Math commands her to step over his magic wand. In so doing she drops a boy-child, and as she makes for the door she again drops something which Gwydion promptly hides in a chest. There he later finds another child. The first boy is baptized and named Dylan, whereupon he immediately makes for the sea and receives the sea's nature—hence his name, Dylan Eil Ton ('Sea son of Wave'). When Gwydion later takes the other child—who seems to be his own son—to Aranrhod's sea-girt fortress, she is so offended with him for thus pursuing her shame that she swears on her son this destiny: that he shall not get a name until he get it from her. Gwydion and the boy again appear at her court, this time in the guise of shoemakers, and she is induced to remark on the deft hand of the fair one, whence his name Lleu Llawgyffes.* Similarly when she swears on the boy a second destiny, that he shall not bear arms till she equip him, it is again Gwydion who by means of his magic illusions brings her to do so, and a third destiny, that he shall not have a wife 'of the race that is now on earth', is circumvented by Lleu's marriage to Blodeuedd ('Flowers'), a woman

---

* Lleu of the Deft Hand (*lleu*: light, fair).

conjured by Math and Gwydion from the flowers of the oak, the broom, and the meadowsweet.

Blodeuedd falls in love with Gronw, lord of Penllyn, and plots with her lover to kill her husband. Feigning solicitude for his safety, she elicits from Lleu how he might be killed. He could not be slain within a house or outside, on horseback or a-foot, and moreover, the spear would have to be prepared during a whole year, but only while people were at Mass on Sunday. Eventually a tub is set under a thatched frame on the bank of a river, and Lleu, half-dressed after taking a bath, is inveigled into taking his stand with one foot on the back of a he-goat and the other on the edge of the tub. Smitten in this position by Gronw's spear, he flies away in the form of an eagle. After a long search, Gwydion, by following on the track of a wayward sow, discovers him in an oak-tree on an upland plain—'nor rain wets it nor heat melts . . . the sanctuary of a fair lord'[45]— his decayed flesh dropping to the ground. Gwydion, with his magic wand, restores him to his human form, and all the good physicians of Gwynedd are brought to heal him. Then Gronw is made to suffer at Lleu's hands the death he had intended for Lleu, and it is said that Lleu later became lord of Gwynedd.

Like the Peoples of the Goddess Danann, the family of Dôn include several wizards, adepts at feats of illusion and transformation. Of Math it is said that whatever whispering, however low, that would be between men, if the wind met it, he would know it. He seems to be related in name to the Irish Mathu, named as one of the three prophets of the heathens, the other two being Nuadu* and Goibniu; also to Matha, the druid who represents the old faith in early accounts of St Patrick, and perhaps to Mathgen, sorcerer of Tuatha Dé Danann in 'The Second Battle of Mag Tuired'.[46] In addition

---

* In another Welsh tale, 'Kulhwch and Olwen', there are brief references to Lludd Llaw Ereint—whose name is equivalent to that of Nuadu Airgetlám, king of Tuatha Dé Danann—and also to another son of Dôn, Amaethon.

to Gwydion, Gilfaethwy, and Aranrhod, the family of Dôn includes Gofannon, whose name, like that of Goibniu, the donor of the Feast of Immortality, comes from the same root as *gof*, Irish *goba*, 'smith'.[47] The story of the slaying of Dylan by his uncle Gofannon, which is alluded to in the *Mabinogi*, is probably cognate with the story of the death of Ruadán at the hands of Goibniu.[48]

The name of Lleu seems equivalent to that of Lug, who is sometimes called Lug Lámfada—'Lug of the Long Arm (or Hand)'. 'Lleu of the Ready Hand' does not manifest the all-round competence of the Irish Samildánach, but the peculiar conditions which govern his death, and the way he survives even when these are fulfilled, show his supernatural quality. Lug too has a wife who proves unfaithful to him with Cermat son of the Dagda. Cermat is killed by Lug (as Gronw is killed by Lleu) and the role of the Dagda who, after searching the world for the means to heal his son, resuscitates him with a magic staff, recalls that of Gwydion, not in relation to Gronw but in relation to Lleu. Lug in turn is killed by the spear of Mac Cuill son of Cermat.[49] The name of Blodeuedd, Lleu's unfaithful wife, is partly equivalent to the Irish *Bláthnat*, which in one story is the name of a wife obtained from 'the House of Donn' for Lug's son, and in another the name of an unfaithful wife who reveals to her lover when her husband (CúRoí) may be slain.[50]

The name of Dôn seems to be a bye-form of *Donwy*,[51] which occurs in *Dyfrdonwy** and, perhaps, in *Trydonwy*, both apparently names of rivers in Wales. *Dyfrdonwy* is certainly given as the name of one of 'the three wells of the ocean'.[52] The other two wells are identified with the sea-flood and the fall of rain through the atmosphere, respectively, while Dyfr-donwy, according to a late text, 'comes (?) through the veins of (the) mountains like the flinty feast made by the King of kings'. The name *Donwy* can be related phonologically to the

* *dyfr*: 'water'.

Irish *Danann* and also to *Dānu*, the name of a goddess who figures in the Rig Veda. In the Veda, *dānu* signifies 'stream' and 'the waters of heaven',[53] and the same root is to be seen in the names of rivers, from the Russian Don, Dnieper, and Dniester to the Danube and to several rivers in England known as Don.[54] The Vedic goddess Dānu is the mother of Vṛtra, the chief adversary of Indra, the king of the gods, but she is also the consort of the sovereign gods Mitrāvaruṇā.[55] Her ambi-valent role is paralleled by that of Danann in Irish tradition. Danann is the mother of the gods of Ireland and gives her name to the wizard Tuatha. On the other hand, 'the Three Gods of Danann' are usually her three sons, Brian, Iuchar, and Iucharba, who appear in Irish story only as the ruthless slayers of Cian, the father of Lug, the saviour of the Tuatha Dé.[56] Nevertheless, in 'The Second Battle of Mag Tuired', the same title signifies the three craftsmen Goibniu, Luchta, and Credne, while in another story, 'The Wooing of Étaín', it signifies Lug, the Dagda, and Ogma, the three leaders of the Tuatha.[57] The Dagda and Ogma, as well as Lug, are some-times described as sons of Ethniu,[58] and in 'The Wooing of Étaín', *Ethniu* (which also occurs as a river name) is said to be another name for Boand, paramour of the Dagda and eponym of the Boyne, the river which, according to the metrical *dind-senchas*, is known as 'Roof of the Ocean' as far as Scotland, as the Severn in England, as the Tiber in Rome, as the Jordan and the Euphrates in the East, and as the Tigris 'in enduring paradise'.[59]

4

The tales of Tuatha Dé Danann and the Children of Dôn and other 'mythological' tales abound in enchantments and trans-formations, and victory is gained by superior knowledge and wizardry. Intelligence and magic are the distinctive features. When we turn to the tales of the Ulster Cycle, on the other hand, though we are again in a world of marvels, the heart of the matter is quite different. The central group of characters are not wizards but warriors who glory in their prowess and their unyielding endurance. It is not primarily intelligence but will-power and fearless action in the face of terrifying odds that are celebrated. Here we are in the world of the hero.

Challenges, taunts, and the vaunting of exploits, already accomplished or to come, serve as the theme in several tales of this cycle, where honour and prestige are the motivating principles. The rivalry between the two northern provinces, Ulster and Connacht, provides the setting for several of the tales, for it is said that 'for three hundred years before the birth of Christ there was war between them'.[60] When Conchobar was king of Ulster, the dominant figure in Connacht was Queen Medb. Her husband, King Ailill is a much less imposing character, and before her marriage to him Medb had been the wife of King Conchobar of Ulster.[61] In 'The Story of the Pig of Mac Dathó',[62] the king of Leinster, Mac Dathó, had a famous hound, the guardian of his kingdom. This hound was sought at the same time by King Ailill and Queen Medb, on the one hand, and by King Conchobar on the other. Mac Dathó's wife suggested that it should be promised to each in turn, and plans were made for the rival parties to come for it on the same day. At the great feast which was prepared for them, the main dish was a matchless pig, nurtured for seven years on the milk of fifty cows. Bricriu, who in several tales is the evil-tongued counsellor who sows dissension among the Ulster heroes, suggested that the pig should be divided 'according to battle-victories'. After a brief exchange of taunts between the Ulstermen and two heroes of Munster, a Connacht man elevated himself above all the men of Ireland, and placing himself knife in hand beside the pig, 'Find ye now', said he, 'one man among the men of Ireland who can contend with me, or else leave to me the dividing of the pig.' This was Cet son of Mágu, of whom it is told elsewhere that he often went into Ulster to seek the slaying of a man, 'for from his initiation he never went without the slaughter of an Ulster-man'.[63] One after another of the Ulster warriors take up his challenge, but each has to retire in shame when he is taunted with some past occasion when Cet brought humiliation upon him. Cet is now ready to carve the pig, when Conall Cer-nach* of Ulster enters the hall and contests the privilege with him: "'I swear by that by which my people swear, since I took spear in hand I have never been a day without slaying a Connachtman or a night without plundering by fire, and I have never slept without a Connachtman's head beneath my knee." "It is true," said Cet, "thou art a better warrior than I. But if it were [my brother] Ánluan who were here, he would match thee with victory for victory. It is bad for us that he is not in the house." "But he is," said Conall, drawing Ánluan's head from his belt; and he hurled it on to Cet's chest so that blood gushed over his lips. Then Conall sat down by the pig and Cet went away from it. "Now let them come to the con-test!" said Conall.'

In 'The Feast of Bricriu',[64] the three rival warriors who con-tend for 'the champion's portion', a huge cauldron filled with the choicest food and drink, are all Ulstermen—Loegaire Búadach,** Conall Cernach, and CúChulainn—and the tale serves to bring out the incomparable fearlessness and power of CúChulainn, the matchless hero of this Cycle. Here again it is Bricriu who brings about the contest and he also sets the wives of the heroes wrangling over precedence at the feast. The three warriors are sent to Ailill, King of Connacht, and later to CúRoí mac Dáiri, King of Munster, for judgement. At Crúachan, the residence of the king of Connacht, three magic cats from the Cave of Crúachan are let loose to attack them during the night. CúChulainn alone stands his ground. When eventually they reach the fort of CúRoí mac Dáiri

---

* Conall the Victorious
** Loegaire the Triumphant.

CúRoí is abroad on his travels as usual: 'Ireland could not contain him for his haughtiness, renown and rank, over‑bearing fury, strength and gallantry.' Following CúRoí's in‑structions, Bláthnat his wife tells them that each of them must take his turn to guard the fort until her husband returns. The first night Loegaire, as the eldest of the contestants, keeps watch, when a huge and horrible spectre appears from the western sea and throws him out over the fort. The next night Conall fares likewise, and on the third night it is CúChulainn's turn to take his place at the look‑out post. This is the night on which it is foretold that the monster of the nearby lake will devour the whole company of the fort, man and beast. CúChulainn first kills three groups of nine attackers, and when the lake monster appears he hacks it to pieces after tearing out its heart with his hand. The spectre then appears from the west, from the sea. As a result of CúChulainn's salmon‑leap, his swooping‑feat with his drawn sword over his opponent's head, and his dizzy circling in mid‑air around him, the spectre is constrained to ask for quarter. In return for his life he grants CúChulainn his three wishes, uttered with one breath: for himself the sovereignty of Ireland's heroes and the champion's portion without dispute, for his wife precedence over the ladies of Ulster for ever. The spectre vanishes, but soon afterwards CúRoí returns and like‑wise gives his verdict in CúChulainn's favour.

When they return to Emain, CúChulainn's rivals still re‑fuse to admit his pre‑eminence and so the matter rests until, at eventide after the assembly and the games, a huge, horrible *bachlach** appears in Conchobar's hall, the Branch‑red, and stands beside the fire like a blazing luminary. He carries a huge tree, a block, and an axe and craves a boon he has not been granted anywhere in the world, namely that a warrior shall be‑head him the first night, he the warrior the following night.**

---

* Shepherd, peasant, boor.
** In its original form the challenge is that one of the warriors should allow he *bachlach* to behead him first, but in the event this order is not followed.

Munremur, Loegaire, and Conall accept the challenge on successive nights, but after seeing the challenger leave the hall carrying his head and his axe, none of them abides to face the ordeal. The honour of the Ulstermen is clearly at stake. CúChulainn now strikes off and smashes the giant's head, and the following night he lays his own neck on the block. The *bachlach* raises his axe till it reaches the roof-tree of the hall. The creaking of the old hide worn by the giant and the crashing of the axe are like 'the loud noise of a wood tempest-tossed in a night of storm'. But the blade is brought down with the blunt side below, and now, in Emain, CúChulainn is awarded the triple prize already adjudged to him in Crúachan and at CúRoí's fort. The *bachlach* then vanishes. He was CúRoí mac Dáiri.

In yet another story,[65] CúChulainn, fresh from his victories over Goll, a one-eyed champion who appears from the sea, and over Garb who has slain many of the Ulster host, appears unexpectedly at the door of the hall where Conchobar and his warriors are feasting. He insists on being announced only as a youth of Ulster—even as Lug declared himself a mere wright— and on being refused admission he forces an entry and threatens destruction to the king and all his company. Reconciliation follows, and as Lug was assigned the seat of the sage, so here CúChulainn is given the seat of the champion.

The central story of the Ulster Cycle is *Táin Bó Cuailnge*, 'The Cattle-raid of Cuailnge',[66] an epic narrative which tells of an expedition by the combined forces of four provinces, led by Medb of Connacht, to carry off by force a great bull possessed by one of the landowners of Ulster. The ambitious and ruthless Queen Medb coveted the bull, Donn Cuailnge,* lest her possessions be one whit inferior to those of her husband Ailill which included the great bull Finnbennach.**

* The Brown One of Cuailnge.
** Whitehorn.

In the Book of Leinster, ten tales are listed as 'preliminary tales', that is tales which precede the *Táin*.[67] There is only a tenuous link between some of them and the great epic, but one of them tells how the story of the *Táin* was recovered from Fergus mac Roich, one of the chief protagonists, who arose from his grave to tell it; in others, such as 'The Adventures of Nera', the *Táin* is prophesied or prefigured, while others again throw light on certain aspects of the situation which is envisaged in the epic. Thus, in the *Táin*, Fergus mach Roich, former king of Ulster, and Cormac son of King Conchobar, together with other warriors of Ulster to the number of thirty hundred, appear on the side of Medb. One of the preliminary tales shows that they were in exile in Connacht because Conchobar had broken faith with them concerning the safe-conduct granted to the sons of Uisliu* and they in revenge had slain many of their own people and burned Emain. Another of these tales accounts for the strange disability which, for three months, prevents the Ulstermen from undertaking the defence of their province. Macha, a woman who had appeared mysteriously in the house of a rich Ulster farmer and brought him great wealth, was later compelled, in spite of her being with child, to run in competition with the king's horses. At the end of the race she gave birth to twins (hence the name of Ulster's royal residence, *Emain Macha*, 'The Twins of Macha') and pronounced a curse on the Ulstermen even to the ninth generation. In their time of greatest difficulty they would be as bereft of force as a woman in childbed and that for the space of a *noínden***—a 'confinement' of warriors which is paralleled in the thought and custom of other peoples.[68] However, CúChulainn and his father are not affected by this torpor. In explanation of this it is said that CúChulainn was not born an Ulsterman, and in other texts he is described as a foster-child of the Ulstermen.[69] This recalls the ambiguous affiliation of Bres

* See pages 280 f.
** Nine days, or four days and five nights, or five days and four nights.

and of Lug—Lug who like CúChulainn is deliberately but
vainly restrained from taking part in his great battle and who,
in the *Táin*, heals CúChulainn's wounds and for three days
takes his place as the defender of Ulster. According to one
tradition, Lug was reincarnated in CúChulainn.

Yet another of the preliminary tales tells of the origin of the
Whitehorn and Donn of Cuailnge,[70] the rival bulls whose
tremendous fight provides a fitting conclusion to the *Táin*.
They had previously appeared in various forms. As the wizard
swineherds of Ochall, king of the *síd* of Connacht, and Bodb,
king of the *síd* of Munster, respectively, they were first friends
and later rivals. Afterwards they appeared as ravens who prophesied the slaughter which would be occasioned by them;
then as water beasts devouring one another—when they fought,
'fiery swords darted out of their jaws and reached the sky'; then
as famous champions each again tested his comrade's might
before the two became demons, and then again water worms.
One of the them, when taken from a spring by Queen Medb,
advised her to marry Ailill; the other, taken from a river in
Cuailnge by Fiachna mac Dáiri, prophesied the fight with the
beast of Connacht. Both of them were then swallowed by cows
and reborn as the finest bulls ever seen in Ireland, Finn and
Dub, 'White' and 'Black'. The Bull of Cuailnge could
shelter a hundred warriors of Ulster from the heat and cold,
and fifty boys could play of an evening on his back. He would
beget fifty calves a day, and these would be born the following
day. During his wanderings on the occasion of the great cattle-
raid, he is counselled by the Morrígan, and in his fight with
the Whitehorn he courses over the whole country, and for a
day and a night he carries the remains of his slaughtered foe in
torn fragments about his ears and horns before scattering them
over the face of Ireland. He ends his career by making a great
slaughter of the women and youths and children of his own
Cuailnge, and then, after he has turned his back to the hill,
his heart breaks in his breast and he belches it out like a black
stone of dark blood.

This clash of two great powers by no means overshadows
either the long series of combats by virtue of which the youthful
CúChulainn, during his long sleepless vigil, stays the advance
of the enemy host single-handed or the final great battle in
which the hosts of Medb are routed by the awakened Ulstermen. In one story,[71] CúChulainn is described as a small
black-browed man, greatly resplendent, and in the *Táin* much
play is made of his youthful and inoffensive appearance, his
beardless countenance and his boyish gaiety. Yet when his
terrible battle frenzy came upon him he changed out of all
recognition. From crown to sole his whole body trembled like
a bullrush in mid-torrent. He made a mad whirling feat of his
body within his skin so that his heels, his calves, and his hams
appeared in front. He drew one eye back into his head, the
other stood out huge and red on his cheek, and his mouth was
distorted and twisted up to his ears so that his throat appeared
in sight and a man's head could go into his mouth. His hair
bristled all over his head like hawthorn, with a drop of blood
on each single hair. The champion's light stood out of his
forehead as long and thick as a warrior's whetstone, and from
the ridge of his crown there arose a thick column of dark blood
like the mast of a great ship. It is no wonder that he was called
'The Contorted One'. When he displays his comeliness to
the women and maidens, the poets, and the men of art, it is a
baroque kind of beauty, as M.-L. Sjoestedt remarks[72]—his
hair, brown at the skin, blood-red in the middle, golden
yellow in the crown; four spots, yellow, green, blue, and purple,
on each of his cheeks, seven pupils in each of his eyes, seven
toes on each foot, seven fingers on each hand, 'with the clutch
of a hawk's claw . . . in every one of them'.

In his rage 'CúChulainn would recognize neither comrades
nor friends. Alike he would strike them before and behind.'[73]
Even so, it is to be noted that he rejects the advances of that
dread figure of destruction, the Morrígan, and so incurs her
hostile intervention when he is hardest pressed in battle. May
it be that sheer destructiveness is an enemy that the warrior

must constantly shun, and that the Dagda, the creative. All-father, the lord of life and death, is the true consort of annihilation? With one end of his staff the Dagda can kill nine men, but with the other he restores them to life.[74]

We have already noted that the qualities revealed in this cycle of stories are violent assertiveness, invincible energy, and power of resistance. Here too one finds the conflict of loyalties which, without the warrior's discipline, would paralyse the will. The host of Medb is guided by her lover Fergus, former king of Ulster, who is constrained to face in battle not only his own stepson, Conchobar, who has ousted him from his kingdom, but also his beloved fosterchild, CúChulainn. CúChulainn himself has to fight to the death his best friend and former companion, FerDiad, and the extreme courtesy with which the grim battle is waged serves only to heighten the personal tragedy. The same theme is typical of the early poems and sagas of the Germanic peoples.[75] Again and again the hero is confronted with a desperate choice between two courses, each of which is felt to be evil and each of which presents itself as a duty. Unlike the wizards of the Mythological Cycle, who display their superiority by the circumvention of destinies, the hero justfies himself by his unhesitating choice between dire alternatives and by the resolute way he follows his chosen path though he fully realizes where it will lead him. It is the apotheosis of the will that is depicted here. Nowhere is it better exemplified than in the short tale of CúChulainn's only son Conlaí.[76] Brought up in his mother's country, the boy is a stranger to the Ulstermen when he arrives in a skiff off the coast of Ireland. There is a charming picture of him shooting down birds without killing them, and then releasing them and bringing them back with his call, but the way he repulses several of Ulster's greatest warriors shows that his skill at arms is prodigious. CúChulainn, the defender of Ulster, cannot evade his duty to compel the stranger to reveal his identity. Conlaí, for his part, has been sworn not to make himself known to any one man or to refuse combat with any. When he is warned that this might well be his own son, CúChulainn replies: 'Even though it were he indeed, I would kill him for the honour of Ulster.' And when the deed is done, he carries the youth back in his arms and throws him down before Conchobar and his warriors: 'Here is my son for you, men of Ulster.'

5

The tales of the Fenian or Ossianic Cycle are similar to those of the Ulster Cycle in that they tell of heroic fighters, but the two groups of stories differ profoundly in their characters, their milieu, their ethos, and their provenance.

The Irish call this third branch of their literature *fianaigheacht*, lore of the *fiana*. The word *fian* (plural, *fiana*) is used of a troop of professional soldiers and also of 'a band of roving men whose principal occupations were hunting and war'.[77] Thurneysen suggested[78] relating the word to the name *Féni* which some-times signifies the Irish people, and sometimes the body of commoners as distinct from the ruling classes. When used in connection with board games, the word *fian* itself sometimes denotes the set of pieces used in the game, but when it is said that 'their *fian* have checkmated our king (*branán*)' in a game in which there was apparently only one king-piece, the term seems to denote the pieces of inferior status.[79] The same word is sometimes found in conjunction with the word *foirenn* and it is interesting to note that the Welsh word *gwerin* which is cog-nate with *foirenn* signifies a set of pieces, a complement, and also the people as distinguished from the nobility. Another Welsh word used for commoners as a body of people is *gwrêng*, and in medieval Welsh this compound of *gŵr* ('man') and *ieuang* ('young') denotes young gentlemen training to bear arms. In Irish too, *óc*, 'young man' could also mean 'a warrior', *óc féne* 'one of a roving band', 'a "fian" warrior', and *óc-aire* 'the lowest grade of freeman of full age and status'.[80] This asso-ciation of juniority with a military group and a social class occurs in other societies. The Roman *juvenes* were men whose age qualified them for military service and marriage, while among the various meanings of the English word *yeoman* ('young man') one finds 'a servant', 'an attendant in a royal or noble household', 'a freeholder under the rank of gentleman', 'a freeholder . . . serving as a foot/soldier', and (in the plural) 'pawns at chess'.[81] The Irish word *fian* is found glossed by *ceithearn* (anglicized as *kerne*) which denotes 'a troop of foot/soldiers', and one distinguishing feature of the Fenian warriors is that they usually fight on foot, never like the Ulster heroes in chariots. Another is the camaraderie which they display, the intense pleasure found in a life shared with members of one's own special group, particularly when that group is 'a picked body of fine young men'.[82] This is in marked contrast with the harsh individualism and clamorous rivalry which char/acterizes so many of the Ulster stories. Finn is pictured as the captain of King Cormac mac Airt's soldiery, his house/troop, his mercenaries, and his huntsmen. His role is very different from that of CúChulainn, the lone champion who commanded no army.

The *fiana* had their peculiar organization and customs. Of 'Finn's people' it is said:[83]

> 'their strength was seven score and ten officers, each man of these having thrice nine warriors, every one bound (as was the way with CúChulainn in the time when he was there) to certain conditions of service, which were: that in satis/faction of their guarantee violated they must not accept material compensation; in the matter of valuables or of meat must not deny any; no single individual of them to fly before nine warriors.
>
> 'Of such not a man was taken into the Fiana; nor admitted whether to the great Gathering of Uisnech, to the Convention of Tailtiu, or to Tara's Feast; until both his paternal and his maternal correlatives, his *tuatha* and kindreds, had given securities for them to the effect that,

though at the present instant they were slain, yet should no claim be urged in lieu of them: and this in order that to none other but to themselves alone they should look to avenge them. On the other hand: in case it were they that inflicted great mischiefs upon others, reprisals not to be made upon their several people.

'Of all these again not a man was taken until he were a prime poet versed in the twelve books of poesy. No man was taken till in the ground a large hole had been made (such as to reach the fold of his belt) and he put into it with his shield and a fore-arm's length of a hazel stick. Then must nine warriors, having nine spears, with a ten furrows' width betwixt them and him, assail him and in concert let fly at him. If past that guard of his he were hurt then, he was not received into Fianship.

'Not a man of them was taken till his hair had been interwoven into braids on him and he started at a run through Ireland's woods; while they, seeking to wound him, followed in his wake, there having been between him and them but one forest bough by way of interval at first. Should he be overtaken, he was wounded and not received into the Fiana after. If his weapons had quivered in his hand, he was not taken. Should a branch in the wood have disturbed anything of his hair out of its braiding, neither was he taken. If he had cracked a dry stick under his foot [as he ran] he was not accepted. Unless that [at his full speed] he had both jumped a stick level with his brow, and stooped to pass under one even with his knee, he was not taken. Also, unless without slackening his pace he could with his nail extract a thorn from his foot, he was not taken into Fianship: but if he performed all this he was of Finn's people.'

Fianship was an honourable institution, recognized in the laws and considered essential to the welfare of the community.[84] According to Keating,[85] who wrote in the seventeenth century, the *fiana* used to be quartered on the men of Ireland from Samain to Beltaine, while in the summer half of the year they engaged in hunting and supported themselves thereby. In both seasons they were expected to police the country. More-over, no girl could be given in marriage until she had been offered to the *fiana*.[86] These last stipulations remind one of the privileges and duties assumed by the traditional youth-groups still found in some rural communities,[87] while the literature of Robin Hood perhaps offers the nearest counterpart in English tradition.

In one story[88] we are told that Feradach Fechtnach, King of Ireland, had two sons, Tuathal and Fiacha. Feradach died and his two sons divided Ireland between them—her wealth and her treasure, her cattle and her fortresses to the one; to the other her cliffs and her estuaries, her mast and her 'sea-fruit', her salmon, her hunting, and her venery. When this story is related to the nobles of Christian Ireland they protest that the partition was not equitable. Whereupon Oisín (the son of Finn) inquires of them which of the two portions they themselves would have preferred. 'Her feasts, her dwelling-houses, and all her good things,' they reply. 'The portion which they would deem the worse,' says the Fenian leader, Caílte, 'that is the one which we should prefer.' In this story (according to the poem included in the same text), the elder brother assumed the kingship, while the younger, Fiacha Finn, chose to cast his lot with the Fiana. Fiacha chose 'rivers, wastes, wilds and woods, and precipices and estuaries'. But this did not prevent him from succeeding to the kingship after the death of his brother. To enter a *fian* was thus a suitable role for those who, because of their junior status, were without land and office.

The partition we have described is comparable with that made between the Sons of Míl and Tuatha Dé Danann, by which the latter received the underground or hidden half of the country. In a Fenian story it is said that St Patrick will relegate Tuatha Dé Danann 'to the foreheads of hills and

rocks'.[89] The *fiana*, the *síd*-folk, Tuatha Dé Danann, and the
Fomoire belong to those parts of Ireland which are outside the
regions of settlement. The *fiana* are depicted as belonging to bygone days, to the pre-Christian past, and their name is found
in association with those of the Fomoire and the fairy host
(*síthchuire*).[90] The mothers of the Fenian heroes are said to belong to Tuatha Dé Danann,[91] and their opponents likewise
belong to the *síd*-dwellers. In a tale now dated to the eighth
century,[92] Finn slays a food-stealing enemy, Cúldub,* as he
enters a *síd*. Finn's thumb is jammed in the door of the *síd* and
when he puts it in his mouth he divines Cúldub's name. This
illumination obtained by Finn as a result of chewing his thumb
recurs in other stories. In several early texts, as O'Rahilly and
Murphy have shown,[93] Finn's enemy has a name or else antecedents which suggest the character of a supernatural malevolent burner. We will merely mention Fothad, one of a trio
of that name who are also called 'Single-god', 'Strong-god',
and 'Fair-god', Dearg ('Red') who used to jump 'to and fro
across the cooking hearth', and Aillén mac Midna who,
blowing fire from his mouth, burned Tara every Samain.
Aillén, like Cúldub, is slain as he enters the *síd*. Finn ousts
from the *síd* of Almu his maternal grandfather, Tadg son of
Nuadu, who was responsible for the slaying of Finn's father
by Goll** mac Morna, a rival *fian*-captain also known as
Aed (*aed* = 'fire'). In tales recorded in the modern period, Balor,
Lug's maternal grandfather, is responsible for the death of Lug's
father, and he also threatens to burn Ireland with his evil eye.
It appears that in all three cycle of stories the hero has to defeat
an antagonist whose one eye and destructive character appear
to connect him with the Fomoire, the representatives of chaos.
In the Ulster Cycle the theme occurs in the story of the slaying
of Goll and Garb.†

* 'Black-hair'.
** 'One-eye'.
† *Supra*, p. 57.

The fact that the *fiana* are warriors links their lore with the Ulster stories, but their close relations with the *síd*-dwellers, and Finn's role as a poet and diviner, seem to connect them with the Mythological Cycle. There is a correspondence between Finn's name and that of the Welsh Gwyn ap Nudd, who is likewise a warrior and a hunter, and Gwyn is the king of Annwfn, the king of fairy.[94] But in the same way as the warrior-ship of the *fiana* is on a lower plane than that of the Ulster heroes, Finn's divination is on a lower plane than the wizardry of the Mythological Cycle. As to the character of the *fiana*'s hunting and their delight in the chase, comparison has been suggested with the hunting on foot and with dogs which is still popular among the small farmers and townsmen of certain districts of modern Ireland.[95]

There is evidence from about the eleventh century that the Fenian tales were even then a part of popular tradition,[96] and they have been cherished by the countrymen of Ireland and Scotland down to our own day. On the other hand, while references dating from the eighth century or earlier show that some of these tales were known also to the literate classes, and while there are references in the Middle Ages to differences between folk and learned versions of the same tales, it seems that this branch of the tradition hardly formed part of the repertoire of the learned *filid*. In a twelfth-century list of more than nine score tales which the *filid* were expected to know, only five belong to the Fenian Cycle.[97] Again, whereas the extant text of *Táin Bó Cuailnge* is apparently based on an earlier ninth-century written version, and the story may well have been in writing before the end of the seventh century, the most comprehensive text of the Fenian Cycle does not appear until the end of the twelfth century. This is *Acallam na Senórach*, 'The Colloquy of the Ancients',[98] a long rambling narrative in which Caílte recounts to St Patrick and others of his period the adventures of the *fiana* in war and the chase, adventures which were associated with the hills and woods and lakes they see as they make their way over the face of Ireland. From the twelfth century on, the stream of Fenian literature flows strongly. On the other hand, the great period of the Ulster stories was nearly over, and it seems that very few of them were ever included in the repertoire of the storytellers of the ordinary people.

The Fenian Cycle differs also in form and temper from the other cycles. It comes into prominence in the period of the poetry of the troubadour and the *trouvère* and the Arthurian romances of Europe. Its greatest story tells of an elopement—'The Pursuit of Diarmaid and Gráinne'—which we shall discuss in a later chapter.* The characteristic form of this branch of the literature (from the twelfth century onwards) is the speech-poem or ballad, usually 'spoken' by Oisín or Caílte or Finn, and often giving expression to a delight in the sights and sounds familiar to those who live an out-door life in the waste and the wild and the woods. The following is a translation of one of the poems in the 'Colloquy':[99]

> 'Arran of the many stags, the sea reaches to its shoulder; island where companies were fed, ridges where blue spears are reddened.
>
> 'Skittish deer upon its peaks, ripe cranberries on its heaths, cold water in its streams, mast upon its brown oaks.
>
> 'Greyhounds there, and beagles, blackberries and sloes of the blackthorn; its dwellings close against the woods, stags scattered about its oak-groves.
>
> 'Gathering of purple lichen upon its rocks, grass without blemish on its slopes, a pleasant covering over its crags; gambolling of fawns, trout leaping.
>
> 'Smooth is its clearing, fat its swine, pleasant its fields, a tale that may be believed; its nuts on the tops of its hazel-wood, sailing of long ships past it.
>
> 'It is delightful when the fair weather comes, trout under the brinks of its streams, seagulls answer each other round its white cliff; delightful at all times is Arran.'

* Page 281.

In the Ulster Cycle, the only poems that are comparable are uttered by a woman whose lover is doomed.[100]

Whereas the Ulster Cycle is characteristically heroic, the Fenian Cycle is characteristically romantic. In the 'Colloquy', for example, everything is tinged with the gentle regret aroused by the remembrance of things past, the cherished memories of a happy life in which one has shared. Thus the three great Irish Cycles between them figure forth the classic triad of faculties: thinking, willing, and feeling. Whereas the Mythological Cycle features intelligence and knowledge, and the Ulster Cycle will-power, the distinctive quality of the Fenian tales is 'human warmth of feeling'.[101]

6

We have seen that Tuatha Dé Danann, the dominant people in the Irish Mythological Cycle, are paralleled by the Children of Dôn in the Welsh *Mabinogi*. The names of some of the individual personages in the two literatures correspond, and also there are broad similarities between some of the stories on either side. There is no correspondence in name between the warriors of King Conchobar and any Welsh heroes, and there is no group of Welsh stories which invites close comparison with the Ulster Cycle. The cycle of poems associated with the name of Llywarch Hen, like *Táin Bó Cuailnge*, tells of lonely vigils at fords and border battles fought in defence of the country or province. Moreover, the milieu and the standards revealed in these poems, as also in the panegyrics and elegies attributed to Taliesin and Aneirin, are thoroughly heroic. But the prose narrative which may once have provided the framework to the Llywarch speech-poems is now lacking, and the elegiac tone of the poems themselves, and their close relationship with certain descriptive and gnomic nature poems, have prompted comparison with the Fenian poems of Ireland rather than with the Ulster stories.[102]

Several scholars have remarked on similarities to be observed between the Fenian stories and the Arthurian stories.[103] In one of the earliest references to Arthur, namely that of Nennius', *Historia Brittonum*, about the beginning of the ninth century,[104] he is described as *dux bellorum*, 'war leader' or 'leader of troops', a title which, as van Hamel remarks, 'would make a very satisfactory equivalent for *rígféinnid*, the Irish title of Finn'.[105] Like Finn, Arthur is here a warrior who defends his country against foreign invaders. In the *mirabilia* or Wonders of Britain (which are included in the same book), and also in 'Kulhwch and Olwen' which was probably written earlier than any other extensive Arthurian story, he figures as the hunter of a boar, Twrch Trwyd (or Trwyth).*[106] According to the latter text this hunt, the greatest of several mentioned in the story, began in Ireland, where the boar had already lain waste a third of the country, and the chase was continued through South Wales and into Cornwall. It required the co-operation of Arthur, his huntsmen, his house-troop, Mabon son of Modron,[107] Gwyn son of Nudd** (in whom God has set the spirit of the demons of Annwfn), the son of Alun Dyfed, and several other notables. Twrch Trwyth, a king transformed into a boar (according to this story), figures also in early Irish literature. In *Lebor Gabála Érenn*, Torc Triath† is described as the King of Boars. A story dated to the ninth century or earlier mentions an assembly or fair known as *oenach Tuirc Thréith*,†† and in Cormac's Glossary the name‡ is interpreted as 'the assembly of a king's son'.[108] This explanation is immediately followed by the only long anecdote concerning Finn to be found in the whole Glossary, and it has been suggested[109] that the reference to the assembly brought memories of Finn to the compiler's mind. In any case, boar hunts have a prominent place in the Fenian

---

* *porcum troit; twrch trwyth.*
** v. *supra*, p. 67.
† *Twrch Trwyd* and *Torc Triath* are equivalent forms.
†† 'The Assembly of Torc Triath (*or of the torc of a triath*)'.
‡ With *orc* instead of the synonymous *torc*.

literature. An account of a great boar-hunt in which all the *fiana* of Ireland took part is the prelude to the story of Finn's death, and Diarmaid's destiny is bound up with the life of a magic boar whose human origin and venomous bristles recall Twrch Trwyth.[110]

The brief references to Arthur in the work of Nennius and in several early Welsh poems show that he was a figure of renown in Welsh tradition at least from the eighth century, but as in the case of the Fenian tradition, which is likewise known from the earliest period of Irish literature, the extensive literary texts of the Arthurian Cycle date from the twelfth century and the Arthurian legend then becomes the dominant story tradition, a tradition which draws mythological person-ages from all types of story into King Arthur's entourage. We have referred to evidence from about the eleventh century that the stories of Finn were even then current among the common people and that these popular versions differed from those of the learned literary tradition. Similarly, learned writers of the early twelfth century in Britain refer to the stories of the common people concerning Arthur and object to what they regard as their distortion of the truth.[111] In Wales, Cornwall, and Britanny, at this period, there was a firm popular belief that Arthur was not dead but would return to deliver his people from their enemies.[112] In the early Welsh poems and in 'Kulhwch and Olwen', Arthur (like Finn) fights witches, giants, magic animals, and the powers of Annwfn, while in twelfth-century folkloristic texts he is himself the king of a subterranean country.[113] Like the Fenian heroes in the 'Col-loquy' and in modern folklore, the Arthurian knights in 'The Dream of Rhonabwy'[114] make their latter-day successors appear as a 'lesser breed', and again in the topographical lore of the modern period Arthur is envisaged as a gigantic figure.

If the tales of Finn and his companions were destined, through the works of Macpherson, to give Celtic literature a European renown in the period of the modern Romantic Movement, the Arthurian tales, the *matière de Bretagne*, became the staple of the romantic literature of Europe in the high Middle Ages. 'The Pursuit of Diarmaid and Gráinne' is paralleled by the still more famous Arthurian story of Trystan and Esyllt,* and in the other Arthurian romances the exploration of sentiment and the celebration of courtly love are seen to have become the chief concern of European poets and storytellers. Like the adventures of the Irish *fiana*, those of the Arthurian knights have as their setting the forest, the wild, and the desert, together with the mysterious dwellings where the knights are received as guests. It is true the knight travels alone, he fights in single combats and is typically a horseman, and one hesitates to press the correspondence too far. But it may be pointed out that the knight's investiture is nowadays traced back to the initiation rite by which a youth took up arms and, leaving his family, began his military apprenticeship[115]—the earliest meanings of the English word *knight* are 'boy' 'youth' 'military servant'—and that the knight of the shire is the traditional representative of the Commons, the third estate.

However, the precise extent of the Welsh, or Celtic, element in the vast Arthurian literature of Europe is still a highly controversial question. The true relation of three of the major Arthurian tales in Welsh, 'The Lady of the Fountain', 'Peredur son of Evrawc' and 'Gereint son of Erbin', to three of the narrative poems of the twelfth-century French poet, Chrétien de Troyes, is likewise problematic.[116] We have not excluded these three tales completely from our purview, but we do not attempt to comment on Arthurian texts written in Germanic and Romance languages, or on Welsh texts which are clearly derived from them, even though the origin of much of their content, and indeed of their mystery, is perhaps to be sought in the lore of the Celtic countries.

* See p. 283.

7

The Irish tales nowadays classified as the Historical Cycle, or the Cycles of the Kings, are in general less magical than the Mythological Tales, less heroic than the Ulster Tales, less romantic than the Fenian. Though these qualities are by no means absent, none of them may be said to be the distinguishing feature of this extensive group of tales. These tales are not only about kings, but about kingship, the founding of dynasties, dynastic succession, and the fortunes of the royal houses of Ireland and her provinces. Stories about several of the renowned kings who figure in these cycles, from Conaire Mór to Conn of the Hundred Battles, Cormac mac Airt, Niall of the Nine Hostages, and Domnall son of Aed, will be told in later portions of this book. For the present we shall confine our attention to tales which are concerned with the nature of kingship as a marriage between the king and the realm.[117]

In their youth, Niall (of the Nine Hostages) and his four stepbrothers, Brian, Fiachra, Ailill, and Fergus, were given weapons by a smith and sent hunting to prove their arms. After losing their way in the forest, the youths lit a fire to cook the game they had killed, and Fergus was sent in search of drinkingwater. He came to a well guarded by a monstrous black hag who would grant him the use of the well only on condition that he gave her a kiss. The lad refused and returned without water. Each of his three brothers in turn went on the same errand, but only Fiachra deigned to give the hag a 'bare touch of a kiss'. For that she promised him a 'mere contact with Tara'—meaning that two of his seed (but none of the descendants of the other three brothers) would be kings. Then it was Niall's turn. Faced with the same challenge, he kissed the old hag and embraced her. When he looked again, she had changed into the most beautiful woman in the world. 'What art thou?' said the boy. 'King of Tara, I am Sovereignty,' '. . . and your seed shall be over every clan.' She sent him back to his brothers but bade him give them no water until they had

granted him seniority over them and had agreed that he might
raise his weapon a hand's breath over theirs.

Sovereignty presents herself as a loathsome hag, and is transformed into a fair lady by the embrace of the destined king, in
the story of another five brothers, sons of King Dáire—and the
same motif recurs in English and French romances. It had
been foretold that a son of Dáire's would obtain the kingship
of Ireland and that 'Lugaid' would be his name. Dáire gave
the name to each of his five sons, but a druid told him that his
successor would be the one who would catch a golden fawn
which would enter the assembly.[118] When the fawn was
hunted, a magic mist was set between the five brothers and
everyone else. It was Lugaid Laígde who caught the fawn, and
it is he who entered the bed of the hag who was revealed as
Sovereignty.

The relation between Irish kings and their realm is often
portrayed as a marriage, and the inauguration feast of a king is
called a wedding-feast. The country is a woman, the spouse of
the king, and before her marriage she is a hag or a woman
whose mind is deranged. When she is united with the king,
her countenance is 'as the crimson lichen of Leinster's crags . . .
her locks . . . like Bregon's buttercups', her mantle a matchless
green.[119] In later literature she is described as a courtesan, and
she has been compared with the Roman Acca Larentia, a
courtesan who endowed Rome with her earnings, and with
Flora whose name was also Rome's.[120] A union between the
king and the goddess of the land was an essential part of the
royal ritual in ancient civilizations of the Near East—and
sacred prostitution belongs to the same complex of ideas.
According to a Sumerian hymn of the second millennium
B.C., the marriage of the king with the goddess Innana, 'the
Lady of the Palace', was consummated 'at the New Year, on
the day of decisions', in the bed-chamber of a chapel built for
the goddess.[121]

There are indications that Queen Medb of Connacht was an
embodiment of Sovereignty. A daughter of a king of Tara, she

is said to have been married to King Conchobar, but 'through pride of mind' she forsook him against his will. Thereafter she mated successively with Tinde son of Connra Cas, with Eochaid Dála and with Ailill mac Máta, each of whom became king of Connacht. She was sought by other suitors too, for she 'never was without one man in the shadow of another'. It is said that Eochaid Dála was appointed king 'with the consent of Medb if he became her husband'. Irish tradition also tells of another Medb, the Leinster Queen Medb Lethderg,* daughter of Conán of Cuala. She was the wife of nine of the kings of Ireland in succession, including Conn's father, his son Art, and Cormac son of Art. 'Great indeed was the power of Medb over the men of Ireland, for she it was who would not allow a king in Tara without his having herself as a wife.' So when Art died, 'until Medb mated with the son, Cormac was not king of Ireland'.[122]

Both Krappe and Coomaraswamy have identified the Sovereignty of Ireland with the Indian goddess Śrī-Laksmī who is 'the personification of the right to rule . . . (the) Spirit of Sovereignty . . . and certainly so when the relationship is . . . a marital one'.[123] She is Indra's consort, and she has many names. As Apālā, the 'Unprotected', she woos Indra, bringing as her sacrificial offering Soma, the drink 'of which none tastes who dwells on earth'. This she prepares by chewing. And Indra 'verily drank the Soma from her mouth'.[124] Here we have another quality of the goddess. Medb's name is cognate with the Welsh *meddw*, 'drunk', and related to the English word *mead*. She is 'the intoxicating one'. Medb Lethderg was the daughter of Conán of Cuala, and an old poem says that no one will be king over Ireland 'unless the ale of Cuala comes to him'.[125] Referring to the water she gives Niall from the well, Sovereignty says: 'smooth shall by thy draught from the royal horn, 'twill be mead, 'twill be honey, 'twill be strong ale.'[126] In a story to which we shall refer again, Conn is confronted

* 'Half-red' or 'Red-side'.

with Sovereignty in a vision. This time the king does not mate with her, but she serves him with food and with a drink called *derg flaith*, a name which can mean both 'red ale' and 'red sovereignty'. She then continues to 'give' the cup to a long line of future kings whose names and reigns are announced by her consort, Lug son of Ethniu. Sovereignty is a bride, the server of a powerful drink, and the drink itself.

8

We shall not concern ourselves in this book with the extensive body of literature called the 'Lives of the Saints', though some individual saints figure as characters in certain stories of the Fenian and Historical Cycles. The role played by the saints in these stories and in the Lives themselves, as scholars, judges, prophets, and controllers of nature and fertility, is comparable in many ways with that of the pre-Christian druids, while they are peers of the Tuatha Dé Danann as masters of wizardry. The legendary material in the Lives has much in common with that of the other Cycles, but it contains elements for which there are no native or biblical parallels. Comparative study will probably show that these owe less to monkish fabrication than has often been supposed. Here we will content ourselves with one illustration taken from the Irish Life of St Moling.[127]

At the end of his period of instruction for the priesthood, Tairchell (who was later called Moling) requested a boon from his fosterer, namely that he be allowed to go on a circuit, to collect alms for the Church. As he proceeded along the road, bearing two wallets and a bowl for the alms, and his fosterer's ashen staff in his hand, he met 'the Evil Spectre' with his mis-shapen household. The Spectre grasped his weapons and entered into a dialogue with the saint, in which each threatened to destroy the other: 'I will drive this spear through thy side,' said the Spectre. 'By my fosterer's hand, I will rap thy head with the staff,' said Tairchell. The saint then requested a boon from the spectres: 'to let me have my three steps of pilgrimage towards the King of heaven and earth, and my three steps of folly also, so that death may be the further from me.' The boon was granted and he leapt his three steps of pilgrimage and his three steps of folly. 'The first leap that he leapt, he seemed to them no bigger than a crow on the top of a hill. The second leap that he leapt, they saw him not at all, and they knew not whether he had gone into heaven or into the earth. But the third leap that he leapt, 'tis then he alighted on the wall of the church enclosure.' The spectres pursued him, but he escaped into the church. Collanach, the priest, recognized him as the prophesied one and said: 'Thou wilt be (called) Moling of Luachair from the leaps* thou hast leapt.'

In Irish tradition St Moling figures as the friend of another celebrated leaper, the mad Suibne Geilt, who, resorting to the woods, grew feathers and so could jump from tree to tree and from hill top to hill top—an Irish counterpart of the Welsh Myrddin Wyllt.[128] But for a parallel to the tale we have just told we must turn to the contest between Vishnu, one of the three supreme gods of Hinduism, and the demon Bali son of Virocana. This is the version related in the *Rāmāyaṇa*:

> Bali, who had overcome Indra, Lord of Gods, en joyed the empire of the three worlds, and he was cele brating a sacrifice when Indra and the other gods, dis tressed with fear, spoke to the great ascetic Vishnu who was engaged in mortification and contemplation in 'The Hermitage of the Perfect'. '"Bali, son of Virocana", they said, "is performing a sacrifice. . . . Do thou, O Vishnu, for the benefit of the gods resort to a phan tom shape and assuming the form of a dwarf bring about our highest welfare . . ." Thus addressed by the gods, Vishnu, adopting a dwarfish form, approached the son of Virocana and begged three of his own paces. Having obtained three paces Vishnu took a monstrous form and with three steps the Thrice stepper then gained

* *ling(im)* = (I) leap.

possession of the worlds. With one step he occupied the whole earth, with the second the eternal atmosphere, with the third the sky. . . . He made that demon Bali a dweller in the underworld and gave the empire of the three worlds to Indra . . .'[129]

The predicament of the gods at the beginning of the Hindu story, which reproduces that of the Tuatha before the Second Battle of Mag Tuired, has no counterpart in the Moling story. Otherwise, the parallelism is well-nigh complete.[130]

MOLING	VISHNU
1 A candidate for the priesthood practising austerities.	1 A hermit perfecting himself in a hermitage.
2 He is collecting alms for the Church.	2 The contest is such as 'is engaged when a man offers the fore-offerings'.
3 He is armed with a staff of ash—a wood used to keep demons at bay.	3 He is armed with a 'thunderbolt' (a ritual term for anything used to destroy spiritual enemies).
4 His contest with the Evil Spectre.	4 His contest with the king of the demons.
5 Three steps granted readily.	5 Three paces granted.
6 The prodigious three leaps.	6 The prodigious three paces.
7 He is named Moling for his leaps.	7 He is called the Thrice-stepper.

In the Life of Moling this episode could be dismissed as a mere story illustrating the superiority of sanctity over evil, and it is as a story that it is told of Vishnu in the *Rāmāyaṇa*. But A. M. Hocart has demonstrated that it has antecedents of the profoundest spiritual significance. Here is some of the evidence he adduces.[131] In the *Śatapatha Brāhmaṇa*, which is vastly older than the *Rāmāyaṇa*, the story takes a different form. The gods (Devas) and the demons* (Asuras), both descended from

* Or counter-gods.

Prajāpati, vied together. The gods were worsted, and the demons proceeded to divide the world between them. When the gods, placing Vishnu, *the sacrifice,* at their head, approached the demons and asked for a share, they were grudgingly granted 'as much as this Vishnu can lie upon'. Though Vishnu was dwarfish, the gods were not offended: 'They have given us much who have given us the extent covered by the sacrifice,' they said. 'They laid Vishnu down and surrounded him on all sides with poetic metres . . . and having piled up fire on the east they went on singing hymns and practising austerities and since by this means they acquired the whole earth . . . hence the name *vedi* for an altar. Hence the saying, "As great as the altar, thus great is the earth," for by the altar they obtained the whole earth. Thus he who so knows this appropriates this whole earth from his rivals, deprives his rivals of a share in it.'

When the fore-offerings are offered, the sacrificer bears a pan containing the sacred fire, which is Vishnu. He then 'strides Vishnu's strides'—the sacrificer becomes the sacrifice and possesses the worlds. The story, and no doubt the ritual too, is as old as the *Rig Veda*: 'Indrāvishnu [sacrificer-sacrifice], this deed of yours is to be praised, in the intoxication of soma you took vast strides . . . you extended the regions of the air that we might live.' 'Friend Vishnu, stride vastly. Sky give room to fix the thunderbolt. Let us slay Vṛtra; let us release the streams.' 'The highest step of Vishnu the sacrificers ever behold like an eye fixed in heaven. The poets rejoicing, wakeful, kindle that which is the highest step of Vishnu.'[132]

If the simple story of Moling is connected with all this, there is no doubt a similar wealth of meaning behind such incidents as the lighting of the sacred fire by St David at Glyn Rhosyn and the ritualistic stratagems by which his wizard opponent tried in vain to resist him.[133] Similarly, the great contest between St Patrick and the druids of Tara, in which the saint forestalls the druids in lighting the sacred fire and defeats them in a series of magical competitions by which he demonstrates his superior command over the worlds of light and darkness, fire and water.[134] Here the pre-Christian druids have become the powers of evil, and the saint has usurped their role, but the story may well be an adaptation of an original in which druids and demons vied with one another for possession of the world. Without the aid of parallels we cannot penetrate behind these tales, but they appear to bring us as near as we shall ever get to some of the mysteries of the Celtic druids.

Part Two

THE WORLD OF MEANING

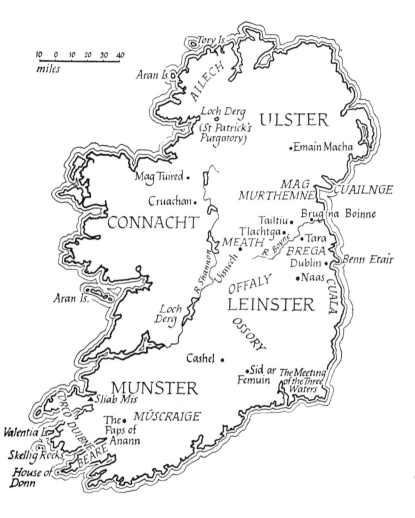

Fig. 1   Sketch-map of Ireland

CHAPTER III

Darkness and Light

> . . . and God divided the light from the darkness. And God called
> the light Day, and the darkness he called Night.
>
> GENESIS, I, 4–5.

THE ALTERNATION of day and night, light and darkness, had a
profound meaning for the Celts as it did for many other
peoples. It manifested a fundamental duality which had a
variety of other expressions. Even now the dead of night is
felt to be nearer to the Other World than is the light of day.
A person born during the night can see ghosts and phantoms
which are invisible to the children of day.[1] Fairies and other
spirits become active after sunset; night, in a very real sense,
belongs to them, and it is fitting that mortals should with-
draw to the security of their own firesides. In Ireland, country
people still say it is inappropriate for persons to be out at all
hours of the night. Such wanderers might disturb the 'little
people', and they run the risk of recognizing among them the
spirits of dead relations. The country people also doubt the
propriety of staying up late at night, because the dead approach
the house silently every hour between ten and twelve o'clock in
the hope of finding that all is quiet, and the way to show them
respect is to retire early, leaving the hearth swept and the seats
arranged for them around a well-made fire. Throwing out
water or ashes at night is prohibited, lest the spirits be disturbed,
and it is dangerous to whistle out-of-doors or to call children
by their names. As dawn dispels darkness, so does the crowing
of cocks send the spirits and elves to their abodes—night seems

to be their day and day their night.[2] Given this atmosphere of belief, it is small wonder that night is the propitious time for divination, witchcraft, wakes for the dead, and the telling of supernatural tales.

As the day consists of two halves, so does the year consist of summer and winter.[3] The first of May is the Calends of summer, the first of November the Calends of winter, and these two festivals divide the year into two seasons of six months each. Summer is the period when nature is awake, and when young people used to leave the winter homestead to spend their time in summer dwellings, tending their herds on the hills and indulging in outdoor pastimes. By November Eve (*Samain*), they returned again to the old home and spent the winter nights plying their fireside crafts, listening to fireside stories and entertaining themselves indoors. The Fiana likewise used to spend the summer season, from Beltaine (First of May) to Samain, hunting and fighting in the forests, but from Samain to Beltaine they quartered themselves upon the settled population. Winter is the dark side of the year, nature is asleep, summer has returned to the underworld and the earth is desolate and inhospitable.[4] In Wales, January was called 'the black month'. November, the first month of winter, was known as the dark or black month in Scotland, Cornwall, and Brittany, and the Scots referred to the depths of winter as *an Dùdlachd*, 'gloom'.[5] It was the season of '*death* revels' presided over by a 'king' with a blackened face, whose emblem of office was a sword, a scythe, or a sickle.[6]

Time as it manifests itself in this way consists of the alternation of opposites, light and darkness, warmth and cold, life and death. The Coligny Calendar (a Gaulish calendar engraved on a bronze tablet which was unearthed in France in 1897) bears witness to a still more thorough-going application of this dual principle to the measurement of months and years. While most of it is inscribed in abbreviations which cannot be interpreted with any certainty, its basic structure is quite clear. It covers five years—a significant period in view of Diodorus's

testimony that the continental Celts held quinquennial sacrifices. The five years consist of sixty months plus two intercalary months, one at the beginning of the cycle and another
in the middle. The second intercalary month thus divides the
cycle into two moieties of two-and-a-half years each. The whole
cycle is inscribed in sixteen columns as is shown in Fig. 2.
The Gaulish names of the months have been inserted and each
column should be read downwards.

It will be observed that the first half of the year begins with
a month called *Samon-*, and the second half with a month
called *Giamon-*, two words which are related to the words for
'summer' and 'winter', respectively, in the surviving Celtic
languages. In accordance with this, early interpreters of the
calendar concluded that *Samon-* was the mid-summer month
and *Giamon-* the mid-winter month.[7] Alternatively, it might
be argued that *Samon-* and *Giamon-* are the *first* months of
summer and winter, respectively, corresponding roughly with
May and November, the two turning points of the traditional
Celtic year. Other considerations, however, suggest a complete
reversal of this order.[8] In Ireland, though *sam* means 'summer',
Samain (cf. *Samon-*) is, strangely enough, November Eve, the
beginning of the winter half-year—the season of storytelling
and feasting, and in Christian times the season to which most
of the major church festivals belong. The Coligny Calendar,
like the Church Calendar, was 'a timetable of ritual', and the
fact that most of the rubrics believed to indicate festivals are
concentrated in the first half of the year suggests that winter
preceded summer, that *Samon-* is, paradoxically, the first month
of winter and *Giamon-* the first month of summer. Such an
arrangement of the seasons would harmonize with Caesar's
testimony concerning the precedence of night over day. The
Gauls, he says, called themselves sons of the god of night and
defined 'the division of every season, not by the number of days,
but of nights; their birthdays and the beginning of months
and years they observe in such order that day follows night.'[9]
The order of the seasons does not seriously concern us here,

(Intercalary month)	RIVROS MAT	GIAMON- ANM	EDRIN- MAT	RIVROS MAT	GIAMON- ANM	EDRIN- MAT	RIVROS MAT
MAT	ANAGAN-TIOS ANM	SIMIVIS-ONN MAT	CANTLOS ANM	ANAGAN-TIOS ANM	SIMIVIS-ONN MAT	CANTLOS ANM	ANAGAN-TIOS ANM
SAMON- MAT	OGRON- MAT	EQVOS ANM	SAMON- MAT	OGRON- MAT	EQVOS ANM	SAMON- MAT	OGRON- MAT
DVMANN- ANM	CVTIOS MAT	ELEMBIV ANM	DVMANN- ANM	CVTIOS MAT	ELEMBIV ANM	DVMANN- ANM	CVTIOS MAT

Fig. 2   The Structure of the Coligny Calendar

but to facilitate description we shall assume that the year and the first half of the five-year cycle began with winter, while the second half-cycle began with summer.

Again, the months of the year were of two kinds. Six of them had thirty days and are distinguished by the rubric *MAT*; the other six had only twenty-nine days and are inscribed *ANM*.[10] *MAT*- (cf. Irish *maith* and Welsh *mad*) probably meant 'good', whereas *ANM* seems to be an abbreviation of *AN MAT*-, 'not good'. We may compare the Athenian calendar in which thirty-day months were 'full months', twenty-nine-day months 'hollow months'. In south-east Asia these two kinds of months, called 'complete' and 'defective' respectively, alternated in a regular sequence.[11] The *MAT* and *ANM* months of the Coligny Calendar are also interspersed except for one adjustment. If the sequence had been preserved throughout, both *Samon*- and *Giamon*- would be *MAT* months of thirty days, but there seems to have been a deliberate rearrangement so that the first half of each year—the ritually important half—and the first half of the cycle as a whole, should begin and end with a *MAT* month, and that the second

(Intercalary month)	EQVOS ANM	SAMON- MAT	OGRON- MAT	EQVOS ANM	SAMON- MAT	OGRON- MAT	EQVOS ANM
MAT	ELEMBIV- ANM	DVMANN- ANM	CVTIOS MAT	ELEMBIV- ANM	DVMANN ANM	CVTIOS MAT	ELEMBIV- ANM
GIAMON- ANM	EDRIN- MAT	RIVROS MAT	GIAMON- ANM	EDRIN- MAT	RIVROS MAT	GIAMON- ANM	EDRIN- MAT
SIMIVIS- ONN- MAT	CANTLOS ANM	ANAGAN- TIOS ANM	SIMIVIS- ONN- MAT	CANTLOS ANM	ANAGAN- TIOS ANM	SIMIVIS- ONN- MAT	CANTLOS ANM

halves of both years and cycle should begin and end with an
ANM month. Excluding the intercalary months, both halves
of the cycle consist of thirty months, a 'month of months',
and on the analogy of the months they are of two kinds,
MAT and *ANM*.

The same pattern appears also in the structure of the months
themselves. Each is made up of two parts, in the first of which
the days are numbered up to fifteen and in the second up to
fourteen or fifteen according to the length of the month. As in
Indian and other calendars, one half is doubtless the 'bright
half' of the lunar month, the other the 'dark half', but as with
the seasons it is difficult to decide which is which. In between
the halves is inscribed the word *ATENVX* which is interpreted either as 'renewal' or as 'the returning night'. The
former interpretation could be consistent with the principle
recorded by Caesar. On the other hand, Pliny says that the
druids used to begin their months on the sixth of the moon,[12]
and if they reckoned from the new moon this would mean
beginning with the light half. In India, however, the month
began with the bright half in the south and with the dark half

in the north.[13] By analogy, it is not inconceivable that even the
year and the cycle should have begun with winter in one half
of a country and with summer in the other. With reference to
principle both concepts are equally valid. Equated with the
primordial chaos that precedes the creation of the cosmos, and
with gestation which precedes birth, darkness comes first,
but as a symbol of death and dissolution it follows at the end
of the day.

We may now summarize our pairs of contraries:

Night	and	Day
Dark half of month	and	Light half of month
MAT month	and	*ANM* month
Winter	and	Summer
Samon-half of cycle	and	*Giamon*-half of cycle

Each half-cycle consisted of five seasons; the one had three
winters, the other three summers:

A. Winter: Summer: Winter: Summer: Winter
B. Summer: Winter: Summer: Winter: Summer

The symbolic meaning of Day and Night as the microcosm
of time, and indeed of the 'whole world', could not be stated
more explicitly than it is in a story preserved in the Book of
Leinster.[14] After the Dagda had apportioned all the *síd*-
mounds of Ireland between the lords of Tuatha Dé Danann,
the Mac Óc came to him and asked for land. 'I have none for
thee,' said the Dagda, 'I have completed the division.' 'Then
let me be granted,' said the Mac Óc, 'a day and a night in thy
own dwelling.' That was given to him. 'Go now to thy following,' said the Dagda, 'since thou hast consumed thy
(allotted) time.' 'It is clear,' said the Mac Óc, 'that *night and
day are the whole world*, and it is that which has been given to
me.' Thereupon the Dagda went out, and the Mac Óc remained in his *síd*. A variant of this story occurs in 'The Wooing of Étaín', but there the meaning is less cryptically expressed.
The Mac Óc claims Elcmar's *síd* in perpetuity on the grounds
that 'it is in days and nights that the world is spent'. Similarly,

Conchobar wrested the kingship of Ulster from Fergus mac Roich after being granted a year's temporary kingship.[15] The consolidation of his position is explained politically, but the logic of the ruse seems to be that it is 'in summers and winters that the world is spent'. As we shall see later King Conchobar personified the Year in himself, and there are grounds for regarding the Mac Óc as a personification of the Day. He was called Mac Óc ('Young Son') by his mother because he was begotten and born all in one day which had been magically lengthened by the Dagda.[16]

2

The dividing lines between the contrasting periods of time are haunted by a mysterious power which has a propensity both for good and for evil. Certain acts were forbidden at sunrise and at sunset because these were moments of danger; on the other hand, morning dew and morning water had a particular virtue, and cures could be effected by remedies sought at sunset.[17] This supernatural power breaks through in a most ominous way on November Eve and May Eve, the joints between the two great seasons of the year. These two Eves (together with Midsummer's Eve) were known as 'spirit nights' in Wales,[18] and throughout the Celtic lands chaos was as it were let loose at these two junctures, fairies were unusually active, witches worked their charms, and the future was foreshadowed by omens of all kinds. The customs of both Eves have features characteristic of New Year celebrations generally; for example, the practice of divinations and the re-lighting of household fires from a ceremonial bonfire. But in atmosphere the two festivals differed fundamentally in that they epitomized the contrasting seasons which they inaugurated.

Hallowe'en, the Calends of winter, was a solemn and weird festival. The *síd*-mounds were open on this '*púca*' night, and their inhabitants were abroad in a more real sense than on any other night. The souls of the dead returned and became visible. In Ireland, until recently, people did not leave the house on this night unless obliged to do so, and if they did they kept clear of churchyards. They should not look behind when they heard footsteps, for it was the dead that were on their tracks.[19] In Wales it was said that there was a phantom on every stile. Food, called *bwyd cennad y meirw*, was left out-of-doors to propitiate the wandering dead, doors were left unbolted, and special care was taken before going to bed to prepare the hearth for the visit of dead relatives.[20]

In Scotland, it was a 'night of mischief and confusion',[21] and its eeriness was intensified by the impersonation of spirits of the dead by young men who went about with masked, veiled or blackened faces, and dressed in white or in disguises of straw. The boundary between the living and the dead was thus obliterated, and so was the separation of the sexes, for boys wore the clothing of girls and sometimes girls disguised themselves as boys. The general disorder was further intensified by mischievous pranks. Ploughs, carts, gates, and other belongings were borne away and thrown into ditches and ponds; horses were led away and left in other people's fields. The peace of the household itself was disturbed: the door was bombarded with cabbages pulled at random from gardens, the chimney was blocked with turf, and smoke was blown in through keyholes.[22]

An extraordinarily wide variety of divinations were practised on Winter's Eve to discover who would die during the course of the year, who would marry, and who the future partner would be. In Wales, anyone bold enough to wait in the church porch until midnight might hear a voice calling out the names of those who were to die during the year—but he ran the risk of hearing his own name among those of the doomed. Marriage divinations were a particular feature of this Eve, but even in these death lurked round the corner; there was always the danger of seeing a coffin instead of the face of the future partner. Hazel-nuts and apples, the fruits of two trees with rich otherworld associations, figured prominently in many of the divinatory pastimes.

A period of disorder in between the old year and the new is a common feature of New Year rituals in many lands,[23] but it is soon followed by the re-creation of an orderly world which lasts for another year. At Hallowe'en the elimination of boundaries, between the dead and the living, between the sexes, between one man's property and another's and, in divinations, between the present and the future, all symbolize the return of chaos. It is noteworthy that the 'day with a night' which the Mac Óc, in the foregoing story, equated with the whole of time, were those of Samain. This day partakes of the nature of eternity. But, bonfires apart, the positive side of the ritual is not evident in the surviving customs. What Hallow-e'en inaugurates is winter, and much of the uncanniness of the night, when man seems powerless in the hands of fate, will prevail until the dawn of another summer.

Summer's Eve, on the other hand, has a positive as well as a negative aspect. Fairies can work mischief and witches can bring misfortune by stealing the year's profit from cattle and from wells, but the dangers of the night are different from the awful imminence of death experienced at Allhallowtide. This world is no longer swamped by the world beyond; one's *luck* in the ensuing year may be in the balance, but one is not brought face to face with an unalterable destiny. And effective measures can be taken to ward off evil. One can keep watch to prevent witches from stealing the first milk and from skimming the well on May morn, and other precautions against the dangers of witchcraft can be taken by refusing to give away fire, water, and food. Branches of the rowan-tree, placed over the doors of house and byre, will keep away witches and fairies alike. Whereas folklore has little to say about what one should do on the first *day* of November, the perils of May Eve are but a prelude to the joys of the first summer's day: a climb up a hill to see the sunrise, washing in the morning dew, drinking from the well before sunrise, the gathering of leaves and flowers and the wearing of greenery instead of the straw of winter. It was the dawn of a new and orderly day, the sun rose early and so should men, and the ritual niggardliness and guarding of property on this day is in marked contrast to the free giving to the living and the dead, and the liberties taken with other people's belongings, on Hallowe'en.

3

While the twofold structure was basic to the Celtic conception of time, other patterns, such as the fourfold division of the day into morning, afternoon, evening, and night, of the moon into quarters, and of the year into spring, summer, autumn and, winter,[24] all had a meaning beyond the purely temporal one. And the moments at which the divisions joined partook in some degree of the significance attached to the great turning-points of the year. Midday and midnight, like sunrise and sunset, were moments when the veil between this world and the unseen world was very thin. Fairy funerals were to be seen at noon, and it was an auspicious moment for banishing fairy 'change-lings'. Midnight was the 'witching hour', fairies and phantoms became visible, and to visit a churchyard at this hour was a challenge to be reckoned with.

St Brigid's Night (The Eve of the First of February) divided the winter half of the year into winter and spring; *Lugnasad* (Lammas, 1st August) divided the summer half into summer and autumn. St Brigid's Day, *Imbolc*, is the old festival of spring, and the Eve is still observed in Ireland with various rituals and divinations. Spring activities are over by the time May gives the trees their 'green livery'. Summer ends in July, and Lug-nasad, the first day of autumn, was a festival of first-fruits which used to rival Beltaine and Samain in importance. By Samain all the crops had been gathered in. Fruit left on the trees after this date was contaminated by the *púca*.[25] Thus the main divisions of the Celtic year were related to the annual round of agricultural life rather than to the movements of the sun, though it is clear from the Coligny Calendar and from folklore that the solstices and equinoxes were also observed.

In Scotland, Quarter-Days still fall in November, February, May and August, but various changes in the calendar during the course of the centuries have resulted in minor displacements, so that the actual dates are now November 11th, February 2nd, May 15th and August 1st. They are known as 'Witches' Days', and fairies hold revels and raid helpless human beings on their Eves. It is said that the fairies remove to different dwellings at the beginning of each quarter. Lending is un-lucky as it is on May Day, rowan crosses are used as a protec-tion against supernatural dangers, and divinations are practised. Changelings can be got rid of on Quarter Days as they can at noon time, but it is unlucky to 'straddle' the beginning of a quarter—for example, by proclaiming a marriage at the end of one quarter and solemnizing it at the beginning of the next.[26]

The turning-points in time have a paradoxical quality everywhere. In one sense they do not exist; in another sense they epitomize the whole of existence. Their significance may be compared with that of the 'Twelve Days of Christmas' each of which prognosticates the weather of the corresponding month in the New Year. These twelve days were marked by mumming, buffoonery, licence, mock-mayors, witchcraft, and other signs of chaos. In Scotland, no court had any power during these days, and in Ireland those who died went to heaven without having to face Purgatory and Judgement.[27] In Wales they were called omen days (*coel-ddyddiau*) and in Brittany 'over-days' (*gourdeziou*).[28] It has been suggested that a period of twelve days between two mid-winter festivals in the Coligny Calendar had a similar significance.[29] Furthermore, the thirty days of the intercalary month which precedes each half-cycle in this calendar bear the names of the thirty months in a half-cycle. The intercalary month is thus a microcosm of a half-cycle, though it has recently been argued that it is a recapitulation of the half-cycle which precedes it rather than a prefiguration of the ensuing one.[30]

In later chapters we shall discuss certain features of the mythological structure of space, but it may be added here that boundaries between territories, like boundaries between years and between seasons, are lines along which the supernatural intrudes through the surface of existence. Water which flows between two or three parishes or townlands has curative qualities, it is used in Hallowe'en divinations, and it has power both to charm away the 'profit' of milk and butter on May Eve and to break such a charm. Again, the fact that unbaptized children used to be buried in boundary fences suggest that these lines, like the unbaptized child, did not really belong to this world.[31] Stiles were favourite perches for ghosts. And territories, like seasons, must have their boundaries ritually redefined every year. In many parts of Ireland May Day was spent in mending fences,[32] and the ceremony of 'beating the bounds' is in the realm of space what new year ceremonies are in the realm of time; both concentrate attention on a line of division. The date of the 'beating of the bounds' varies from place to place, but the most usual day is Ascension Thursday,[33] which usually falls in May—at the end of winter, when the world is created anew. This mysterious character of boundaries (which usually follow rivers and streams) enhances the significance of combats fought at fords, which are a recurrent feature of Celtic story. Fought at such a place a combat partakes in some measure of the nature of a divination rite, as do contests engaged in at the boundaries of seasons. Thresholds have a similar significance, and in several Fenian tales the hero overcomes his fairy adversary as he is entering the *síd*.

CHAPTER IV

Coming into Existence

'Bear us across the Sea as in a ship, thou Comprehensor.'

RIG VEDA, IX, 70, 10.

CELTIC TRADITION has preserved no native story of the creation of the world and of man. Even in the oldest documents that have survived, the Biblical Adam and Eve have already been accepted as the first parents of mankind. Nevertheless, *Lebor Gabála Érenn*, 'The Book of the Taking of Ireland', is un-doubtedly a laborious attempt to combine parts of the native teaching with Hebrew mythology embellished with medieval legend. It begins with *In principio fecit Deus caelum et terram* and proceeds from the Creation to the story of Noah and the Flood, the Dispersal of the Nations, and the descent of the Gael of Ireland from Japheth son of Noah. For the early Christian Celts, as for Africans and others of our own day, the acceptance of the new Faith, which has a cosmogony of its own, inevitably involved severing the stem of native tradition at some point or other and grafting it on to the Christian roots through which it would henceforth draw its sustenance. *Lebor Gabála Érenn* performed this grafting so far as the Irish were concerned. It demonstrated to them genealogically that they too were descendants of Adam, and that the Biblical theo-phany had to do with their destiny. And there can be no doubt that it fulfilled a need, for the memorization of the long arti-ficial genealogies, and the (to us) tedious exploits of the des-cendants of Japheth in the Mediterranean lands,[1] became a part of the education of the *filid*, the official custodians and trans-mitters of the mythological tradition. This work of bringing the Gentiles into the Christian family by linking up their diverse traditions with those of the Hebrews and synchronizing them with the ancient history preserved in the writings of classical historians was, of course, going on throughout Christendom, and it was achieved for Britain by Nennius and Geoffrey of Monmouth.

This biblicized 'history', as set out in *Lebor Gabála*, culminates in the story of 'The Sons of Míl'.[2] After journeying through Egypt, Crete and Sicily, these ancestors of the Irish eventually reached Spain, and one of their company, Bregon, built a tower there. From the top of this tower Íth son of Bregon saw Ireland across the sea and set sail to investigate the land he had seen. At that time Tuatha Dé Danann were in occupation of the country, and they, suspicious of his motives, killed him. Then his kinsmen, the eight Sons of Míl, invaded Ireland to avenge his death. The most prominent among them were Donn the king, Amairgen the poet and judge, Éremón the leader of the expedition, and Éber. They were accompanied by Lugaid the son of Íth, their own sons, the sons of Bregon, and a number of champions. On reaching Ireland, they defeated the Tuatha, here associated with Demons and Fomoire, and then proceeded to Tara. On their way they met in turn the three goddesses, Banba, Fotla, and Ériu, each of whom extracted from Amairgen the promise that her name should be a name for the island. At Tara they encountered the three kings of the Tuatha, Mac Cuill, Mac Cécht, and Mac Gréne, who 'pronounced a judgement against the sons of Míl' to the effect that they should leave the island in peace for three days. The justice of the case was referred to Amairgen, on pain of death if he judged falsely. 'I pronounce it,' said Amairgen, 'Let this island be left to them.' 'How far shall we go?' said Éber. 'Past just nine waves,' said Amairgen. This was the first judgement he gave in Ireland. And so they withdrew and went through the motions of landing again as though they were performing a ritual. Their first landing had been resisted, for every time they came up with Ireland the demons made the port as it were a hog's back, and they had skirted round the island three times before coming ashore. Now the druids and poets of the Tuatha sang spells against them, and a magic wind carried them far out to sea, but Amairgen countered with a poem which calmed the wind. The invaders landed for the second time and, after a further victory over the Tuatha, took possession of the country.

The repeated landing, which may have a significance comparable to that of the 'second birth' in the life-story of individual personages, is not the only feature which reveals the pre-Christian origin of the tale. As the invaders raced for land for the first time, Donn showed envy of his brother Ír who had gained the lead. The oar broke in Ír's hand and he fell backwards and died. He was buried in 'Skellig of the Spectres' off the west coast of Munster, and his brothers judged that it would not be right for the envious Donn to share in the land. After they had landed, Donn offended Ériu, the queen of the Tuatha Dé Danann, and she prophesied that neither he nor his progeny should enjoy the island. When he again spoke threateningly of the Tuatha before landing the second time, a wind arose and his ship was wrecked. *Lebor Gabála* also says that the youngest brother, Erannán, climbed the mast to reconnoitre and fell to his death. But according to the *dindsenchas*[3] it fell to the lot of Donn to climb the mast, to chant incantations against the Tuatha, and as a result of the Tuatha's curse an ague came into the ship. Donn asked that his body be carried to one of the islands lest the disease remain in Ireland, 'and my people will lay a blessing on me for ever'. After his ship had foundered, his brother Amairgen declared that his folk should come to the high rock, *Tech Duinn*, 'the House of Donn', whither his body was carried, and so, according to the heathen, the souls of sinners visit it and give their blessing to Donn before going to Hell, while the souls of the penitent behold the place from afar and are not borne astray. There are references to the House of Donn as the assembly-place of the dead in earlier sources: 'To me, to my house ye shall all come after your death.'[4] And the belief has survived in Ireland that on moonlit nights the souls of the dead can be seen over the Skellig

rocks, on their way to 'The Land of the Young' (*Tir na nÓg*).[5]
Until recently, people used to resort to one of these precipitous
little islands to perform a mountain-climbing ritual the symbolism of which is manifestly pre-Christian. Leaving votive
offerings at sacred wells at the foot of the mountain, the pilgrim ascended by a narrow track, squeezed himself up through
a chimney-like chasm called The Needle's Eye, crossed the
'stone of pain' which projected perilously over the sea, and
mounted the dizzy pinnacle known as The Eagle's Nest,
where stood a stone cross. The ordeal reached its climax with
the pilgrim sitting astride a ledge overhanging the sea, which
lay some 460 feet below, and kissing a cross which some bold
adventurer had cut into the rock. By making this pilgrimage
in life, the pilgrim was believed to expedite the progress of his
soul through Purgatory after death.[6]

The Celtic substratum of our story is particularly evident in
an obscure poem which Amairgen utters as he first sets his
right foot upon Ireland, a poem which gives the coming of the
Sons of Míl a significance beyond that of a mere historical
invasion. R. A. S. Macalister translates it as follows.[7]

> I am Wind on Sea,
> I am Ocean-wave,
> I am Roar of Sea,
> I am Bull of Seven Fights,
> I am Vulture on Cliff,
> I am Dewdrop,
> I am Fairest of Flowers,
> I am Boar for Boldness,
> I am Salmon in Pool,
> I am Lake on Plain...
> I am a Word of Skill,
> I am the Point of a Weapon (that poureth forth combat),
> I am God who fashioneth Fire for a Head.
> Who smootheth the ruggedness of a mountain?
> Who is He who announceth the ages of the Moon?

And who, the place where falleth the sunset?
Who calleth the cattle from the House of Tethra?
On whom do the cattle of Tethra smile?
Who is the troop, who the god who fashioneth edges . . .?
Enchantments about a spear? Enchantments of Wind?

Potentially, the whole creation is bound up in Amairgen, and
Indian parallels preclude the dismissal of his speech as simply
an expression of 'the pride of the sorcerer'. Thus Śrī Krishna
in the *Bhagavad-Gītā*[8] declares himself to be the divine seed
without which nothing animate or inanimate exists. He is the
Ātman, he is Vishnu, Shiva, Brahma and all the gods, the
beginning, the life-span and the end: 'I am the radiant sun
among the light-givers . . . among the stars of night, I am the
moon . . . I am Meru among mountain peaks . . . I am the
ocean among the waters . . . Of water-beings I am Varuna:
Aryaman among the Fathers: I am Death . . . I am the
Wind . . .' He is pre-eminent among hymns, poetic metres,
the letters of the alphabet, the months and the seasons: 'I am
the dice-play of the cunning, I am the strength of the strong . . .
I am the silence of things secret: I am the knowledge of the
knower. . . . What I have described to you are only a few of my
countless forms.' Vishnu, dormant during the interval of non-
manifestation between the dissolution and recreation of the
universe delivers himself of a similar series of 'I am' utterances.
He is the cosmic juggler or magician and he is all those
appearances through which the true essence of existence manifests itself—the cycle of the year, light, wind, earth, water, the
four quarters of space, and so on. 'And whatever you may see,
hear or know in the whole universe, know me as Him who
therein abides.'[9] Similarly Amairgen on the ocean of non-
existence embodies the primeval unity of all things. As such
he has the power to bring a new world into being, and his
poems are in the nature of creation incantations. With one
of them he conjures fish into the creeks, with another of them

the attributes of the land of Ireland are re-created by being spoken, or rather twice-spoken, anew:[10]

> 'I seek the land of Ireland,
> Coursed be the fruitful sea,
> Fruitful the ranked highland,
> Ranked the showery wood,
> Showery the river of cataracts,
> Of cataracts the lake of pools,
> Of pools the hill of a well,
> Of a well of a people of assemblies,
> Of assemblies of the king of Temair;
> Temair, hill of peoples,
> Peoples of the Sons of Míl,
> Of Míl of ships, of barks;
> The high ship Ériu,
> Ériu lofty, very green,
> An incantation very cunning . . .'

In the new era that is being inaugurated Ériu will be the 'high ship' of the Sons of Míl, and to them and to Lugaid son of Íth will be traced the lineages of all the tribes of Ireland.

After they had gained possession of the island, a contention arose between Éremón and Éber concerning the kingship. Amairgen, as arbitrator, said 'The heritage of the chief, Donn, to the second Éremón; and his heritage to Éber after him,' but Éber insisted upon a division. Here we have the inception of a territorial dichotomy which is fundamental to the cosmo-graphic structure of Ireland. Éremón took the kingship in the North and Éber in the South, or according to some texts, Éber took the South and Éremón took the North *with the kingship*.[11] In any case the precedence of the North appears in other ways. Seven chieftains went with Éremón to the North and six with Éber to the South.[12] A further contention is said to have arisen between the two brothers concerning three ridges, 'shining treasures with a cantred to each of the three'.[13] The northern half had two ridges whereas the South had only one. Dis-satisfied with his lot, Éber rebelled and was slain by Éremón, but the feud is said to have continued between the descendants of the two brothers. Throughout the period of Irish independ﹀ ence, dynastic succession usually took the form of an alter﹀ nation between two lines which traced their descent from two brothers.[14] The division of the country into two halves is also said to have given distinct attributes to the North and South of Ireland. Before parting, the two brothers cast lots upon their artists, a poet and a harper. The poet, 'learned man of mighty power', went with Éremón northward, 'so that henceforth in the North he secured dignity and learning'; the harper went to Éber southward: 'string﹀sweetness of music . . . in the South part of Ireland; thus shall it be till the mighty Judgement'.[15]

Throughout Irish literature the Northern Half of Ireland is known as *Leth Cuinn*, 'The Half of Conn', and the Southern Half as *Leth Moga*, 'The Half of Mug'. As a common noun *conn* means 'head', 'chief', 'sense', 'reason', while *mug* means 'servant'. The traditional boundary﹀line between the two halves runs along Eiscir Riada, a broken ridge of low mounds running between Dublin and Galway Bay, and the names of the two halves are explained by the story of a struggle between Conn, the eponymous ancestor of the Dál Cuinn dynasties of the Northern Half, and Mug Nuadat ('Servant of Nuadu'), also known as Eogan, the eponymous ancestor of the Eoga﹀ nachta, the rulers of Munster. Mug Nuadat, by storing up pro﹀ visions for a coming famine, gains the Southern kingdom for himself.[16] To quote a verse from Keating's 'History of Ire﹀ land':[17]

> 'Eoghan transcended Conn,
> Not in number of battles and conflicts—
> More plenteous the food of adventurous Eoghan
> Was being distributed according to the laws of peace.'

Thus the 'Servant' king gains his position by the peaceful occu﹀ pation of providing food for the country. Later he renews war against Conn, but is defeated and slain—another case of a

Southerner being dissatisfied with his lot and suffering ultimate defeat.

The division of societies into moieties symbolized as upper and lower, heaven and earth, male and female, summer and winter, senior and junior, north and south, right and left, and so on, is world-wide, and the dichotomy is expressed in a two-fold division of countries, provinces, cities, villages, temples, halls, kindreds, and other phenomena.[18] Often there are two kings, or a senior king ruling over the whole realm, but particularly over his own half, and a junior king over the other half. The superiority of one moiety over the other is, however, formal and ritualistic rather than political, and it is often the case that the lower in status wields the greater power. The two halves have distinct and complementary duties and privileges, and they perform various services for each other. But there is also an antagonism between them which manifests itself in mock-conflicts, team-games and other contests. Such a dual organization seems to underlie the common division of Welsh cantreds into 'above' and 'below' the wood, or 'above' and 'below' the river. 'Great' and 'little', 'within' and 'without', or 'upper' and 'lower' are commonly used to differentiate between two neighbouring villages or parishes of the same name, or to describe subdivisions of villages or parishes—and rivalry between the two halves is common. We have already met an example of this kind of duality in our discussion of the relationship of Tuatha Dé Danann with the Fomoire.

2

In *Lebor Gabála Érenn* the story of the Sons of Míl is not, as we have implied here, a continuous narrative. After tracing the fictitious history of the Gael until they are ultimately at Bregon's Tower in Spain on the eve of their voyage to Ireland, the narrative is interrupted: 'Let us cease from the stories of the Gael, that we may tell of the five peoples who took Ireland before them . . .',[19] and we are taken back to another *in principio* when, notwithstanding what had been going on in Biblical lands, Ireland was still empty and without form, and we are told of

Fig. 3 Leth Cuinn and Leth Moga

five earlier ages during which the island gained its familiar features, its archetypal inhabitants, and its culture. When that has been done, we are returned to Bregon's Tower to pick up the story of the Gael and their occupation of Ireland. But the native tradition has not been allowed to go unedited. The pedigrees of all the five peoples, including Tuatha Dé Danann, are traced back, like that of the Gaels themselves, to the Biblical Noah, and scholars have been tempted to dismiss the whole composition as 'a medieval work of fiction'. But it is well to remember that the monks or poets who compiled it lived much closer to the pre-Christian world than we do. The work still retains features which the study of other mythologies would lead us to expect in myths about the beginnings of things, and the more one studies it the more one is persuaded that the compilers had some understanding of the nature of the material they were endeavouring to reconcile with the new Christian teaching.

As we have already mentioned, the five invasions of Ireland before the advent of the Gael were those of (1) Cessair, (2) Partholón, (3) Nemed, (4) Fir Bolg and (5) Tuatha Dé Danann. We shall mention some of their general character-istics before proceeding to a fuller discussion of their individual and collective symbolisms. Ireland at the 'time' of these 'inva-sions' was vastly different from any Ireland that men have known. We are taken back to a prehistoric condition of things, when the island had not been completely fashioned, when its virgin ground had not yet been divided into provinces and when its features remained nameless. From a mythological point of view, nothing really exists until it has been 'formed', 'defined', and named,[20] and in as much as *Lebor Gabála Érenn* is concerned with the origin of physical features, bound-aries, and names, it retains some of the essentials of a cosmo-gonic myth. When Partholón arrived, there were only three lakes and nine rivers in Ireland. Seven more lakes burst forth in his day, four in the time of Nemed, and three in the time of Tuatha Dé Danann—a recurrent motif is the eruption of a lake at the digging of a grave and the naming of the lake after the person buried therein. The making of clearings is a further aspect of the process of shaping the country. Partholón cleared four plains and Nemed twelve, for when Partholón landed there was in Ireland only the old plain of Elta, made by God the Maker, on which no twig ever grew. Throughout the book we find hills, mounds, plains, promontories, lakes, and the very country itself acquiring names and significance from their connection with the lives, deaths, and burials of the personages in the myth. *Division* of the land is another aspect of the process of creation and definition and there is mythological authority for almost every division of Ireland. We have already mentioned that the Sons of Míl divided it into two, but it had already been divided into four by Partholón's sons, into three by the remnants of the Nemedians, and into five by Fir Bolg— 'As everyone does (says one redaction), they partitioned Ireland.' 'And that is the division of the provinces of Ireland which shall endure for ever, as the Fir Bolg divided them.'[21]

The invasions also provide the genesis of much of the everyday culture, such as cultivation, building, trading, grinding, and churning. The origin of the kingship and the administration of justice are accounted for, as well as knowledge, poetry, arts and crafts, battleshouting, chessplay, ballplay, horseracing, and the holding of assemblies. In *Lebor Gabála* care is taken to commemorate the occasions when things were done or experienced for the first time and to record the names of the persons concerned—the first to land, the first to die, the first to be king, the first to pass judgement, and so on. In this way the prototypes of existence in this world are established one after another. As with other traditional cultures, Celtic society could not function without precedents. A dispute over boundaries could not be settled on grounds of expediency; the oldest and most learned historians had to be called upon to recount how Ireland was divided in the beginning. When the original model had been recalled, there could be no further argument: 'It is thus it has been, and will be for ever.'[22] That the need for archetypal precedents of this kind persisted even when the old tradition had been supplanted by Christianity is clearly seen in the incantations and charms of Scottish crofters. Cures derive their efficacy, and daily activities their meaning, by being regarded as repetitions of what members of the Holy Family and the Saints did once upon a time:

'I bathe my face
In the nine rays of the sun
As Mary bathed her Son
In the rich fermented milk . . .'

'I am smooring the fire
As the Son of Mary would smoor . . .'

'I will pluck the gracious yarrow
That Christ plucked with His one hand . . .'[23]

This is the way of all ancient cultures. Life is meaningful in as much as it is an imitation or re-enactment of what the gods did in the beginning: 'reality is acquired solely through repetition or participation; everything which lacks an exemplary model is "meaningless", i.e. it lacks reality'.[24] And one need only think of Greek mythology to realize that these models are not confined to what is morally approved; they relate to all human situations. It is said that Partholón went hunting and fishing one day, leaving his wife and Toba, his henchman, to guard the island. The woman seduced the man, and that was the first adultery that ever was in Ireland. A great thirst possessed them in their guilt and they drank of the vessels and tubes of Partholón. On his return, Partholón perceived the taste of their mouths on the drinking-tubes and, incensed by their misdeed, he killed his wife's lap-dog. That was the first jealousy in Ireland. Then Partholón upbraided his wife, but she put up the defence that it was her husband's fault for leaving her in a situation in which the inevitable had happened:

'Honey with a woman, milk with a cat,
food with one generous, meat with a child,
a wright within and an edged tool,
one before one, 'tis a great risk.'

'The one with the other will go together.' Therefore it is right to guard them well from the beginning. 'Not upon us is the blame . . . but it is upon thee.' And that was the first judgement in Ireland, 'the right of his wife against Partholón',[25] a judgement which seems to echo the words of the Indian Laws of Manu: 'the adulterous wife throws her guilt on her (negligent) husband'.[26]

The five pre-Gaelic peoples may be compared with the Indian 'Five Kindreds' which are spoken of in the *Rig Veda* as immigrants who have come from another place across the waters and have settled and tilled the lands on the hither shore. This was no historical invasion, but a crossing over from one form of being to another, a crossing variously described as having been accomplished in a ship and in a heavenly chariot. As we shall see when we discuss voyages to the Other World, 'in metaphysical formulation a "crossing of water" always implies change of state and status'. The voyage of the Five Kindreds seems to be the other-world voyage in reverse, a coming into existence, a change from infinite possibility to actual manifestation.[27] It is indeed a far cry from the hymns of the *Rig Veda* to the pedestrian prose of *Lebor Gabála Érenn*, but the patently artificial derivation of the five peoples of Ireland from Scythia, Greece, Egypt, and so on, may well have been substituted for a tradition that they too hailed from the 'other shore'. The four cities of the northern islands of the world, whence Tuatha Dé Danann came with their supernatural talismans, certainly have no place in terrestrial geography, and there was a divergence of opinion as to whether the Tuatha came in ships or in clouds through the air.

The *Rig Veda* also speaks of the eight supreme Hindu gods known as Ādityas as crossing over the waters in an amphibious chariot 'with seats where eight may sit'.[28] These may be compared with the eight Sons of Míl. Donn, the eldest of Míl's sons, recalls Vivasvat, the eighth Āditya. Vivasvat was the first to offer sacrifices and those men, his descendants, who follow his example postpone their death, that is the moment when they will be received by Yama, his son. Donn sacrifices himself for the Gaels, and when they die their journey takes them to, or past, the House of Donn. Éremón, the leader of the Sons of Míl, has been compared with Aryaman, another of the Ādityas, and some philologists have suggested that their names may be cognates.[29] Aryaman is also the chief of the Fathers, as Éremón is the chief of the ancestors of the Irish. Indeed, inasmuch as the Sons of Míl are the ancestors of mortal men, they bear a closer resemblance to the 'Fathers' (*Pitris*) of Indian mythology than to the sovereign gods. Donn, who is described as 'king' of the Sons of Míl, may then be com- pared with Yama himself, 'king of the Fathers', 'the first of men that died, the first that departed to the other world . . . the gatherer of mankind'. 'Yama chose death, and found out the path for many, and he gives the souls of the dead a resting place.'[30]

3

In the story of the five primeval peoples of Ireland, the waters of the Flood separate Cessair and her company from the four peoples who came after her. Partholón and his people, though they came after the Flood, also perished from the earth leaving no descendants. But the three remaining groups of settlers, Nemed's company, Fir Bolg and Tuatha Dé Danann, belong together. After the death of Nemed, the leader of the first of these groups, and the destruction of most of his people in a conflict with the Fomoire, a remnant led by this three sons, Starn, Iarbonél the Soothsayer and Fergus Lethderg,* escaped in a ship. Fir Bolg and Tuatha Dé Danann were descendants of the first two of these sons, while the descendants of the third are said to have settled abroad.

Unlike all their predecessors, Fir Bolg and Tuatha Dé Danann were ruled by kings, and the two peoples seem to be complementary to one another. We have already seen that the

---

* Fergus Half-red or Fergus Redside.

Tuatha were divine wizards or druids. It was Fir Bolg, on the contrary, who instituted the political division of Ireland into five provinces, established the kingship, and first administered justice. The most imposing figure among their kings was Eochaid son of Erc: 'There was no wetting in his time save only dew: there was no year without harvest. Falsehoods were expelled from Ireland in his time. By him was executed the law of justice for the first time.'[31] Another of their kings was

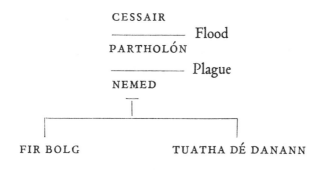

Fig. 4 The Five Peoples

Rinnal: 'In his time weapons were first given points' (*rinn=* 'spear-point').[32] In the First Battle of Mag Tuired,[33] Fir Bolg and Tuatha Dé Danann oppose one another. Nevertheless they are kinsmen who speak the same language; they approach one another with mutual respect and they agree to forge weapons for one another. One of the Tuatha voices a eulogy of the Fir Bolg javelins, but the Fir Bolg sorcerers, on the other hand, play only a minor and negative role in the battle in comparison with Badb, Macha, the Morrígan, and the wizards of Tuatha Dé Danann.

Among the five peoples, Tuatha Dé Danann and Fir Bolg are clearly the spiritual and temporal élite. In comparison with them the peoples of Partholón and Nemed are inferior groups who have no kings, and in some ways they 'look like doublets of one another'.[34] Both leaders have to contend with the

Fomoire, both clear plains, both die of plague. But Nemed's name means 'holy' or 'sacred', or as a noun 'privilege', 'sanctity', 'sanctuary', and in the earliest Irish law tracts it occurs as a term signifying all persons of free status. As MacNeill remarks:[35] 'We can hardly doubt that freemen were "holy" [*nemed*] in the sense of being qualified to participate in public religious rites. Caesar tells us how those who refused obedience to the judicial decisions of the Druids were excluded from the sacrifices, and how this exclusion involved the loss of *jus* and *honos*.' Partholón cleared four plains, but Nemed cleared twelve and also built two royal forts. This seems to signify that Nemed cleared four plains for each of his three groups of descendants and prepared forts for the two royal groups among them. In other words, the immediate company of Nemed subserved the two groups which succeeded them and which were included in them *in potentia*.

The character of Partholón's people is more clearly indicated. There were seven labourers in his company, two ploughmen, two plough-irons and four oxen. Though, like the Fomoire, they engaged in hunting and fishing, they were obviously tillers of the soil. But Partholón is also described as 'chief of every craft'[36] and many crafts were first practised in his time. The first guesting-house was made, beer was brewed and flesh cooked in a cauldron for guests. 'Under the taking of Partholón was building first done in Ireland, and a quern, and churning, and ale.' Duelling was instituted, and of Partholón's two merchants, one is said to have got gold in Ireland, the other cattle and kine.[37] The eldest of his chieftains was the son of Senboth, a name which seems to signify a serf or servile tenant.[38] Partholón's people have no place in any independent Irish story, but in modern Ireland the day of Parthanán falls at the end of harvest time, when the dread Parthanán comes to thresh all corn left standing. He is an agricultural demon, like the better-known *cailleach* or hag who falls to the lot of the last to finish with the harvest, and the *púca* who befouls all fruit left on the trees on Hallowe'en.[39]

In terms of social functions we thus have the druid Tuatha, the Fir Bolg rulers, the people of Nemed to whom we have as yet ascribed no distinctive role other than privilege and service to the two royal groups, and lastly the husbandmen and craftsmen of Partholón. Turning to the social system of the Irish as it is known from the early laws and sagas, we find three types of freeman, namely, *druí*, 'druid' (or in later times *fili*, sage and poet), *flaith*, 'lord' or 'person exercising authority', and *bó-aire*, 'freeman'. *Druí* is probably derived from a root meaning 'to know', and *flaith* is related to the Welsh *gwlad* 'country', *gwledig* 'ruler', and the German *gewalt* 'force', 'violence'.[40] The word *aire* in *bó-aire* means 'every freeman, "commoner" as well as noble ... who possesses an independent legal status'.[41] Similarly, the Sanskrit *arya* covers the three 'noble' or sacrificial classes, though philologists are not agreed as to whether the two words are cognate. *Bó-aire* means 'cow *aire*', and comparative studies show that cattlemen typify the free commoners from IndoEuropean times.[42] This third estate, we submit, is represented among the invaders by the people of Nemed—who were despoiled of their corn and their milk and their progeny, by the Fomoire.[43] This is borne out by what is said about five names which were given successively to Tara, names which are correlated with the invasions as follows:[44]

The Sons of Míl ... called it Temair.

Tuatha Dé Danann called it Cathair Crofhind.

Fir Bolg . . . . called it Druim Cáin, 'whither chieftains used to go'.

Nemed . . . . called it Druim Léith, after Liath son of Laigne Lethanglas, who cut down its tangled wood so that *'its corn was rich corn'*.

Before that it was called Fordruim—'there was a time when it was a pleasant hazel wood in the days of the noble son of Ollcán'.

Professor Georges Dumézil has related the three free classes in Celtic society with the *brāhman* (priest), the *kṣatriya* (warrior, royal) and the *vaiśya* (farmer) castes in Indian society.[45] In a series of books and articles published during the past twenty years he has traced the ramifications of a system of three func tions in the mythologies of various peoples who belong to the Indo-European linguistic family. These 'functions' he des cribes as:[46]

> *I The Sacred.* The relations of men with the sacred and with one another under the surveillance and protection of the gods—on the one hand, cult, magic, and on the other, law, government; also the sovereign power exercised by the king or his deputies in accordance with the will or the favour of the gods, and again, more generally, knowledge and intelligence, here inseparable from the manipulation of sacred things.
> *II Physical force.* The use of main force, primarily though not solely in war. [Also the executive aspects of kingship and government.]
> *III Fertility.* This covers a wide range of related qualities in which the unifying principle is less apparent. It includes fruitfulness in human beings, animals and plants, but also food, wealth, health, peace and the fruits of peace, as well as voluptuousness and beauty. There is also the important idea of 'large number', applied not only to goods (abun dance) but also to the men who compose the social body (mass).

This hierarchic structure serves as a framework of concep tion and a support for all sorts of beliefs, rites and institutions, so that the harmonious and orderly working of each function is necessary for the welfare of society and the world.

In Ancient India the three sacrificial castes which embodied the three functions were subserved by a fourth. This was the *śūdra* caste of agricultural workers, craftsmen, entertainer sand other menials. 'We hear of carpenters, wheelwrights, potters, smiths, fishermen, dog-leaders, and hunters. There were drum-mers, conch-blowers and flute-players.'[47] Similar skills were covered by the fourth class in ancient Rome. In his *De lingua latina*, Varro lists in succession words relating to officers of the state and then to (1) priests, (2) military affairs, and (3) per-sonal fortune (degrees of wealth). After these come words for artisans and men of special skills such as jugglers, 'namers', boxers, trackers, runners, hunters, and fruit-pickers.[48] Likewise in early Ireland there was a fourth class which comprised a variety of people in addition to agricultural serfs. 'The folk of vocal and instrumental music besides, jockeys and charioteers and steersmen and followers in feasts and retinue (?), and mummers and jugglers and buffoons and clowns and the lesser arts besides, it is in regard of the honour of those who keep them that *díre* (honour-price) is paid for them. Otherwise they have no franchise apart.'[49] Certain kinds of craftsmen attained the status of subject *nemed* ('subject freeman') by virtue of their art. They were 'house-builders, builders of ships and boats, and of mills, wood-carvers, chariot-makers, turners, leather-workers, fishermen, smiths and metal-workers, and some others; among musicians, harpers only'.[50] Some of Partho-lón's craftsmen perhaps correspond to this intermediate grade, but in the over-all social system as symbolized in the Invasions he and his labourers and his craftsmen fall naturally into the fourth class.

Even the addition of the fourth function does not complete the picture. *Lebor Gabála Érenn* speaks of *five* peoples, as does the *Rig Veda* of a totality of 'Five Kindreds'. In Hindu writings these enigmatic Five Kindreds are variously explained as five orders of divine beings, created beings in general, the ancestors of humanity, the four castes and the barbarian Nishadas.[51] Thus, when the fifth group is included in the Indian social system, it is the aborigines utterly beyond the pale. Similarly with the Irish invasions, the one that remains to be considered is the primordial Cessair.[52] Her company consisted of fifty women and three men, namely Fintan son of Bóchra, Bith son of Noah and father of Cessair, and the pilot Ladra. The main action of their story in Ireland turns on the division of the women. Fintan took Cessair and sixteen others; Bith took her companion Bairrfhind and another sixteen, whereas Ladra was left with a mere sixteen and was dissatisfied with his lot. Nevertheless it is of him that it is said that he died of excess of women—'or it was the shaft of the oar that penetrated his buttock'. After Ladra's death, Fintan and Bith shared the remaining women between them so that they then had twenty-five each. Bith went north and he was the next to die. When the women returned to Fintan and Cessair, Fintan escaped 'afleeing before all the women' until he came to the Hill of the Wave (*Tul Tuinde*). Bereft of her father and her husband, Cessair broke her heart, and all her maidens died, and then forty days after they had arrived in Ireland, came the Flood. Fintan spent a year under the waters in a cave called 'Fintan's Grave' above Tul Tuinde, and so survived.

In its overwhelmingly female character, this company bears a resemblance to the Fomoire in the time of Partholón, among whom women outnumbered men in a proportion of three to one. Cessair was the first to bring sheep into Ireland and it is noteworthy that the Fomoire in Nemed's time turned Ireland into a sheep land.[53] As we have seen, the Fomoire are closely associated with the sea and its islands, and their name suggests 'under-sea'. Cessair is connected with the Flood-waters and in this story women and water seem to belong together. The division of the women, like the other divisions we have mentioned, was an act of creation, a separating out. Their re-union symbolizes a return to an undifferentiated chaos. All this took place at 'The Meeting of the Three Waters'. Ladra's death was caused by women or by the oar with which he plied the waves; Fintan fled from the reunited women and was overwhelmed by the Flood. His flight before the women is reminiscent of inundation tales in which a person is pursued by irrupting waters.

According to the lost early manuscript, 'The Book of Druim Snechta', the name of the woman who settled in Ireland before the Flood was not Cessair but Banba, and she, as eponym of Ireland, is to be identified, not with water, but with the land that would emerge from the waters, 'the island of Banba of the women'. She survived the Deluge on the mountain peak of Tul Tuinde—'To this present mound the waves of the Flood attained'—and she lived to proclaim to the Sons of Míl that she was older than Noah.[54] The peak recalls the 'primeval hill' of Near Eastern cosmogonies, the first land to rise out of the waters of chaos.[55] In other words, the first woman symbolized both water and land, and the two basic elements seem to be further personified by Cessair's husband, Fintan son of 'Ocean' (*Bóchra*), and her father whose name means 'World' (*Bith*).

In some versions of *Lebor Gabála* which include Cessair's expedition as one of the five invasions, it is observed that 'others do not accept it among the invasions',[56] and Nennius's *Historia Brittonum*, which contains one of the earliest records of these traditions, begins with Partholón and does not mention Cessair. Fintan, who lived to tell the tale, is duplicated in Tuan (of Partholón's group) who survived all subsequent invasions and recounted the story in the time of Colum Cille. The whole scheme is thus feasible without Cessair. So too in the social system, in India and elsewhere, the aborigines (like the outcastes) stand outside the four principal castes; yet they must be represented in any complete symbol of the whole of mankind.

The antecedents of the five Irish invaders offer a further clue to their status.[57] Tuatha Dé Danann came from a land of magic learning, Fir Bolg came to gain freedom from the oppression of overlords, but Partholón was an outlaw who fled from his homeland after killing his father, and the plague which overtook his people is seen as retribution for his crime. The company of Cessair also left their homeland in disgrace. Noah, so the story goes, had refused to admit them into the ark, declaring that 'this is no ship for robbers and no den of thieves'.

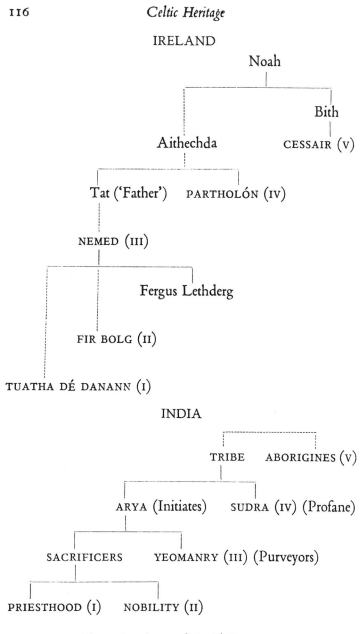

Fig. 5 Invasions and Social Structure

Sundering themselves from the God of Noah, the outcasts set up an idol and worshipped it, and then proceeded to build an ark of their own.[58] While Bith, the father of Cessair, is an *apocryphal* son of Noah, the ancestry of all the post-diluvian invaders is traced back to Aithechda son of Magog son of Japheth son of Noah.[59] *Aithechda*, the first unbiblical name in this pedigree, is a derivative of *aithech*, 'churl', 'rent-payer'. Aithechda was the near ancestor of Partholón (Function IV) and the remote ancestor of Nemed. Nemed was the immediate ancestor of Fergus who settled abroad—so that his people (Function III) took no part in the later struggle for supremacy —and the remote ancestor of the two ruling peoples, Fir Bolg (Function II) and Tuatha Dé Danann (Function I). As will be seen from the diagrams opposite, this is almost a replica of Hocart's analysis of the relationship between the Indian castes.[60]

CHAPTER V

A Hierarchy of Provinces

'Whatever exists is fivefold.'
TAITTIRÎYAKA-UPANISHAD, I, 7.

MODERN IRELAND comprises four great provinces, Connacht, Ulster, Leinster, and Munster, whose origin lies beyond the beginning of recorded history. Yet, the Irish word for 'province' is *cóiced*, which means a 'fifth', not a 'fourth', and the expression 'five fifths of Ireland' is familiar to all who speak the Gaelic tongue. The antiquity of this five-fold conception cannot be doubted, but tradition is divided as to the identity of the fifth fifth. *Lebor Gabála Érenn* attributes the original division into five provinces to Fir Bolg.[1] These settlers were led by five brothers and they shared Ireland between them. The fifth province of that division consisted of a subdivision of Munster, and in accordance with this, Ireland is represented throughout most of the early literature as consisting of Connacht, Ulster, Leinster, and 'the two Munsters' (East Munster and West Munster). It was held that all five provinces met at the Stone of Divisions on the Hill of Uisnech, which was believed to be the mid-point of Ireland.

The alternative tradition[2] is that the fifth province was Meath (*Mide*), 'the Middle'. This is a common belief among present-day Irishmen who are unfamiliar with the historical literature, and it is not a recent invention. A poem which is attributed to Mael Mura, a ninth-century poet, tells of a revolt of the vassal tribes of Ireland under the kings of the *four* provinces, a revolt in which Fiachu, King of Tara, was killed. After a period of misrule, the legitimate dynasty was restored in the person of Fiachu's son, Tuathal Techtmar, who defeated the vassal tribes in each of the four provinces—Connacht,

Ulster, Leinster and Munster. According to some medieval texts, it was Tuathal who created the central province of Meath by taking a portion of each of the other provinces; Keating states that before Tuathal's conquest Meath was but a minor kingdom (*tuath*) around Uisnech. We must, however, con- sider a body of comparative evidence before accepting the view that the central province, without which no province could be called a 'fifth' in this scheme, was the result of a military con- quest in the second century A.D.

What we have to try to understand is the meaning of the sub- division of an island into four parts each of which is called a fifth, and the existence of two apparently incompatible tradi- tions—neither of which can be shown to be more authentic than the other—which, respectively, locate the implicit fifth fifth at the centre and as an entity within one of the other four. In the Middle Irish text called 'The Settling of the Manor of Tara',[3] which relates how the territorial divisions were con- firmed at the beginning of the Christian era by a supernatural authority, both these conceptions of the five-fold structure of Ireland are re-authenticated, and there is no indication that the writer of this remarkable document was aware that the one is inconsistent with the other. The text relates that, in the reign of Diarmait son of Cerball (A.D. 545-565), the nobles of Ire- land protested against the extent of the royal domain, and that Fintan son of Bóchra was summoned to Tara, from his abode in Munster, to define its limits. Seated in the judge's seat at Tara, Fintan reviewed the history of Ireland from Cessair to the Sons of Míl, and told of a strange personage called Tre- fuilngid Tre-eochair who suddenly appeared at a gathering of the men of Ireland on the day when Christ was crucified. This stranger was fair and of gigantic stature, and it was he who controlled the rising and the setting of the sun. In his left hand he carried stone tablets and in his right a branch with three fruits, nuts, apples, and acorns. He inquired about the chronicles of the men of Ireland, and they replied that they had no old historians. 'Ye will have that from me,' said he. 'I

will establish for you the progression of the stories and chronicles of the hearth of Tara itself with the four quarters of
Ireland round about; for I am the truly learned witness who
explains to all everything unknown.' And he continued:
'Bring to me then seven from every quarter of Ireland, who are
the wisest, the most prudent and most cunning also, and the
shanachies of the king himself who are of the hearth of Tara;
for it is right that the four quarters (should be present) at the
partition of Tara and its chronicles, that each may take its
due share of the chronicles of Tara.'

It will be observed that the basic idea here is that Ireland
consists of four quarters and a centre—the provinces of Connacht, Ulster, Leinster, Munster, and Meath. This arrangement was confirmed by Trefuilngid, and in leaving that
ordinance with the men of Ireland he gave Fintan some berries
from his branch. Fintan planted them where he thought they
would grow, and from them are the five trees: the Ash of
Tortu, the Bole of Ross (a comely yew), the Oak of Mugna,
the Bough of Dathi (an ash), and the Ash of populous Uisnech. Though the location of most of these five places is uncertain, there can be no doubt that the underlying idea is that
the trees symbolize the four quarters around the centre.

The confirmation of this pattern by Fintan on Trefuilngid's
authority at Tara was not, however, the end of the matter.
'Then the nobles of Ireland came . . . to accompany Fintan
to Uisnech, and they took leave of one another on the top of
Uisnech. And he set up in their presence a pillar-stone of five
ridges on the summit of Uisnech. And he assigned a ridge of it
to every province in Ireland, for thus are Tara and Uisnech in
Ireland, as its two kidneys are in a beast. And he marked out a
forrach there, that is, the portion of each province in Uisnech,
and Fintan made this lay after arranging the pillar-stone.' In
the lay Fintan defines the extent of each of *these* five provinces,
and they are not Meath and the four quarters but the provinces
of the Fir Bolg division—Connacht, Ulster, Leinster, and the
two Munsters. 'So Fintan then testified that it is right to take

the five provinces of Ireland *from Tara and Uisnech*, and that it is right for them also to take them from each province in Ireland!' The two alternative ideas may be represented as follows— and they *are* alternatives, for to merge them together six provinces must be reckoned with, and that would belie the very name for a province—'a fifth'.

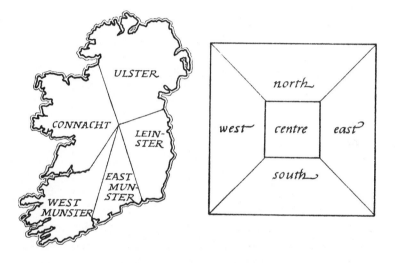

Fig. 6 The Five Provinces

The reader will no doubt have observed the coincidence in number between the Five Pre-Gaelic Invasions of Ireland and the five provinces as described in *Lebor Gabála Érenn*. The authenticity of four of the invasions and of four of the provinces is beyond dispute, whereas the disagreement of the authorities as to whether the prediluvian Cessair should be reckoned among the invasions may be compared with the uncertain status of the second Munster as the fifth of the five provinces. The analogy may be carried a step further. If we exclude Cessair, there are still the Sons of Míl to turn the remaining four invasions into five. Similarly with the provinces, if we exclude the second fifth of Munster there is room for the central fifth of Meath. These correspondences may be tabulated as follows:

INVASIONS	PROVINCES
The Sons of Míl	Meath
Four Pre-Gaelic Invasions	Four Provinces
Cessair	The second Munster

2

Leaving Cessair and the second Munster aside for the moment, it can be shown further that the four great provinces and the centre constitute a hierarchic system which corresponds to that of the invasions from Partholón to the Sons of Míl. When the representatives of the four quarters and of the Manor of Tara had been assembled together as we have just described, the supernatural Trefuilngid asked: 'O Fintan, and Ireland, how has it been partitioned, where have things been therein?' 'Easy to say,' said Fintan, 'knowledge in the west, battle in the north, prosperity in the east, music in the south, kingship in the centre.' Then Trefuilngid proceeded to indicate in detail the attributes of each quarter and the middle. There is some overlapping in these descriptions which blurs the clear distinctions drawn by Fintan, but we will give them in full, italicizing the items to which we wish to draw attention.

WEST (*Connacht*)

LEARNING (Fis), foundations, *teaching*, alliance, *judgement, chronicles, counsels, stories, histories, science,* comeliness, *eloquence,* beauty, modesty (lit. blushing), bounty, abundance, wealth.

NORTH (*Ulster*)

BATTLE (Cath), *contentions, hardihood, rough places, strifes, haughtiness, unprofitableness, pride, captures, assaults, hardness, wars, conflicts.*

EAST (*Leinster*)

PROSPERITY (Bláth), *supplies, bee-hives* (? ceasa), contests, feats of arms, *householders,* nobles, wonders, *good custom, good manners, splendour, abundance, dignity,* strength, *wealth, house-holding, many arts,* accoutrements (?), *many treasures, satin, serge, silks, cloths* (?), *green spotted cloth* (?), *hospitality.*

SOUTH (*Munster*)

MUSIC (Séis), waterfalls (esa[4]), *fairs* (oenaigi), nobles, *reavers,* knowledge, subtlety, *musicianship, melody, minstrelry,* wisdom, honour, *music,* learning, teaching, warriorship (fiansa), *fidchell-playing,* vehemence, fierceness, poetical art, advocacy, modesty, code, *retinue,* fertility.

CENTRE (*Meath*)

KINGSHIP, stewards, dignity, primacy, stability, establish-ments, supports, destructions, warriorship, charioteership, soldiery, principality, high-kingship, ollaveship, mead, bounty, ale, renown, fame, prosperity.

Learning and Battle clearly refer to the aristocratic functions of the druids and the warriors, and their ascription to Connacht and Ulster fully accords with what we have said about the superiority of Conn's Half. In Chapter II we observed that the Mythological Cycle of Tuatha Dé Danann was characterized by wizardry, the CúChulainn Cycle by heroism and the Fenian Cycle by romance. It remains to add that Tuatha Dé

Danann first appeared in Ireland on a mountain of Con‚ maicne Réin in Connacht and that Mag Tuired, the scene of the great battles which form the central theme of this cycle is also in Connacht.[5] The warrior Cycle of CúChulainn is the Ulster Cycle, while the Fenian Cycle, the tales of the ordinary people, are located mainly in the South of Ireland.[6] The three qualities which we have discerned in these three cycles thus have their respective provenance—thinking in the West, willing in the North, feeling in the South.

The correlation of provinces with functions makes the great epic of the CúChulainn Cycle more intelligible. It comme‚ morates a struggle between the two aristocratic provinces of Connacht and Ulster, in which the protagonists are Queen Medb of Connacht on the one hand, and King Conchobar and his nephew CúChulainn on the other. Professor Dumézil has singled out 'Sovereignty' in its magical and judicial aspects as the primary attribute of Function I, and we have seen that Medb personifies Sovereignty. It is said that Conchobar had been Medb's first husband, and her desertion of him against his will is said to have been the first cause of the *Táin*.[7] On the other hand, the immediate cause of the *Táin* was that Medb coveted Ulster's great bull. The bull symbolizes the warrior function both in Rome and in India.[8] Thus the *Táin* appears as an example of the classic struggle between the priestly and the warrior classes, each of which tends to usurp the functions and privileges of the other. It may be compared with the First Battle of Mag Tuired between the Tuatha wizards and the Fir Bolg warriors. That battle belongs to the Mythological Cycle and in it the warriors are defeated, but the warriors are victorious in the struggle of the warrior Cycle.

It will be remembered that Mug Nuadat gained possession of the Southern Half, the Half of Mug, by feeding the people, and that when Éremón and Éber originally divided the country into two, the harper went to the South and endowed the Southern Half with music in perpetuity. In the fivefold divi‚ sion which we are now discussing, these two attributes,

'Prosperity' and 'Music' are separated and allocated respectively to Leinster and Munster, the two provinces of the Southern Half, here identified with 'East' and 'South'. 'Prosperity', com-bined in our text with such other attributes as wealth, abun-dance and hospitality, singles out Leinster as the province of the Farmers, the third estate, and this is in full agreement with what is told of Leinster. Laigne Lethan-glas, father of Liath, the representative of *the people of Nemed* in a text quoted in Chapter IV,* is the eponym of the Leinstermen (*Laigin*). We have noted that the usual term for ordinary freeman is *bó-aire*, 'cow-freeman', and it is recounted that throughout the early centuries of Irish history the people of Leinster were obliged to render to the high-king of Ireland a tribute known as the *bórama*, 'cow-counting'. Several tales are told about Leinster's revolts against this obligation, among them the story of the Battle of Dún Bolg.[9] In this story, young Leinstermen are smuggled into the king of Ireland's camp, hidden in baskets loaded on to three hundred teams of twelve oxen each. Straw is laid over the men and food upon the straw. 'What are the Leinstermen doing?' asks the king of Ireland of a Leinster spy who has been sent ahead to collaborate with the attackers. 'They are preparing food for you, and never have you had more satisfying meat: they are boiling their swine, their beeves and their bacon-hogs.' 'Who goes there?' cry the men of Oriel as the procession makes it way to the king's camp. 'Soon told,' comes the answer, 'Leinster's servants laden with the king of Ireland's provisions.' Feeling the baskets, the challengers find nothing but food. 'It is the food that's come,' says the spy, as the intruders reach the middle of the camp. The oxen are un-loaded, wild horses are set loose to bring confusion into the camp, and the Leinstermen arise out of the baskets and rout the king of Ireland's men. Here the Leinstermen identify them-selves with the products of the third 'function'. Thus the *Śatapatha Brāhmana*: 'the king is the eater, the yeomanry food',

* Page 111.

'the yeomanry is another's tributary, another's food', and again, 'whatever belongs to the yeomanry, the nobleman has a share in it'.[10]

Two of the most famous hosts of Irish story, Mac Dathó and Da Derga, had their abode in Leinster,[11] while the tale called 'The Melodies of Buchet's House'[12] brings out the oppressive as well as the benevolent side of the relationship between the king and the third estate. Buchet, *bó-aire* of the high-king, was a Leinsterman 'rich in kine',[13] and a paragon of hospitality. With him in fosterage was Ethne, daughter of Cathaer Mór, King of Ireland, and Cathaer's twelve sons used to come guest-ing with large companies, so that his seven herds of cattle were reduced to seven cows and a bull. It was in vain that Buchet sought redress from the aged king who, unable to restrain his sons, advised him to leave the country. Buchet, with his old wife and Ethne, then dwelt in a hut in the forest until they were discovered there by Cormac mac Airt, the future king of Ireland. As a bride-price for Ethne, Cormac gave Buchet so many herds that he could not take them all back to Leinster.

> 'The song of Buchet's house to the companies: his laughing cry to the companies: "Welcome to you! It will be well to you with us! Let it then be well to us with you!" The song of the fifty warriors with their purple garments and their armours, to make music when the companies were drunk. The song, too, of the fifty maidens in the midst of the house, in their purple dresses, with their golden-yellow manes over their garments, and their song delighting the host. The song of the fifty harps afterwards till morning, soothing the host with music.'[14]

If Leinster represents the third function, the only function left for Munster is the fourth, that of the Serf. And it is note-worthy that Mug Nuadat ('Servant of Nuadu') is the epony-mous ancestor of the ruling peoples of Munster only, while Leinster, the East, is often inconsistently counted as part of Conn's Half.[15] In the succession of mythical Nunster kings, the son of Mug Láma is followed by Mug Néit and then by Mug Nuadat.[16] It has recently been argued[17] that *Mugain*, the name of a matriarch of Munster, is a feminine form of *Mug*. While Munster and her rulers signify the South, Leinster's position is ambiguous, like the role of Nemed in the story of the Invasions, and like the status of the *bó-aire* who, though a freeman, was normally a client (*céle*) of a ruling noble and therefore a rent-payer (*aithech*).

The story of 'The Expulsion of the Déssi'[18] also helps to define the position of Munster in the hierarchy. The Déssi's name means 'vassals' and they may be compared with the Vedic *dāsas* and *dasyus* ('foes', 'demons', 'slaves') who were both ter-restrial enemies and demons. The champion of the Déssi kills the high-king's son, who has taken his niece without his con-sent, and he maims the high-king himself. As a result, the Déssi are expelled from Brega, the seat of the high-king. Like the lowly Partholón, the slayer of his king, they become out-laws. Wandering in the South of Ireland, they acquire terri-tory for a while in Leinster, but it is in Munster they eventually settle and there they claim equal freedom with the ruling people. Though Macdonell's remark concerning the Vedic references to the *dasyus* 'the line between what is historical and mythical is not clearly drawn',[19] may be equally applicable to the Déssi, the story purports to show why the Déssi were to be found as vassal peoples in the southern half of Ireland. They were also to be found in Meath—for Meath was a replica of the whole.

Again, the characterization of Munster as the province of Music identifies it with the fourth function. We have already drawn attention to the association of craftsmen with low-class musicians in Irish and other societies.[20] Among the 'folk of vocal and instrumental music' in Ireland, only the harpist could aspire to the rank of freeman—and he only on condition that he 'accompanies nobility'.[21] A gloss in the Laws defines the unfree musicians as singers of *crónán*. The word *crónán* is also used of the buzzing of a fly.[22] In Wales, minstrels were called *clêr*, and a homonym *clêr* means 'flies'.[23] At the bottom of the social scale in Ireland were the disreputable *crossáin*, lewd, ribald rhymers or buffoons who went about in bands. There is an account[24] of a band of nine of them, jet-black and hairy, chanting from nightfall till dawn upon the grave of a king after his burial. They are likened to demons of hell, and when they are dispersed by Mass and holy water they appear in the air above in the form of jet-black birds. Though satire was permissible to all poets, the satirist as such is classed with 'the sons of death and bad men'—fools, jesters, buffoons, outlaws, heathens, harlots—who hold demon banquets.[25] In India too, the labourer caste, with its lowly musicians, personifies the demons.[26]

A medieval text, which gives the characteristics of the king-ships and peoples in Ireland, assimilates Munster's two king-ships to flies and its peoples to bees.[27] Flies are believed to be embodiments of demons, witches, or the souls of the dead by many peoples, including South American Indians, and not all these beliefs[28] can be derived from the notoriety of Beelze-bub, king of gnats and flies, in medieval Europe. Ahriman, the Persian god of darkness, used to appear in nature as a fly, and it was in the form of a fly that the demon of death brought decay and destruction to dead bodies. (It is said that Adam, who was given dominion over all animals, had no power over insects.) The five regalia of the king in India and Burma[29] seem to correspond to the four castes together with the king-ship: crown (kingship), umbrella (priest), sceptre (warrior), sandal (commoner) and *fly-wisk* (serf). Whereas the symbols of the first three castes represent their respective functions, that of the fourth is an instrument with which to exclude them. It is in several countries a symbol of rank.

We now leave the four quarters and turn to the 'Centre', whose key word is 'Kingship'. Most of the attributes ascribed to this province, apart from 'high-kingship' which is peculiar to itself, have already been met with in the quarters. The Centre combines the outstanding features of all the functions. Except for the inclusion of the fourth function,[30] this accords with the nature of kingship, whether central or local.[31] In his comparative study of kingship,[32] Hocart demonstrates that over a great part of the world kings, who were believed to be divine, had three essential attributes: justice, victory, and the power to give fruitfulness to the earth and health to mankind. Kings personify justice, whether they themselves exercise the judicial function or not; victory too belongs to them even though the actual defence of the realm may be in other hands, and however remote they may be from agricultural labours, the fertility of the earth depends upon them. Of these three attributes the primary one is justice, and it is from the king's justice that victory and prosperity ensue.

So it was with the king of Ireland, and also with the lesser kings. Thanks to the righteousness of Cormac mac Airt's government and judgements, calves were born after only three months' gestation, every ridge produced a sackful of wheat, the rivers abounded with salmon, and there were not enough vessels to hold the milk that flowed from the cows.[33] As Professor Dillon has pointed out,[34] texts offering 'Instructions to a Prince' lay great emphasis on the power of Truth as a prerequisite for a successful reign. The oldest of them declares:

'By the prince's truth great peoples are ruled.

'By the prince's truth great mortality is warded off from men.

'By the prince's truth great battles are driven off into the enemies' country.

'By the prince's truth every right prevails and every vessel is full in his reign . . .

'By the prince's truth fair weather comes in each fitting season, winter fine and frosty, spring dry and windy, summer warm with showers of rain, autumn with heavy dews and fruitful. For it is the prince's falsehood that brings perverse weather upon wicked peoples, and dries up the fruit of the earth.'[35]

Similar testimony could be adduced from a variety of Irish texts, and in Wales a vaticinatory poem in the Black Book of Carmarthen speaks of years to come when there will be 'false kings and failing fruit'.[36] So much did the stability of the realm depend on righteousness that in one Irish story the part of the house of Tara where a king pronounced a false judgment 'slid down the deep declivity' where it stood 'and will so abide for ever'.[37] As in other lands, the falsehood which brought catastrophe was not limited to lying and wrong judgement. Wrongful succession and wrongful marriage had the same results. During the reign of the usurper Cairbre Caitcheann there was only one grain on each stalk of corn and one acorn on each oak, the rivers were empty of fish, the cattle milkless.[38] As the result of Conn Cétchathach's marriage with the sinful Bécuma 'there was no corn or milk in Ireland'.[39] But 'a prince's truthfulness—it is known—is a conflict which brings debility on (enemy) hosts; it brings milk into the world. it brings corn and mast'.[40]

The three qualities essential to a king are defined in a negative way in Queen Medb's requirements in a husband. He must be 'without jealousy, without fear, and without niggardliness'.[41] Jealousy would be a fatal weakness in a judge, as would fear in a warrior and niggardliness in a farmer. The higher the status, the more exacting are the standards that go with it, and it is noteworthy that the most reprehensible sin of each class is to indulge in the foibles of the next class below it. Meanness may be excused in a serf, but it is a denial of the farmer's vocation; fear is not incompatible with the peaceful role of the farmer, but it is the warrior's greatest disgrace; jealousy, as we have seen, is a trait of the warrior's character, the correlative of his virtue, but it can undermine the impartiality required in a judge. A king must have the virtues of all the functions without their weaknesses. The same doctrine may be found in the ancient laws of India. Transgressors of high caste are liable to heavier penalties than those of low caste, and from this point of view it is the serf, not the king, who can do no wrong.[42] And with this we must call a halt to our digression on the nature of kingship, a digression prompted by the need to consider why all the 'functions' are represented among the attributes of the central province.

The text on which we have based our discussion of the hierarchy of provinces, survives only in late medieval manuscripts, though there is mention of 'The Story of the Manor of Tara' in the *dindsenchas*.[43] The provincial distribution of functions can, however, be shown to be older than the Middle Ages. Its main outlines appear in a poem ascribed to the ninth-century poet, Mael Mura:[44]

> 'Éremón took the north
> As the inheritance of his race,
> With their ancient lore, with their good fortune,
> With their laws.
>
> 'With their fortresses, with their troops,
> Fierce, active;
> With their rash fights,
> With their cattle.
>
> 'Éber took the south of Ireland,
> The order was so agreed upon,
> With its activity without power,
> With its harmony.
>
> 'With its excellences, with its grandeur (humility),*
> With its hospitality,
> With its vivacity combined with hardiness (without
>   harshness),
> With its loveliness (festivity), with its purity.'

Comparative evidence shows that the system is of even greater antiquity. An Indian text-book for kings gives a detailed account of the lay-out of a royal fort.[45] In the centre of the fort is the apartment of the gods and the 'honourable liquor house'

---

* The words in brackets are alternative readings from the Book of Lecan.

(like the mead-circling hall of Tara), with the king a little to the north of centre. Around all this are arranged the quarters of the four castes: the priests in the North, the warrior-nobles in the East, the farmers in the South and the serfs in the West. The order, proceeding in a clockwise direction, is the same as in the Irish scheme, but whereas the Irish scheme begins with the priests (learning) in the West, the Indian priests are placed in the North. The evidence at our disposal does not enable us to account for this difference.[46] But more remarkable than any divergence in detail is the presence both in Ireland and in India of the curious idea that social classes have to do with the points of the compass.

The correlation between peoples, functions and provinces which we adumbrated earlier in this chapter can now be tabulated in more detail:

People	Function	Caste or Class	Province
The Sons of Míl	—	Kings	Meath
Tuatha Dé Danann	I	Priests	Connacht
Fir Bolg	II	Warriors	Ulster
Nemed	III	Farmers	Leinster
Partholón	IV	Serfs	Munster
Cessair	—	Aborigines	The second Munster

3

We have still to consider the alternative location of the fifth fifth. Modern historians regard the allocation of two fifths to Munster as a spurious tradition invented by the ancient historians, but we have already suggested that the analogy between

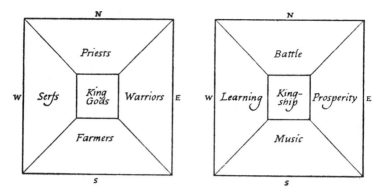

Fig. 7 Classes and Directions (India and Ireland)

what may be called the 'central fifth' and the 'outer fifth', on the one hand, and the invasions of the Sons of Míl and of Cessair on the other, is a sufficient justification for considering both traditions seriously. To equate the royal central province with the Sons of Míl, ancestors of the kings of Tara, is appropriate enough, and if one had to search on the face of Ireland for a territory to correspond to the pre-diluvian Cessair, whom we have equated with the chaos that preceded the emergence of the castes, it would be impossible to find a more fitting location than the farthermost extremity of the province of the 'Servant' king. It behoves us therefore to look more closely at some of the traditions concerning Munster as a whole, and West Munster in particular.

In discussing the Five Primeval Invasions we observed that whereas Nemed's people, Fir Bolg, and Tuatha Dé Danann belong together, Partholón and Cessair are separated from them by plague and Flood. Similarly, the province of Munster stands apart from the other provinces. The current opinion is that the over-lordship of the king of Tara was not recognized in Munster until the ninth century.[47] Munster has a measure of autonomy and it has a hierarchy of its own which reproduces that of the superior realm. Like Ireland itself, it is divided, not only into two, but into five[48]—North, South, East, West, and

Middle; Temair Luachra in Munster is the only Temair of note besides Temair Brega (Tara) and in the two stories about five brothers encountering the Sovereignty of Ireland, the king who is revealed is, in the one case, Niall ancestor of the Uí Néill who for many centuries were able to assert their claim to the kingship of Tara, in the other Lugaid Laígde, ancestor of the Érainn of Munster. In the text on which we have based this chapter the attributes of Munster are almost as all-embracing as those of the Central Province—they include knowledge, wisdom, learning, teaching, and poetic art, warriorship, and fertility, as well as attributes which connect it with the fourth 'function'. It is a world in itself.

This separateness and self-sufficiency of Munster is nevertheless a concomitant of its peculiar role in the wider cosmology—a role which has many facets. Firstly, Munster is associated with the dead. The House of Donn and the world of the dead lie off the coast of West Munster, and a story which tells of the return of the dead Caílte to confirm a statement made by Mongán in Ulster says that he was first heard approaching in Corco Duibne in West Munster.[49] 'The House of Donn' occurs too as a name for Munster or its royal house.[50] MacNeill reckoned that five-sixths of the *ogam* inscriptions on memorial stones in Ireland are located in the three south-western counties of Waterford, Cork, and Kerry, and they are particularly numerous in the barony of Corco Duibne.[51] Among the invaders it was the companies of Cessair and Partholón who perished utterly.

Secondly, Munster is pre-eminently the province of female supernatural personages. 'The Síd of Munster' is known as 'The Síd of the White Women'. Ireland is sometimes called 'the land of Anann', and Anann, described in Cormac's Glossary as 'the mother of the gods of Ireland', is commemorated in the name of two hills, 'The Paps of Anann', near Killarney in Munster. Also associated with a Munster district is Ébliu, sister of Lug, who was a wife of Fintan son of Bóchra ('Ocean'). Áine, variously described as wife and daughter of

Manannán mac Lir, and grand-daughter of Donn of Uisnech, gave her name to the Munster hill Cnoc Áine which, like the Paps of Anann, was a *síd*-dwelling.[52] The *Caillech*, or Old Woman, of Beare is known not only in Ireland but also in Scotland, where she is said to be 'the most tremendous figure in Gaelic myth to-day'.[53] Mountains, lakes and islands owe their existence or their location to her, and cairns are said to be stones that have fallen from her apron. Beare is a peninsula of West Munster, and a note in the medieval Book of Lecan says the *Caillech* was of the Corco Duibne, to whom it was bequeathed that 'they shall never be without some wonderful *caillech* among them'.[54] 'This is why she was called the Old Woman of Beare: she had fifty foster-children in Beare. She passed into seven periods of youth, so that every husband used to pass from her to death of old age and so that her grand-children and great-grandchildren were peoples and races.'[55]

Munster is the primeval world, the place of origin. On its west coast are the landing places of several of the mythical in-vaders, including Dún na mBarc in Corco Duibne where Cessair came to land. Under the name of Banba, this first woman lived to meet the Sons of Míl on Sliab Mis, again in Corco Duibne. Tul Tuinde where Fintan, or alternatively Banba, survived the Flood, is likewise in West Munster, accord-ing to the Fir Bolg division of Ireland. On Valentia Island off the west coast of Munster dwelt the wizard Mug Ruith who lived through nineteen reigns.[56] *Sen* means 'old', and Sen, Sengann, Ro-shen, Senach, Sengarman, Senláech, Senan, Senfiacail—who appear in diverse stories—are all Munster characters.[57] Again, the Érainn are believed by historians to be aboriginal inhabitants who were already in Ireland when the Gaels arrived. Unlike other tribes, their pedigree is traced, not to the Sons of Míl, but to Lugaid, the son of Íth[58]—the fore-runner who was killed by Tuatha Dé Danann. Their name is traditionally linked with that of Ireland (*Ériu*), and their pre-sence is recorded for many parts of the country, but the *Sen Érainn*, 'the Old Érainn', belonged to Munster.[59]

To describe Munster as the province of the dead, and as the province of female and ancient personages, is to stress only some of the more obvious pecularities of its character. It is a land of surprises, as was dicovered by King Fedlimid and his men when they approached the house of Gulide of West Munster, in a snowstorm. Gulide was the sharpest and bitterest lampooner in Ireland, ready to ask anything of anybody, but 'not good at giving'. He had three daughters, 'Fly', 'Smasher' and 'Scream', and he sent one of them to parley with the visitors, 'to see whether they will pass us by tonight'. She confronted the king with a most discouraging account of the poverty of the household—the old food had gone, the new had not come, the women were pregnant, the cows barren and devoid of milk, the mice were active, and even the hard benches were rotten. Eventually, the girl led the king by the hand into the house. He stayed for three days and three nights, and never during his reign did he fare better as regards whitemeat.*[60]

The paradoxical nature of Munster manifests itself in many ways. If the kingship of Munster is 'like a fly', the people are 'like bees', and in Celtic tradition, bees have a secret wisdom and hail from Paradise.[61] The supernatural beings of Munster have a dual nature. Cessair, the outcast, is also Banba the queen, Fintan the idolator is the sage of the ages. Mug Nuadat, the 'Servant' king is also known as Eogan the Great (*Eogan Mór*). Mugain, the Munster queen, seems to be the same person as Mór of Munster.[62] The story goes that the kings of Ireland were seeking Mór. Her 'House' is pointed out at the western extremity of Corco Duibne, and when the sun is shining it is said that 'Mór is on her throne'. Fintan changes his form, and the Old Woman of Beare renews her youth, time and time again. A similar metamorphosis appears in a Fenian story in which Finn's destiny is revealed by a visitant from the Other World. This stranger was Crónánach—his name is suggestive —from Síd ar Femuin, the Síd of Munster, and he appeared, an

* i.e., milk food.

enormous, black, mis-shapen churl, upon Finn's hunting-mound. He brought out two pipes and played 'so that wounded men and women in travail would have fallen asleep at the exquisite music which he made'. Later, 'As the light of day came there came upon the churl a beautiful form and shape-liness and radiance, so that there was a delightful beauty upon him . . . and he had the demeanour of a high-king, and there was the charm of a youth in his figure.'[63]

We have connnected the Music of the South with low-class entertainers, but this gives only one side of the picture. Time and again, both in the early literature and in folktales, sweet music is revealed to be one of the essential attributes of the Other World. Its sound often heralds the approach of the supernatural, and by means of it the *síd*-folk place men and women under enchantment. Just as, in the story of the Sons of Míl, the learning of the North is set over against the music of the South, so the *Rig Veda* bears witness to the fundamental opposition of the brahmans and the *Gandharvas*[64]—beings who dwell in a world apart and whose name is also used with reference to human musicians. In the *Śatapatha Brāhmaṇa*, Words and Chant (*Rik* and *Sāman*) are equated with Earth and Heaven, respectively,[65] and in China 'right behaviour' (*Li*) and music are similarly contrasted: 'Music . . . is of the order of heaven, *Li* . . . is of the order of earth. . . . Music was made manifest in the genesis of all things, and *Li* has its abode in their completion.' It is a universal belief that words have a creative power; they symbolize the manifest world. Music, on the other hand, brings us into harmony with the non-manifest, and 'to understand music is to be at the secret source of *Li*'.[66]

In the time of Conchobar and the warriors of the Ulster Cycle, two kings are said to have ruled in Munster, Eochaid mac Luchta and CúRoí mac Dáiri. Some texts say that they were the kings of the two Munsters, respectively, others men-tion only one or the other as the king of Munster.[67] The pedi-gree of Eochaid is traced to Íth son of Bregon, but we are told

little about him. He was one-eyed, a defect which would dis-
qualify a person for the kingship in other provinces. He shares
this Fomorian feature with the primeval Fintan and Partholón,
with Mug Ruith the 'giant slave' and sorcerer, with Nár
('Shame') the swineherd of Bodb of the Síd of Munster, and
with 'Ill-omen', 'Damage', and 'Want', the three sons of
Uar ('Cruel'), of Tuatha Dé Danann, who plundered Finn
in Munster.[68] The latter three are described as 'three foemen
... lame-thighed ... left-handed, of the race of wondrous evil,
from the gravelly plain of Hell below'; 'venom on their weapons, and venom on their dress, and on their hands and feet,
and on everything they touched'. Personages with one eye do
not belong exclusively to Munster in the stories, but they
characterize the role which is Munster's.

The other king, CúRoí, is more of an enigma than any of
the Munster personages. In one context he is a giant herdsman or peasant (*bachlach*), who may be compared with the giant
lords of animals who direct Arthurian heroes as they approach
the confines of the Other World.[69] In another context he is the
'King of the World'.[70] His remarkable fortress at Sliab Mis in
Corco Duibne recalls the rotating cosmic palaces of Asiatic
legend. 'In what airt soever of the globe CúRoí should happen
to be, every night o'er the fort he chaunted a spell, till the fort
revolved as swiftly as a mill-stone. The entrance was never to be
found after sunset.'[71] He himself is a sorcerer and a master of
illusions. Standing in Conchobar's hall he *looks* like a blazing
luminary, but at the same time the noise of his movements
sounds like a great storm. As the high-king of Temair Luachra,[72]
he belongs to Ireland, and yet he is not of it. From the time he
took up arms at seven years of age until his death, he had not
reddened his sword in Ireland, nor had the food of Ireland
passed his lips.[73] He is addressed as 'thou man who traversest
the stream of brine'.[74] CúRoí has close affinities with the
Indian god Pūśan,[75] who is sometimes represented as god of
the *śūdra*. Pūśan too is a cowherd and a protector of cattle;
he carries an ox-goad. On account of his lack of teeth he does

not eat ordinary food but feeds on a kind of gruel. On the other hand, he is the distributor of portions to the gods, and he and Soma have the guardianship of living creatures. He is the protector of all this world—and he is a patron of conjurors. Born on the far paths of heaven and earth, he sees all creatures clearly at once and he is a guide on journeys to the Other World. He also aids in the revolution of day and night, the epithet 'glowing' is frequently and exclusively applied to him, and he is sometimes identified with the sun.

CúRoí plays diverse roles. He appears as CúChulainn's helper in battle, as one who brings contempt upon him, as his challenger and tester, and as his rival and victim.[76] We have already told the story of CúRoí as the challenger in a beheading contest, a motif which also appears in the Middle English poem of Gawain and the Green Knight. A. K. Coomaraswamy has interpreted this theme in the light of Indian parallels, and in the giant herdsman he sees the Cosmic Man or World Giant who is identified with Varuṇa, Prajāpati, Ātman—the highest gods—'*in their sacrifical aspects as the source from which all things come forth*'.[77] And so we reach the ultimate formulation of the paradox of the fourth 'function'. Personified by serfs and outcastes, it is the lowliest in the hierarchy, but as the embodiment of the sacrifice it is at one with the highest gods. Divided into two, one half of Munster symbolizes serfs, the other the Other World. But as one province it is a land of contradictions. In one of the earlier law tracts, its king is described as 'a master (*ollam*) over kings'.[78] After Tuatha Dé Danann have repaired to the *síde*, leaving the daylight world to the Sons of Míl, it is Bodb of the Síd of Munster they have as king. The visiting high-king who instructs their rulers is not a king of Tara, but Manannán mac Lir, the god of the sea.[79] In the occult, Munster and the powers beyond it are supreme. There, the last *is* first.

CHAPTER VI

Involutions

THE CORRELATION OF THE PROVINCES of Ireland with functions and social classes was, of course, symbolical. We are not suggesting that all the inhabitants of Connacht were druids, or that all the inhabitants of Munster were minstrels! There are units within units. Thus, there is a story of the division of Ireland into twenty-five parts among the children of Ugaine Mór, a division which is said to have lasted for three hundred years.[1] Indian texts sometimes speak, not of the 'five peoples' but of the '*five* five-peoples',[2] and there are many divisions and subdivisions within the four main castes. Whereas the five peoples of Irish tradition symbolize the major functions in the hierarchy, there are indications that each was also a complete society in itself, a replica of the entire series. Kingship belonged pre-eminently to the central province, but every province had a king of its own. If, in the larger unity, the king of Munster's part was that of the 'Servant', in his own province his role no doubt corresponded to that of the central king. Similarly, each province had its druids, warriors, farmers and serfs.

Furthermore, the social classes themselves were not homogeneous groups. Each had a structure which seems to have reproduced that of the larger society. Just as there were high-kings, provincial kings and tribal kings, so were there grades within the learned class. We hear of druids, *filid*, and bards, and these seem to correspond to the druids, *vates*, and bards of Celtic Gaul, of whom classical writers give somewhat confusing accounts.[3] The druids and the *vates* were apparently closely related in function, though the former seem to have been held in highest honour. Both were learned philosophers, but whereas the druids, who apparently presided at sacrifices, were judges in public and private disputes, the *vates* were probably

140

seers who foretold the future by augury and the sacrifice or
victims. We have already noted that the name *druid* probably
comes from a root meaning 'to know'. On the other hand,
words cognate with *vates* in other languages are connected with
prophecy, inspiration and poetry. The third class, the bards,
accompanied their songs with instruments resembling lyres,
and they praised some and reviled others, and so too in medieval
Ireland, praise poems (then composed by the *fili*) were sung
by the bard and there was a harp accompaniment. Indeed
the original meaning of the word *bard* appears to have been
'singer of praise'.[4] The preoccupation of *vates* (and probably of *filid*) with inspiration, with prophecy, and with the
temporal, seems to connect them with the function of the
warrior—*débordant*, berserk—while the praises of the bard are
analogous to the food-gifts of the third function and the acclama-
tion by which the third estate confirms the actions and status
of its rulers.[5] Thus, within the learned class there were grades
corresponding to those of priest, warrior, and farmer—and beneath them were disreputable entertainers such as the *crossáin*.

With the advent of Christianity such a pattern would inevitably become blurred. The druid, as priest of the old religion,
lost his function, and in the Irish laws he is degraded to the
subject *nemed* class, while the *fili*, who seems to have inherited
something of the druid's role, ranks with the upper *nemed*
class.[6] Later still, the role of the *fili* became assimilated to that
of the bard, so that the thirteenth century *fili* was above all a
composer of praise poetry. However, 'The Book of Rights',
compiled or edited in the eleventh century, states that 'knowledge about kings and their privileges is proper to the *fili* and
not to the bard'. According to other texts, the honour-price of a
bard was but half that of a *fili*, and moreover, a bard could
claim nothing on the ground of being a man of learning but
should be satisfied with what his native wit might win him.[7]

The pattern is again mirrored with varying degrees of clarity
in the composition of the successive companies of invaders.

In Cessair's company, Fintan (the sage) and Bith (who went north) are clearly superior to Ladra, the pilot, who went south and was the first to die. Partholón is said to have had three sons and a hireling, a company which, including himself, made five. Another version states that he had four sons (with no mention of a hireling) and their names appear again as those of the four sons of Éber who were granted rule in Munster.[8] Among Nemed's four sons, Iarbonél the Soothsayer, ancestor of Tuatha Dé Danann, represents the First Function, Starn, ancestor of Fir Bolg, the Second Function, Fergus Redside the Third, and Annind, the first to die, the Fourth. The five Sons of Dela who led the Fir Bolg invasion divided Ireland into five. Two of them, Gann and Sengann, who took the two provinces of Munster, have the same names as two Fomo-rian kings, antagonists of Nemed. Sláine and Rudraige, who took Leinster and Ulster, respectively, are namesakes of two of Partholón's sons. *Sláine* means 'health' and Partholón's Sláine is described as the first physician of Ireland,[9] while *Rudraige* was also the name of the founder of the royal house of Ulster.

We have identified Tuatha Dé Danann with Function I, but the other functions are represented within them. When Lug appears on the scene, their leaders are Nuadu (the king), the Dagda (god of druidism), and Ogma (the champion), to-gether with Dian Cécht (god of health) and Goibniu (the artisan).[10] Lug's birth was made possible by the alliance which the Tuatha made with the Fomoire before coming to Ireland from the islands of magic arts, and in the Second Battle of Mag Tuired he assumes the form of his mother's people by going on one leg and with one eye closed. In some versions of the tradi-tion he returns for the battle from the Land of Promise.[11] At Tara he declares himself to be a wright. Though the crafts-man's status is, as a rule, a humble one, he can rise socially by mastering more than one craft: 'Whose art is many, his honour-price is many. It increases franchise.'[12] As the Samildánach, the master of all arts—including the arts of the scholar and the warrior as well as the humble crafts—Lug ascends to the seat of the sage, and the king rises before him till the end of thirteen days—an honour which recalls the twelve 'omen days', and a régime which recalls the temporary kings of other lands. The reign of such kings coincides with a period of ritual chaos during the course of which they are expected to defeat the powers of evil and ensure the growth of crops. In some cases, standing upon one foot is an essential part of their ritual.[13]

The polarity of the outer fifth and the central fifth is trans-cended in Lug. The outer realm is the original unity in which all statuses and destinies have their being *in potentia*. At the centre is the kingship which synthesizes all the functions and upon which the destinies of the realm depend. Between these two poles lies the cosmos, in which each province, each func-tion and each craft has its separate existence. Assemblies, as we shall explain, represent both a return to the original unity and the re-creation of order. They are presided over by kings, but in 'The Settling of the Manor of Tara' they are listed among the attributes of Munster. Their originator was Lug. Again, *fidchell* is a game of kings, but in the list of provincial attri-butes it is ascribed to Munster. It was invented by Lug, and it was he too who instituted horse races, an important feature of assemblies, and ball-games.[14] He has been compared with Varuṇa,[15] the possessor of creative magic (*māyā*) and the *asura* par excellence among the *Devas*. In Lug, king and crafts-man, Tuatha and Fomoire, unite.

Julius Caesar, who numbered a druid among his friends, observes[16] that the god whom the Celts of Gaul worshipped most was Mercury, whom they declared to be the inventor of all arts, the guide on journeys and the greatest power in com-mercial affairs. After him they set Apollo who warded off diseases, Mars who controlled wars, Jupiter the ruler of heaven, and Minerva who supplied the first principles of trades and crafts. Professor Dumézil has pointed out[17] that whereas these five deities do not figure as a group in Roman religion, and the Roman Mercury is not described as the inventor of all arts, the five leaders of the Tuatha who confer before the Second Battle of Mag Tuired do correspond to them as regards functions. Thus, Lug the master of all arts and the institutor of fairs was joined by the Dagda and Ogma, and to these were summoned Dian Cécht and Goibniu. Mercury is named also by Tacitus as the god who was most venerated by the Germans, and it is clear that the god referred to is Wodan,[18] whom Dumézil has equated in 'function' with Varuṇa.[19] What has been said above about Lug's paradoxical nature helps to explain why the greatest of all Gaulish gods was the inventor of the arts.

The figure antithetical to Lug in the Cycle of Tuatha Dé Danann is Bres. Both Lug and Bres are half Fomoire, but whereas the former has a Fomorian mother and a Tuatha father, the latter has a Fomorian father and a Tuatha mother. Each in the event supports his father's side against his mother's. Whereas Lug's inferior connections are with crafts, those of Bres are with agriculture as we saw in Chapter II. But his niggardly behaviour is as discordant with the generosity of the third function as it is with the magnanimity of a king. In him the negative, Fomorian side is dominant.

The prominent part played in various situations by the sister's son or daughter's son of a king will appear in Part III of this book. Generally speaking, there is a conflict, as in the cases of Lug and Bres, between the hero and his maternal kin. Even CúChulainn, the great protagonist of his mother's people, sometimes displays hostility towards Conchobar, his maternal uncle.[20] The term by which Bres is described is *gormac* which means 'a dutiful son', 'an adopted son' (adopted for the support of the adopter), or 'a sister's son'. Words which have a comparable range of meaning are *nia* and *gnia*, both of which mean 'champion' and 'sister's son'.[21] Among the Germans, according to Tacitus, the sons of sisters were highly honoured by their uncles, and this tie of blood was regarded as particularly sacred.[22] Bres does not live up to the epithet of 'dutiful son', and we are reminded again of the ambivalent attitude towards cross-cousins and uterine nephews in societies where a man's choice of spouse is limited to the daughters of his mother's brothers or of his father's sisters. The cross-cousin is a god, yet like Bres he steals the offering and is treated like a scapegoat.[23] Hocart, at the conclusion of a discussion of these uterine relations in Indian mythology, suggests that Christ fulfils the role of cross-cousin in the Christian tradition, and it is noteworthy that in Irish literature there are references to Christ as 'our sister's son'.[24]

The fact that every unit, however small, tends to have a structure which mirrors that of the whole[25] makes the over-all picture extremely complicated. Personages and sub-groups can have associations with a function other than their primary one. For example, the bard belongs to Function I, but in the sub-division of that function he corresponds to Function III; the Fiana belong to Function III, but in as much as they represent the military aspect of that function they have affinities with Function II.[26] All this offers unlimited opportunities for confusion in the transmission and interpretation of a tradition which has been only partially preserved.

And there is yet another complication to be noticed. Finn is associated chiefly with the southern half of Ireland; his principal residence is said to be the *síd* of Almu in Leinster.[27] His chief adversary, Goll mac Morna, on the other hand, is represented as the leader of the Connacht *fiana*.[28] That is, in the *lower* cycle of stories, the one-eyed antagonist *within the fiana* is located in the North of Ireland, the hero in the South. This inversion of the relationship between North and South hitherto considered is in accord with the belief that in the Other World[29] everything is inverted. For example, we have already noted, with regard to ghosts of the dead and other spirits, that our day is their night. In Hindu belief '"left" on earth corresponds to "right" in the beyond',[30] while according to the Dyaks of Borneo, in heaven 'no means yes, black becomes white'.[31] Such inversions have to be borne in mind in any attempt to account for contradictory beliefs concerning 'right' and 'left' as well as 'north' and 'south'.[32]

CHAPTER VII

The Centre

IN 'THE SETTLING OF THE MANOR OF TARA', Fintan declares that it is 'right to take the provinces of Ireland from Tara
and from Uisnech', two sites which are for Ireland like 'two
kidneys in a beast'. Uisnech, the mid-point of the island, is in
Meath, Tara is in Brega, but this territorial duality does not
seem to have been absolute, for, according to 'The Book of
Rights',[1] Brega is included within the larger unity of Meath.
It behoves us therefore to look more closely at the roles of the
two great 'centres' of Irish mythology. We will begin with Tara.

In discussing the feminine nature of kingship, we observed
that the kings of Ireland were men who showed favour to, or
were accepted by, the lady who personified the realm. Installa-
tion was a 'king-marriage'. In the ritual of Tara, on the other
hand, the king must be acknowledged by an embodiment of the
masculine principle. Ireland, in addition to bearing the names
of various goddesses, is called the 'Plain of Fál', or the 'Island
of Fál', the Irish are 'the men of Fál', the king 'the ruler of Fál'.
Fál[2] is the name of a stone on the Hill of Tara. It is characterized as 'the stone penis', and in later tradition as 'the member
of Fergus'. This is the 'Stone of Knowledge' which cries out
under the destined king. One story speaks of a more elaborate
ritual in which the cry of Fál is preceded by a symbolical re-
birth. There were two flagstones at Tara, called Blocc and
Bluigne, which stood so close together that one's hand could
only pass sideways between them. When they accepted a man,
they would open before him until his chariot went through.
'And Fál was there, the "stone penis" at the head of the chariot-
course (?); when a man should have the kingship, it screeched
against his chariot axle, so that all might hear.'[3] Similarly in

India, notwithstanding the personification of sovereignty by a goddess, 'the essence of kingship . . . was also believed to reside in a *linga*, a sort of palladium of the kingdom, which was regarded as a presentation of Śiva himself. This linga (phallus) was placed on the top of a pyramid, in the very centre of the royal residence, which was supposed to be the spot where the axis mundi reached the earth.'[4]

The court of Tara, the centre of the Plain of Fál, was the *quint*essence of the state. A medieval source tells how King Domnall son of Aed established his seat at Dún na nGéd, on the banks of the Boyne, because Tara had been cursed by all the saints of Ireland. 'And he drew seven great ramparts about that fort after the manner of Tara of the kings, and he designed even the houses of the fort after the manner of the houses of Tara: namely, the great Central Hall, where the king himself used to abide with kings and queens and ollams and all that were best in every art; and the Hall of Munster and the Hall of Leinster and the Banquet-Hall of Connacht and the Assembly-Hall of Ulster.' In addition to the Central Hall and the Halls of the four Great Provinces there were 'the Prison of the Hostages and the Star of the Poets and the Palace (*Grianán*) of the Single Pillar (which Cormac son of Art first made for his daughter) and all the other houses'.[5]

It seems likely that the four provincial halls at Tara were arranged around the Central Hall, and the plan of the whole state was further reproduced within the Central Hall itself. 'And he (Domnall) summoned the men of Ireland to this feast at Tara. A couch was prepared for Domnall in the midst of the royal palace at Tara and afterwards the host were seated. The men of Munster in the southern quarter of the house. The men of Connaught in the western part of the house. The men of Ulster in the northern. The men of Leinster in the eastern side of it.' And in the middle of the hall sat the five kings. 'The *centre of Ireland* around Domnall in that house. Thus was the court made. The king of Leinster on the couch opposite in the east, the king of Munster on his right hand, the king of

Connacht at his back, the king of Ulster on his left hand.'[6] Thus the orientation of the group accords with the dual meaning of the usual Gaelic terms for the four directions, north, south, east, and west, meaning also left, right, before, and behind, respectively. These kings may not have had the political power of a Louis XIV, but in the realm of symbolism they could legitimately proclaim: *l'état c'est nous.*

The division of a city, a land, or the world, into four quarters with a central fifth is anything but unique. The *Rig Veda* speaks of the *five* directions, north, south, east, west, and 'here', and this is echoed in such Gaelic sayings as 'the five parts of the world' and 'into the five points', which correspond to our 'four corners of the earth', and 'in all directions'.[7] In India, realms and cities used to be divided into four quarters, 'sometimes with the king's country in the middle making a total of five'.[8] The same concept is fundamental to the elaborate cosmology of China and there is a striking resemblance between the five halls of the Irish court and the 'Hall of Light', the cosmic palace of Chinese tradition. This also consisted of five halls 'which were for the worship of the spirits of the five *Ti*,* who ruled in the five directions'.[9] Again, the Grail Castle as pictured in *Sone de Naussay* is a complete cosmic symbol. It is built on an island, with four towers on the outer wall, and a central round tower (elsewhere given as square), which 'is the palace'.[10] Evidence of this kind which could be quoted from many other parts of the world leaves us in no doubt as to the cosmological significance of the four and central fifth in Ireland.[11]

The story of 'Bricriu's Feast' preserves a different tradition about the arrangement of the Banqueting Hall at Tara. Bricriu of the Poison Tongue, trouble-maker of the Ulster Cycle, made a great feast for King Conchobar and his men in Ulster, and he built a new palace for the occasion. 'The house had been made on the plan of *Tech Midchúarta* (Tara's Banqueting Hall),

* Deified Emperors.

having *nine* compartments from fire to wall. . . . A royal com⁄
partment had been constructed for Conchobar in the fore⁄part
of that palace, higher than all the compartments of the house.
. . . The twelve compartments of the twelve chariot⁄warriors of
Ulster had been constructed around it. . . . A sun⁄chamber
belonging to Bricriu himself had been made on a level with the

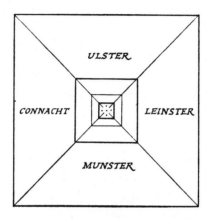

Fig. 8 Tara and the state

compartments of Conchobar and the champions. . . . Glass
windows had been placed looking out on every side of it, and
one of these had been cut above Bricriu's couch, so that he
would have a clear view of the great hall from his compart⁄
ment; for he knew the Ulstermen would not permit him to
enter the house.'[12]

The assertion that Tara's Banqueting Hall had nine com⁄
partments does not tally with the plan we have already des⁄
cribed, but a glance at Chinese and Indian cosmologies re⁄
solves the apparent contradiction. The evidence concerning the
Chinese 'Hall of Light' is particularly striking. Its division
'seems at first to have been into five, and afterwards into nine,

rooms or halls, the symbolism of these numbers being that of the directional and seasonal schemes. . . . Certainly the Nine Rooms represent the co-ordinate scheme of eight directions of the compass (quarters and half-quarters) plus the centre, just as the five rooms represented the simpler scheme of the four cardinal points plus the centre.'[13] The Hall of Light also had an upper chamber, an astronomical observatory—'Skyward House', 'Skyward Look-out', 'Spirit Tower', 'Bright Palace'[14] —to which Bricriu's many-windowed sun-room seems to bear some affinity. Notwithstanding the pre-eminence of the number five in Chinese symbolism, nine too is a 'perfect number' and the country was divided into nine departments corresponding to the nine rooms of the Hall of Light.[15] In Java also the 'Holy Five' becomes the 'Holy Nine' by the addition of the four secondary points of the compass. Similarly in India, we have alongside the four/five-fold conception of cities and lands a tradition that the city and the military camp consist of nine sections. We are also told that the king's quarters were in the northern ninth of the central ninth, while the gods dwelt in the actual centre.[16] The plan would therefore be as in Fig. 9 and it is similar to that of the Hall of Light and the Chinese state.

Around Conchobar's couch in Bricriu's Hall were the couches of the twelve heroes of Ulster, an arrangement which is paralleled by the beds of the Twelve Peers of France set around the magnificent central bed of Charlemagne. It also brings to mind King Arthur and his twelve knights, Oðin seated in a circle with his twelve god-councillors, Hrolf and his twelve berserks, Odysseus and his twelve companions, as well as the Biblical twelves.[17] Mrs Mary Danielli has shown that a four/five-fold conception of the state is also combined with a twelve/thirteen-fold conception in cosmologies as widely sepa-rated as those of Iceland, China and Madagascar.[18] Like Ireland, Iceland consisted of four quarters, north, south, east, and west, but every quarter was further divided into three

sections, making twelve in all. These twelve sections, or
'Things', sent a given number of men to the annual meeting
known as the Allthing, which was held at the theoretical
centre of Iceland under the direction of the Lawspeaker. Here
a temporary town was set up which reproduced the pattern of
the state, the four quarters, the twelve magistrates, and so on,

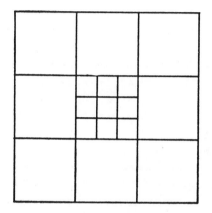

Fig. 9 The ninefold plan

and the area seems to have been elaborately laid out for this
purpose. Conchobar and his twelve heroes are by no means the
only example of a king as the centre of twelve in Irish tradition.
According to *Críth Gablach*, twelve was the company of a king
of a *tuath* and there were twelve couches in a royal house.[19] In
'The Wooing of Emer' we hear of a king of Munster and twelve
under-kings of Munster'[20] When Conaire proceeded to the
bull-feast of Tara, where he was chosen king, three kings were
waiting for him on each of the four roads to Tara with clothes
to cover him. Before his death at Da Derga's Hostel, four sets
of three men were stationed all round his room.[21]

The Irish are said to have had twelve free or noble races—
six in the Half of Conn, and six in the Half of Mug. 'These

are the free states of Ireland.'[22] The country was divided into twice six parts when five chieftains went to the North with Éremón and five to the South with Éber. According to other versions, there were seven in the North and six in the South, making a total of thirteen.[23] In agreement with this, there are indications that at least three of the four great provinces of Ireland were once tripartite. We hear of the 'three provinces of Ulster (East, North, and West)' and there were 'the three Connachts'.[24] At the Fair of Carmun in Leinster, the king of Ossory (a province in south Leinster) sat on the king of Leinster's right, and the king of Offaly (a province in north Leinster) on the king of Leinster's left,[25] an arrangement which implies the conception of a tripartite Leinster. The Life of St Patrick also speaks of 'a twelfth part of Ireland';[26] there were twelve mountains of Ireland, twelve rivers, twelve lakes, twelve winds, and the firmament was divided into 'twice-six parts' corresponding to the 'twice-six months'.[27]

In China and Madagascar the twelve divisions around the cosmic square represent the twelve months of the year.[28] That a correlation of the twelve divisions with the calendar was also known in Europe is attested by Aristotle's observation that the Athenians had distributed their four tribes in imitation of the seasons of the year. By dividing each of them into three phratries they had twelve subdivisions corresponding to the months. Each phratry comprised thirty families of thirty men each, as the months had thirty days.[29] We know of no direct evidence connecting the divisions of Ireland, or the court of the king of Tara, with the calendar. But it should be remembered that the very division of the year into *four* seasons, like the division of a land into four quarters, is an *idea* and not a natural phenomenon. The account of the construction of Bricriu's Hall certainly embodies a calendrical symbolism. It took *seven* of the Ulster champions to carry every single lath, and *thirty* of the chief artificers of Ireland were employed in constructing and arranging the building. The hall contained the couches of the *twelve* heroes and it was built in the course of *one* year.

The connection between Conchobar and the calendar is further attested by a text from the Book of Leinster.[30] Conchobar's mother, Ness, had *twelve* foster-fathers; he himself became king of Ulster by first being granted a nominal kingship for *one year*. There were *three-hundred-and-sixty-five* persons in his household—'that is, the number of days in the year is the number of men that were in Conchobar's household'. Each man provided food and drink for the household for one night, 'so that the first to feed them . . . would come again at the end of the year'. But Conchobar himself provided the feast when the great host assembled at Samain, the year's turning. In the

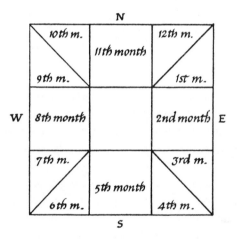

Fig. 10 Cosmos and calendar (China)

household was the gigantic Fergus mac Roich, from whom Conchobar acquired the kingship for a year as a bride-price for his own mother. Fergus seems to have symbolized the week, for all the measurements of his huge body are given in sevens—'the heptads of Fergus'. Unlike the others, he fed the household for a week. But while Fergus was the embodiment of seven, the number is connected in a less emphatic way with Conchobar himself. Seven prophets foretold his advent seven years before his birth, he attained the kingship at the end of his seventh year, and the feast he gave at Samain lasted for seven days—Samain itself and three days before and after. He was both the year and the week.

Was the identification of the king and his household with the year peculiar to Ulster? Comparative evidence disposes us to the view that the king of Tara and his court, no less than Conchobar and Bricriu's Hall (which was modelled on Tara's Banqueting Hall), symbolized the year, with the four quarters corresponding to the four seasons.

Although the four great provinces and the centre constitute the state, the ordered cosmos, they do not comprise all that is. Beyond the confines of Ireland and beneath its surface lies another 'world' and, as we shall see in Part III, Celtic stories are largely concerned with the intrusion upon the cosmos of strange chaotic beings and with the adventures of mortals who enter that Other World. Similarly, beyond the ramparts of Tara, the microcosmic symbol, there is a world that is 'other' and often hostile. The opposition between these two worlds is expressed by another analogy, which likens Tara and Ireland to the board on which the game called *Brandub* was played. This was a game in which a king-piece and four supporting pieces occupied the centre of the board, and comparison with the Welsh *Tawlbwrdd* and Swedish *Tablut*, about which more is known,[31] suggests that there were eight opposing pieces distributed along the sides of the board. Comparison with these games also suggests that a board with forty-nine 'holes' or squares (7×7), like the one recovered from a lake-dwelling in Westmeath, is the appropriate size. 'The Settling of the Manor of Tara' states that the green of Tara had 'seven views on every side',[32] while according to a poem which portrays Ireland as a *brandub* board, Tara is the central square, the four squares around it are the provincial capitals, the king-piece is the king of Ireland and his four defenders are the four provincial kings:[33]

'The centre of the plain of Fál is Tara's castle, delightful hill; out in the exact centre of the plain, like a mark on a parti-coloured *brannumh* board. Advance thither, it will be a profitable step: leap up on that square, which is fitting for the *branán* (king), the board is fittingly thine. I would draw thy attention, O white of tooth, to the noble

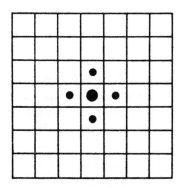

Fig. 11 Probable plan of *brandub* board

squares proper for the *branán* (Tara, Cashel, Croghan, Naas, Oileach), let them be occupied by thee. A golden *branán* with his band art thou with thy four provincials; thou O king of Bregia, on yonder square and a man on each square around thee.'

The game implies that Tara and the cosmos of which it is the centre are surrounded by hostile forces. These board games were favourite pastimes in the households of kings and nobles, and the evidence of Welsh and Irish Laws shows that they were invested with considerable significance. Originally, their purpose may have been similar to that of the ritual dice contests of Tibetan festivals, whereby the Dalai Lama defeated a man from among the people, who played the part of the King of the Demons. In India, too, sovereignty was related to the decision of the dice. During the inauguration ritual the priest handed the king five dice saying, 'Thou art the master; may these five regions be thine . . .'[34]

It is said that Conn, the high-king, used to mount the rampart of Tara every day lest the people of the *síd* and the Fomoire should take Ireland unawares.[35] Potentially, Tara was always in a state of siege. The great 'Feast of Tara' was held at Samain, a time of year when the citadel was more than usually prone to attacks from *síd* folk such as Aillén mac Midhna who used to come at Samain every year to burn up the fort and all its gear.[36] The description we have quoted of the seating arrangements at Tara comes from an account of one of these Hallowe'en feasts. On this night of mischief and confusion, the four provincial kings and their people sat four-square around the king of Ireland, symbolizing and asserting the cosmic structure of the state and of society while chaos reigned outside. Precedences were of prime importance in this setting, and controversy over precedences is the favourite theme in stories about feasts. No transgression of the customary hierarchy could be allowed to go unchallenged, for it had the force of an omen of the way things would be in the ensuing year or period.

2

Whereas Tara is the seat of kingship, several considerations associate Uisnech with the druids. It was at Uisnech that Mide (eponym of Meath), chief druid of the people of Nemed, lit the first fire. The fire blazed for seven years, 'so that he shed the fierceness of the fire for a time over the four quarters of Ireland'. From that fire were kindled every chief fire and every chief hearth in Ireland. 'Wherefore Mide's successor is entitled to a sack (of corn) with a pig from every house-top in Ireland.' And the indigenous druids said: 'Evil (*mí-dé*, a pun) to us is the fire that has been kindled in the land.' On Mide's instructions, these druids were marshalled into a house and their tongues were cut out. He buried the tongues in the ground of Uisnech and sat upon them.[37] Another story of the lighting of a symbolical fire is linked with the neighbourhood of Uisnech. It is told to explain how Delbaeth got his name. Banished with his five sons from Munster 'he went to the cairn of Fiachu and kindled there a druidical fire, out of which burst five streams of flame. And he set him a son to each stream. From these descend the five Delbnas. Hence the name Delb-aed, "shape-fire", clung to him.'[38]

The lighting of a fire as a ritual proclamation of the ascend-ancy of the one who lights it occurs in several other Celtic stories. For example, St David on taking possession of the land which bears his name lit a fire, to the dismay of the local chieftain—'the kindler of that fire shall excel all in powers and renown in every part that the smoke of his sacrifice has covered, even to the end of the world'.[39] Similarly St Patrick, through lighting the Paschal fire, usurped the privileges of the druids who were preparing a fire at Tara.[40] The story of the founding of the monastery of Loch Ree by St Ciarán recalls Nemed's company of eight. 'With eight upon the loch Ciarán travelled but with twelve hundred on land. . . . A fire was lit by the clergy. . . . Said his wizards to Diarmait: "The purpose for which yon fire is kindled tonight is such that it will never be put out." '[41] According to the Welsh laws, the right to enter and occupy land which one's father occupied until his death was the right to uncover the fire (*datanhud*).[42] Men-tion may also be made of the firm tradition that a humble squatter who builds a house on the waste during the course of one night, and has smoke rising from the chimney by the dawn of a new day, gains possession of the site and the land around to the distance to which he can throw an axe from his cabin door.[43]

In the *Rig Veda* the arrival of the Five Kindreds and the Eight Ādityas marks the birthday of the Universe, the origin of months and days, 'the Spring-tide of the Cosmic Year, when dawn first shone for Man'. On landing, their first concern is to establish on earth a ritual in 'imitation of the First Sacrifice'. They erect a fire-altar, and by this sacrificial act they gain possession of the land and secure their legal title to it.[44] In Irish tradition, Partholón, Tuatha Dé Danann, and the Sons of Míl are all said to have struck the land of Ireland at Beltaine, the beginning of a new summer, the time of year when it is the custom to rise early to see the dawn breaking—and when 'ship-processions' used to form a part of the folk-ritual in several of the coastal districts of Britain.[45] It is said that the Great Assembly of Uisnech used to be held at Beltaine,[46] and though we are not told at what time of the year the people of Nemed landed, it is a safe presumption that Mide's fire is the archetypal Beltaine fire. Cormac's Glossary, as well as Keating's History, states that Beltaine fires served to preserve cattle from disease throughout the following year, and the Glossary also says that the druids chanted spells over the fires.[47] The custom of kindling them with a fire-drill survived in some districts until modern times,[48] and Beltaine continued to be *the* occasion when the lighting of the fire on the hearth of every home was charged with danger and significance.[49]

The druids of Gaul used to hold a central assembly which was no doubt the counterpart of the Great Assembly of Uisnech mentioned in medieval texts. Caesar testifies that 'on a fixed date in each year they hold a session in a consecrated spot in the country of the Carnutes which is supposed to be the centre of Gaul. Those who are involved in disputes assemble here from all parts and accept the druids' judgements and awards.'[50] It is noteworthy that among the few details that have survived concerning Uisnech is the tradition that it was at a great meeting held there by the three noble tribes who divided Ireland that the first judgement respecting distress was passed in Ireland.[51] According to the *dindsenchas* it was at a great peace-making assembly held there that the death of Lug was encompassed by the three grandsons of the Dagda,[52] an event which would doubtless contribute to the sanctity of the spot in pre-Christian times.

Giraldus Cambrensis records that the Stone of Divisions at Uisnech 'is said to be the *navel* of Ireland',[53] and in a poem Fintan says:[54]

> 'It is long since I drank a drink
> Of the Deluge over the *navel* of Uisnech.'

This is no chance metaphor. The centre of the world is sym-bolized as the 'navel' (*omphalos*) in many other traditions ranging from Indonesia to Greece and Peru.[55] Nor is the choice of Uisnech as the site of the original fire fortuitous, for the belief that there is a hearth or a fire-altar at the midpoint is also common to other cosmologies. According to the Pythagoreans there is fire at the centre of the universe.[56] Agni, the Vedic sacrificial fire, is the navel of the earth; 'this altar is the further-most border of the earth, the sacrifice is the navel of the world'.[57]

Agni is also a pillar at the parting of the ways, and is com-pared to a column supporting the (five) kindreds.[58] The pillar-stone at Uisnech was five-ridged, symbolizing the five pro-vinces at the centre.[59] Around it was marked out a measure of land consisting of the portion of each province in Uisnech. Here, as at Tara, the world was symbolized by a series of microcosms, each set within the other. In the cosmologies of other lands the centre is often an axis which extends from the netherworld to the heavens above, uniting the universe vertically as well as horizontally. Or at the centre there is a shaft which is the mouth of the nether regions into which the waters of the Deluge flowed, a hole in the ground like the Roman *mundus* into which the spirits of the dead depart, or an oracular cave as at Delphi.[60] No tradition of this kind survives at Uisnech, unless it be that the tongues of the aboriginal druids beneath it have that significance. But we would suggest that the Other World is represented there in another way. West Munster, the 'outer fifth' province which leads to the House of Donn, has its place at Uisnech along with the other four provinces. It is perhaps significant that whereas the Sons of Míl encountered

the kings of the Tuatha Dé Danann at Tara, it was in West
Munster and at Uisnech that they held converse with the
queens. At Tara, the bounded cosmos is represented by four
within four within four; at Uisnech, the cosmos together with
its source in the primordial chaos is represented by five within
five within five. In the stories, Uisnech has no ramparts.
It differs from the four-sided Mount Meru of Indian tradition
and other pyramidal symbols of the centre, and compares
rather with the five-pointed star and the five-petalled flower
with which the alchemists sometimes represented the 'quintessence' in the centre of the cross of the elements.[61]

In diverse cosmologies the mountain in the centre of the
earth is the source of the world's rivers. The centre is symbolized
not only by a mountain, a pillar, a fire-altar, and a tree, but
also by the well of life.[62] There is more than a suggestion of this
in the derivation of twelve chief rivers from a mythological
event which occurred at Uisnech. It was during an assembly
held there at the accession of Diarmait son of Cerball that a
great hail-storm fell upon the gathering. 'Such was its greatness
that the one shower left twelve chief streams in Ireland for
ever.'[63] Another version of the story attributes the streams to a
miracle wrought by St Ciarán to relieve a drought, and just as
Mide who lit the first fire was entitled to a hearth tax, so Ciarán
was entitled to a general cess throughout Ireland.[64] In 'The
Colloquy of the Ancients',[65] when Caílte, Patrick, and their
companions were 'at the pillar-stone of Uisnech', Oisín went
in search of water for the feast. He went alone and kept his
face turned backwards to see that no one watched him. In this
fashion he came to the 'white-rimmed' well of Uisnech, which
no one had found since the battle of Gabhra. There he saw
'eight beautiful salmon clothed in their diversely shaded hues,
the intricacy of the place being such that they needed not to
fear anything'. He took eight sprigs of watercress and eight
of brooklime, and dipping a pail into the well he scooped up
the eight salmon alive and plunging madly. On his return,
he set the vessel with the cress and brooklime floating in it

before the king of Ireland, and the night was spent in feasting and story-telling.

Uisnech is not in fact the hydrographic centre of Ireland, but the derivation of the twelve streams from a miracle wrought there would appear to endow it with that significance. Further-more, the secret well brings to mind the mysterious Well of Segais, or Connla's Well, which nobody durst visit except Nechtan and his three cup-bearers. Like Mimir's Well at the root of the Scandinavian world-tree, this well was the source of inspiration and knowledge. Over it grew the nine hazels of wisdom, 'out of which were obtained the feats of the sages'. The hazel-nuts dropped into the well and caused bubbles of mystic inspiration to form on the streams that issued from it. Alternatively, the nuts were eaten by the salmon in the well, or they passed into the River Boyne. Those destined to partake of the nuts or of the salmon obtained the gifts of the seer and the poet. The location of the well is variously described. It is the source of the Boyne, the source of the Shannon, the source of the seven chief rivers of Ireland, and it has its counterpart in the Land of Promise where the five rivers that flow from it are the five senses.[66]

Though Tara was the centre of political power, Uisnech may once have equalled it in prestige. According to the eleventh-century Book of Rights, Meath, of which Uisnech is the centre, *contained* Brega, the province of Tara. Meath proper consisted of five free kingdoms and five tributary king-doms; Brega consisted of six tributary kingdoms only, one of which was that of the Déssi.[67] The two seem to have had com-plementary roles in the national ritual. According to the *dindsenchas*, 'when all were bidden by the king of Ireland to the feast to Tara, a feast used to be celebrated by the king of Meath' on the hill of Slemain Mide. Unlike the other kings of Ireland, the king of Meath did not contribute to the feast of Tara, yet it was a calamity (a violation of *geis*) for the king of Ireland if the feast of Slemain were not celebrated by the king of Meath when he himself held the feast of Tara.[68] A fairly early text[69]

tells us that the provincial kings, and apparently the king of
Tara, had 'seats in Uisnech'. They 'had a claim on the king
of Tara to hold the feast of Tara for them. And it was after
that that the kings of the provinces used to purchase their seats
at Uisnech. The tax and purchase price was this: the warrior's
gold armlet which was worn on the arm of every prince in
Ireland, he used to leave it in his drinking-place.' Whereas the
festival of Tara was a feast (*feis*), at which, perhaps, the
marriage of the king with the realm was celebrated,[70] the great
assembly of Uisnech was an *oenach*, a '(re)union' of the people.
The fire of Uisnech was first kindled for the clans of Nemed
(i.e. the householders, or those admitted to the sacrifice),
whereas it is said that it was Eochaid, the ideal king of Fir
Bolg, who 'sat in the beginning in Tara'.[71]

The duality of Uisnech and Tara is strikingly paralleled by
dual ritual sites both in Rome and in India.[72] In the *Brāhmaṇas*
it is a strict rule that every sacrificial site must comprise two
essential fires and one accessory fire. One of the two essential
fires, namely the fire of the householder or sacrificer, is the
original hearth from which every fire is kindled; it is proof
of the possession of the land, and it symbolizes the world of
men. The other, kindled to the east of it, is the place of offerings;
it symbolizes the celestial cosmic world of the gods, and its
inauguration is marked by the same wealth of numerical
symbolism as we have observed in the arrangement of the court
of Tara. The first of these two fires, that of the householder,
must be kindled with a fire-drill and the spot is sprinkled with
salt (among other things), for 'salt is cattle and one places
cattle in this world'. This hearth is circular, whereas the other
is square and *orient*ated. As regards the association of Uisnech
with Ériu, it is noteworthy that whereas the eastern fire was
for the worship of the gods, the western fire, by which the
sacrificer's wife sat during the rites, was for the worship of the
consorts of the gods.[73] Professor Dumézil has compared these
two Indian fires with two types of ritual sites known in ancient
Rome, the first represented by the hearth of Vesta, the second

by the *templa quadrata* of which the original city or its central symbol was the prototype. The former was round, it symbolized the earth as the home of men, and it was the centre of the world. If the Vestal fire went out, it had to be re-kindled by *Ignis Vesta*, that is by means of the fire-drill. As its name implies, the other type of site was square and *orient*ated, and it was there that the great rites of the national political life were performed.

With regard to the implicit identification of Tara with the world of the gods, it must be remembered that whatever 'celestial' beliefs the Celts may have had have been lost, or at least 'grounded'. In India, the king is a personification of Indra, the king of the gods, and his courtiers are embodiments of the corresponding members of the celestial hierarchy.[74] And it is Tara, not Uisnech, that has the greatest resemblance to the Heavenly Jerusalem of the Christian Apocalypse, which stands four square and orientated—a walled city from which sinners, sorcerers, and the legions of hell are excluded. It would appear that Tara originally symbolized the cosmos of the gods as opposed to the chaos of the demons. Uisnech was the primeval unity, the principle in which all oppositions are resolved.

3

Whether Hallow'en fires were ever kindled at Tara itself, we do not know. Keating says that it was the custom to assemble the druids of Ireland at Tlachtga, some twelve miles away, on that eve, and that a fire in which offerings were burnt was kindled there. This was a 'prelude' to the Feast of Tara. Keating maintains further that all the fires of Ireland were quenched on that night and that the men of Ireland were forbidden to re-light them except from the fire of Tlachtga.[75] If this is right, the summer fires of Ireland emanated from Uisnech, the winter fires from Tlachtga. The account given by Keating of the arrangement of things in the central province does not fully harmonize with the concept of Uisnech as the navel of Ireland.

He alleges that Tuathal Techtmar built four fortresses in Meath, one in each of the portions taken from the four great provinces. In this scheme Uisnech is connected with Con, nacht, Tara with Leinster, Tailtiu with Ulster, and Tlachtga with Munster.

The authenticity of Keating's arrangement has been con, tested by modern scholars, who ridicule the idea of connecting Tlachtga geographically with Munster.[76] There are other con, siderations, however, which suggest that Keating's testimony

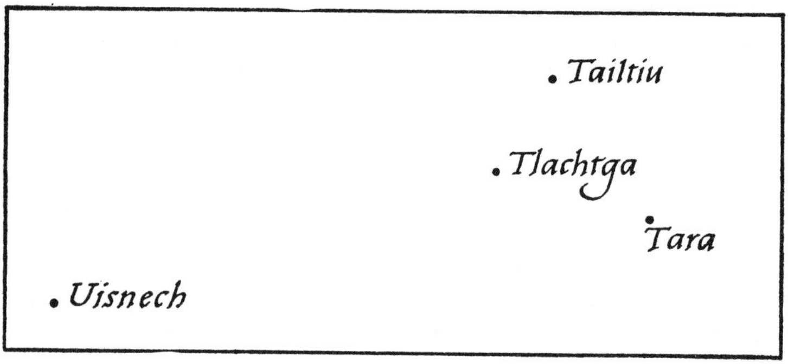

Fig. 12 The four centres in Meath

may not be a complete fabrication. Tailtiu was the queen of the most illustrious king of Fir Bolg,[77] the warrior aristocracy who founded the kingship, and it is appropriate that the assembly centre which bears her name should be associated with Ulster, and that it should be the burial place of the Ulstermen.[78] It is also appropriate that in the two stories of an encounter between five brothers and the Sovereignty of Ireland the brothers after their testing should proceed to Tailtiu,[79] and that the assembly of Tailtiu, convened by the king of Tara, should be held at Lugnasad—the time when Fir Bolg, and Fir Bolg only, landed in Ireland.[80]

The ascription of Uisnech to Connacht, the province of the

priesthood, is natural enough, while Tara is situated in Brega which medieval writers, as well as Keating, regard as a part of Leinster.[81] The personification of Sovereignty whom the kings of Tara were obliged to wed was Medb Lethderg of Leinster.[82] Again, while Fál is a symbol of kingship—and its heart is in Tailtiu—its sexual symbolism connects it with the third function, the embodiment of fertility. As a warrior the king's closest affinities are with Ulster, but as the giver of fertility and prosperity he belongs to Leinster.[83]

Tlachtga (which is associated with Munster), owes its origin and name, according to the *dindṡenchas*, to Tlachtga, daughter of Mug Ruith of West Munster, 'who had been with her father learning the world's magic'.[84] For her, 'Church legend had a hatred not found against [any] other of the Celtic gods and heroines.'[85] Another sorceress from Munster intimately associated with Hallowe'en was Mongfind daughter of Fidach of Munster, the wife of King Eochu Muigmedón and hostile stepmother of Niall of the Nine Hostages. She died on Samain Eve, by taking poison which she had prepared for her royal brother. Samain-tide was called by the common people 'the Festival of Mongfind' because she, 'so long as she was in the flesh, had powers and was a witch: wherefore it is that on Samain Eve women and the rabble address their petitions to her'.[86] All this accords with what we have already adduced about the association of Munster with serfs, witches, and demons. Samain Eve is the night when these nefarious agents are at large, and it is fitting that the Samain fire, kindled, in modern parlance, 'to burn the witches', should be on the site which symbolized Munster. Furthermore, Tlachtga may be equated with the accessory third fire of Indian sacrificial rites, the fire from which the eastern fire which we have equated with Tara was kindled. Offerings to the ancestors were made on this third Indian fire, while its name and location associate it with the South. It was intended to defend the sacrifice about to be offered on the eastern fire against the evil powers of the southern regions.[87]

Keating's association of Tlachtga with the feast of Tara harmonizes with medieval statements that Ireland had *three* great festivals, those of Uisnech, Tailtiu, and Tara.[88] The sacred rites belong to the first three functions, and it is understandable that Tlachtga, which represents Munster and the fourth function, should have no independent status as the centre of a fourth festival. The fact that the assemblies of Uisnech and Tailtiu, the two sites associated with the provinces of Conn's Half, are summer festivals held at Beltaine and Lugnasad, respectively, while the two southern sites are involved in the celebration of Winter's Eve, suggests an identification of the North with summer and the South with winter—and we may note that it is in winter that the commoners are expected to provide hospitality for their lords. In India the North is day, the South is night, the North is male, the South is female; spring and summer, respectively, correspond with the priesthood and the nobility, the rainy season with the common people.[89] But there is no evidence from the Celtic lands of any such systematization, and the inversions to which we have referred make it unprofitable to speculate. The imminence of the supernatural at night and in winter suggests the correlation of these periods, like the South, with the Other World. Conversely, the Other World is depicted as a land of summer, especially when it is winter on earth.

With regard to the inconsistency between the two-fold and the four-fold conceptions of the middle province and its centres, it may be added that the co-existence of contradictory cosmological systems is by no means peculiar to Celtic tradition.

4

The provincial capitals of Ireland had many features in common with those of the centre. Almost without exception they stood on hills, or at least on artificial mounds. They were burial places, a feature which they share with the churches, rather than with the palaces, of our own time. Like churches, too, they were dedicated to the memory of founders, who were in most cases believed to be buried in them. The founders were almost invariably female.[90] In the centre we have Ériu at Uisnech, Tea at Tara, Tailtiu at Tailtiu and the sorceress Tlachtga at Tlachtga. Emain Macha, capital of Ulster, was founded by Macha the war-goddess, Naas was the burial-place of Naas, wife of Lug, while Cruachan was said to have derived its name from Cruacha, a handmaiden who accom-panied Étaín when she eloped with Midir of Tuatha Dé Danann.[91] The names and exploits of women also figure in traditions about less well-known sites, such as Carmun, in Leinster, about which we shall have more to say presently. Continuing our analogy with churches, most of the Irish centres were 'notre dames', like so many of the great eccles-iastical centres of latter-day Gaul.

In most cases the female founder, like Cessair, the first to occupy Ireland, had an untimely end. Tailtiu's heart broke under the strain of clearing the plain that bears her name; Carmun died of grief in exile, and death 'came upon her in ungentle shape'; Macha died in giving birth to twins after being forced to run a race against the king's horses; Tlachtga had been ravished by the three sons of Simon Magus, and when she had journeyed to the hill that now bears her name she died giving birth to triplets—and over her the fortress was built. There is a widespread belief that the victims of miserable and violent deaths are restless in their graves, and the corpses and graves of women who have died in childbirth are particularly feared in many parts of the world.[92] That this fear existed among the Celts is indicated by the fact that such women were not permitted to be buried in graveyards founded by some of the Celtic saints.[93] These considerations gave the places we are discussing a proximity to the supernatural which hallowed them and enhanced the significance of words uttered, and actions performed, upon them.

Assemblies similar to those of the great centres of Meath were held at provincial capitals and at lesser centres,[94] and as far as their dates are known, they were held at sacred points in time. The folk-customs observed at Beltaine, Samain and Lugnasad are thus popular versions of a solemn ritual which was fundamental to the well-being of the community and which formerly required the participation of kings, officials of the court, and all classes. To neglect these assemblies brought dire consequences. 'Everyone of the Ulstermen who would not come to Emain at Allhallow-Eve lost his senses, and on the morrow his barrow and his grave and his tombstone were placed.'[95] A poem preserved in medieval manuscripts[96] describes one assembly, namely that of Carmun, which was held at Lugnasad, and it is clear from the more meagre information available about others that the description is representative of assemblies generally. Through the holding of this assembly the Leinstermen were assured of an abundance of corn and milk, freedom from conquest, the enjoyment of righteous laws, comfort in every house, fruit in great abundance, and plenty of fish in their lakes, rivers, and estuaries.

> 'There comes for neglect of it
> baldness, weakness, early greyness,
> kings without keenness or jollity,
> without hospitality or truth.'

Like the 'truce of the god' which ensured safe conduct to all who attended the Olympic games and other sacred assemblies in Greece, an armistice was imposed. Samain was 'a day of peace and amity between the men of Ireland, on which none is at enmity with his fellow'.[97] Similarly at Lugnasad at Carmun, deeds of violence, abductions, the repudiation of husband or wife, and the levying of debts were all prohibited —and the penalties were severe:

> 'Whoever transgresses the law of the kings
> Benén prescribed firmly for ever
> that he should not thrive in his tribe,
> but should die for his mortal sin.'

The festival was a return to the beginning of things. In the first place it was a commemoration and re-enactment of the mythological event in which the sanctity of the site had its origin. It was a wake for the dead founder, and the races and other competitions were her funeral games.

> 'Thither came, for the delight of her beauty,
> to keen and raise the first wailing over her,
> the Tuath Dé over this noble plain eastward:
> it was the first true assembly of Carmun.'

The poet is at pains to recall the hundreds of times the same scene was enacted after that inauguration, and in the following three stanzas he seems to invoke the presence of the universe and all its component parts, as does the Christian *Benedicite*.[98]

> 'Heaven, earth, sun, moon, and sea,
> fruits of earth and sea-stuff,
> mouths, ears, eyes, possessions,
> feet, hands, warriors' tongues.

> 'Horses, swords, chariots fair,
> spears, shields, and faces of men,
> dew, mast, sheen on leaf,
> day and night, ebb and flow—

> 'The hosts of Banba, free from enduring sorrow,
> gave all these completely [as pledges]
> that it should not lie under gloom of disputes
> to interrupt it, every third year.'

There in the presence of the kings, the nobles, and the people, the whole mythological and chronological past of the nation was conjured into the present by the shanachies:[99]

'Lore of Finn and the Fiana, a matter inexhaustible,
Destructions, Cattle-raids, Wooings,
tablets and wooden books,
satires, keen riddles:

'Proverbs, maxims of might,
and truthful teachings of Fithal,
dark lays of the Dindsenchas for thee,
teachings of Cairpre and Cormac;

'The great feast of Tara and other feasts,
the assembly of Emain and other assemblies;
annals there, this is true;
every division into which Ireland has been divided:

'The story of the household of Tara, that is not scanty,
the knowledge of every cantred in Ireland,
the chronicle of women, tales of armies, conflicts,
Hostels, Prohibitions, Invasions:

'The ten-fold Testament of hundreded Cathair
to his right pleasant offspring kingly of stature:
[assigns] the estate of each man as is due,
so that all may listen to it . . .

'Violent Deaths and Slaughters, strains of music;
accurate knowledge of the goodly race;
his royal pedigree, a blessing through Bregmag
his battle and his stark valour.'

This declamation clearly had the force of a creation rite to re-
establish the foundations of the tradition at the inception of a
new period of time. The social order was also re-affirmed.
The emphasis on 'the estate of each man as is due' is in accord
with the careful observance of precedences at Tara and the
seating of each 'in due order by rank in his place' at the assembly
of Tailtiu.[100] In addition to confirming the status quo, the
assemblies were also occasions for granting new statuses. It is
said that candidates were received into the *fiana* at the assemblies
of Uisnech, Tara and Tailtiu.[101] There were horse-races and

chariot-races through which new orders of merit were established, and at Carmun poets, pipers, fiddlers, tympanists,
bone-players, horn-players, and roarers, all exerted their powers
before the king and he bestowed upon each art its rightful
honour. The competitions at eisteddfodau, 'gatherings of the
clans', sports, shows, and fairs in our own day are clearly
survivals of such rituals as these.

Evidence concerning legislation and the administration of
law at the Irish assemblies is, on the face of it, somewhat contradictory. Of the feast of Tara it is said: 'Here too is the reason
for which the feast of Tara was made at all: the body of the
law which all Ireland enacted then, during the interval between that and their next convention at the year's end none
might dare transgress, and he that perchance did so was out-
lawed from the men of Ireland.'[102] It is known that laws and
statutes were proclaimed upon local meeting-hills within
historical times,[103] and the promulgation of the law from Tyn-
wald Hill has remained a feature of Manx ceremonial to the
present day. The settling of disputes is the only function of the
assembly of the druids of Gaul that Caesar mentions, and
an early Irish text says that at the feast of Tara the kings of
Ireland 'used to settle the affairs of Ireland for seven years, so
that debts, suits and adjustments used not to be submitted for
judgement until the next feast seven years later . . .'.[104] Similarly at Carmun, dues and tributes were discussed and legal
enactments settled.

On the other hand, the poem on Carmun emphasizes the
importance of avoiding quarrels and the levying of debts,
while the assembly of Tailtiu was held, not only 'without
wounding or robbing of any man, without trouble, without
dispute, without reaving', but also 'without challenge of property, without suing, without law sessions, without evasion,
without arrest'.[105] The most feasible explanation seems to be
that the references to the avoidance of litigation appertain only
to the opening stages of assemblies, symbolizing the conclusion of the preceding year and its affairs. In the same way as

the stopping of the clock in a house which death has visited indicates the supervention of a world where time does not exist, so profane time with its debts and quarrels was suspended during the sacred phases of the assembly when the whole heritage of the people was accurately and vividly remembered. And we may infer that this unifying experience promoted a state of mind which was conducive to the settlement of differences and the recognition of law. Fortified by its tradition and purified of its contentions, society could begin its life anew.

CHAPTER VIII

Five Peaks

WALES, UNLIKE IRELAND, is a peninsula of a larger island. It was occupied by the Romans, invaded by the Saxons, subjugated by the Normans, and eventually united with England under the Tudors. If we were dealing merely with an original geographical pattern, the prospect of finding it in Wales would be very dim. But we are concerned not with geography but with a conceptual framework which was by no means confined to the Celts and which could be impressed anew upon whatever territory was considered a unit. We have no evidence as to how Britain was conceived of in pre-Roman times, but it is noteworthy that Roman Britain was divided first into 'Upper Britain' and 'Lower Britain', then into four provinces, and eventually into five. The names Essex, Sussex, Wessex, and Middlesex are an abiding reminder of the existence of the pattern in the world of the Saxons.

Britain has her primeval invasion in the legend of Brutus. According to Geoffrey of Monmouth's *Historia Regum Britanniae,*[1] Brutus, prince of Troy, was incestuously conceived; his mother died at his birth and he was destined to kill his father. Voyaging to Britain with a company of his people, he was joined en route by a further group of four generations of Trojan exiles under the leadership of a champion fighter named Corineus. In accordance with prophecy, they eventually landed in Britain which was thinly peopled by aboriginal giants. Brutus built a city for himself at London and divided the island. Corineus chose Cornwall as his province because 'it was there the giants were most numerous', and when, twenty-four years later, Brutus died and the island was shared between his three sons, the first of them was given England, the second Wales, and the third Scotland. These three sons may perhaps be compared with the three Nemed groups, leaving Corineus the giant-killer to be equated with Partholón, the first adversary of the Fomoire. Geoffrey derives Caerludd, a Welsh name for London, from the name of King Lludd who built the walls of the city. This same Lludd, according to a Welsh story, by measuring the length and breadth of Britain, ascertained that Oxford was the mid-point of the island.[2]

Míl and his eight sons may be compared with Cunedda and his eight sons who are said to have invaded Wales and settled there in the early fifth century.[3] Tybion, Cunedda's eldest son, like Donn the eldest son of Míl, died before the family settled in the new country, but in the Welsh story the dead man's son, Meirion, takes his father's place (as Lugaid son of Íth took the place of his dead father in the Irish story).Cunedda, however, is the founder of the northern dynasty of Gwynedd only, and his sons and his grandson are eponymous founders of territories in North Wales, with the exception of one son whose name is borne by Ceredigion (Cardiganshire).

In Wales as in Ireland—and indeed in France, England, Germany, Egypt, Israel, and India—the main traditional division is into North and South, rather than into East and West. We mentioned that when Éremón and Éber divided Ireland between them there were two ridges in the North and one in the South, and there is a tradition that Éremón shared the North with another brother named Ír, while Éber had the South. The proportion of two in the North and one in the South also appears in another Irish story, which tells of the massacre of the nobles of Ireland by tributary peoples.[4] Three pregnant wives escaped to Alba, and their three sons eventually returned to Ireland and were granted their birthright. They were the ancestors of Conn (eponym of Connacht), Araide (of Ulster) and Eogan Mór (of Munster). The Second Branch of the *Mabinogi* contains a similar story of the birth of *five* sons to five pregnant women, the only people left alive in Ireland after a disastrous war. The sons grew up and in due course united with one another's mother, and from them are the five provinces of Ireland.[5]

Conn of Connacht, Araide of Ulster, and Eogan Mór of Munster are described as 'the three free-born ancestors of Ireland', and they may be compared with 'the three royal tribes of Wales' referred to in early modern manuscripts.[6] The three tribes are the dynasties of Gwynedd and Powys in the North, and of Deheubarth, the one southern province. Giraldus Cambrensis attributes the same division of the country to the three sons of Rhodri Mawr in the ninth century, and it also appears in the law-books.[7] The eleventh-century protonyms of the three tribes are said to have raised two others to the same dignity, making a total of 'five royal tribes'. One of the two additional protonyms was Lord of Glamorgan in the same period. Of the other, Elystan Glodrydd, there is no reliable historical evidence, but his realm was in east Central Wales—'Between the Wye and the Severn'.[8] The correspondence between these five realms and the five provinces of Ireland can hardly be fortuitous.

The central province apart, the fourfold division is further reflected in the medieval bishoprics: Bangor (North-West), St Asaph (North-East), Llandaf (South-East) and St David's (South-West). In the centre of Wales, near the point where the north-western, north-eastern and south-western provinces and bishoprics met, is the mountain of Pumlumon ('Five peaks'),* in which the Wye and the Severn have their source. Like the Stone of Divisions on Uisnech Hill, not to mention the five-peaked world-mountain of Chinese tradition, Pumlumon symbolizes the whole. (Extending westward from its top is a commote called Perfedd ('Middle'),[9] and the ancient mother church of Llanbadarn Fawr in this commote has historic claims to be the centre of a fifth bishopric.) To the south-east of the mountain, in the fifth province, 'Between the Wye and the Severn', is the commote of Gwrtheyrnion, the land of

---

* Or, possibly, 'Five Banners (or Beacons)'.

Gwrtheyrn (Vortigern), the ruler of Britain at the time of the Saxon invasion.[10] His name, as Dr Nora K. Chadwick has recently observed, is the virtual equivalent of the Irish *ard-rí* ('high-king') and 'may originally have been a title'.[11] If Pumlumon has some affinity with Uisnech, what little is known about Gwrtheyrnion entitles it to comparison with Brega of the kings.

In his study of Irish dialects, O'Rahilly comes to the conclusion 'that historically there were but two main dialects in Irish, a Northern and a Southern, and that each of these (but especially the Northern) was divided into two lesser dialects'.[12] In Wales too, the major linguistic cleavage is that which divides the Northern and the Southern dialects, and within these two main dialects there are features which indicate a less marked division between Gwynedd and Powys and between Glamorgan and Dyfed.

2

In the 'Four Branches of the Mabinogi', three groups of characters predominate, two in the North and one in the South, though there is one episode in which a fourth appears, namely Teyrnon and his wife in the South-East.[13] The wizard children of Dôn, the equivalents of Tuatha Dé Danann, are located in Gwynedd. The Children of Llŷr, who figure in the Second Branch, the only branch which has anything of the heroic qualities of the Ulster Cycle, are also located in Gwynedd in the story, but modern place-names seem to link them with Powys,[14] which is also the province of the Llywarch Hen heroic poems. In the *Mabinogi*, it is in the two branches which tell of the northern families that one reads of stormy passions and violent deeds, interludes of timeless bliss and tragic deaths. The southern family of the Mabinogi, that of Pwyll, has to counter with submission, self-restraint and patient persistence the antagonism of the mysterious powers of Annwfn, on the

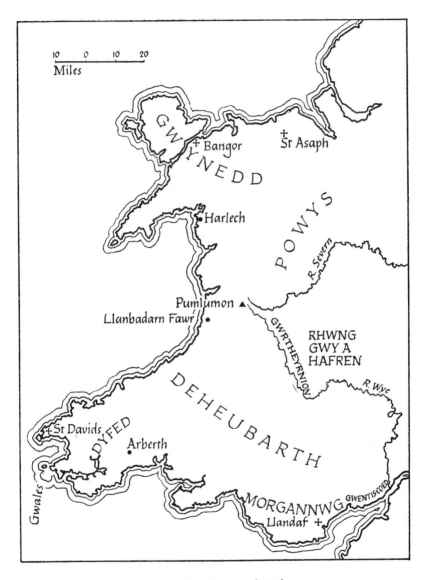

Fig. 13 Sketch-map of Wales

one hand, and of villein craftsmen on the other. Pwyll's son, Pryderi, finding himself duped by Gwydion son of Dôn, wages war on Gwynedd and, like Mug and Éber in Ireland, is defeated and slain.

Arthur belongs to many parts of Britain, but in Welsh tradition his court is located either in Cornwall or in south-east Wales. In the work of Nennius, Arthur appears in the place-lore of the Builth district and of Ergyng (now in Hereford-shire);[15] in the early Welsh poem 'The Spoils of Annwfn' he is associated with the lords of Dyfed, and in the story of Kul-hwch and Olwen his great boar-hunt ranges over South Wales.[16] His geographical background in Wales is thus comparable with that of Finn in Ireland.

Like Munster, Dyfed in the south-west has a mysterious realm within it or beside it. Pwyll, Lord of Dyfed, loses his companions while hunting and finds himself face to face with Arawn, King of Annwfn. He does not recognize him, and when they exchange roles for a year and a day, Arawn's realm comes as a revelation to Pwyll, though it appears to be within easy reach of Dyfed. Henceforth Pwyll is known as the Head of Annwfn, and the new friendship between the two rulers leads to an exchange of gifts, including swine which are sent from Annwfn. Elsewhere,[17] Pryderi son of Pwyll is described as the swineherd of his foster-father, Pendaran Dyfed, and as one of the three renowned swineherds of the Isle of Britain. In an Irish story,[18] a vision seen by a swineherd fore-shadows the coming of Conall Corc to Cashel and to the kingship of Munster. The swineherd is given freedom for himself and his children, and it is he who proclaims the king of Munster and receives his garment. His people (the Mús-craige), the first to offer a hostage to Conall, are also freed. In short, swine belong to the Other World; tending swine is a servile occupation,[19] but in Dyfed the chief is a swineherd and in Munster swineherds are freemen closely associated with the kingship. The paradoxical character of Dyfed appears in other ways, for not only is its ingenuous ruler[20] known as the

Head of Annwfn, but Manawydan, the correlative of Manan-nán, the 'outer' high-king of Tuatha Dé Danann, appears there as a 'humble lord' who engages in hunting and agriculture and readily learns a craft.[21]

Off the west coast of Dyfed, the island of Gwales, which in the *Mabinogi* is a station on the route of the seven survivors commissioned to bury the head of Brân, brings to mind the House of Donn.[22] Off the coast of Dyfed too lies the land of Plant Rhys Ddwfn—the name is probably a corruption of *Plant yr Is-ddwfn* or *Plant Rhi Is-dwfn*, 'The Children of (the King of) the Nether World'—a fairy people who had the power to make their country invisible except from one small patch of ground in Dyfed.[23]

3

In describing the division of Wales into three provinces, Gwynedd, Powys, and the South, between the three sons of Rhodri Mawr, Giraldus Cambrensis states that the South was given to Cadell 'with the blessing of all the people and his brothers. For although this last portion was by far the largest in size it was nevertheless counted the worst' because the gentry (*uchelwyr*), 'who teemed in this province', were habitually in revolt against their lords.[24] The association of rebellion with the South is clearly not peculiar to Ireland. At every court in North Wales there were five officers, of whom the fifth was an official judge, but in the courts of the South there were only four officers, together with a host of judges, to wit, every owner of land.[25] Here the mass of landowners indicates the democratic third function.

An undated poem (published in *The Myvyrian Archaiology of Wales*)[26] gives the characteristics of the different parts of Wales. It does not provide a clear and simple picture, but we may note that it attributes to Gwynedd boastful words, timid (?) men, and great intentions, and to Anglesey high birth, wise men, and relics. To Powys are attributed brave men setting out for battle and also a welcome for minstrels; to Glamorgan, genial men, women in majesty, and churls (?) and rich men in market, while the people of two of the westernmost divisions of Dyfed are described as serfs. It may be noted incidentally that the statute which in the early sixteenth century governed the training, conduct, and privileges of poets was ascribed to Gruffudd ap Kynan,[27] the protonym of the royal tribe of Gwynedd. On the other hand, a twelfth-century poem on the privileges of the men of Powys[28] emphasizes their aristocratic and martial qualities. These privileges included exemption from certain royal dues, from providing quarters for huntsmen and from receiving royal ladies on circuit, together with the right to be in the first onset in battle, to be in the van of the hosts, and to guard the rear when withdrawing. The qualities traditionally associated with Glamorgan are generosity, courtesy, and festivity.[29]

One of the poems we have quoted ascribes a position of honour to women in Glamorgan. One of the very few explicit differences betweeen North and South Wales in the Laws is that in the South a woman who married independently was assured of her bridal gift (from her husband) exactly as if she had been given in marriage by her family, whereas in the North, unless she had secured an agreement in advance, she could claim only three steers.[30] Similarly, only in the southern versions of the Laws is it stipulated that for lack of male heirs a daughter could inherit all her father's property, while the poem on the privileges of Powys definitely states that 'a share to the brother his privilege commands, a share to the sister is not had from Powys.'[31] This evidence suggests that, in some sense, the southern half of the country may have been regarded as the female half, and this would be in accord with Irish tradition. Munster, as we have seen, has associations with goddesses and with the Fomoire.[32] Matrilineal succession is attributed to the Cruithne in particular, a people who are said to have first appeared in these islands as allies of the Leinstermen.[33] They were allowed to settle in Leinster because of the cure they introduced for mortally wounded warriors, which was to make them lie in trenches filled with milk. According to one early text, they stole the wives of the Sons of Míl; according to other sources, Éremón, who banished them from Ireland,[34] gave them wives on condition that succession with them should be through the female line as well as through the male, or through the female line only—the versions differ.

In Wales as in Ireland, there were grades within the learned class. In the preChristian society the highest was doubtless that of the druids, but even in the earliest Welsh records the druids are hardly mentioned. The 'chief poet' (*pencerdd*), 'a poet who has won in a contest for a chair',[35] was at least equal in honour to the highest court officers. He seems to correspond to the Irish *ollam* or chief *fili*. Beneath him was the poet of the household or housetroop (*bardd teulu*), who was one of the twentyfour court officers. When the *bardd teulu* took office he received from the king a harp, with which he was never to part.[36] He sang for the troop when it went on a raid, and before it set out for battle he sang 'The Monarchy of Britain'. The term *cerddorion* seems to cover yet another class of minstrels who recognized the *pencerdd* as their lord, and there are references in the laws to the lowly *croesaniaid*.* In medieval tracts on the art of poetry, slightly different terms seem to refer to the same classes: *prydydd* 'poet', *teuluwr* 'poet of the household or housetroop', and *clerwr*, 'minstrel'. Three duties are assigned to the *teuluwr*:[37] to gladden the company, to be generous,** and to make courteous supplication—terms which recall the festive music of Buchet's House in Leinster. The *teuluwr*, who also composed love poems, was the disciple of a *prydydd*, but the *prydydd* should shun the chaotic art of the *clerwr* (Function IV), for 'their arts are opposed to one another'.[38] With the

* Cf. *supra*, p. 127ᶜ.
** Literally 'generᴄ sity'—? 'to promote generosity'.

eclipse of the superior functions of the master-poets, their art
became for the most part confined to the composition of praise-
poems. When the law and the prophets belong to the past, the
psalms remain.

In Ireland in the early seventeenth century, the traditional
precedence of the North was challenged by a southern poet,
and this led to a sustained and wide-ranging poetic disputa-
tion concerning the relative claims of Leth Cuinn and Leth
Moga.[39] Towards the end of the following century a similar
case for the greater importance of the southern contribution to
the *Welsh* literary tradition was elaborated, not without
fabrication, by Iolo Morganwg. In the context of the fourfold structure we have discussed, Iolo's claim for Glamorgan
as the seat of bardism may well be correct, provided the 'bard'
is duly assigned to the third place in the learned hierarchy.
And it is fair to add that Iolo particularly claimed for his
native province a wealth of pleasant 'household poetry' (*canu
teuluaidd*)[40]—the poetry of the *teuluwr* or bard.

The dichotomy manifested in the division into North and
South appeared too in the division of the Welsh royal hall.
One of the terms used for the partition that separated the two
parts of the hall was *corf*, a word which is also used of 'a wood
on the steep brink of a stream',[41] such a wood as often formed
the boundary between the upper and lower halves of territorial
units. The king and his heir, his judge, his chief poet, and other
dignitaries, sat in the upper part of the hall; the captain of the
house-troop and his men, and the household bard, sat in the
lower part.[42] When the king wished to hear a song, the chief
poet sang two songs in the upper hall, one of God and the
other of kings, and then the household bard sang a third song
in the lower hall. It was also the household bard who, with a
quiet voice, sang for the queen in her room. The two songs—
of God and of kings—in the upper hall and the bard's one
song in the lower hall hardly call for further comment, and
the same is true of the association of the bard with the queen
and with the troop. One officer connected with the court,

the *maer biswail* ('dung officer'), was responsible for the king's mensal land. There the villeins came under his jurisdiction and he ordered their ploughing, sowing, and other activities. He had charge, under the steward, of the maintenance and supplies of the court, but he belonged to the villein class; scant respect was shown to him in the precincts of the king's hall.[43]

4

The centre of the mysterious adventures of Pwyll and Pryderi is the throne-mound (*gorsedd*) which was outside the court of Arberth. Whoever sat on it would see a wonder or suffer wounds and blows. It was from this mound that Pwyll, the Head of Annwfn, first saw Rhiannon on her magic horse. There sat Pryderi when enchantment fell upon Dyfed, and it was there that Manawydan was on the point of executing a supernatural, thieving 'mouse' when the land was disenchanted and his lost companions restored to him.

The association of a ritual mound with Annwfn appears in Ellis Wynne's *Gweledigaetheu y Bardd Cwsc* (1703), which tells of three visions—of the World, of Death and of Hell. The poet falls asleep and sees a crowd of people whom he takes to be Gypsies or witches until, noticing their beauty and recognizing among them the faces of deceased acquaintances, he realizes they are fairies (*tylwyth teg*). They are dancing on the 'play mound' (*twmpath chwareu*), but they now take hold of the poet and they carry him over land and sea until he espies below him the most beautiful castle he has every seen. Meanwhile they try to get the poet to satirize his own king, when he is rescued from their clutches by an angel who informs him that they were the Children of Annwfn. A 'play mound' used to be found near or inside graveyards in Wales. The mound was banked up, with turf seats for the spectators arranged around an open floor where the games were played.[44] It appears to be a simple version of the Cornish *plen an gwary* ('the place of the play'), the examples of which have been described as 'the only surviving medieval theatres in Britain'.[45] The Irish word *oenach* (assembly) is glossed by *theatrum*, and the Welsh word *gorsedd* which means 'assembly' and 'court' as well as 'throne-mound', occurs as the equivalent of *théâtre*.[46] That 'mound', theatre, and place of general assembly should be closely related, or indeed identified with one another, is not peculiar to Celtic tradition.[47]

In Irish tales, mounds outside courts are scenes of games and visionary encounters which do not belong to the round of mundane existence, and the holding of assemblies on hills and mounds is a commonplace of Irish history. It may be assumed that every local community had such a traditional assembly place, but it is to Munster that assemblies are attributed in 'The Settling of the Manor of Tara', and the *gorsedd* celebrated in Welsh story is in Dyfed. Moreover, CúRoí, herdsman and King of Munster, has been compared with the giant herdsman in Arthurian stories who sits on a mound and directs the hero to the strange palace where his mettle is proved. In the story of 'The Lady of the Fountain', this director is a big, black, ugly forester, one-footed and one-eyed, and wild animals 'numerous as the stars in the firmament' assemble and disperse at his command.[48] In both Celtic and Norse tales,[49] the person who sits on a mound is usually a king or a herdsman (or both at once), while many a Fenian wonder-tale begins with Finn seated on his hunting-mound when his company follow the chase.

Like the throne-mound outside the court, the sun-chamber (*grianán*) outside the banqueting-hall has features which suggest comparison with the 'outer fifth' province.[50] In some contexts, the *grianán* is the women's part of the court. Again, it is from his *grianán* that Bricriu, the master of ceremonies who always stands aside from the conflicts he initiates, watches the proceedings in the hall from which, though he built it, he is excluded.[51] Bricriu and CúRoí seem to have their Norse counterparts in Loki and Útgarða-Loki, respectively. Útgarða-Loki is the colossal lord of an outer world, and his conduct towards Thorr, the champion god,[52] is in some ways similar to that of CúRoí towards CúChulainn. Loki, a ruthless deceiver and creator of conflict, is of the gods and yet not of them. They vainly try to exclude him from their feast, and later he seeks refuge from them in a mountain where he builds himself an observatory from which he can see in every direction.[53] It is no accident that Bricriu and Goll, in the Ulster Cycle, are both sons of Carbad (i.e. they have the same patronymic); that in the Fenian Cycle, Conán Mael, the reviler and trouble-maker, and Goll, the slayer of Finn, are both sons of Morna, and that Kei, the churlish seneschal[54] in the Arthurian Cycle, is concerned with the service of the king's table.

CHAPTER IX

Numbers

'Every moment beginneth existence, around every "Here"
rolleth the ball "There". The middle is everywhere.'

NIETZSCHE

At Uisnech and Tara we found a concentration of symbols.
Not only did the provinces and their kingships converge upon
these centres and fuse together, but there was an assemblage of
such symbols as a hill, a stone, a palace, a seat, a tree, a well,
a fire—and they were places of contact with the supernatural
world. The other great centres had similar concentrations. For
example, some of the principal features of Cashel, capital of
Munster, may be gleaned from two tales. The first[1] tells of the
return of Conall Corc to Munster after a sojourn in Scotland.
On that day the swineherd of Aed, King of Múscraige, was
tending his swine and at night he told the king of a wonderful
sight he had seen. He saw a *yew tree* on a *rock* and in front of it
an oratory with a *flagstone* before it and angels ascending from
the flagstone and descending upon it. The vision was interpreted by a druid: the place (Cashel) would be the residence
of the kings of Munster for ever, and the kings would be the
descendants of the first man to kindle a *fire* under that yew tree.
Aed would have gone there at once, but the druid advised
him to wait till morning, and Conall unwittingly forestalled
him. The second story[2] says that when St Patrick mounted
the flagstone legions of demons flew out from beneath it. The
saint blessed the stone with the virtue of counsel and ordained,
firstly, that an angel should pass over it every even-tide;
secondly, that if the king of Munster accompanied by the nine
sons of a great chief fasted upon it he should have whatever

boon he craved, and lastly, that its fire should be one of the three that would be alive in Ireland until the end.

On the other hand, in Ireland one may still be confronted with the riddle: 'Where is the middle of the world?' The correct answer is 'Here' or 'Where you are standing.'[3] The same question appears in versions of the medieval European tale of the 'Abbé Sans Souci', including one recorded in Brittany, and to explain the answer a finger is placed on the surface of a ball, showing that the centre is wherever the finger touches.[4] The riddle is in harmony with the *Rig Veda*'s five points: north, south, east, west, and 'here'. The directions are orientated around wherever one 'is'. Similarly, significance is not confined to the great ceremonial centres. Every ritual place or cult object is endowed with what Professor M. Eliade has called 'the prestige of the Centre',[5] be it a local meeting-hill, a pillar-stone, an inauguration tree, a sacred well, a grave, or what it may. The identity of the domestic hearth with the central one is expressed in the re-kindling of its fire from the central fire. For the purposes of this ritual the centre of any locality is the hill or cairn on which the bonfire is lit, and in the house the *focus* is the hearth. In recent folk-belief a priest's house assumed something of the role of ancient Uisnech, for when a pestilence broke out in south-western Ireland it was customary to quench the fires in the homes and to light them anew with embers obtained from the house of a priest.[6]

Temair (Tara), which is mythologically derived from the name of Éremón's queen, Tea, is a fairly common hill-name, and it is said that every other Temair which exists in Ireland was given to Tea, as well as Temair Luachra and Temair in Brega.[7] In as much as Tara is a hill, it can be symbolized by whatever hill is chosen for the purpose. Every beehive tomb in Greece is a symbol of the *omphalos* ('navel' of the earth); every *stupa* (gravemound) in India is a miniature of Mount Meru in the middle of the world.[8] In Yorubaland, Frobenius found little clay cult objects which consisted of a central cone, representing the god of world order, with four smaller cones around it representing the gods of the cardinal points.[9] Similarly every *cairn* in Ireland represents the whole. A cairn is a mound of stones erected over a burial or at some other point with other-world associations, such as wherever a man has died out-of-doors or where a coffin has rested. But, in a discussion of the title *Nia in Chairn*—'The Champion of the Cairn'—given to Conchobar's son Cormac, it is noted that 'some of the learned assert that every place wherein there are five stones, or any other five things, or the five provinces of Ireland, is properly called a cairn.'[10] Therefore Cormac as *Nia in Chairn* was 'champion of the five provinces'. A pillar-stone at Keimaneigh (South of Cork) is said to be a petrified woman and in it are five cavities with five oval stones in them.[11] That, according to this definition, constitutes a cairn. Even children playing 'fivestones'[12] are unwittingly playing with symbols of the whole of Ireland.

The pattern of the whole was again mirrored in the houses maintained by kindreds of the *fuidir* tenant class. 'A *fuidir* does not incur liability of his kindred, unless they maintain five dwellings. If it is with five complete dwellings, they share their family lands.'[13] The subdivision of land into quarters also is symbolic. In Wales, according to the law-books, there were four acres in a homestead, four holdings in every township, and so on.[14] In the Isle of Man four quarterlands at one time formed a *treen*, the smallest unit for administrative purposes. Similarly in Ireland and the Western Highlands of Scotland the quarterland is regarded as the primary division of farmland (though it is further subdivided into eighths, sixteenths, and so on). The Irish *baile biatach*, like the *davach* or ounce-land in Scotland and the Hebrides, comprised four quarterlands and was a tax unit.[15] There are also traces of the existence of this fourfold system in medieval England where four wards, four townships, or four villes constituted a unit for various legal purposes. 'There is definite evidence that the number four was associated in the medieval mind with the four quarters.'[16] While the dominant idea in these cases is the four quarters, the elusive fifth is not altogether absent. The Irish *faithche* consisted of four fields, one on each side of a *homestead*,[17] and a similar concept is implied in the Welsh system of four acres to one homestead. We also know that in at least one district of South Wales the inhabitants of four adjoining sharelands used to meet at a *focal point* on three annual holidays to play games and to listen to songs.[18]

Five is not the most prominent number in Celtic tradition, but it nevertheless appears in a large number of significant contexts. Ireland had five great roads and five celebrated hostels.[19] There were five paths of the law, and five prohibitions for each of the four provincial kings (but seven for the king of Tara).[20] Both Finn and the fairies counted by fives.[21] Finn was one of the *five* masters of every great art, and was killed by the 'five sons of Uirgriu', each of whom 'planted a spear in the royal fian-chief'.[22] The unitary character of five is also suggested by an episode in the *Táin* in which the Gálioin, whose loyalty is suspect, are distributed among the other troops 'so that no five men of them shall be in one place'.[23] Mythical personages wore fivefold cloaks, and CúChulainn had five wheels on his shield, which is particularly note-worthy when we remember that Achilles' shield was made in five layers and that shields representing the cosmos were wide-spread in the iconography of the ancient world.[24] When his wife, Ethne, and three champions of Ulster visit CúChulainn on his sick bed, they arrange themselves around him, Fergus between him and the wall, Conall Cernach between him and the bed-rail, Lugaid Reoderg between him and the pillow, Ethne at his feet—one at each point, with CúChulainn in the middle.[25]

The secret fifth also has its counterpart in the fifth of the five 'families' (or groups) of five signs each which constitute the *ogam* alphabet.[26] The first three groups of five stand for the different consonants, the fourth group for vowels. The fifth set of five, called the 'supplementary family', is said, in the medieval tracts, to denote diphthongs. Early Irish stories con-tain several references to the use of *ogam* to convey secret messages or for divinatory purposes. In one case four sticks are used, in another a four-sided stick. Vendryes notes the importance of twenty in the Celtic numerical system, and also in the numerical system of certain peoples in India, and the five 'supplementary letters' (*forfeda*) are dismissed as a later addition,[27] just as the fifth province has been accounted a later addition. The signs in this fifth group are different in character from those of the four other groups, thus:

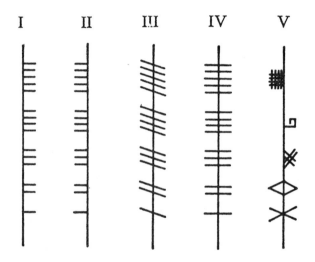

Fig. 14 The *ogam* characters

Are we to consider it an accident that each of these five characters of the fifth group is formed by a cross (single, double or quadruple), a diamond or circular enclosure, or a rudimentary spiral—all apt symbols of the mystic centre?

A medieval tract on language teaches that 'five words are adjudged to be a breath of the poet.' 'And when dithyramb or metrical rhythm was present, how was it measured? for there is not couplet rhyme or caesura rhyme in it. Not hard.

By a word completing a breath which was indicated by the fifth word . . .'[28] Again, there are five kinds of language, namely: 'the language of the Féni, the precedents of the poets, the language of separation, the hidden (?) language of the poets, in which they speak with one another, and *iarmberla*, such as *cuich* [? *cóic* 'five'], that is a secret, and *ballorb*, a member which completes the poet . . .'[29] The fifth kind of language was learned by the poet in his fifth year of training.

In a Fenian story,[30] a spell involving the number five is chanted upon a spear; the spear moves from the chanter's hand and impales the enemy. Modern card games are played with four suits, but in Irish a 'trick' in these games is known as *cúig*, 'five'.[31] In Indo-European languages the first four numerals were declined, with feminine and masculine forms. Five was thus the first number that had only one form, and it was by invoking this number, which was both masculine and feminine, that Indra defeated the Asuras in a ritual counting-contest. Hence, according to the *Śatapatha Brāhmaṇa*, the Sacrificer when the first fore-offering has been performed, says: 'One (*unus*) for me!' and 'One (*una*) for him we hate!' 'Two (*duo*) for me!' and 'Two (*duae*) for him who hates us and whom we hate!' and so on to the fourth fore-offering. Then, 'Five for me' and 'Nothing for him who hates us and whom we hate!' 'For, there being "five" to "five", he (the enemy) is defeated, and *whoever knows this* appropriates to himself everything that belongs to that (enemy of his), strips his enemies of everything.'[32]

There are Indian rites in which groupings of five gods are placed in a cross formation with the principal symbol in the centre,[33] while in Buddhist teaching the human body and the human heart have the same five-fold structure: 'O nobly-born, these realms are not come from somewhere outside (thyself). They come from within the four directions of the heart, which, including its centre, make the five directions.'[34] Again: 'This fundamental idea of the four cardinal points and the central area (below and above) which forms the fifth . . . is found in all the religious expressions of the Aztec peoples.'[35] In Vou-doun: 'The figure five is as the four of the cross-roads plus the swinging of the door which is the point itself of crossing, the moment of arrival and departure.'[36]

2

The number nine figures so prominently in Celtic tradition that it has been described as the 'northern counterpart of the sacred seven' of Near Eastern cultures.[37] Bricriu was not the only subject who built a ninefold residence for his king. It is stated in the Welsh Laws that the serf class should build nine houses for the king, while the serf's own house should also consist of a hall plus eight penthouses.[38] Repeated allusions to houses comprising 'nine houses (or rooms) in one', in the fifteenth-century poems of Guto'r Glyn,[39] confirm the exist-ence of a Welsh tradition that a complete house should consist of nine component parts. A holding consisting of a homestead and eight acres (*erwau*) is sometimes mentioned in the Welsh Laws as an alternative to the more usual unit of a homestead and four acres, while in Ireland there are instances of kingdoms which consisted of nine cantreds.[40]

Apart from sporadic pointers of this kind, and the sub-division of quarterlands into eighths, the eight/ninefold con-ception of things has not left an enduring impression on the territorial divisions of the Celtic lands, but it is to be found in a great many other significant contexts, among which the following are but a small selection. We have mentioned the nine hazels of wisdom that grew at the heads of the seven chief rivers of Ireland.[41] There is also a story[42] of a marvellous tree which grew from above downwards, like an inverted Yggdra-sill. It had nine branches, of which the highest was the most beautiful, and in them pure white birds listened to the melodies to be heard there. The story is interpreted allegorically, the tree being Christ, the nine branches the nine grades of heaven, and the birds the souls of the just, but the symbol of the inverted tree is as old as the *Rig Veda*.[43] An early Welsh poem which mentions the Cauldron of the Head of Annwfn says that 'by the breath of nine maidens was it kindled', and in the *Vita Merlini* the Fortunate Isles are governed by nine sisters, the first of whom was Morgen.[44] In the *dindsenchas*[45] there is a tale of Ruad son of Rigdonn who rows north of Ireland with three boats and finds they have no power to move. He swims to a secret spot and finds nine fair and strong 'female forms' with whom he sleeps nine nights 'without gloom, without tearful lament, under the sea free from waves on nine beds of bronze.' One of the women bears him a child.

Irish literature abounds with 'companies of nine', and in a considerable number of cases it is made clear that the nine consist of a leader and eight others. This is strikingly illustrated in a description of Medb's mode of travel in *Táin Bó Cuailnge*:[46] 'and nine chariots with her alone; two of these chariots before her, and two behind, and two chariots at either side, and her own chariot in the middle between them'. King Loegaire, when setting out to arrest St Patrick, ordered nine chariots to be joined together 'according to the tradition of the gods'.[47] Eight swordsmen guarded Bricriu on his way to the feast he had prepared in his nine-chambered hall.[48] CúChulainn had nine weapons of each kind, eight small ones and one large one.[49] Cathbad the druid had eight disciples and Finn appears with eight Caíltes gathered around him.[50]

Nine, like five, symbolized the whole. In Welsh medieval society the ninth generation was the recognized limit of kin relationship, and even the human body had nine principal parts.[51] The number also appears in traditional British games such as Ninepins, in which the middle pin is called the 'king', and Nine Men's Morris which was played on a square divided into eight sections around a central 'pound'.[52] In Scotland, the need-fire was kindled sometimes by nine men and sometimes by nine nines of first-begotten sons.[53] The number was also connected with the Beltaine fire in Scotland, and in Wales, as in parts of Scandinavia, the fire was made with nine sticks collected by nine men from nine different trees.[54] Nines, and particularly the 'ninth', were very important in divinations and in folk cures,[55] and even the waves of the sea broke in series of nine, the ninth wave being larger and more fortunate than the rest.[56]

Almost as common as nine in Celtic tradition is twenty-seven, frequently expressed as 'three nines'. Three times nine plus a leader, making twenty-eight in all, seems to have been a numerical arrangement of considerable significance. Calatín with his twenty-seven sons (and his grandson) insist on their being regarded as a single warrior, claiming that all Calatín's offspring were constituent parts of his own body.[57] In 'The Wooing of Emer', CúChulainn was opposed by the lady's father together with her three brothers each of whom had eight men—a company of twenty-eight altogether.[58] Again, Bran set out on his voyage with three companies of nine, each commanded by one of his foster-brothers.[59] Companies of nine, comprising a leader and eight others were customary among the Fiana; these, however, were grouped into larger units comprising three companies of nine plus a leader.[60] Thus, time and again we encounter the arrangement: $[(8 + 1) \times 3] + 1 = 28$.

The number nine may at one time have had a place in the calendar of the Celtic peoples. In the Welsh Laws, the ninth day of the month often marks the end or the beginning of a period, and a period of nine days or nine nights is certainly in evidence in the literature as a significant unit of time.[61] In Wales the period of bright moonlight during the harvest moon is called *y nawnos olau* (the nine light nights), and in Irish the terms *nómad* and *noínden* stand for units of nine time-spaces (? days or half-days).[62] From such evidence as this, Rhŷs and others long ago drew the conclusion that the Celts had a nine-day week, or rather a nine-night week, for they reckoned by nights.[63] Three weeks of nine nights would give a twenty-seven-night month, and the importance of the number twenty-seven in Celtic mythology is perhaps related to the twenty-seven constellations of the lunar zodiac, as it is in Hindu mythology where the moon, King Soma, has twenty-seven star wives with each of whom he spends one night every month.[64]

Apart from traces of an ancient nine-day week alongside the present seven-day week, seven and nine appear as alternatives in a number of contexts. The Hostel of Da Derga is variously described as having nine doors and seven doors.[65] In some contexts in the Welsh Laws it is said that the serfs should build seven houses for the king,[66] not nine. Similarly, the limits of kin for purposes of the blood-fine are variously defined as nine generations and seven generations.[67] Seven is as popular a number as nine in some branches of Celtic literature and there can be no doubt that it had a significance for the Celts, as for other Indo-European peoples, long before the introduction of Christianity. Among the Greeks, the relative antiquity of seven and nine is not known; both appear side by side as meaningful numbers in Homer and in the oldest cults.[68] Seven sometimes alternates with five. By reckoning Fir Bolg as three peoples, some texts speak of seven invasions instead of the usual five.[69] The basic division of Scotland was into seven, between the seven eponymous sons of Cruithne.[70] England and Ireland also have had their respective heptarchies. Again, in contradistinction to the twenty-seven lunar constellations, we have the more usual lunar zodiac of twenty-eight 'mansions' (4×7) which is believed to have originated in Babylonia and to have spread to lands ranging from China to medieval Europe.[71] Gildas, writing in the sixth century, says that Britain was adorned with twenty-eight cities.[72] Unlike Bricriu's hall, the splendid house of Ailill and Medb in Cruachan has 'seven compartments from the fire to the wall in the house all round'. In one story[73] a quarter of it is allocated to the guests, and this together with its sixteen windows (plus a skylight) suggests a fourfold division with perhaps seven compartments in each quarter making a total of twenty-eight. The magni-ficent four-pillared compartment of Ailill and Medb stood

in the middle of the house. Medb had seven sons, the seven
Maines, and it has been suggested that they personified the
days of the week. Everything connected with Medb's lover,
Fergus mac Roich, was also reckoned in sevens.[74] Thus,
whereas the royal household of Ulster figured the solar year,
that of Connacht may have figured the lunar month.

3

The figure of twelve individuals around a king which we discussed in connection with Bricriu's Hall is reproduced in the
tradition of Crom Cróich of Mag Slécht:[75]

> 'Mag Slécht, whence was it named? Answer: It is there
> the king-idol of Ireland was, i.e. Crom Cróich, and the
> twelve stone idols around him; but he was of gold. And
> until the coming of Patrick he was the god of every people
> that occupied Ireland. It is to him they used to offer the
> first-born of every stock and the first-born of every family.
> It is to him that the king of Ireland, Tigernmas son of
> Follach, came at Samain, together with the men and
> women of Ireland, to adore him. And they all bowed
> down before him, until their foreheads, and the soft part
> of their noses, and the caps of their knees, and the points of
> their elbows, broke; so that three-fourths of the Men of Ire-
> land died of these prostrations. Hence Mag Slécht.'

The metrical version adds the detail that the twelve subsidiary
idols were arranged in four rows of three,[76] forming the now
familiar pattern of a centre and three in each direction. Through
a miracle performed by St Patrick, the central idol 'bowed
westwards to turn on its right side, for its face was from the
south, to wit, to Tara. . . . And the earth swallowed the twelve
other images as far as their heads.'[77]

With the number twelve, as with the number seven, there is
always the possibility that native tradition has been affected
by Christianity. A recent writer dismisses the story of Crom

Cróich as 'an *ad hoc* invention to account for a circle of twelve low boulders surrounding an inner taller one tilted over west⁄ wards on its right side.'[78] If the story is an invention, the twelve stones around a thirteenth which are said to have given rise to it still have to be accounted for. That the number is not fortuit⁄ ous is suggested by a ritual of circumambulating a sacred hill, which has survived at Locronan in Brittany. The path around the hill was twelve kilometers long and it was punctuated by twelve stations marked by sacred stones. The circumambula⁄ tion was performed every seven years, beginning in the west, rising northwards, descending eastwards, and proceeding south. The participants then climbed the hill and descended westwards. On their way down, they went three times round a massive stone, representing the moon, which stood close to a wood called Nevet (Sacred place).[79]

The symbolism of twelve, like that of seven, is certainly older and more widespread than Christianity. A knowledge of the zodiacal twelve is found throughout Eurasia, and it was firmly established in Scandinavia in pre⁄Christian times. That it should have been unknown to the pre⁄Christian Celts is hardly probable.

4

Finally, we shall turn our attention to the numbers seventeen and thirty⁄three. Partholón and Nemed between them cleared sixteen plains, which together with the 'Old Plain of Elta', fashioned by God before any of the invaders arrived, make a total of seventeen.[80] According to the 'Book of Rights', seventeen kings accepted annual gifts from the king of Cashel and there were seventeen kingdoms in Meath (including Brega as one).[81] Cairbre Crom is said to have conferred seventeen townlands upon St Ciarán.[82] Seventeen may thus have been a significant territorial unit. Seventeen days, the seventeenth of the month, and seventeen years occur in a number of interest⁄ ing contexts. For example, both Partholón and the sons of

Míl arrived in Ireland on the seventeenth of the moon, the Battle of Tailtiu began on the seventeenth of the moon, and there are several examples of reigns of sixteen or seventeen years' duration.[83] *Lebor Gabála* lists sixteen triads of Tuatha Dé Danann, together with the three gods of Danann.[84] Finn's womenfolk numbered seventeen, and seventeen chieftains in succession commanded Ireland's Fiana.[85]

In Ireland, as in Rome, youths became men at the age of seventeen years. Fosterage came to an end and marriage could be contemplated. This transition is marked in CúChulainn's life by his great exploits during the cattle-raid of Cuailnge, and the first of these was to thrust into the ground a forked tree which Fergus, himself an exile for seventeen years, tried seventeen times in vain to pull up.[86] Mongán, fostered in The Land of Promise, was brought back to Ireland after sixteen years, and then betrothed.[87] A druid advised Maeldúin to take only seventeen men with him on his celebrated Voyage, and his three foster-brothers who insisted on joining the crew against this advice were lost on the way. When the company reached the Island of Women they found seventeen maidens, in addition to the queen of the island.[88] In this tale seventeen is clearly a fated number, though Maeldúin himself and the queen are not included in the reckoning.

A division of the heavens into sixteen regions appears in the cosmic systems of the Greeks, the Romans and the Germans, and among the Etruscans these divisions were used for divinatory purposes. The Egyptians knew of sixteen giants who were closely connected with the celestial regions. Sixteen perfect lands were created by Ahura Mazda. Given a centre, such cosmologies[89] become seventeenfold. In the *Śatapatha Brāhmaṇa* we have the now familiar play of the odd and even number:[90] 'Let him (the sacrificer) seize seventeen victims for the central stake, in order that he may secure everything; for seventeenfold is Prajāpati and seventeen (stoma) is everything; and sixteen at each of the other (stakes) in order that he may gain and secure everything, for everything consists of sixteen parts,

and the Aśvamedha is everything.' The Brahmanas also un-
ceasingly reiterate: 'Prajāpati is the year, so Prajāpati is seventeen.' The correlation of the year with seventeen was achieved
by adding the twelve months and the five seasons. Sometimes,
however, Prajāpati is declared to be eighteen, comprising the
twelve months, the five seasons and the year itself.[91] Similarly
in some Irish instances, seventeen is as it were further completed
by an eighteenth. For example, it was on the eighteenth attempt
that Fergus succeeded in uprooting the forked tree, and
Maeldúin himself constituted an eighteenth member of his
ship's crew. CúChulainn broke all the seventeen chariots
which King Conchobar kept in reserve, and was satisfied only
when given the king's own chariot.[92] The force of Medb in
the *Táin*, including the Ulster exiles, was seventeen units;
the Gálioin were the eighteenth.[93]

In Ireland, the 'sixteenth' and 'seventeenth generation', like
the 'ninth generation' in Wales, marked the limits to which
kin could properly be reckoned, and even in modern times:
'There is not an old *seanchaidhe* (storyteller) in Tirconaill that
has not heard times without number of the *seiseadh glun deag*,
i.e. the sixteenth generation.' Curses are invoked to the seventeenth generation.[94] Indeed, the ancient Irish kinship system
incorporates all the uneven numbers which we have hitherto
discussed. It classifies kindred into four categories according to
their degree of remoteness:[95]

1   'The *geilfine* extends to five persons.'
2   'The *deirbhfine* extends to nine persons.'
3   'The *iarfine* extends to thirteen persons.'
4   'The *innfine* extends to seventeen persons.'

The system is conceived of as expanding in ever-widening
circles, the outer ones containing the inner ones. In other
words, the innermost circle of the *geilfine* comprises five persons,
while each of the other three contains four additional ones,
making a combined total of seventeen. A great deal has been
written in an endeavour to identify the seventeen 'persons', but

while it is now generally agreed that they represent classes of kin rather than individuals, the evidence as to the nature of these classes remains inconclusive.

Time and again the numbers we are discussing have resolved themselves into multiples of even numbers, plus an odd one.

$$4 + 1 = 5$$
$$(4 \times 2) \quad 8 + 1 = 9$$
$$(3 \times 4) \quad 12 + 1 = 13$$
$$(8 \times 2) \quad 16 + 1 = 17$$

If we take the process a step further we get:

$$(16 \times 2) \quad 32 + 1 = 33$$

—a number which would take account of, among other things, relationships on the mother's side as well as the father's. According to Giraldus Cambrensis there were thirty-two 'cantreds' (*trícha cét*) in each of the five provinces of Ireland, and sixteen in Meath.[96] As listed in the *Táin*, the muster of the men of Ireland consisted of thirty-three threes.[97] Thirty-two leaders of the Tuatha Dé Danann are listed in the story the First Battle of Mag Tuired,[98] and this list does not include Lug—their saviour in the Second Battle. With them may be compared the company of thirty-three men, all seemingly thirty-two years of age, who sit at tables in the otherworld island-castle in *Perlesvaus*.[99] Nemed reached Ireland with only one ship; thirty-three of his ships were lost on the way.[100] CúChulainn slays thirty-three of Labraid's opponents in the *Síd*, and a late account of the Second Battle of Mag Tuired names thirty-three leaders of the Fomoire—thirty-two plus their high-king.[101]

In the story of the Wandering of the Déssi we are told that it was thirty-three years after their expulsion from Tara that they again fought the Leinstermen. The divisions of Fiachu Suidge, their rulers, numbered thirty-three, and it is perhaps significant that to the name of the middle or seventeenth man in the list of eponyms is appended the observation 'namely a man who went into a *síd*-mound'.[102] In a poem, the two great rival groups of Fiana—Clann Mhorna, who had the support of the high-king, and Clann Bhaoisgne—are each represented by sixteen men.[103] Another poem lists the leaders who in succession commanded the Fiana during its history of 320 years (and a half) to the death of Finn, while Oisín's ten years would extend the period to 330 years. For thirty-two successive years included in this reckoning Clann Mhorna had the command; Goll later held it for ten.[104] The story of Bricriu's Feast includes a list of the names of the thirty-two heroes who accompany King Conchobar to Bricriu's hall.[105] So too in 'The Dream of Maxen Wledig', 'thirty-two crowned kings, his vassals at that time,' accompany the Emperor in a hunt which leads to a vision.[106]

The number thirty-three has a time-honoured place in the traditions of other Indo-European peoples. In Rome, thirty lictors representing the thirty *curiata* acted in conjunction with three augurs. Thirty, or thirty-three, days (*iusti dies*) intervened between a declaration of war and the departure of the full army. The Vedas speak of the thirty-three gods (*Visve devah*—'All-the-gods'), and these have their counterparts in Persian mythology.[107]

5

We have implied that each of the odd numbers we have discussed is, so to speak, the completed form of the next even number below it. This is borne out by the fact that, both in old authorities and in modern Gaelic, seven persons are sometimes referred to as *mór-sheis-ear*, which means literally 'great six persons', while the dialect word *mór-ochtar*, 'great eight persons' signifies 'nine'.[108] The unit which transforms an even number into an odd number is more than a quantitative addition. In the majority of the examples we have cited, it is the centre or leader, the unifying principle. The inferiority of even numbers is suggested by such details as that after the massacre of the nobles by the *aithech-thuatha* ('tributary tribes')

Ireland is said to have had four associated kings,[109] that Niall of the Nine Hostages was so called because he held five hostages from Ireland and four from foreign lands, that there were five officers in the courts of North Wales and only four in those of the South, and that in the board-games to which we have referred the number of pieces in the 'king's party' is odd or even according to whether the king-piece is counted or not, while, lacking a king, the number of opposing pieces is un-ambiguously even. For Pythagoras odd numbers were mascu-line, even numbers feminine, and it is perhaps noteworthy that when the plague destroyed Partholón's people they numbered five thousand men and four thousand women. In the Indian story of the contest between Indra and the Asura, it is the feminine forms attributed to the latter which give out with 'four', while Indra goes on to win with 'five'. The Chinese express the fundamental duality of *Yang* and *Yin* in terms of odd and even numbers, while 'In Voudoun one *and* one make three; two *and* two make five; for the *and* of the equation is the third and fifth part, respectively, the relationship which makes all the parts meaningful.'[110]

Yet, compelling as it is, the concept of the additional unit as the unifying or superior factor by no means exhausts the symbolism of numbers. In many of the groupings and divisions described in this book there is a category which stands apart from the rest not by virtue of its superiority but because it is external in some way or other. And this tends to occur whether the total number be odd or even. As we have seen, two is constituted of 'upper' and 'lower'. Among the three men of Cessair's company, Ladra was inferior to the other two; of the three Nemed groups one settled abroad, and in the division of Wales and Ireland into three, the third portion represents the 'lower' element. Similarly with the four 'functions', the fourth, represented by the unfree class, is external to the other three. Death separates Partholón and his people from the three sub-sequent pre-Gaelic settlers who are all of the same stock, and

we have noted that Munster stands apart from the other provinces. Again, of the five peoples who took Ireland before the
Gaels, one was prediluvian and was led by a woman, and in
the Fir Bolg division the fifth province is the 'outer' one. In the
Mabinogi, the Island of the Mighty is left in the care of seven
overlords 'and Pendaran Dyfed as a young lad with them'.
Cunedda, founder of the dynasty of Gwynedd, had nine sons,
but of these the eldest died before the family came to Wales and
the number was completed by the inclusion of his son. Eight
Sons of Míl set out to Ireland; the ninth member of the expedition was Lugaid, son of their late kinsman who had recon-
noitred the country. But, Lugaid apart, there was one of the
eight sons whose portion was the land of the dead.

The completing unit changes the structure of a number, but
its identity is often problematic. The Welsh laws speak of
seven generations of kindred, but only six are clearly identi-
fiable.[111] According to one version the seventh is 'nephew son
of fifth cousin' (*nei vab gorchaw*) who marks the limit to which
kin is reckoned. But other versions ignore this category and
the seven can then be accounted for only by counting 'the man
himself' at the centre of the web of relationships. One of the
most puzzling problems of the Irish kinship system is the
identity of the fifth person of the *geilfine*, and in reading the
medieval and modern commentaries one is reminded of the
enigma of the fifth province. But here too on the fringes of the
kin is an elusive category called the 'finger-nails'—a term which
also occurs in Germanic laws.[112] Similarly with the classification of land: odds and ends of unused lands associated with
English villages were called 'no man's land', 'anyone's land',
or 'Jack's land', and in Scotland such fields were left undis-
turbed to the service of the devil. G. L. Gomme compares
them with fragments of uncleared land which villagers of some
parts of India left as habitations of the dead and other supernatural beings.[113]

Thus we return again to the fact that the excluded, the wild,
the dead, the young, the female, the Other World have their

place in the total scheme of things. The significant unit can be the last as well as the first, and it can be both at once. Niall of the Nine Hostages was inferior to his four half-brothers in that his mother was treated as a slave, and superior to them in that he was destined to be high-king. The ninth wave is the greatest, but it comes from the outermost limits of the cosmos. What lies beyond the bounds of the cosmos is, in a sense, inferior to it, but it is also the source of all things. Thus, whereas the centre turns multiplicity into unity, the external factor sets it in the context of infinity, and between unity and infinity there is a strange identity.*

* It remains to be said that the symbolism of numbers is not confined to the principle to which our evidence points in this chapter. Thus, while there are instances of three as two-plus-one the number was also conceived of as a unit of three equals, as for example in the 'triads' and in the 'triskele' figures. Again, nine was envisaged as three threes as well as eight plus one, and three nines occur frequently without a completing twenty-eighth. Although the Celtic examples of thirty-three illustrate the concept of $32 + 1$, this number is also interpreted in Indian texts as $30 + 3$, and 3×11. We have also excluded from our discussion the larger numbers, such as fifty, which was a unit of considerable significance in ancient Greece and the Near East generally as well as among the Celts. On the analogy of certain other numbers we have mentioned, it could be conceived of as five decades, but there is no clear evidence of this. In Irish texts there are numerous examples of 'three times fifty' while 'three times five' is rare. Numbers, like other symbols, have more than one meaning.[114]

Part Three

THE MEANING OF STORY

CHAPTER X

The Storyteller's Repertoire

'Now I suppose most people will think I am but entertaining myself
with a toy, and using much the same kind of licence in expounding
the poets' fables which the poets themselves did in inventing them.
. . . But that is not my meaning. Not but that I know very well
what pliant stuff fable is made of, how freely it will follow any way
you please to draw it, and how easily with a little dexterity and discourse of wit meanings which it was never meant to bear may plau-
sibly be put upon it . . . All this I have duly examined and weighed . . .'

FRANCIS BACON

In the first part of this book we have introduced to the reader
the main personages which figure in Celtic mythology, group-
ing them according to the 'cycles' to which they belong.
Though the ancient storytellers were doubtless aware of the
existence of these separate 'cycles', each with its distinct
dramatis personae, there is no mention of them as such in the
extant literature. In the classification of tales that has survived,
the stories are not grouped according to cycles, nor are the
events in the life-stories of individual personages arranged
chronologically, as they are in the Lives of the Saints. Instead,
the stories are grouped according to the subjects with which
they are concerned—as in a modern index of folktale types.
There is no way of estimating the antiquity of this mode of
classification. All that can be said is that the two extant
medieval versions of it, nowadays designated List A and List
B,[1] are probably derived from an original which was already
in existence in the tenth century.

The order of classification is different in the two lists, each
of which contains some subject-headings which are absent
from the other. List A contains seventeen types of tales, List

B fifteen, thirteen types being common to both. There is no reason to suppose, however, that types recorded in only one of the lists, such as Conceptions and Births, Voyages, and Tragic Deaths, are less authentic than the others, and little weight can be attached to the omissions. The two lists may be collated as follows:

Types in Lists A and B
Destructions (Togla)
Cattle-raids (Tána)
Courtships (Tochmarca)
Battles (Catha)
Feasts (Fessa)
Adventures (Echtrai)
Elopements (Aithid)
Slaughters (Airgne)
Irruptions (Tomadma)
Visions (Físi)
Loves (Serca)
Expeditions (Sluagid)
Invasions (Tochomlada)

Types in List A only
Caves (Uatha)
Voyages (Immrama)
Violent Deaths (Oitte)
Sieges (Forbassa)

Types in List B only
Conceptions and Births (Coimperta)
Frenzies (Buili)

A preamble to List A in the Book of Leinster indicates that the poets memorized the tales under these headings:[2]

'Of the qualifications of a Poet in Stories and in Deeds, here follows, to be related to kings and chiefs, viz.: Seven times Fifty Stories, i.e. Five times Fifty Prime Stories, and Twice Fifty Secondary Stories; and these Secondary Stories are not permitted (assigned) but to four grades only, viz., an *Ollamh*, an *Anrath*, a *Cli*, and a *Cano*. And these are the Prime Stories: Destructions, and Cattle-raids, and Courtships, and Battles, and Caves, and Voyages, and Violent Deaths, and Feasts, and Sieges, and Adventures, and Elopements, and Slaughters.'

After listing the tales under these twelve headings, five more headings are introduced with the statement that:

'It is as Prime Stories these below are estimated; namely, Irruptions, and Visions, and Loves, and Expeditions and Invasions.'

While the preamble asserts that there were 250 Prime Stories and 100 Secondary Stories, less than 200 of the Prime Stories, and none of the Secondary Stories, are listed. It is possible that certain categories of Prime Stories are missing from both lists. For example, a section of the *Táin* is devoted to the *Macgnímartha* ('Youthful Exploits') of CúChulainn, and there is a tale called *Macgnímartha Finn*. In any case, the absence of any reference to the nature of the hundred 'Secondary Stories' (*foscéla*) constitutes a serious gap in our knowledge. The omission of these tales from the lists, together with the fact that they were the prerogative of the first four grades of poets, suggests that it may not have been considered proper to tell them to the public generally, and there seems to be no justification for regarding them as 'secondary' in any pejorative sense.

Again, the body of the traditional lore recounted at the Assembly of Carmun includes such subjects as Assemblies, Annals, Prohibitions, and Divisions, which do not seem to be fully covered by the headings in the Lists. It also mentions the important class of tales known as *Dindsenchas*, stories of places, to which there is no reference in the lists. Thus, important as they are as an indication of the way in which the poets organ-ized their material, the lists as we have them cannot be regarded as a complete canon of the traditional literature, though evi-dence we have considered in Chapter IX suggests that List A with its seventeen types made up of twelve plus five may be an attempt to arrange the tales in accordance with a cosmo-logical pattern.

2

The question arises as to why the poets learnt the tales classified in this way according to events or deeds. Why was it not more

convenient for them to memorize them according to cycles, or
at least as narratives about the entire careers of individual
heroes? The concluding passages of the Irish burlesque 'Vision
of Mac Conglinne' seem to offer a clue to the answer to this
important question. There it is satirically claimed that 'Nothing
sorrowful shall be heard by anyone who has heard [that story];
it will be a year's protection to them.' The narrator goes on to
say that

> 'the married couple to whom it is related the first night
> shall not separate without an heir; they shall not be in
> dearth of food or raiment. The new house in which it is
> the first tale told, no corpse shall be taken out of it; it shall
> not want food or raiment; fire does not burn it. The king
> to whom it is recited before battle or conflict shall be
> victorious. On the occasion of bringing out ale, or of feasting
> a prince, or of taking an inheritance or patrimony, this
> tale should be recited.'[3]

We may conclude from this that a wedding-night, the 'warm-
ing' of a new house, the eve of battle, the bringing out of ale,
feasts, and the taking over of inheritance were some of the
occasions when tales were traditionally told. The poem quoted
in Chapter I shows that they were also told before setting out
on a voyage and before going to a court of law or to a hunt.
Again, storytelling was a feature of the celebration of seasonal
festivals, while it has been the custom at wakes for the dead,
at christenings, and at weddings down to our own day.[4]
Although the sources we have cited prescribe the same tale
for a variety of different occasions, we would suggest that
originally there were tales appropriate to each occasion. In
the 'Colloquy of the Ancients', in which St Patrick and his
company move from place to place in Ireland, it is legends of
places that are told at every session, and in modern folk-custom
ghost-stories are considered particularly appropriate to November Eve. Is it therefore not likely that it was 'Battles' in particular that were related to kings about to embark upon war,

their significance. The
Lleu Llaw Gyffes have
II. Of the birth of Lug,
e of Mag Tuired' is that
the Fomoire, that Balor
on of Dian Cécht, and
l, Lug.[2] We must there-
ich has preserved more
er, there is no marriage
ad motif of 'the secluded
n of a woman who has
e gist of the story.[3]

Balor, who had one eye
ther, which would cause
the back of his head. It
e would be slain by his
aughter Ethne (Ethniu)
en to see that she learned
Glas Gaivlen, the mar-
o lived on the mainland
n and Mackinealy (Mac
lord of that district. By
Mackinealy, helped by a
ing access to Ethne and
ys. These Balor gave to a
out of the sheet in which
Mackinealy and brought
y was captured by Balor
ckinealy sleeps with the
fall into the water and
t thrive until it is taken
et another version, Cian,
helper that the boy will
him by name. Cian en-
who, however, does not
day the boy very nimbly

that 'Cattle-raids' were told before undertaking a cattle-raid, 'Voyages' on setting out to sea, 'Conceptions and Births' at births, 'Wooings' at weddings, 'Death Tales' at wakes, and so on? Arranged as they were in the Lists of his memory, the storyteller could easily select his stories to fit the different occasions as they arose. We are not suggesting that the telling of each type of tale was ever restricted to the circumstances that corresponded to it in real life. Indeed, we have noted that at the Assembly of Carmun, and probably at other great ceremonial gatherings, the whole repertoire of tales was declaimed. In this respect the custom among the early Celts may not have been very different from what it is in our own Christian ritual. The Baptism of Jesus in the Jordan is cited at every christening, the miracle at Cana of Galilee at every marriage, the Resurrection at every funeral. Each allusion is appropriate to the occasion, but the relevance of these scriptural events was never confined to birth, marriage, and death.

Evidence to which we have referred in Chapter I shows that the narrator of 'The Vision of Mac Conglinne' is parodying what was once a serious belief when he claims that to listen to the tale will bring life, offspring and prosperity. But concrete benefits apart, the stories served as mythical models. In the words of van Hamel,[5] they provided examples of which 'the deeds of other men must be regarded as a reflexion'. Van Hamel's further statement, that the heroes were intended to be 'imitated' by people in early Celtic society, must nevertheless be qualified. We shall speak later of correspondences between myth and ritual, but outside the ritual the deeds of mythical heroes cannot be repeated by mortal men. As events in ordinary life they are, as often as not, fantastic, anti-social, immoral and catastrophic. Yet, as we shall show in the following chapters, it is one of the great paradoxes of human life that it derives its deepest meaning from a mythological realm the inhabitants of which conduct themselves in a way that is antithetical to what is normal in every-day behaviour and experience.

In Welsh, the very word for 'meaning' (*ystyr*) comes from

the Latin *historia* which has given the English langu:
'story' and 'history'. 'History' has now been emptied
of the original extra-historical content of *historia*, whicl
from a root meaning 'knowing', 'learned', 'wise man',
The old Welsh word for 'story', *cyfarwyddyd*, means 'gu
'direction', 'instruction', 'knowledge', 'skill', 'prescrip
stem, *arwydd*, means 'sign', 'symbol', 'manifestation',
'miracle', and derives from a root meaning 'to see'.[7] TI
teller (*cyfarwydd*) was originally a seer and a teacher whc
the souls of his hearers through the world of 'mystery'.

In the remaining chapters we shall follow the class
of tales adopted by the ancient storytellers, but sinc
three-quarters of the tales in the Lists are not knowr
many of the tales which have survived are not include
Lists, we shall take the liberty of applying the tra
classification to the material as we have it. Space does no
us to deal with more than a fair sample of the type:
We have referred to the great 'Battles' of Mag Tuired
most famous of all 'Cattle-raids' in Part I, while 'In\
'Divisions', 'Feasts' and 'Assemblies' have figured in
The remainder of the book will be devoted mainly to th
of tales which are most directly concerned with the life-
the individual.

Myths belong to the world of symbols, and one's
hension of them is a matter of insight. The 'scope' of a s
reference cannot be limited to a particular concept, o
concepts, and we need hardly stress that the comr
offered here is of necessity neither final, nor comple
exclusive of other approaches. We shall consider, for ex
the light which the hero's birth-story sheds on the my
human birth, but this does not mean that birth-mytl
not also be valid symbols of initiation, conversion, or 're
The full 'content' of a myth can never be adequately ex
'in other words'. There can be no definitive exegesis.

most important before examining
remarkable births of Pryderi and
already been mentioned in Chapter
all we are told in 'The Second Bat
the Tuatha made an alliance with
gave his daughter Ethniu to Cian
that she brought forth the gifted chi
fore fall back on later tradition v
elaborate accounts. In these, howe
alliance. Instead we have the widesp
maiden', and Lug, like Lleu, is be
been deemed to be a virgin. Here is t

On Tory Island dwelt a robber,
in the middle of his forehead and an
the death of those he looked upon, i
had been revealed, by a druid, that
grandson, and so he confined his
in a high tower and set twelve won
nothing about men. Balor coveted
vellous cow of Gavida the smith w
with his two brothers, Mac Samtha
Cennfaelaidh), the latter being the
trickery, Balor stole the cow. Then
druid and a fairy, succeeded in gai
in due time she gave birth to three b
servant to drown, but one of them fe
they were wrapped and he was taken t
up as a smith by Gavida. Mackine
and killed. (In another version, M
twelve women as well; their childr
become seals. Ethne's child does r
back to Tory Island to be nursed. In
the child's father, is told by his dru
not thrive until his grandfather call
gages himself as a gardener to Balo
like having any child near him. On

that 'Cattle-raids' were told before undertaking a cattle-raid, 'Voyages' on setting out to sea, 'Conceptions and Births' at births, 'Wooings' at weddings, 'Death Tales' at wakes, and so on? Arranged as they were in the Lists of his memory, the storyteller could easily select his stories to fit the different occasions as they arose. We are not suggesting that the telling of each type of tale was ever restricted to the circumstances that corresponded to it in real life. Indeed, we have noted that at the Assembly of Carmun, and probably at other great ceremonial gatherings, the whole repertoire of tales was declaimed. In this respect the custom among the early Celts may not have been very different from what it is in our own Christian ritual. The Baptism of Jesus in the Jordan is cited at every christening, the miracle at Cana of Galilee at every marriage, the Resurrection at every funeral. Each allusion is appropriate to the occasion, but the relevance of these scriptural events was never confined to birth, marriage, and death.

Evidence to which we have referred in Chapter I shows that the narrator of 'The Vision of Mac Conglinne' is parodying what was once a serious belief when he claims that to listen to the tale will bring life, offspring and prosperity. But concrete benefits apart, the stories served as mythical models. In the words of van Hamel,[5] they provided examples of which 'the deeds of other men must be regarded as a reflexion'. Van Hamel's further statement, that the heroes were intended to be 'imitated' by people in early Celtic society, must nevertheless be qualified. We shall speak later of correspondences between myth and ritual, but outside the ritual the deeds of mythical heroes cannot be repeated by mortal men. As events in ordinary life they are, as often as not, fantastic, antisocial, immoral and catastrophic. Yet, as we shall show in the following chapters, it is one of the great paradoxes of human life that it derives its deepest meaning from a mythological realm the inhabitants of which conduct themselves in a way that is antithetical to what is normal in everyday behaviour and experience.

In Welsh, the very word for 'meaning' (*ystyr*) comes from

the Latin *historia* which has given the English language both 'story' and 'history'. 'History' has now been emptied of most of the original extra-historical content of *historia*, which derives from a root meaning 'knowing', 'learned', 'wise man', 'judge'.[6] The old Welsh word for 'story', *cyfarwyddyd*, means 'guidance', 'direction', 'instruction', 'knowledge', 'skill', 'prescription'. Its stem, *arwydd*, means 'sign', 'symbol', 'manifestation', 'omen', 'miracle', and derives from a root meaning 'to see'.[7] The story-teller (*cyfarwydd*) was originally a seer and a teacher who guided the souls of his hearers through the world of 'mystery'.

In the remaining chapters we shall follow the classification of tales adopted by the ancient storytellers, but since about three-quarters of the tales in the Lists are not known, while many of the tales which have survived are not included in the Lists, we shall take the liberty of applying the traditional classification to the material as we have it. Space does not permit us to deal with more than a fair sample of the types listed. We have referred to the great 'Battles' of Mag Tuired and the most famous of all 'Cattle-raids' in Part I, while 'Invasions', 'Divisions', 'Feasts' and 'Assemblies' have figured in Part II. The remainder of the book will be devoted mainly to the classes of tales which are most directly concerned with the life-cycle of the individual.

Myths belong to the world of symbols, and one's appre-hension of them is a matter of insight. The 'scope' of a symbol's reference cannot be limited to a particular concept, or set of concepts, and we need hardly stress that the commentary offered here is of necessity neither final, nor complete, nor exclusive of other approaches. We shall consider, for example, the light which the hero's birth-story sheds on the mystery of human birth, but this does not mean that birth-myths may not also be valid symbols of initiation, conversion, or 're-birth'. The full 'content' of a myth can never be adequately expressed 'in other words'. There can be no definitive exegesis.

thereby became pregnant. (Another text says that King Fachtna Fáthach was her lover and that he caused her pregnancy). The pangs of childbirth came upon Ness when she was journeying with Cathbad over the plain of Muirthemne to a meeting with Eochu, but Cathbad said that if the birth were delayed until night the child would become king and the most renowned in Ireland, because a glorious child, Jesus Christ, would be born the same night in the east of the world. So she reached a flagstone at Mag-Inis and gave birth to a boy with a worm in each of his fists. (According to the other text, Ness declared that the child would not be born until the auspicious time unless it came out through her side, and she sat on a flagstone on the bank of the River Conchobar, while Cathbad uttered a poem prophesying the illustrious future of the child about to be born. At birth the child went head over heels into the river, but he was seized by Cathbad and named Conchobar after the river. In a further poem extolling his future greatness, Cathbad curiously addresses the child as 'my son and my grandson'.)

There are also two versions of the story of the conception and birth of CúChulainn.[8] The first begins with the repeated appearance of a flock of birds which grazed the plain of Emain to the roots. The warriors of Ulster pursued them in nine chariots, Conchobar's grown-up daughter, Dechtine, serving as his charioteer. The beautiful sweet-singing birds, each two linked with a silver chain, were divided into nine flights of twenty each and were headed by two birds joined by a silver yoke. In the evening, three of the birds detached themselves from the rest and flew before the pursuers to the End of the Bruig. There night came upon the Ulstermen and it began to snow. The only shelter they found was one new house, occupied by a couple, where they were entertained until they were merry and drunk. Then the man of the house told them that his wife was in labour. Dechtine went to her and a boy-child was born. At the same time, a mare outside the house dropped two foals, which the man gave to the child. By morning, both house and birds had disappeared, and all that remained with the Ulstermen at the End of the Bruig were the child and the two foals. With these they returned to Emain.

Dechtine reared the child, but to her grief it fell ill and died. On her return from the lamentation she felt thirsty and tried to drink from a copper vessel, but each time a little creature, which was invisible when the vessel was removed, sprang into her mouth with the drink. During the night a man came to her in her sleep and declared himself to be Lug son of Ethniu. It was he who had brought her to the Bruig, it was with him she had stayed the night, and the little child was his son. He would now enter her womb and she would bear a child whose name would be Setanta. The Ulstermen could not understand how it came that Dechtine was with child and suspected that her father had slept with her in his drunkenness. Conchobar betrothed her to Sualdaim mac Roich, but she, ashamed of her condition, induced a miscarriage. Then she conceived again and bore a son. (This was Setanta who was later named CúChulainn).

The triple conception of CúChulainn does not figure in the other version of the story, and Dechtire (as she is called in that version) is not Conchobar's daughter and charioteer but his sister. She and fifty maidens had disappeared from Emain three years before the events which we have just told began, and it was they that plagued Emain in the form of birds. When the pursuing Ulstermen had been made welcome by a man and a woman in a small house at nightfall, Bricriu went out and guided by a low plaint saw before him a magnificent house. There he was greeted by a nobleman and his wife, and learnt that the latter was Dechtire, that her fifty maidens were with her and that they were the birds which had allured the Ulstermen thither. When he rejoined his comrades, Bricriu, withholding a part of the truth, spoke only of the beautiful woman and her splendid entourage. Conchobar asserted that, as the warrior was his vassal, he was entitled to have the woman to sleep with him. Fergus went to fetch her, but as he was returning with her she complained that she was in travail, and a delay was granted. The Ulstermen lay down to sleep, and when they awoke they saw a little boy in Conchobar's lap.

Conall Cernach's mother was Findchoem, daughter of Cathbad and wife of Amairgen.[9] She suffered from 'hesitation of offspring', and when a druid told her that she should bear a noble son if she paid him a good fee, she accompanied him to a well over which he sang spells and prophecies. He then told her to wash in the water, and 'you will bring forth a son, and no child will be less pious than he to his mother's kin, that is to the Connachtmen'. Findchoem then drank a draught from the well and swallowed a worm. That worm was in the boy's hand in his mother's womb and it pierced the hand and con/sumed it. Druids baptized the child into heathenism, pro/phesying as they did so the havoc he would eventually wreak upon the men of Connacht. Cet, the mother's brother, who, although he knew of the prophecies, had protected his sister until her delivery, now drew the child towards him and put it under his heel and bruised its neck. Thereupon the mother exclaimed: 'Wolfish (*conda*) is the treachery (*fell*) you work, O brother.' 'True,' said Cet, 'let Conall (*Con/feall*) be his name henceforward.' Whence he was called wry/necked Conall.

Many strange births appear in the Cycles of the Kings. This is how Cormac mac Airt was born.[10] Before the battle against Lugaid Mac Con, in which he was slain, Art son of Conn of the Hundred Battles spent the night as guest of a smith named Olc Acha. It had been prophesied that a great honour would derive from the smith and he asked Art to lie with his daughter Étaín that night. This he did and Cormac was con/ceived. Before departing to the battle in which he knew he would die, Art instructed Étaín to take the child to be fostered by his friend Lugna in Connacht. When her time drew near Étaín set out for Lugna's house so that the child might be born there, but as soon as she arrived in that country her pains took her and she gave birth to her son on a bed of brushwood collected by her maid. Thunder boomed, and Lugna on hearing it exclaimed: 'Noise—thunder—birth of king', and realizing that it was Cormac that was born he set forth to seek him.

Meanwhile, Étaín went to sleep, leaving the child in the care of her maid. But the maid also fell asleep and a she-wolf came and carried the child away and thereafter brought him up with her whelps in a cave. Lugna found the distraught mother, took her home, and offered a reward for a clue to the infant's whereabouts. One day a man named Grec chanced upon the cave, and in front of it he saw a child on all fours amidst gam-bolling wolf-cubs. The child, together with the cubs, was brought to Lugna's house and Lugna hailed him as Conn's victorious representative. He named him Cormac, which was in accordance with Art's instructions.

The story of the birth of King Fiacha Broad-crown[11] begins in the same way as that of Cormac and ends like that of Conchobar. The night before the battle in which he (as well as Art) was killed, Eogan, King of Munster, cohabited with the daughter of a druid at her father's request. The girl con-ceived and when her time came her father said it was an ill thing she was not brought to bed the following morning, for had it been then, the child would have overtopped all Ireland. She replied that the child would not be born before then unless it came through one of her sides. She sat astride a stone in the mid ford, appealing to the rock to maintain her. When she was loosened next day she died, and the child's head had been flattened against the stone—hence he was called Fiacha Broad-crown.

There are a number of conflicting traditions about the parent-age of Mes Buachalla and her son Conaire Mór, King of Ireland.[12] According to 'The Destruction of Da Derga's Hostel' she was the daughter of Cormac mac Airt and his wife Étaín. Étaín had proved barren until she conceived this daughter after being given a pottage by her mother, a woman from the *síd*-mounds. Cormac married again and ordered his daughter to be abandoned in a pit. Two servants were entrusted with the task, but they lost heart when the child laughed as they were putting her in the pit and they left her instead in the calf-shed of the cowherds of Eterscél, great-grandson of Iar, king of Tara. The cowherds reared her and she was named Mes Buachalla, 'the cowherd's foster-child'.

According to other sources Mes Buachalla was the daughter of Ess, who conceived her either through incest with her father, Eochaid Airem, King of Tara, or through intercourse with the *síd*-folk of Brí Léith. Eochaid ordered the destruction of the child, but she was left in a kennel, with a bitch and her whelps, at the house of a herdsman.

We now revert to 'The Destruction of Da Derga's Hostel'. The cowherds kept the girl concealed in a house of wicker-work which had only a roof-opening, but King Eterscél's folk discovered her and told him of their find. It had been prophesied that a woman of unknown race would bear Eterscél a child, so he sent people to break into the wicker house and bring her to him. Before this was done, a bird came through the skylight and told the girl what was being planned. He shed his bird-plumage on the floor and she gave her love to him. He told her that she would have by him a son, whose name would be Conaire, and that he should not kill birds. She was then betrothed to King Eterscél. Others say, however, that Eterscél was Mes Buachalla's father and that it was he who got her with child.

Another king who was believed to have had a supernatural father was Mongán.[13] Fiachna Finn, King of Ulster, was sorely pressed in battle in Lochlann when a tall warrior, who transpired to be Manannán mac Lir, appeared on the battle-field and offered victory if Fiachna would allow him to go to Ireland to sleep with Fiachna's wife. He would go in Fiachna's shape and beget a glorious child who would be called Mongán son of Fiachna Finn. The king agreed and secured his victory. In due course a son was born to Fiachna's wife, but when he was three nights old Manannán came and took him to be reared in the Land of Promise until he was twelve years of age.

According to another version, Manannán first went to Fiachna's wife and offered to save her husband's life if she consorted with him. He then went and told Fiachna what had taken place and gave him the victory.

The shape-changing motif also occurs in Geoffrey's story of King Arthur's conception.[14] His mother was Igerna, wife of Gorlois Duke of Cornwall, and she was being guarded in Tintagel castle against the amorous intentions of King Uthr Bendragon. Uthr, aided by Merlin's magic, visited her in the form of her own husband, and 'that night was the most renowned Arthur conceived'. Merlin himself had been begotten upon a king's daughter by a mysterious youth who visited her in the dormitory of her nunnery and united with her in her sleep.[15]

Features similar to those which recur in these tales are found in many others. A druid had foretold that the death of Ragallach, King of Connacht, would be caused by his own child. When a female child was born to his wife, the king ordered her to kill it. The child was cast into a bag and given to a swineherd to be destroyed, but the swineherd left the bag at the door of a pious woman and she reared it religiously. This daughter later became Ragallach's own concubine.[16] Before the birth of Sechnasach, his destined mother, Mór of Munster, fled from home under the influence of voices threatening her with evil. She regained her senses, and Sechnasach was begotten, when she slept with King Fíngen mac Aeda.[17] Again, Fingel, who was to be the mother of Noidhiu Nae-mBreathach,* was closely guarded lest anyone should make her conceive, but she was visited by a phantom from over the sea and was pregnant for nine months and nine years. When her son was born she suggested that he should be put to death, but the child spoke, uttering nine judgements.[18] When Aí mac Olloman, a poet of Tuatha Dé Danann, was in his mother's womb, a blast of wind shook the house, and a druid prophesied the birth of a wonderful child. The king would have slain the

* Noidhiu of the Nine Judgements.

child, but its father hindered him, and the child demanded a boon from the king.[19] Ségda Saerlabraid was the son of a 'sinless couple', for his parents, the king and queen of the Land of Promise, never came together except when he was conceived.[20]

Some of the most striking features we have encountered in these tales may be tabulated as follows:

1 The advent and future greatness of the hero have been fore-told.

2 His advent is destined to bring death or misfortune to a presiding power, his grandfather, his uncle, or his own mother.

3 Certain difficulties have to be overcome before his future mother can fulfil her destiny:

    (*a*) She is closely guarded or confined in a fortress.

or (*b*) She has to be induced to leave home.

or (*c*) Her own resistance has to be overcome by force or by cunning.

or (*d*) She is married, but barren.

4 There is a mystery about the hero's begetting:

    (*a*) Whether he has an earthly father or not, he is usually begotten by another—a king, a man from another race, or a supernatural being.

    (*b*) Others say he is born of incest.

    (*c*) Others again attribute his conception to a creature swallowed by his mother in water.

5 There is an auspicious time for his birth, which is heralded by signs in the natural world; his birth is delayed until the appropriate time.

6 Certain animals are associated with his birth and up-bringing.

7 He is lost at birth, or an attempt is made to kill him; he is thrown into the sea or borne away in a boat.

8 At birth and in his youth he displays qualities that reveal his extra-ordinary nature.

9 Difficulty is sometimes experienced in securing a name for him, or he is given a name in peculiar circumstances.

Stories of the coming of saints into the world (recorded in the Lives of the Saints) have a great deal in common with those of the 'secular' heroes. Their births are foretold by an angel, another saint, or a druid. St Beuno's father and mother had been continent for twelve years before the saint was begotten in their old age.[21] St David and St Cynog were the products of rape, St Cadoc's mother was abducted and St Lonán's mother was tricked into having intercourse with a man other than her lover.[22] St Budoc's mother was accused of infidelity.[23] St Cennydd and St Cuimíne Foda were born of incest and St Déclán's ancestry was traced back to the incestuous Clothra.[24] St Fínán's mother was impregnated by a 'red-gold salmon' when she was bathing in Loch Léin.[25] In several cases, the saint's mother has a vision or dream at the time when her child is conceived. She sees a star falling into her mouth, a ball of light descending upon her head, or 'her bosom full of gold and her paps shining like snow'.[26] During her pregnancy, St Columba's mother received from an angel a marvellous mantle which then floated away from her to heaven.[27]

St Senán's mother, like the Buddha's, was delivered from the pains of travail,[28] and other miracles are characteristic of the births of saints. The child may speak at birth, or a spring may burst forth and he is baptized in it.[29] There is often a plan to kill the child[30] and in some cases, like those of St Budoc and St Cennydd, he, or his mother before he is born, is set adrift on the sea. When St Brendan was born, a cow cast thirty calves and they were given to him. When he was five years old, a wild doe came daily to provide him with milk.[31] St Cennydd was fed in the same way;[32] Saints Ailbe, Bairre and Ciwa were all suckled by wolves.[33]

Needless to say, tales of this kind are not peculiar to Celtic mythology. They are the common stuff of birth myths the world over, and if one went into detail one would find strange similarities between the Celtic stories and stories collected from the far ends of the earth. Lest anyone should too readily dismiss the visions of saints' mothers as the fanciful imaginings of Christian hagiographers, we will just mention that a Chinese dynasty traced its origin to an egg, dropped by a heaven-sent bird, which was swallowed by a girl while bathing; that several Tartar tribes ascribe their lineage to a virgin who was awakened one night by a light which embraced her and, entering her mouth, passed through her body. The Aztec deity, Huitzilopochtli, was conceived by a mother who caught and hid in her bosom a little ball of feathers that floated down to her through the air. Her children conspired to kill her, but Huitzilopochtli, issuing forth from her womb all armed, like Pallas from the head of Zeus, slew them and enriched his mother with their spoils. The virgin mother of the great Mexican hero, Quetzalcoatl, was visited by a god who breathed upon her and so quickened life within her.[34] The mother and father of the Hindu god Krishna were imprisoned in a castle because it was prophesied that their son would kill the king, his own mother's brother. When he was born, the boy stood up before his parents in the full glory of his divinity. He then became a human child again, the doors were opened and his parents were freed of their fetters. The father took the child across a river, which rose as they went through it and almost overwhelmed them, and he left it to be reared by cowherds.[35] Tales of this kind could be multiplied indefinitely without touching either Classical or Biblical sources, and they could be augmented by stories of heroes born of incest and of heroes set adrift at birth or reared with animals.

2

From the point of view of the established order of things in this world, the way in which the hero is conceived and born is 'all wrong'. Ordinary children are born of married parents who are not blood-relations. The hero is more often than not

conceived 'illegitimately' by an unmarried girl and born out
of wedlock. If the mother is married, he is begotten through
what would normally be called adultery, and the irregularity
of the union is often accentuated by violence and trickery.
To make matters worse, even the integrity of the family is
violated: a father begets a hero upon his daughter, a son upon
his mother, a brother upon his sister. A mockery is made
even of the laws of biological nature, for a barren woman may
conceive a hero by drinking water, by swallowing worms,
or by eating a fish or a grain of wheat.

Yet, these were originally religious stories which were believed to have a liberating and elevating effect upon their
hearers. We have inferred that it was appropriate to recount
them at the birth of human children and have suggested that
they had a validity as exemplars in the light of which the meaning of ordinary births could be apprehended. But they were
obviously not patterns to be emulated in real life. To resolve
the paradox the myths must be regarded as symbols of the
transcendental meaning of birth, of what birth is from the
point of view of the unseen world. From an earthly standpoint
a child is conceived inadvertently during the course of its
parents' conjugal relations, without the intervention of any
other agency. But from the point of view of the supernatural
world, the child's birth is destined, the parents are chosen, the
time and place are ordained, and the earthly life of the child is
'pre-figured' before he is conceived. The hostility of earthly
powers cannot prevent his advent; his mother has no choice and,
in a sense, is violated.

And in every conception there is a third factor. The child
may derive its biological inheritance from its earthly parents,
but it is also the incarnation of a supernatural essence. This
doctrine, that a spirit enters the womb at conception, is widespread among both 'primitive' and highly sophisticated peoples.
To the Indian, 'three things are required for conception, viz.
conjunction of father and mother, the mother's period, and
the presence of the Gandharva: of which the first two may be

called depositive and the third an essential cause'. 'Man and the Sun generate man,' says Aristotle; 'Call no man father upon earth,' says St Paul, and according to St Thomas Aquinas, 'The power of the soul, which is in the semen through the Spirit enclosed therein, fashions the body.'[36] The myths are concerned with this third factor, symbolized by the mysterious begetter and by the fructifying substance which is swallowed by the mother. In some of the stories, the begetter is a super-natural being—Lug, Manannán, a bird-man, or one of the *síd*-folk. In others he is the king or a stranger from another race. These latter invite comparison with widespread rituals by which supernatural powers were given access to women through the agency of such human personifications as kings, priests or strangers.[37] Traces of rituals of this kind in the Celtic lands have survived both in the mythological literature itself and in later tradition. It is said that King Conchobar, who was regarded as a 'terrestrial god', was entitled to the first night with the bride of every Ulsterman, 'so that he became her first husband'.[38] According to oral tradition, Balor's two deputies exercised the same right.[39] The Fenians had the option on the women of the tribe and claimed either a ransom or the right to cohabit with even a princess the night previous to her mar-riage.[40] Boswell refers to a Scottish laird who insisted that the *Mercheta Mulierum* mentioned in old charters did really mean the privilege of a lord to have the first night with his vassals' wives, and that on the marriage of each of his own tenants a sheep (or a payment of five shillings) was still due to him.[41] In Ireland, there are still 'widespread traditions of the days when landlords excercised the *jus primae noctis* over their tenants' wives, and one hears of leases which contained clauses govern-ing the right.'[42]

There are indications that these rights were not confined to the time of marriage. 'When any man of Ulster used to give him (Conchobar) a night's hospitality, he used to sleep that night with the man's wife,' and there is mention of a king of Ireland's son who came to his father and said: 'I desire to make "a stripling's free circuit of Ireland" and the wife of every king in Ireland shall pass a night with me.'[43] As Mrs Chadwick has argued in her recent study of Pictish and Celtic Marriage, there is a great deal of evidence which 'suggests the right of a king or his *fili* to beget children ritualistically among married couples'.[44] The 'Devil' of the medieval witch cult exercised a similar right over his female subjects,[45] and tales of *incubi*, demons which assumed the shape of men and held carnal converse with mortal women,[46] seem to be related to this practice. In Geoffrey of Monmouth's *Historia Regum* it is suggested that Merlin was begotten by one of these demons.[47]

The begetting of a hero is, however, nowhere attributed to such rites as the *jus primae noctis*, and to derive the stories from the rites is to confuse cause and effect. It is rather that the mythological realities with which the stories are concerned are also the *raison d'être* of the correlative rites. Stories in which the supernatural factor is symbolized as entering through the mother's mouth also seem to have their counterpart in custom. A belief in the fructifying potentialities of water has driven childless women throughout the ages to bathe and to drink at sacred wells in the hope of conceiving, and a belief in the embodiment of the supernatural essence in worms and flies seems to account for the fact that in Wales it is still said of a pregnant girl that she has swallowed an insect (*pry'*) or a spider (*corryn*).[48]

In the stories, the role of the earthly father is minimized or discounted altogether, as though to stress the third factor in conception—the mother is a maiden, she is secluded from contact with men, or, though married, she has proved barren until the intervention of the third factor. But an inconsistent passage in 'The Wooing of Étaín' combines all three factors. Étaín, a Tuatha woman transformed into a fly, fell into the cup of the wife of Étar, an Ulster champion, and was swallowed by her. 'In this way she was conceived in her womb.' But the story adds paradoxically that she was called Étar's daughter and *was begotten by him*.[49] In other cases too, where the mother is married, the child is often called the son of her husband. Thus

CúChulainn, though begotten by Lug, was called Setanta son of Sualdaim, and Mongán, though begotten by Manannán, was Mongán son of Fiachna Finn.

In some of these tales, the supernatural essence in the child is personified as the incarnation or reincarnation of a particular deity. Individual reincarnation is also implied in the story of Daolgas[50]—and there is perhaps a hint of the rebirth of the begetter in the birth-stories of Finn, Cormac mac Airt, and Fiacha Broad-Crown, whose fathers were destined to die as soon as they had begotten their sons. When Daolgas son of Cairril lay dying, his daughter stooped over him and kissed him As she did so, a spark of fire flew from his mouth to hers and she became pregnant. In due time she gave birth to a broad-crowned boy, and, since no other name was found for him, he was called by his father's name, Daolgas. Tuan, the sole survivor of Partholón's company, after successive trans-formations into a deer, a boar, and an eagle, was eventually eaten in the form of a salmon by the wife of King Cairell and reborn of her. He was called Tuan son of Cairell, but he bore within him the whole history of Ireland since the coming of Partholón.[51] It will be recalled that the two rival swineherds who finally became the two great contending bulls of *Táin Bó Cuailnge* passed through similar transformations before they were swallowed in the form of water-worms by the cows from which they were reborn. In the Welsh Story of Taliesin,[52] the witch Ceridwen prepares in her cauldron a magic brew which, after a year's boiling, will yield three blessed drops. Whoever swallows these drops will know all the secrets of the past, the present, and the future, and she intends them for her ugly son Morfran ('Sea-crow') who is nicknamed Afagddu ('Blackness'). The drops fly out of the cauldron and fall on the finger of Gwion Bach, the boy who has helped to tend the fire underneath the cauldron. He puts his finger in his mouth, and then, realizing his danger, flees. Ceridwen sets out in pursuit. Gwion transforms himself successively into a hare, a fish, a bird, and a grain of wheat; she gives chase in appropriate forms—a greyhound, an otter-bitch, a hawk, and a hen. In this last form, she swallows the grain of wheat, and in the fulness of time, Gwion Bach is reborn of her as the wizard-poet Taliesin.

While individual beings in some of these stories retain their identity through diverse incarnations, the child Taliesin, in a poem replying to the king's question as to who he is and whence he has come, envisages himself as a ubiquitous presence which has witnessed the history of the world and will endure to the end. The blessed drops did no more than make him aware that he was there when it all happened. The poem, like several others in the same strain preserved in the medieval Book of Taliesin, exalts him to a plane which transcends that of finite human beings.

> I have been teacher to all Christendom
> I shall be on the face of the earth until Doom,
> And it is not known what my flesh is, whether flesh or fish.

In a poem in the Book of Taliesin he claims to have witnessed the fall of Lucifer, the Flood, and the birth and the Cruci-fixion of Christ. And, while in another poem he says that he was created by Gwydion, he here says that he was in the Court of Dôn before Gwydion was born. Some of the poems in this Book are replete with utterances beginning with 'I have been', and the things he has been include inanimate objects—stock, axe, chisel, coracle, sword, shield, harp-string, raindrop, foam; animals such as bull, stallion, stag, dog, cock, salmon, snake, eagle—and a grain which grew on a hill. He declares that he was not made of father and mother but was created of nine things—fruits and various flowers, earth, and water from the ninth wave.[53] Like Amairgen whose poem we have quoted before, Taliesin is everything, and it is a fair inference that among the Celts, as in India and other lands, there existed alongside the belief in individual reincarnation, a doctrine that there is essentially only One Transmigrant. As Ovid expresses it: 'The spirit wanders, comes now here, now there, and occupies whatever frame it pleases. From beasts it passes into human bodies, and from our bodies into beasts, but never perishes.'[54]

The supra-personal character of the incarnating spirit is also indicated by other motifs. Thunder peals when Cormac is born, and at the birth of certain saints a spring wells forth, a wood lights up, or a rod held in the mother's hand bursts into leaf and flower,[55] like the trees that blossomed and fruited when heaven and earth rejoiced at the birth of Krishna. Animals are born simultaneously with the hero—a colt with Pryderi, two colts with CúChulainn, a dog with Finn, a fish-like brother with Lleu, and with Lug twelve half-brothers who become seals. In other tales the hero's animal connections are established after his birth. He is suckled by a she-wolf and goes on all fours, he is left in a kennel with a bitch and her pups, or he comes up from the loch with a fish in his hand. Some heroes and heroines are named from their association with animals: Kulhwch is so called because he was born in a pigstye (*kil-hwch*); CúChulainn is 'the hound of Culann', Mes Buachalla 'Cowherds' Fosterchild', Oisín 'Little Deer', and Oscar 'Deer-Love'. And there are many whose animal names are not explained, such as Ruadchoin 'Red hounds', Conchenn 'Wolf-head', MacCon 'Son of Wolfdog', March 'Horse' (he had horse's ears), Bran 'Crow', Echbél 'Horse-lip'.[56]

So close is the affinity of some heroes with particular species that they are not permitted to eat their flesh. CúChulainn was forbidden to eat dog;[57] Conaire was forbidden to kill birds, which should be dear to him because of his father.[58] It was fatal for Diarmaid to hunt swine, because of a prohibition laid upon him as a boy. It happened in this way. Finn's dogs fell to fighting and Diarmaid's foster-brother, seeking refuge between the knees of Diarmaid's father, was squeezed to death. The dead boy's father transformed the corpse into a grey cropped pig and pronounced an incantation over him giving him the same life-span as Diarmaid. The latter eventually met his death in a boar hunt in which he killed this pig and was himself mortally wounded by it.[59] As a youth, Finn tasted of the salmon of knowledge; according to one tradition he was slain with a fishing-gaff.[60] St Ailbe, suckled by a wolf, acknowledged to the end of his days this 'kinship by the milk'; St Ciwa, suckled in the same way, had a great nail like a wolf's claw on one of her fingers and was called the 'Wolf Girl'.[61]

In mythology, animals are not mere brutes; they are possessed of a supernatural intelligence and power. Their association with the birth and infancy of heroes is world-wide, and in many cases they befriend or serve their heroic 'kinsmen' beyond the days of childhood. We need only mention Cormac's wolves, Conaire's birds, Finn's dog, and Pryderi's colt. CúChulainn's celebrated chariot-horses have been identified with the two foals dropped on the night of his birth. According to another story, one of them emerged from a lake, the other from the Great Glen, and they returned there at the time of their master's death.[62] These animal correlatives of the hero may be said to symbolize the extra-human, otherworldly or unconscious ground of his nature, a symbolism which is well illustrated in the stories of the Welsh twin brothers, Lleu and Dylan, and the Indian half-brothers, Krishna and Balarāma. The moment he is baptized, Dylan makes for the sea and receives the sea's nature, swimming as well as any fish, and because of this he is called Dylan Eil Ton, 'Sea son of Wave'. No wave ever broke beneath him.[63] Though Balarāma lives on earth with Krishna until both have grown to manhood, he disappears into the same element. As he sits one day under a tree by the sea-shore, lost in thought, a snake crawls out of his mouth, leaving his body lifeless, and winds its way to the sea. 'The ocean itself arises in the form of a mighty serpent king to salute the great guest, its own higher Self, the serpent of the universal waters. The serpent essence of the divine hero goes back into the form-lessness of the Abyss—returning into itself after having accom-plished the momentary role of companion and supporter to a human avatar.'[64]

The universality and oneness of the otherworld progenitor has a bearing upon the incest motif which appears here and there in the birth stories. This is a world-wide feature of the conception of heroes, and, treating it as we have treated the other motifs, we must accept the proposition that the conception of every child is in a sense incestuous. If the begetter of the divine in each individual is fundamentally one, it follows that mother, child, husband, wife, plants, and animals are spiritually brothers and sisters. Incest is thus 'inevitable because of the kinship of all the manifest principles, *ab intra*'.[65] The same truth can also be expressed cosmogonically. Incest and kinship with animals, and with nature generally, symbolize the primeval unity before animate and inanimate, plant and animal, man and beast were separated out. Many cosmogonic myths represent the beginning of things as a division of the original whole into two: heaven and earth, land and water, male and female. The first couple are brother and sister, and from their incestuous union mankind is descended. So far as we know, no story of this kind has been handed down in Celtic tradition, but it is noteworthy that incestuous unions are frequent in lineages of the Mythological Cycle, and that certain Irish tribes traced their descent from a founder born of incest.[66]

When the world comes to an end, its manifold forms will be reabsorbed into the unity which cannot but appear as chaos when viewed from within the framework of the world itself. It is implied in an ancient Irish charm—the charm by which Tuatha Dé Danann took away the kingship from Fir Bolg, and by which the Sons of Míl took away the kingship from the Tuatha—that the world, or an age, endures till *ogam* and *achu* be mixed together and till sun and moon be mixed together.[67] And in a poem in which the Badb prophesies the end of the world, incest appears among the disorders that presage the end:

> 'Son will enter his father's bed,
> Father will enter his son's bed,
> Every one his brother's brother-in-law.[68]

Thus, the incestuous birth of the hero again symbolizes the presence in the child of a universal, the beginning and the end, which recognizes neither brother nor sister, father nor mother—and in the last synthesis, neither species nor gender nor element.

Unions between brothers and sisters are alluded to enigmatically in the above poem: 'Every one his brother's brotherinlaw.' Similarly, those who told or listened to the birth stories were intrigued by the curious ways in which incest confuses kinrelationships, and causes categories that are usually distinct to overlap. In the context in which it has been preserved, the story of Daolgas's incestuous birth is told by Finn as the answer to a riddle: 'What man was the son of his own daughter?' Similarly Cuimíne, born of a union of father and daughter, is alluded to in a quatrain: 'This Mugain was his mother, he to her was brother.'[69] Mes Buachalla was 'granddaughter of her father, sister of her mother'.[70] Although there is no incest motif in the birthstory of Conchobar as we know it, Cathbad addresses him at birth as 'my son and my grandson', which would be literally true only if Ness were his daughter. The most remarkable case of incest in Irish story is that of Clothra who slept with each of her three brothers unknown to the others. Her son was called Lugaid of the Red Stripes (*Lugaid Riab nDerg*) because he had two red lines round his body which marked off the portions in which he resembled his three fathers. When he grew up, he in his turn begot a son —named Crimthann—upon his own mother:[71]

> 'Lugaid Riab nDerg to fair Crimthann
> Was father and was brother,
> And Clothra of the comely form
> Was grandmother to her son.'[72]

This interest in the enigmatic implications of incest is by no means confined to the Celtic lands. For example, stories of fatherdaughter incest are expressed in the form of the following riddle in Hebrew, Islamic, and Christian contexts:

'A woman said to her son,
"Thy father is my father,
And thy grandfather is my husband;
Thou art my son and I am thy sister." '[73]

Arabs in North Africa and Negroes in Central Africa justify the exposure of children born of incest on the grounds that the child would be, for example, 'So and so's son and his nephew', making it clear that the existence of such a living contradiction among them could not be contemplated.[74] Mythology on the other hand, as we shall see later, is largely concerned with persons, things, and acts which are both 'this' and 'that', or neither 'this' nor 'that', and the principle can be extended to birth myths generally. Most of the tales we have recounted could be envisaged as answers to paradoxical riddles. For example:

'A dog that was not a dog, born of a woman that was not a woman, in a house that wasn't there; he was begotten by a man that was not a man; his father was reared by his mother as a child, a child which died and did not die; his mother swallowed a worm that was not a worm—and his father was also his uncle.'

The answer to the riddle would be the complicated stories of the birth of CúChulainn. It would be wrong to try to make sense of these traditions by tearing them to fragments on the assumption that they are a confusion of unrelated motifs. Their very ambiguity is of the essence of mythology.

CúChulainn's mother entered the realm of Lug in the form of a bird, and the story of Cathbad's interception of Ness, between the spring in which she was bathing and the place where she had left her weapon, is reminiscent of a world-wide folktale in which a mortal surprises a swan-maiden when she is bathing, steals her bird-dress, and makes her his wife.[75] The supernatural lover of Mes Buachalla visits her in a bird-dress, and, as we shall recount in a later chapter, it was in the form of swans that Midir and Étaín absconded from Tara's court to the *síd*. There is no suggestion that a swan form is the norm in the Other World. The implication is rather that the form of a swan—perhaps because it is that of a creature of land, water and air, a creature whose milieu has no boundaries—is appropriate for communication *between* two worlds, and that, at the time of the hero's conception, the mother as well as the supernatural father is in that transitional zone, neither completely in this world nor in the other. Girls are metaphorically described as 'swans' both in Irish and in Greek literature, but whether they were ever ritually dressed in swan clothing we do not know. What we do know is that Irish poets had cloaks of bird feathers and that such clothing was worn by shamans in Siberia and North America for their excursions to the world beyond.[76]

The mothers of Lug, Conaire, and Arthur, like the mothers of Perseus, Gilgamesh, and many others, were secluded in special buildings, while the virginity of some of the mothers who are not said to have been confined was closely guarded. The seclusion of a maiden in a high tower is also a widespread motif in marriage tales, and we shall recount later an Irish tale in which the bride is confined in 'an ingenious, bright, shining bower set on one pillar over the stead'. We have already mentioned that the buildings of the Court of Tara included the 'Palace of the Single Pillar' which Cormac mac Airt made for his daughter. The reasons given for these confinements, in the stories, vary a great deal—the girl's marriage, or her destined son, will bring death or misfortune to her father, to her mother, or to some presiding power, or it is prophesied that she will marry a commoner, or that she will be impregnated by the sun.[77] But the seclusion motif itself invites comparison with a profusion of customs, from many parts of the world, arising out of a wellnigh universal belief that women at certain periods—puberty, menstruation, and childbirth—do not belong entirely to this world. They are both holy and unclean. They can be a great source of harm to themselves and to others, yet, controlled by ritual, their condition can be made a source of power for good. In custom they are excluded from society, they are *confined* in separate huts, they must not touch the earth, or they are 'forbidden the sun'. They are ceremonially 'taboo', like divine kings and priests. 'The uncleanness, as it is called, of girls at puberty and the sanctity of holy men do not differ materially from each other. They are only different mani/festations of the same mysterious energy which becomes bene/ficent or maleficent according to its application.'[78] Puberty rules in widely separated parts of the world require that a girl should be secluded for a period of days, months, or even years, and the place of confinement is sometimes a dark cage raised above the ground, or a hammock suspended from the roof. 'The general effect of these rules is to keep her suspended, so to say, between heaven and earth.'[78]

When the tale of the hero's conception has been told, his origin remains a mystery. Merlin is enigmatically described as 'a boy without a father',[79] which, taken literally, implies that he was born without being begotten. In other cases the mystery lies, not in the absence of a cause, but in an embarrassing multiplication of contradictory causes to produce an effect which by the dictates of common sense can only have one cause. And there are other enigmas. The Welsh Lleu seems to have been born from the afterbirth.[80] If so, he could be said to have been born of his mother and not born of his mother. The Irish Furbaide is said to have been brought forth through his mother's side,[81]—like Goll mac Morna, Julius Caesar, the Egyptian god Set, Indra, and Buddha.[82] Indian gods are indeed brought forth in all kinds of fantastic ways: through the forehead, the hand, and the armpit.[83] In Shakespeare's play, the witches assure Macbeth that he cannot be killed by 'a man born of woman'. The paradox is resolved when it transpires that Macduff was 'from his mother's womb untimely ripped'—and that a forest which is not a forest can move. It is along this knife/edge line between being and non/being that the gods appear, and the impossible becomes possible.

3

The advent of the hero is almost invariably an embarrassment to someone or other, and an attempt is made to get rid of him. To the examples we have recounted we could add Niall of the Nine Hostages who was exposed naked beneath the green of of Tara because of the jealousy of his step-mother. After he had been there for three days, Torna the poet took him to his home and reared him.[84] Morann, destined to become chief judge of Ireland, was born with a caul, and his father, deeming him a monster, ordered two of his men to cast the child into the sea. When this was done the wave broke the helmet and the child spoke, saying, 'Rough is the wave.' Then they took him and left him at the door of a smith, who reared him and eventually restored him to his father.[85] The infant Taliesin was sewn up in a water-tight bag or coracle by his mother, Ceridwen, and thrown into the River Dyfi. The river bore him down to the sea, and he was found by Elffin in the weir of his father, Gwyddno Garanhir.[86]

The hero is disposed of in the same ways as peoples in many parts of the world dispose of children whose existence is an affront to what is considered normal. Exposure was a widespread practice, and so was committal to the waters. It is said that the continental Celts used to submit the question of the legitimacy of their offspring to the judgement of the Rhine. 'Bastards were drowned, but the river bore the true born on its surface to land.'[87] Speke mentions a similar practice observed in Africa, and it is said that in India children were sometimes placed in wicker baskets and set adrift on the river, the child's future caste being determined by the place where it was washed up.[88] In Ireland too, in the case of certain categories of incestuously conceived children, 'the law is that he be put in a leather box out to sea as far as a white shield will be visible on the sea. But if it is in the same land he chances again he gives the service of a "fuidir" to the sons of his father's first wife and he is like every illegitimate son in the kindred.'[89]

Just as both gods and demons are supernatural, and both the 'inner' and 'outer fifth' extra-territorial, so the bastard and the hero are both beyond the social order. This affinity of the higher and the lower category of outsider manifests itself in diverse ways. Not only are bastards, like heroes, *exposed* instead of being simply destroyed, but traditional methods of executing criminals are analogous to sacrificial rituals. Outside the Indian caste system there are outcasts who have transgressed the laws of their castes and also homeless 'holy men', some of whom wear rags or the traditional ochre-coloured garb of the condemned criminal as a sign that they are dead to the social hierarchy.[90] The hero and the way he is treated cannot be explained away in terms of bastardy, but there is a connection between the two categories—the affinity of extreme opposites.

The personification of the hostility with which the advent of the hero is greeted varies. In some stories, the resistance is offered by his mother, or his maternal grandfather or uncle; in others it is offered by his father, or his stepmother, or by the king. Equally various are the motives for resisting his coming. But the resistance itself is one of the most constant features of birth-stories, not only in the Celtic lands, but throughout the world.[91] It is inevitable that the intrusion of the universal into the world of particular things should be resisted. The phenomenon is a miracle, an incongruity which challenges all the pre-suppositions of that world as a self-contained and self-sufficient reality. The intruder must be repelled as a potential danger, an illegitimate who has no right to be there, an in-cestuously conceived enigma, or a monstrosity. And as we have shown, these reactions are by no means groundless. From the worldly point of view, the universal cannot but appear chaotic. In the interest of law and order, normality and morality, the disturbance from the Other World must be repressed and forgotten. And so, the infant prodigy is expelled to the wilder-ness beyond the confines of ordered life, or to the waters of non-existence, the otherworld chaos to which he belongs.

Alternatively, he is denied a name and thus kept outside the cosmic pale where everything that exists has a name.

Unlike the ordinary unwanted children, the infant hero does not die. Notwithstanding, or indeed by virtue of, his abnormal origin, he comes to land again. But this time he arrives *incognito*—a foundling whose parentage is unknown or concealed. His voyage is his 'invasion', the process whereby he comes more assuredly to earth. Oftener than not, the people who find him are of humble status and he is reared by these before he claims his birthright in more exalted circles. If he was an outcast before, he now takes his place in the home of a smith or among fishermen, cowherds, or swineherds. This accords with the social doctrine of India: 'Before initiation a boy was theoretically a Sudra; that is, one not admitted to the ritual. On initiation he becomes a Brahman, or a nobleman, or a farmer'[92]—he is admitted into one of the three castes of the 'twice-born'. There is evidence from India too that the children of some high castes were given to a pastoral people or a cowherd caste for fosterage, and it is significant that an edict incorporated in the Theodosian Code forbids parents to entrust their children in this way to the care of shepherds. The Welsh Laws contain a stipulation concerning the rights of a free-born child fostered by the king's villeins, and there is a Norse saying that 'he is a lesser man who fosters another's child.'[93]

On the other hand, not all heroes are reared among the lower orders. Niall was found by a poet, Pryderi by a lord, Cormac by a king, and Taliesin by a king's son, while in tales wherein the hero is actually given in fosterage the foster-father is usually of high rank, though the hero may have foster-brothers of a status inferior to his own. Fosterage was a very important institution in Ireland, but, apparently, the Irish Laws give no clear indication of the social standing of the foster-parents to whom the upbringing and education of the sons of kings and nobles was usually entrusted. Some sources show that it was a mark of status for a child to have several fosterers.[94] Four of Conchobar's warriors contest the honour of fostering

CúChulainn, an honour already granted to the child's aunt, Findchoem, and it may not be fanciful to discern in their claims traces of the pattern of functions discussed in Part II. The first to speak is Sencha, who in various stories is the peace-maker who acts as a foil to Bricriu the creator of discord. Like Bricriu, Sencha stands aside from the contentions of the chief warriors. He claims that besides being strong, noble, and skilful in combat he is an *ollam*, wise and not forgetful. He addresses people in the king's presence; he arbitrates before the king in battle and he judges for the Ulstermen. Blaí the Hospitaller (*Briugu*), the next to speak, protests that if the child is entrusted to him, neither neglect nor contempt shall destroy him. It is he who calls together the men of Ireland; he entertains them for a week; he supports their skills and their plunderings and sustains them when they are defamed and in honour contests. Next, Fergus boasts of his valour and his prowess, his rank and his wealth. He is a champion who gives protection against every evil; he lays low the mighty and upholds the weak. Finally, Amairgen claims that he is praised not only for his valour but also for his wisdom, his good fortune, his age and his eloquence. He is a poet and the bane of every chariot-warrior. In the event, each of them is given the share in the boy's up-bringing that befits the particular qualifications he claims.[95]

During childhood the extraordinary nature of the hero is revealed, not so much by his ancestry as by his own preco-ciousness. Though an infant, he speaks like a sage, expressing himself in poetry and pronouncing judgments. He grows with superhuman rapidity and becomes the master of various skills at an absurdly early age. While still a child, he can don the king's armour, slay a monster, or present himself at the king's court with an assurance that leads to the recognition of his identity. Taliesin when taken from the sea claims to know more than his rescuer can ask him, and at the age of thirteen he dumbfounds the king's bards and again reveals that he bears within him the history of the world and the lore of the ages.[96] 'I am old, I am new. . . .' 'I have been dead, I have been alive. . . . I am Taliesin.'[97] Such a being had no need to grow up. Neither is what is essential in man subject to the processes of physical growth.

When he is expelled or lost, the hero is still a nameless nonentity. But he acquires a name when he reappears. Conchobar is named from the river from which he is rescued. Elffin on finding the nameless child in the bag in his father's weir exclaims: 'What a beautiful brow (*tâl iesin*).' 'Taliesin be it,' says the child, accepting the name. Lug after being taken back across the sea to Tory Island gains a name from his unwitting grandfather. Lleu, arriving at Aranrhod's fortress by sea in Gwydion's magic ship, likewise wrests a name from his hostile mother. Conall Cernach is given a name from the assault by his uncle which nearly kills him, Pryderi from his mother's first remark on hearing of his return. In each case it seems to have been thought appropriate to name the child from an exclamation made on the spur of the moment, as though truth were unwittingly revealed in a moment of thoughtlessness.

A comparison between the exposure of the hero, particularly by immersion or by setting him adrift, and the sacrificial ritual of baptism is therefore inescapable. Baptism is a death and rebirth ceremony by which a child is named and is given new 'parents' who accept responsibility for the way in which he is brought up. In the West of Ireland to the present day a new-born child is palpably within the grip of unseen forces, and precautions have to be taken lest it be borne away by the fairies.[98] It will be remembered that it was a supernatural claw that snatched Pryderi from his mother's side. The danger of abduction is greatly reduced by baptism, and the child is sometimes given a temporary name, or a lay baptism is resorted to, to protect it until the proper ceremony can be arranged. Baptism is also widely believed to be efficacious in restoring a child to health, that is, in preventing it from slipping back into the unseen world. By being returned through water to the world beyond and brought back again by the appropriate ritual, the child is separated more completely from its uncanny associations with the unseen world. From now on, its relations with that world will be channelled through the proper rites.

When the fairies steal a child, they are prone to leave one of their own progeny in its stead. These 'changelings',[99] ugly, old-looking, peevish, and insatiable as they are, resemble in their precociousness the infant hero. They are recognizable by their adult speech, and they are sometimes induced to speak, and thus to reveal their true identity, through the performance in their presence of some absurd act, such as cooking in an egg-shell. Their remarks betray an agelessness like Taliesin's. 'I remember seeing an acorn before an oak, a nut before a hazel, but have never seen brewing done in an egg-shell.' Or, according to a Breton variant: 'I remember when they were building Babel, and never heard before of a brewery of egg-shells.' To the suggestion that he should be christened, one of them is said to have responded with roaring and screeching that would frighten the Danes. (It will be recalled that it was through baptism that Dylan returned to his element.) Methods of banishing the changeling and retrieving the lost child included abandoning the former on a dung-hill or in a boundary ditch, exposing it to fire or casting it into a river or lake. The real child would then be restored. If we are right in interpreting the changeling as a personification of the other-wordly side of the human child's nature, these tales may refer to a pre-Christian rite analogous to baptism, whereby the human child itself was ritually 'expelled' or 'exposed' so as to separate it from the supernatural and save it from being possessed by its mysterious 'other' self.

CHAPTER XII

Youthful Exploits

BORN WITH THE WISDOM of a sage or the strength of a champion and growing twice as fast as his fellows, the hero soon abandons childish things, and his triumphant intrusion upon adult society is one of the universal themes of mythology. The spectacular 'epiphany' of Lug described in Chapter II is a notable example. Wizard prodigies in particular seem to require no education in their art. While still a child, Taliesin could dumbfound all the king's wise men with his poetic eloquence.[1] Ambrosius (the Merlin of Geoffrey of Monmouth) was called a boy without a father in the course of a quarrel with one of the boys with whom he happened to be playing ball. The taunt was overheard by emissaries who were searching for such a boy to serve as a foundation sacrifice for a new citadel which was being built for King Vortigern. All efforts to build the citadel had proved of no avail, for whatever materials were gathered to the site by day disappeared during the night, and Vortigern's druids had declared that the building would never be accomplished unless the ground were sprinkled with the blood of a child without a father. Brought thither, the boy asked the king who it was that had instructed him to kill him. 'My wise men,' he replied. 'Order them thither,' said the boy. He then asked them by what means the procedure they had proposed was revealed to them. Promising the king that he would unfold everything to him, he questioned them further: 'What is hidden under this pavement?', but they did not know. 'There is a pool. Come and dig.' They did so and found the pool. 'Now tell me what is in it,' but they were ashamed and made no reply. 'There are two vases in the pool.' These were found, and while the druids remained silent to his questioning he revealed that in the midst of the vases there was a tent and in it two serpents (*vermes*), the one white and the other red. The serpents began to struggle with each other; at first the white one seemed to be the stronger, but at length the red one rallied and drove its adversary from the tent and through the pool. Ambrosius asked the wise men what the omen signified, but they admitted their ignorance. He then explained that the pool was the world, the tent Vortigern's kingdom, the red serpent Vortigern's dragon, the white that of the English who eventually would be expelled. The boy ordered Vortigern to depart and to build himself a fortress elsewhere. 'I, to whom fate has allotted this mansion, shall remain here.' And the king assigned him that city and all the western province of Britain.[2]

It was a playmate's jibe about his obscure parentage that initiated the course of events which led to the Mac Óc's being recognized by the Dagda as his son and to the ousting of Elcmar from the Bruig.[3] Similarly, Cormac struck one of his foster-brothers at play and the latter cried that he had been stricken by a fellow 'whose clan and race are unknown, except that he is a gentleman without a father'. Cormac complained to his foster-father and learned that he was King Art's son and that he was destined to the kingship which Lugaid Mac Con had usurped. Accompanied by his foster-father and by the wolves with whom he had been suckled, he came to Tara, where Mac Con took him into fosterage. It then happened that Mac Con pronounced judgement on a woman whose sheep had eaten the queen's crop of woad. The judgement was that the queen should have the sheep in compensation for the woad. 'No,' said Cormac, 'the shearing of the sheep is sufficient to offset the cropping of the woad, for both will grow again.' 'That is the true judgement,' exclaimed all, 'it is the son of the true prince who has given judgement,' and the part of the house where the false judgement had been given fell down the slope. Mac Con was then deposed in favour of Cormac.[4]

We read in 'The Destruction of Da Derga's Hostel' how the young Conaire was called from his play to attend a 'bull feast' at Tara. This was a divination rite in which a bull was killed and a man ate his fill of it and drank the broth. A spell of truth was sung over the man and in his sleep he would see the destined king. On this occasion the diviner had seen a stark naked man with a stone in his sling going along one of the roads to Tara. As Conaire rode in his chariot, he saw some great white-speckled birds and pursued them into the sea. The birds cast their bird-skins and turned upon him with spears and swords, but one of them protected him, saying: 'I am Nem- glan, king of your father's birds.' And he explained that Conaire must not cast at birds because they were his kin. Directed by the bird-man the boy went his way naked, and three kings were waiting on each of the four roads to Tara with royal garments to clothe him. He was placed in a chariot and in- stalled as high-king.[5]

In another account of Conaire's inauguration[6] the boy is not received with such a demonstration of good will. He pro- ceeded to Tara accompanied by his mother, who was a sor- ceress, and a formidable army which, presumably, she had conjured from the *Síd*. The hosts of Tara withdrew, leaving the chariot of kingship to them. This chariot would tilt up before anyone not destined to receive the kingship, the horses would spring at him, and the king's mantle that was in the chariot would be too big for him. But the horses stayed for Conaire, and the chariot received him. Standing in the pre- sence of the hosts he donned the mantle and it fitted him. The chariot moved towards the two stones Blocc and Bluigne and they opened before him. Fál cried out, and the hosts cried 'Fál has accepted him'. Declining to give battle, the hosts in Tara made submission to Conaire and gave him his father's heritage.

2

While we hear little of the childhood of most mythological personages, the 'Youthful Exploits' (*Macgnímartha*) of CúChu- lainn and Finn are stories in their own right. The careers of

these two heroes from infancy to young manhood could appro-
priately be described as successions of epiphanies. The Ulster
exiles, Fergus and his companions, recount the boyish feats of
CúChulainn to the anxious Queen Medb before she sets out
to oppose him in the fateful Cattle-raid of Cuailnge.[7] In his
fifth year he had set out alone to Emain Macha to join King
Conchobar's boy-corps, playing with his toy weapons as he
ran. Breaking the rules of entry into the corps, he gate-crashed
into the boy's game, carrying all before him, and when the boys
threatened him with death as an intruder he scattered the whole
hundred-and-fifty of them. At the demand of the four-year-old,
Conchobar placed the boys under his protection, and in no
time he was the king's favourite, doing what he liked with the
boys at play, giving mortal hurt to fifty of them in a fight and
defeating the whole corps single-handed at team games. One
day in the following year, Conchobar and his men went to a
feast given by Culann the smith, leaving CúChulainn (or
Setanta as he was called until then) to follow when he had
finished his game. When Conchobar's party were safely in the
smith's house, and had forgotten all about the lad, their host
let loose the monstrous hound which guarded his land. As
CúChulainn arrived, the hound charged at him with open
jaws, but the boy threw his ball into its throat and taking hold
of the creature by two of its legs he dashed it to pieces against
a pillar-stone. Conchobar and his men rejoiced at finding the
child alive; the smith lamented the loss of his watchdog.
CúChulainn then assumed the dog's duty, and from that
he was named CúChulainn, 'The Hound of Culann'; his
guardianship of the smith's domain symbolized his future role
as the guardian of Ulster.

In his seventh year the boy happened to overhear Cathbad
the druid tell his pupils that the life of the youth who took arms
that day would be short, but that he would win eternal fame.
CúChulainn went at once to Conchobar to demand arms.
Fifteen sets were offered him in succession but he smashed each
one of them and was satisfied only when furnished with the

king's own weapons. Then he shattered twelve chariots and was given the king's war-chariot. After a ride to the playing-fields to receive the salutations of the boys, he bade the king's charioteer drive him to the Look-Out Ford on the frontier, where Conall Cernach, the Ulster champion, was keeping watch and ward of the province. There the lad broke the shaft of Conall's chariot so that he could not follow him, and entering alien territory he challenged the three terrible Sons of Nechta Scéne to combat. The first could be harmed neither by the points nor by the edges of weapons; the second, if he were not defeated with the first blow, would never be defeated, and the third could traverse the sea with the swiftness of a swallow. CúChulainn slew all three of them. On his way home he ran down two stags and shot down a number of swans without killing them. With the wild deer tied behind his chariot, the tethered swans flying over it, and the heads of the three sons of Nechta Scéne in the chariot, he approached Emain Macha in battle rage. To subdue his fury, the Ulstermen sent their women forth naked to meet him, and when he hid his face from them he was plunged into three vats of cold water. The staves and hoops of the first vat burst asunder with the heat, the second vat boiled, and even in the third the water became hot. When he had been calmed, they dressed him in fresh raiment and henceforth he took his place between the two feet of the king.

The youthful hero's departure from his mother's home, the threat to his life when he joins the youth group, the contests, the acquisition of a new name, the taking of arms and the first foray, all recall variants of the world-wide rites by which boys are initiated and sent out to blood their weapons and to win a scalp or a head. CúChulainn's assumption of the role of Culann's dog compares with the magical identification of the Scandinavian *berserkir* with wolves and of members of African men's societies with leopards and other beasts of prey, while his slaughter of the dog with his bare hands brings to mind the initiation test of unarmed combat, with a wild boar or wolf, which prevailed among the Heruli. 'Wolf', in particular, is 'the cognomen of members of Indo-European military frater-nities.'[8]

CúChulainn's crossing of the frontier and his combat with the three supernatural Sons of Nechta Scéne has been identi-fied as an ancient Indo-European initiation *scenario* of a struggle with three monsters or with one three-headed monster.[9] The battle fury in which he returns to his people is analogous to the ' "extreme heat" and "rage" which, on other levels of sacrality, characterizes the incarnation of power.'[10] This asso-ciation of heat with the warrior's frenzy has been shown to exist both among Indo-European peoples and among peoples who cannot be shown to have had any historical connection with them. Professor Dumézil has drawn the analogy between the cooling of CúChulainn's ardour and certain features of the initiation rites of the secret Cannibal Society of the Kwakiutl of British Columbia.[11] After rituals involving seclusion in the bush, the consumption of human flesh, entry into the cult-house and a symbolical ascent to the world of the gods, the initiate is no longer a mere human being. When he returns to the village after three or four months' absence, he behaves like a wild beast, biting the arms of whomsoever he meets and swallowing bits of the flesh, and it takes four men to hold him. The woman who has served him in the bush now appears and dances naked before him, with a corpse in her arms. He climbs on to the roof of the cult-house, removes a few of the planks, jumps into the interior and dances in ecstasy, trembling in every limb. To calm him the 'Attendant' seizes him by the head, drags him out until they are both up to their waists in the salt water, and plunges him four times in the water.

Macgnímartha Finn[12] has a number of features in common with the story of CúChulainn. Thus Finn encounters a group of boys on the green of a fort. He beats them all together at their games, and when the man of the fort incites them to kill him and they all throw their hurleys at him, he again defeats them. In response to a challenge, he even drowns nine of them. It is during this encounter that he is named Finn ('the Fair'): hitherto he was called Demne. Like CúChulainn, Finn cap⁄tures two wild stags, and on another occasion he brings home a live duck after shooting it.[13] But the story as a whole is less spectacular than CúChulainn's.

Finn was brought up secretly in a forest by two warrior women because his hereditary enemies, the Sons of Morna, were lying in wait for him. On leaving the women he wandered *incognito*, but his skill as hunter and *fidchell*⁄player betrayed his identity when he entered the service of one king after another. Then he came to a chief smith who gave him his daughter to sleep with and made two spears for him. After bidding farewell to the smith, he slew an extraordinary sow which was devastat⁄ing the country, and returned with its head as a bridal gift to the smith for his daughter. Going his way again, Finn met and slew the warrior who had dealt the first wound to his father in his last battle.

At last, after a visit to some of the old *fian* in a desert wood, Finn came to learn poetry from Finnéces on the Boyne. For seven years Finnéces ('Finn the Poet') had been watching the salmon of Féc's Pool; for it had been prophesied of him that he would eat the salmon of Féc, when nothing would remain unknown to him. The salmon was found, and Demne (as Finn called himself) was ordered to cook it but not to eat any of it. The youth brought the cooked salmon. 'Have you eaten of the salmon, my lad?' said the poet. 'No', said he, 'but I burned my thumb and put it into my mouth afterwards.' 'What is your name my lad?' said he. 'Demne', said the youth. 'Finn is your name, my lad,' said he, 'and to you was the salmon given to be eaten, and truly you are Finn.' Finn then ate the salmon. It was thus that knowledge was given to Finn: whenever he put his thumb into his mouth, and sang through *teinm laída*, then whatever he did not know would be revealed to him.

After this, Finn went to the poet Cethern son of Fintan for further teaching. At that time there was a beautiful fairy maiden in Síd Breg Éle. Many of the men of Ireland had tried to woo her on Samain Eves when nothing could be hidden in the *síd*-mounds, but the only reward that each had got for his pains was that one of his people was slain, while no one knew by whom it was done. When this happened to Cethern, who 'like everyone else' went to woo the maiden, Finn sought the advice of the champion Fiacail mac Conchinn, and was instructed to go and sit down between the two mountains called the Paps of Anann. Sitting there on the Eve of Samain, Finn saw the two fairy hills (that were between the two Paps) open, revealing a great fire inside each, and he heard voices on either side of him discussing an exchange of gifts between the inhabitants of the two *síde*. Then a man came out of one of the hills and proceeded towards the other, carrying a kneading trough and on it a pig, a cooked calf, and a bunch of garlic. Finn threw Fiacail's spear at him and heard wailing in the fairy-hill from which he came. It transpired that the victim was the slayer of the wooers' men.

Fiacail set out to a tryst with the *fian*, and Finn insisted on going along too in spite of Fiacail's belief that the lad could never keep pace with him. Fiacail carried twelve leaden balls around his neck to curb his swiftness, and as they went along he threw off one ball after another. Finn picked them up, bringing the twelve with him to the end of the journey, and Fiacail's running was no swifter than Finn's. Keeping watch that night, Finn heard three fairy women wailing on a fairy-mound, and he snatched the brooch of the cloak of one of them as she was entering the mound. As a reward for returning the brooch, she presented him with a vessel full of gold and silver which he divided among the *fian*.

Here again we have typical initiation motifs—separation from motherly care, the new name, the acquisition of arms, and victory over a wild beast. The story tallies at several points with the ritual by which youths were admitted into the *fiana*,[14] a ritual which involved the severing of family connections, and tests, not only in athletic and soldierly skills but also in the twelve forms of poetry. Particularly noteworthy is the parallel between the story of the boys throwing their hurleys all to- gether at Finn and the test in which nine warriors threw their javelins at the candidate while he defended himself with a shield and a stick. But there is nothing in the extant accounts of the rites to correspond with Finn's encounter with the adverse forces of the unseen world as he sits between the two Paps of Anann, on the borders of West Munster, during a night which does not belong to mundane time. Such an encounter is an essential feature of initiation rituals generally, and it figures in other youthful exploits of Finn, such as his victory over Aillén mac Midna (who used to burn up Tara every Hallowe'en), the victory which brought him the chieftainship of the Fiana.[15] Folktales of the Fenian Cycle also describe a visit of the youthful Finn to a strange land of giants, where after being swallowed by a monster he cuts his way out through its side and gains a magic healing cup.[16] This motif again has a wide distribution, both in story and in actual ritual. For example, ceremonial re-birth from the inside of an artificial cow was practised in India. Certain tribes in northern New Guinea[17] initiate their youths in a hut modelled in the shape of a mythical monster which symbolically swallows and disgorges them. Circumcision is explained to the uninitiated as the bite of the monster.[18] In the initiation rituals of the Bushong of the Congo, the youths pass naked through a tunnel which symbolizes the inside of a leopard and are reborn from it. Inside the tunnel, 'hammering out new men', is a smith who personifies the first ancestor, the originator of the rites.[19]

A smith plays a decisive role in the Youthful Exploits of both CúChulainn and Finn, and this is not surprising when it is realized that smithcraft has a supernatural quality and that in many parts of the world there is a close connection between iron-working and alchemy and between smiths and initiation into 'men's societies'.[20] A further Irish example of a smith as initiator occurs in the story of Niall and his four step-brothers.[21]

Mongfind sends the boys to Sithchenn, a smith who is also a magician and a seer. He gets them all into the forge and sets fire to it. Niall comes out with the anvil, and the other four brothers with the sledge-hammers, a pail of beer and the bellows, the spearheads, and a bundle of dry sticks with one green twig in it, respectively. From this the smith foretells their future. Mongfind sends them to the smith a second time to obtain arms, and he sends them forth to prove their prowess, an expedition which culminates in a further test—the encounter with the hag at the well. In several traditions the forge is symbolical of the womb,[22] and the smith's test may be regarded as a re-birth of the boys, through fire, into their respective roles.

3

Before leaving the subject of the initiation of youths, we must consider the story of 'CúChulainn's Training'. It appears as an independent tale in eighteenth century manuscripts, but we will outline the older version which is incorporated in the story of CúChulainn's wooing of Emer.[23]

Discovering that his daughter, Emer, was being wooed by CúChulainn, Forgall Monach* went to Conchobar's court in disguise and, hoping to get rid of his daughter's suitor, he recommended that the lad should go to Domnall the Warlike in Alba to complete his military education. CúChulainn set out, accompanied by Loegaire the Victorious and Conchobar.** 'When they had come to Domnall they were taught by him one thing on a flagstone with a small hole, to blow bellows. Then they would perform on it till their soles were all but black or livid. Another thing on a spear, on which they would climb. They would perform on its point; or dropping down on their soles.' Domnall's loathsome mis-shapen daughter, Dornoll ('Bigfist'), fell in love with CúChulainn, and when he refused her she vowed revenge on him.

* ? Forgall the Wily.
** In other versions: Conall Cernach.

Then Domnall told CúChulainn that he would not be fully trained until he came to Scáthach ('Shadow'), and at this the three companions set out to the abode of this female champion in the East of Alba. Then a vision of home, conjured up as it seems by Dornoll, caused his friends to forsake CúChulainn. He went on alone. On his way he encountered a dreadful beast like a lion, which fought with him, and he was subjected to foul-play by youths who laughed at him. (According to some versions the beast carried him on its back for four days, until they came to the uttermost bounds of men.) He came to a house in a glen and was welcomed by a maiden who declared that she was a foster-sister of his. He was also welcomed by a warrior and from him he learned how to cross the 'Plain of Ill-luck' that lay before him. On one half of that plain men would freeze fast; on the other half they would be raised on the grass. The warrior gave him a wheel and an apple. By following the wheel he crossed the first half of the plain, and the apple guided him the rest of the way. Then, after traversing a Great Glen by a narrow path and crossing a terrible stony height, he reached the fortress of Scáthach. (In other recensions the house was on an island and could be reached only by a perilous bridge which threw people from it unless they leapt from one side on to its middle and reached the other side by a second leap. CúChulainn successfully negotiated the bridge, much to the surprise of FerDiad and other Irish youths whom he found playing on the green before it.)

As CúChulainn knocked at the door of the fortress, his spear-shaft went through it and he was admitted by Uathach* daughter of Scáthach, who soon became his mistress. As she served him with water and food on his arrival he broke her finger, and her shriek brought the champion Cochor Crufe to combat with him. CúChulainn slew him, and when Scáthach (like Culann the smith) bewailed her loss, the youth offered to take on the man's services. On the third day, the maiden

* 'Spectre'.

advised CúChulainn to go through his salmon-leap at Scáthach when, reclining in the great yew tree, she was teaching
her two sons. He was to set his sword between her two breasts
until she gave him his three wishes: the first, that she should
teach him without neglect; the second, that she (presumably
the daughter) should wed him without payment of bride-
price; the third, that she should say everything that would befall him, for she was also a prophetess. All this was granted.

A battle broke out between Scáthach and the people of the
princess Aife,* the hardest woman-warrior in the world.
To keep him out of harm's way, Scáthach gave CúChulainn
a sleeping potion and bound him, but this only put him out
of action for an hour and he was soon fighting against three of
Aife's warriors. Then he overcame Aife herself by a trick, and
carrying her on his back he exacted from her 'three wishes':
first, that she should give hostages to Scáthach and never
oppose her again; second, that she should be with him that
night before her own fort; third, that she should bear him a
son (Conlaí) and send him to Ireland at the end of seven years.
All this was granted. On his way back, he met an old woman,
blind in her left eye. She told him to beware and not to be in
her way. 'As there was no footing on the cliff of the sea he let
himself down from the path so that only his toes clung to it.
When she passed over them she hit his great toe to throw him
down the cliff. Then he leapt the chariot-chief's salmon-leap
up again, and struck her head off.' Before CúChulainn departed for home, Scáthach foretold the great perils that awaited
him there.

The version of the tale preserved in eighteenth-century manuscripts[24] says that CúChulainn began his training 'with
Uathach of the Glen in the great fierce province of Munster'
before he set out for the land of Scáthach. Both of these places,
together with the 'Terrible Valley', the 'Green Isle', the

* 'Reflection'?

'Lonesome Isle' and the 'Eastern World', which figure in analogous adventures in Celtic folktales,[25] may be equated with the Other World entered by noviciates during initiation ceremonies. For example, the secluded forest initiation-lodges of the *ndembo* secret society of the Lower Congo are 'The Country of the Dead',[26] and descent into the infernal regions is a well-known feature of initiation, be it into shamanism or into the Mysteries of antiquity.[27]

Like CúChulainn in the land of 'Shadow', noviciates in initiation ceremonies are confronted by hostile initiators in monstrous disguises, and are taught secrets by their 'super-natural' instructors. The later texts of our story explain that the feat taught by Domnall (or his daughter) involved resting with the chest on the point of a spear without tearing dress or raiment—a feat which recalls the ordeals of Indian wonder-workers. CúChulainn 'leapt aloft hoveringly, so that he laid his breast and bosom on the sharp point of the spear, and he cared little if that were his place of rest for the whole fair day.'[28] After crossing the Bridge of the Leaps, which becomes as narrow as a hair and as slippery as an eel's tail, he is left by Scáthach's daughter at the house of the 'barbers', with the injunction that they should 'deal gently with him tonight'. They, however, throw him on to the top of the house and they all throw their spears and darts at him—a hardening process after which he will be calm though there be many armies before him.[29] In this, as in his other exploits, the hero turns the tables on his testers and vanquishes them, but it may not be without significance that they were barbers, for hair-cutting seems to have been an initiation rite in Celtic as in many other societies—we have already mentioned the humiliating hair-cut which CúChulainn received at the hands of the giant CúRoí. Furthermore, CúChulainn appears to have returned to Ireland with an 'initiation scar' upon his arm. In a mortal combat with Scáthach's gigantic son, the latter 'fell with his face on CúChulainn, so that a foretooth of the big man chanced on the top of CúChulainn's shoulder and took a piece of flesh and skin completely from him as far as the tip of his fingers. So that was CúChulainn's Shearing.'[30]

The sexual content of initiation rites is well-known, and there are sexual episodes in the tales we have told—the naked women in the story of CúChulainn's first foray, Finn's union with the smith's daughter, the quest for the woman whom everyone woos at his peril, and Finn's capture of a fairy woman as she enters the *síd*. CúChulainn consorts with Scáthach's daughter and with Aife, and according to the later texts he even wrests from Scáthach herself 'the friendship of her thighs'.[41] The feminine aspect of the Other World and the appearance of mysterious women in each class of tale are mentioned elsewhere in this book. Here we will simply observe that the union of CúChulainn with the female warriors, like Niall's union with 'Sovereignty',[32] is a marriage between an apprentice and his vocation. Craft initiations generally have a strong sexual reference, and the relation of the craftsman to his craft and materials is that of husband to wife. The farmer is the 'husband' of his land, the smith the husband of his forge. For example, among the Chishinga of Northern Rhodesia, a smith would be guilty of adultery if he slept with a human wife while his forge was 'pregnant with iron'.[33]

Initiation involves both a humiliation and an elevation to a higher plane of being; it is both a terrifying experience and the means of triumph over terror. Though the hero is exposed to foul-play, mockery and mortal danger, it is the positive, victorious side of the ordeal that is celebrated in the myth, rather than the submissiveness that one usually associates with youths undergoing initiation. During the course of initiation, the noviciate learns that many of the frightening trials to which he is subjected are really hoaxes, and that his formidable initiators are really his elders disguised as ghosts and other supernatural beings. These secrets must not be disclosed to women and non-initiates generally; on the contrary, the latter are often regaled with deliberately exaggerated reports of the cruelty of the ordeal and the heroism of the noviciates. Sometimes the noviciates themselves, at the end of the ceremonies, put on masks and invade the village to terrify the uninitiated.[34] It may also be note-worthy that Finn, in the land of giants, 'put his finger under his wisdom-tooth and found out that they were people under glamour (*sgleo*), that they were not really bigger than other people and that he could kill them all if he tried.'[35] The dis-covery that the truth of myth belongs to the realm of drama rather than to ordinary life should not, however, be dismissed as a disillusionment in the modern sense of the word. While it brings a liberation from childish fears it also exalts the novi-ciate. As an initiate into the mysteries he can now identify himself with supernatural beings and personify them in the rites.

The function of initiation as a means of education in the be-haviour appropriate to everyday adult life is well known. Equally important, however, is the ritual transgression of taboos, the indulgence in excesses which break the bounds of everyday life. The Kwakiutl noviciate into the Cannibal Society eats human flesh, an 'inhuman' act which the un-initiated contemplate with horror, but an act through which the noviciate attains a god-like transcendence over the rights and wrongs of ordinary life.[36] In Buddhist Tantric rites the devotee partakes of the sacrament of the 'five forbidden things' —wine, meat, fish, parched grain, and sexual intercourse— and in so doing rises to a height which is beyond the law.[37] If we view the audacity and the excesses of the hero from this standpoint, he seems to personify not only the initiate but the inner meaning of initiation. He is the victory, the embodiment of a spirit which no boundaries can contain.

CHAPTER XIII

Wooings

IT WILL BE REMEMBERED that CúChulainn's perilous adventure in the land of Scáthach was contrived by Forgall
Monach, the hostile father of his future bride Emer, when he
discovered that the young hero had been to his fort to woo the
maiden. Forgall was a nephew of Tethra, King of the Fomoire,
and his fortress in Brega was called Luglochta Loga, 'The
Gardens of Lug'. Before CúChulainn drove to it in his
chariot, nine men had been searching every province in Ireland
for a whole year in the hope of finding in some stronghold a
maiden it might please CúChulainn to woo, but their search
had been of no avail. Though Forgall's fortress was in Ireland,
the journey there was a metaphorical adventure into a mysterious world. Conversing in riddles with Emer, CúChulainn
says that he passed the night in 'the house of a man who calls
the cattle of the plain of Tethra', and he has come 'between the
Two Props of the Woodland, from the Darkness of the Sea,
over the Great Secret of the Men of the Gods, over the Foam
of the Two Steeds of Emain, over the Field of the Morrígan,
over the Back of the Sea Pig, over the Valley of the Great Ox,
between the God and his Prophet, over the Marrow of the
Woman Fedelm, between the Boar and his Dam, over the
Washing-place of the Horses of the Gods, between the King
of Ana and his Servant, to the Food Storehouse of the Four
Corners of the World, over Great Ruin and the Remnants of
the Great Feast, between the Vat and the Little Vat, to the
Daughters of the Champion of Tethra, King of the Fomoire,
to the Gardens of Lug.'[1] When the hero goes a-wooing, the
drive from Ulster to Brega becomes a ceremonial progress into
the world beyond.

On returning from the land of Scáthach, CúChulainn set
out again in his scythe chariot for Forgall's fortress, leaped over

the three ramparts of the fort and 'dealt three blows in the fort, so that eight men fell from each blow, and one escaped in each group of nine, namely Scibur, Ibur, and Cat, the three brothers of Emer.' Forgall fell to his death from a rampart as he fled from CúChulainn, and the triumphant hero carried off Emer and her foster-sister with their weight in gold and silver. Escaping towards Ulster, they were pursued by Forgall's men, and CúChulainn had to pause at various historic places on the way to do battle with them. But the incidents of the struggle were no mere contingencies. During the punning conversation of the lovers at their first encounter, CúChulainn had seen the breasts of the maiden over the bosom of her smock. And he said: 'Fair is the plain, the plain of the noble yoke.' 'No one comes to this plain,' said she, 'without leaping the hero's salmon-leap, bringing out two women with their weight in gold and silver, and at one blow slaying three times nine men but saving one man in each group of nine.' In the event, CúChulainn and his adversaries were simply going through the motions of a drama, the course of which had been pre-ordained before the action began.

Before we comment on the prodigious difficulties encountered by the most admired young man in Irish story when seeking the bride of his choice, we will outline two other tales of a similar character as a basis for discussing the salient features of a hero's marriage. The first is an Irish tale in which the winning of a bride is the direct objective of a journey like CúChulainn's journey to the land of Scáthach; the second, the best known 'wooing' in Welsh, is an elaborate version of the widespread type of tale in which the fulfilment of difficult tasks is a condition of marriage.

While Art son of Conn is playing *fidchell* at Tara with his stepmother Bécuma (a woman from the Land of Promise), the *Síd*-men steal the pieces and he loses the game. Bécuma lays a *geis* on him to search for Delbchaem* daughter of Morgan,

---

* 'Fair Shape'.

who dwells on an isle amid the sea. He sets out and finding a coracle on the shore he travels in it from island to island until he comes to a strange island full of apple⁄trees and lovely birds and bees, where a company of ever⁄beautiful women dwell in a house thatched with bird⁄feathers and equipped with a crystal bower and inexhaustible vats. Among the women is Créide Fírálaind.* She gives him a splendid mantle and, seeing that it fits him, she welcomes him as Art son of Conn—'and it is long since that thy coming has been decreed'. As he takes his leave after staying with her for six weeks, she warns him of the perils ahead and advises him how to deal with them. 'There is sea and land between you (and her). . . . There is a great dark ocean between you, and deadly and hostile is the way there; for that wood is traversed as though there were spear⁄points of battle under one's feet, like leaves of the forest under the feet of men. There is a luckless gulf of the sea full of dumb⁄mouthed beasts on this side of that immense wood. And an enormous oak forest, dense and thorny before that mountain, and a narrow path through it, and a dark house in the mysterious wood at the head of the same path, with seven hags and a bath of lead awaiting you, for your coming there has been fated. And there is somewhat more grievous still, even Ailill Dubhdédach** son of Mongán Mínscothach.† And weapon cannot harm him. And there are two sisters of mine there. . . . There are two cups in their hands—a cup filled with poison, and one filled with wine. And the cup which is on your right hand drink from it when you have need. And near at hand is the stronghold of the maiden. It is thus: with a palisade of bronze round about it, and on every stake of it the head of a man slain by Coinchend, save on one stake alone. . . .' Coinchend, wife of Morgan, was a monstrous warrior⁄woman. She was fated to die when her daughter married.

* Fírálaind: 'Truly Beautiful'.
** 'Black⁄toothed Ailill'.
† Mínscothach: 'Tender Blossom'.

On his way, Art also crosses a sea full of monsters, a forest in which he encounters evil hags, an icy mountain, a forked glen full of toads, a mountain infested with lions, and a narrow bridge over an icy river. He then overcomes the giant door-keeper of Morgan's fort, whom he finds sharpening his teeth with a pillar-stone. Despite all obstacles and opponents, he arrives at the stronghold in the Land of Wonders where Delb-chaem, the king's daughter, is housed in a bower set high on a single pillar. He slays Coinchend and Morgan and after taking possession of the Land of Wonders he brings Delb-chaem to Ireland as his bride and banishes his stepmother from Tara.[2]

In the story of Kulhwch and Olwen, the stepmother of Kulhwch son of Kilydd swears upon him a destiny, that he shall never win a wife until he wins Olwen daughter of Ysbad-daden Benkawr,* and love of the maiden enters his every limb. He sets out in splendid array to the court of Arthur, his first cousin, and after a parley with the porter he boldly enters the hall on horseback, regardless of the rules, when Arthur and his warriors are feasting. The boon he asks for is that Arthur shall trim his hair and that he shall get him Olwen—invoking her in the names of Arthur's warriors, with whom are included a host of the supernatural *personae* of Welsh tradition.

For a whole year, messengers search in vain for the where-abouts of Olwen. Then Kei, Bedwyr, Kynddylig Kyfar-wydd,** Gwrhyr Gwalstawd Ieithoedd,† Gwalchmei and Menw set out with Kulhwch, declaring that they will not leave him until she is found or until he says she does not exist. They approach a great fort, and not far from it they meet the shepherd Custennin tending sheep on top of a mound. From him they learn that Ysbaddaden and Olwen dwell in

---

* Ysbaddaden 'Chief Giant' or 'Giant Head'.
** 'Kynddylig the Guide'.
† 'Gwrhyr Interpreter of Languages'.

the fortress, and that no one on such a quest as theirs has ever returned from there alive. They enter Custennin's house, and with his wife's connivance Olwen is brought to meet them there in all her glory. Kulhwch recognizes her: 'Ah maiden, it is you I have loved. Come with me.' But she has promised not to leave without the counsel of her father, who is destined to die when she is married.

Silently slaying the gatemen and the watchdogs, Kulhwch and his companions enter the presence of Ysbaddaden and declare their quest. Servants raise the giant's eyelids with forks, so that he may see his prospective son-in-law, and he promises to give his answer next day. As they leave, he throws a poisoned spear at them. Bedwyr catches it and hurls it back, wounding Ysbaddaden in the knee. A similar exchange takes place on the next two days, when Menw throws back a second spear, wounding the giant in the chest, and Kulhwch pierces his eye with a third. On the fourth day, Ysbaddaden agrees to give his daughter to Kulhwch if he will accept his conditions.

In a long parley, the giant sets Kulhwch thirteen difficult tasks. As each task is prescribed, Kulhwch makes the 're-sponse': 'It is easy for me to get that, though you think it is not easy,' and the giant proceeds to the next task with: 'Though you get that, there is something you will not get.'

The accomplishment of these major tasks is a preparation for the nuptial feast. A great thicket must be cleared and the ground tilled to provide meat and drink for the guests; scattered linseed must be collected and resown to produce flax for the wedding-veil; honey nine times sweeter than that of a virgin swarm must be found to make bragget. Kulhwch must bring the cup of Llwyr son of Llwyrion to hold the drink, the horn of Gwlgawd Gododdin to pour it, the hamper of Gwyddneu Garanhir* in which everyone finds the meat he likes, the caul-dron of Diwrnach the Irishman to boil the meat, and the harp of Teirtu and the birds of Rhiannon to give entertainment.

* Long-legged Gwyddneu.

Ysbaddaden's hair must be cut and washed and his beard shaved. For this, Kulhwch must obtain the tusk of Yskithyr⁄wyn Chief Boar as a razor, the blood of the Black Witch to dress the beard, and the shears and the comb that are between the ears of Twrch Trwyth.*

No less than twenty⁄six subsidiary tasks must be performed to provide the means to accomplish those necessary for the feast—special oxen for the ploughing, special horses, dogs, leashes, a special collar and a special sword for hunting Twrch Trwyth, and the services, not only of Arthur and his huntsmen, but of supernatural personages such as Amaethon son of Dôn, Gofannon son of Dôn, Mabon son of Modron (who was taken from his mother when three nights old and whose whereabouts are unknown), and Gwyn son of Nudd (who cannot be spared from Annwfn).

With the co⁄operation of allies ranging from ants and the oldest animals to the supernatural powers invoked at the out⁄set, the tasks are successfully performed, Ysbaddaden is slain, and Olwen becomes Kulhwch's wife.[3]

Features which appear in one or more of these three tales— the dangerous journey through a strange land, the guides on the way, the initial encounter with the bride, the difficult tasks, and the escape with the bride—also appear in various combina⁄tions in a wide range of folktales. Sometimes there is an un⁄expected connection between the guides and the female side of the hero's own world. Custennin's wife is Kulhwch's mother's sister, while in a folktale the hero spends three successive nights in the dwellings of three giants who are his mother's brothers.[4] The maiden who helps CúChulainn on his way to the land of Scáthach introduces herself as his long⁄forgotten foster⁄sister. Though Créide who receives Art to the otherworld house of women is not said to be his kinswoman or his foster⁄sister, she knows his name, she has a mantle to fit him, and she has been

* Cf. *supra*, p. 70.

expecting his coming. Art succeeds in his quest thanks to her connections with, and knowledge of, the other underworld which holds the bride in its clutches. With her we may compare the faithful Luned of Arthurian romance who befriends Owain and brings about his marriage with the Lady of the Fountain,[5] or again the young kinsman who, in the form of a maiden, repeatedly brings Peredur back to the true path of his destiny.[6] In folktales the helpers are sometimes an old man, or a succession of three old men, an old woman or three old women, animals or kings of animals. We have interpreted the animals connected with the hero's childhood as expressions of the extra-conscious side of his being, and it is noteworthy that the animals that help him now are not entirely independent of him. In many cases their help is the repayment of a debt of gratitude which they owe him for the consideration and respect he once showed them when they themselves were helpless in his world.

After passing through this comparatively friendly world of the animal, the aged, and the feminine, the hero forces his entry into the hostile Other World of the bride, an Other World which is ruthlessly masculine. The bride's mother is not mentioned, or she is under enchantment, or she is a fierce Amazon who resembles the manlike Scáthach of CúChulainn's military initiation. The bride's father is a grotesque and cunning giant. If we were to interpret the mother's kin and women-helpers as the feminine substratum of man's soul, these monstrous and wily creatures, male and female, would personify the dark masculine substratum of the feminine soul. The bride herself, on the other hand, is the embodiment of all that is good, beautiful, and feminine in woman. But she too is otherworldly, albeit in a different way, and the hero must negotiate the gulf that separates her from him—he must bring her to earth from her high tower. Kulhwch first meets Olwen in the house where his mother's sister and the giant Custennin live in matrimony, a house where two worlds join, and CúChulainn makes contact with Emer through a dialogue composed of riddles whereby two worlds are spoken of at once. In the Welsh story of Llyn y Fan, the lady from the lake refuses the hero's offer of bread when she first appears before him, and again his offer of dough on her second appearance. When she appears the third time, he offers her half-baked bread—bread which is at once both baked and unbaked—and with that the gulf between their two worlds is bridged.[7] In other folktales there is yet another symbolism. A number of swans alight by a lake and, doffing their swan's dress, they bathe in the lake as maidens. The hero steals the dress of the most beautiful of them and constrains her to take him to her father.[8] As we have already noted, transformation into a swan is a mode of communication between two worlds.

After they have been brought together in this way, the girl helps the hero to avoid various perils. For example, she instructs him that, lest he be slain, he must meet her father with one foot inside and the other outside the doorway; in some cases she helps him to overcome the obstacles which her father places in the way of their marriage. Yet, her attitude towards her father is strangely ambivalent. She refuses to be abducted until his preposterous terms have been fully complied with, but she can then contemplate his death with the most unfilial indifference. Alternatively, she and her bridegroom, sometimes aided by her enchanted mother, elude the pursuing father in a magic flight.

In the popular ballads of England, Scotland, and other European countries, and in the folktales of lands ranging from Europe to Polynesia, the solving of riddles sometimes takes the place of the difficult tasks which the hero must perform to win his bride. There are also many examples of the converse of this motif, where a clever girl, by ingeniously answering her suitor's questions, or matching the tasks he sets her, wins herself a husband.[9] Finn, in wooing Cormac's daughter Ailbe, asks her a number of riddles before he invites her to share his forest life.[10] Scottish tradition connects the same motif with Finn's wooing of Gráinne, of which we shall speak in the next chapter—and it is said that Finn would not marry any lady but one who could answer all his questions.[11] In the oldest Irish version of this wooing, on the contrary, it is Gráinne who sets Finn a difficult task. She hates him and demands as her bridal gift that a couple of every wild animal should be brought to the rampart of Tara.[12]

2

In medieval Ireland and Wales, the most highly esteemed form of marriage was a contract between consenting kin-groups—marriage 'by gift of kin' (as it is termed in the Welsh laws)—and between partners of comparable status, with proper arrangements about marriage payments. Abductions were known and there were procedures whereby such *faits accomplis* could be legalized, but these were inferior kinds of marriage.[13] Similarly in more recent centuries, although temporary marriages and other irregular unions existed, the approved union, even among the common people, was a 'match' negotiated by two families. There was shrewd bargaining over brideprice and dowry, and a 'good match' in the material sense seems to have counted more than mutual attraction between bride and bridegroom.[14] How different are the marriages of mythology! Just as the hero's birth has an outward resemblance to the most disgraceful births in human society, so does his marriage have more in common with abductions and elopements than with the socially approved forms of marriage.

Yet some wedding customs express attitudes towards marriage which are strangely reminiscent of the stories we have related. As a counterpart to the sober contract, there are displays of mock-hostility. Gates are tied and rope-barriers and other obstacles impede the bridegroom's progress to church and his return with his bride, and forfeits must be paid for safe conduct. Hostile powers threatening the success of the marriage must be banished with gunshots. In parts of Ireland, on the day of bringing home the bride, the bridegroom and his friends

would ride out and meet the bride and her friends at the place
of treaty. 'Having come near to each other, the custom was of
old to cast short darts at the company that attended the bride,
but at such a distance that seldom any hurt ensued; yet it is not
out of the memory of man that the Lord of Howth, on such an
occasion, lost an eye.'[15] This brings to mind the spear-throwing
contest in 'Kulhwch and Olwen', while the escape with the
bride in the tales is recalled by Lady Wilde's description of the
bride 'placed on a swift horse before the bridegroom while all
her kindred started in pursuit with shouts and cries.'[16]

Similar accounts are given of the ceremonies observed in
eighteenth-century Wales on the morning of the wedding day.

> 'The bridegroom, accompanied with his friends on horse-
> back, demands the bride. Her friends, who are likewise on
> horseback, give a positive refusal, upon which a mock
> scuffle ensues. The bride, mounted behind her nearest
> kinsman, is carried off, and is pursued by the bridegroom
> and his friends with loud shouts. It is not uncommon, on
> such an occasion, to see two or three hundred sturdy
> Cambro-Britons riding at full speed, crossing and jostling,
> to the no small amusement of the spectators. When they
> have fatigued themselves and their horses, the bridegroom
> is suffered to overtake his bride. He leads her in triumph
> and the scene is concluded with feasting and festivity.'[17]

In Ireland the ride of the bridal party is termed 'dragging home
the bride'.[18] Thus, in the same way as CúChulainn's ride
from Emain Macha to Brega is elaborated into an invasion
of another world, so in the wedding rituals friendly neighbours
are split up into two 'hostile' forces, the bride's people are
'overcome' and the bride is abducted 'by force'.

Just as the hostility of the bride's family is expressed in ritual
rather than in earnest, so in the stories the powers of the Other
World do not make a concerted attack to destroy the hero. As
if there were rules to the game, he is given a chance to overcome
his adversaries one by one or a few at a time; or, instead of

being met with an unequivocal refusal, he is promised the girl if he can perform feats which, though apparently impossible, can nevertheless be accomplished. A curious heptad in Irish law implies that mythological suitors were not the only ones to be faced with such a challenge. Among the seven kinds of women to whom neither compensation nor honour-price was due in case of their being cohabited with unawares is 'a woman who offers upon a difficult condition, i.e. she deems it impos-sible to come to her by force, because of her strength, and she has defied him: "If thou wert able to force me I would lie with thee." She offers herself for a wonderful or difficult dowry, i.e. a bed-tick full of harp strings; a fistful of fleas; or a white-faced jet-black kid with a bridle of red gold on it; or nine green-tipped rushes; or the full of a "carrog" of finger-nail scrapings; or the full of a crow's house of wren's eggs.'[19]

In ordinary wedding customs, however, the obstacles placed in the path of the bridegroom were of a more modest kind, and impossible tasks could by their very nature be accomplished only in a figurative sense—as in the solving of riddles. In parts of Wales, the bridegroom's representatives were at first refused admission at the bride's home and a contest in verse between the two parties ensued.[20] Such contests 'in the doorway' also featured in certain seasonal rituals, and riddles were sometimes embodied in the verses.[21] Riddle contests took place in the marriage rituals of parts of Russia and central Asia until modern times, and in some cases the riddles consist of requests for impossible things. Thus, in one of the villages of the Government of Yaroslav, the 'bride-seller', sitting by the bride, invited the best man to 'bid for the bride', offering him the choice of trading either in riddles or in gold. The choice always fell upon riddles, and half a dozen or more tasks were then set by the 'bride-seller'. For example: 'Give me the sea, full to the brim, and with a bottom of silver.' The best man gave him a bowl full of beer with a coin at the bottom. 'Tell me the thing, naked in itself, which has a shift over its bosom.' He gave him a candle. 'Give me something which the master of this house lacks.' The best man then brought in the bridegroom—presumably to remedy the lack of a son-in-law.[22]

The function of impossible tasks as a means of keeping apart the denizens of two worlds is well illustrated in Indian ritual. To prevent the malevolent ghost of a woman who has died in childbirth from returning from the cremation ground, mustard seeds are strewn along the road behind her bier, for the belief prevails that the ghost can succeed in returning only if it can gather all the scattered seeds. In some places, loose cotton wool is used in the same way and, like the difficult tasks in so many stories, its collection must be accomplished in one night. Since this is deemed impossible, there is no fear of the return of the ghost once the cotton has been scattered.[23] The gathering of scattered linseed is a favourite task in Celtic stories, and this may well have a bearing upon the Hallowe'en divination rite in which a girl scatters linseed or hemp seed and calls on her future husband to come and collect, rake, or mow it. The husband's phantom form then becomes visible.[24]

In folktale versions of the Giant's Daughter theme, the hero, after the tasks have been accomplished, is confronted with the further superhuman test of seeing a distinction where there is no difference. His bride is presented to him as one of three or more sisters, pigeons, or swans, who are exactly alike, and he must identify her.[25] This too seems to have a counterpart in marriage customs. It used to be the practice among many European peoples to substitute a false bride for the real one when the bridegroom or his emissary came to fetch her from her home. In Wales, the bride was disguised, sometimes as an old woman, and the bridegroom's attendant had to identify her,[26] while it was the custom in Brittany to substitute first a young girl, then the mistress of the house, and lastly the grandmother.[27]

In sum, whereas marriage is from the overt social point of view a happy and amicable affair uniting two people who wish to be united and establishing a new bond between two kindreds, myth and ritual are at one in proclaiming the converse of this view. Peaceful and friendly on the surface, marriage symbolizes the victory of a principle from an upper realm over the sinister powers of a lower one, a victory won on the conditions set by those powers themselves. The prize is the emancipation from that lower realm of the opposite principle and the consummate union of the two. Formulated in these abstract terms, the meaning is not inconsistent with our own characterization of marriage as signifying 'the mystical union that is betwixt Christ and his Church', a Church which has been emancipated from the clutches of the Devil by a victory won against him on his own ground.

The recitation of these stories at the wedding-feasts of humble folk enlarged the meaning of the contingent act. Yet the relevance of the stories is not confined to the union of male and female. The bride as a rose among thorns may be compared with the quest-objects of other adventures, such objects as the Sword of Light, Vessels of Plenty, or the Water of Life. Like Psyche in her search for Cupid, Jason in his quest for the Golden Fleece has to perform tasks very similar to those imposed upon Kulhwch by Ysbaddaden Benkawr, and quests for marvellous objects, no less than 'Wooings', often end with a magic flight from the pursuing forces of the underworld. 'Wooings' are thus a variant of the quest for 'the treasure hard to obtain' which man needs for his wholeness and fulfilment, a treasure which must ever be wrested from the grasp of an indefatigable foe.

3

We shall now turn to the most extraordinary of all early Irish 'Wooings', a tale which, while it contains a number of elements in common with those we have already discussed, is informed by a new theme—that of the supernatural rival.[28]

The Mac Óc invites his foster-father, Midir, to spend a year at the Bruig as his guest. Midir agrees to do so if the Mac Óc will reward him with a worthy chariot, a mantle befitting him, and the maiden that surpasses all the maidens of Ireland in beauty and gentleness, namely Étaín Echraide, daughter of

Ailill, King of Ulster. The Mac Óc goes to Ulster to seek Étaín, but her father raises difficulties. The Mac Óc offers to buy her, and Ailill sets him the three tasks of clearing twelve plains, draining the land by making twelve rivers flow from it to the sea, and paying the maiden's weight in gold and silver. With the help of the Dagda, each of the first two tasks is accomplished in a single night and, with the bride-price duly paid, the Mac Óc brings Étaín home to Midir. After his first night with her, Midir is also given the chariot and the mantle he asked for.

When the year is ended, Midir departs with Étaín to his own land at Brí Léith. But his first wife, Fuamnach, who is skilled in magic, resents Étaín's presence and, striking her with a rod of scarlet quicken-tree as she sits on a chair in the middle of the house, she turns her into a pool of water. Fuamnach then goes to her foster-father, the wizard Bresal, and the wifeless Midir leaves the house to the pool into which Étaín has been trans-formed. Presently, the pool turns into a worm and the worm into a purple fly as big as a man's head. The sound of her voice and the hum of her wings give forth sweet music, her fragrance and bloom banish hunger and thirst, and the spray shed from her wings cures all sickness and disease. In this form Étaín be-comes Midir's constant companion—and he knows that she is Étaín. But Fuamnach comes again to Midir and with powerful spells from Bresal she wafts Étaín away in a magic wind so that for seven years she is unable to settle anywhere save on the rocks and waves of the ocean.

At last, the fly alights on the breast of the Mac Óc on the mound of the Bruig. He welcomes her as 'Étaín, the careworn wanderer', takes her to his house, dresses her in purple raiment and lodges her in his 'sunbower', which he takes with him wherever he goes. Presently, Fuamnach hears of the love and honour the Mac Óc bestows on Étaín, and, pretending that she wishes to make peace between her husband and his foster-son, she induces Midir to summon the Mac Óc to him. Meanwhile, she goes secretly to the Bruig and blasts Étaín out of her sunbower on the same flight as before for seven years. Ultimately, in the time of King Conchobar, she lands on the rooftree of a house in Ulster and falls into the golden beaker that stands before the wife of the champion Étar. The woman swallows her with the drink and she is reborn of her. One day when Étaín, now daughter of Étar, is bathing in the estuary with her fifty maidens, a splendidly-dressed horseman approaches and utters a lay alluding to her pre-history and the strife that will ensue because of her.

The scene now moves to Tara where Eochaid Airem is high-king. The king's subjects refuse to convene the festival of Tara because he has no queen. Eochaid dispatches envoys to seek the fairest maiden in Ireland, saying that none shall be his wife save a woman that none of the men of Ireland has known before him. They find Étaín daughter of Étar for him and he marries her. At the festival of Tara the king's brother, Ailill, falls in love with Étaín and he becomes ill lest his honour should be stained. The king's physician finds that he is suffering from one of the two pains that kill a man and that no physician can heal—the pain of love and the pain of jealousy. Then the king goes on a circuit of Ireland, leaving Étaín to look after the dying man and to perform his last rites. But Étaín's presence alleviates Ailill's sickness, and after eliciting the cause of his trouble she promises to become his paramour on a hill above the court. Thrice Étaín goes to the trysting-place at the agreed time, but on each occasion sleep prevents Ailill from keeping his appointment. Instead, a man in Ailill's form appears to her. He addresses her as Étaín Echraide, daughter of King Ailill, and declares himself to be Midir of Brí Léith, her former husband. It was he who had caused Ailill's love-sickness and his sleep, and he has come in his place to ask her to join him in his own land. She refuses to elope with him, but says she will go willingly if her husband bids her.

One summer day, King Eochaid arises and climbs the terrace of Tara, and there he is surprised to see a finely-dressed stranger, for the courts have not yet been opened. The stranger announces himself as Midir of Brí Léith and tells the king he has come to play *fidchell* with him. When Eochaid says his board is in the queen's room and that she is still asleep, Midir produces his own silver board with men of gold and bronze. It is left to Midir to fix the stake and he promises the king fifty beautiful dark grey steeds with their enamelled reins. Midir loses and departs with his board. Next morning Eochaid finds him again on the terrace and with him the fifty steeds. This time Midir offers a still more marvellous stake, but Eochaid, warned by his foster-father to be careful, imposes the famous great tasks on Midir, namely, to clear Meath of stones and to put rushes over Tethba, a causeway over Móin Lámraige and a wood over Bréifne. Midir protests, but undertakes the tasks on condition that no one watches. Eochaid, however, bids his steward spy, and it appears to him as though all the men in the world are at work, with Midir directing operations from the top of a mound they have made with their clothes. The tasks completed, Midir comes again to Eochaid with 'an evil look on him' and rebukes him for the unreasonable hardship he has imposed on him. Eochaid is ready to make amends, and again they play *fidchell*. 'What shall the stakes be?' asks Eochaid. 'The stake that either of us shall wish,' says Midir. Eochaid loses, and Midir then declares his wish: 'My arms around Étaín and a kiss from her.' After a silence, Eochaid promises: 'Come a month from to-day and that shall be given thee.'

On the appointed day Eochaid locks the courts and sets the best warriors and the war-bands of Ireland each encircling the other around Tara. Étaín serves that night, for the serving of drink is a special gift of hers. To the astonishment of the hosts, Midir appears in the midst of the house in all his splendour and demands what has been promised. When Eochaid prevaricates, Midir discloses that Étaín has agreed to join him if Eochaid sells her. 'I will not sell you indeed,' says Eochaid, 'but let him put his arms round you in the middle of the house as you are.' 'It shall be done,' says Midir. Taking his weapons in his left hand, and with the woman in his right arm, he bears her away through the skylight of the house. The hosts rise up in shame around the king, but all they see are two swans flying round Tara and going in the direction of Síd ar Femuin.

It is decided to dig up every *síd*-mound in Ireland until Étaín is regained. Eochaid and his men spend more than a year and three months searching and digging—and what they dig by day is replaced by night. Eventually, as they are razing Síd Breg Léith, Midir appears and reproaches them for the wrong they are doing him. Did Eochaid not sell him his wife? When Eochaid refuses to yield, Midir tells him that, on the understanding that the king will do him no more harm, his wife will be returned to him at the third hour on the morrow. When the hour comes, Eochaid and his company are baffled by the appearance of fifty women all in the form and raiment of Étaín, with a grey slut before them. They tell Eochaid to choose his wife now, or bid one of them stay with him. Eochaid recalls that his wife was the best in Ireland at serving drink: 'I shall recognize her by her serving.' Twenty-five of the women are placed on either side of the house with a vessel filled with liquor in the middle between them, and they serve from each side in turn. It comes to the last but one and Eochaid says of her: 'This is Étaín, though it is not her serving'—and the rest of the women depart.

It is Midir, however, who gets in the last sally. One fine day he appears to Eochaid and his wife and after again rebuking the king for his unfair behaviour he tells him that Étaín was pregnant when he took her away and she had given birth to a daughter. It is not his former wife but his own daughter that Eochaid has chosen as his present wife. By this time the daughter is herself with child—and the rest of the tale has already been told in this book as the story of the incestuous birth of Conaire Mór.

Unlike the stories we have already discussed, this tale does not say that King Eochaid married a woman from another world. On the contrary, his wife was to him the daughter of

Étar, a champion of Ulster, and he had to undertake no arduous journey to the Other World to win her. Yet, the tale appears to demonstrate the same principle as we found in the previous tales—that the woman, though in mortal guise, is essentially a being from another world. As Olwen hails 'geographically' from the Other World, Étaín hails from it 'historically', and it has by no means finished with her. She turns out to be as mysterious as any fairy bride, for she has a complicated history of previous existences. Of all this she her-self has no conscious memory, and her husband, who has made a point of marrying 'a woman that none of the men of Ireland had known before him', is unaware of the fact that he has a supernatural rival.

The supernatural suitor seems to correspond to the Indian *Gandharva*, whose presence, as we have observed, is considered necessary for conception. At weddings, the Gandharva is a kind of rival who, to the last, disputes the bridegroom's pos-session of the bride.[29] The few references to the Gandharvas (in the plural) in the *Rig Veda* show them to be spirits of the air or of the waters, but other texts associate them with moun-tains, caves, and forests, with the world of the dead, and with animals. They are half-man and half-bird. Their wives or mistresses, the Apsaras, appear as water nymphs. The Gand-harvas have charge of *soma*, or they steal *soma*; they are skilled in medicine and they are fond of women. They also appear as singers and musicians who attend the feasts of the gods, while from the time of the *Mahābhārata* their name also denotes human musicians. The Centaurs of Greek mythology are said to be cognate figures; one of the exploits most frequently attributed to them is the abduction of a betrothed woman or a bride. In the Celtic countries there are stories of the abduction of brides by fairies,[30] while the 'straw-boys' (youths disguised in straw suits and masks) who appear as uninvited guests at wedding festivities, the leader claiming the right to dance with the bride,[31] seem to have a role which corresponds still more closely to that of the Gandharvas.

While the Gandharvas are the special personifications of the supernatural lover, it is said in India that a woman is never without a husband. Until she is four years of age she is the wife of Candra (Soma); then she becomes in turn the wife of the Gandharva and of Agni, after which she becomes the wife of her human husband.[32] The order of these four seems to symbolize a process of descent or of coming to earth, for Candra is the moon, the Gandharvas are spirits of the air, while Agni (fire) presides over the earth. The details of Indian marriage rites also imply the possession of the bride by each of these divinities in turn, and such a doctrine would explain the nuptial continence which used to be customary in many parts of Western Europe. The order of precedence in Brittany is striking in the light of the Indian teaching. The first night was the night of the Good God, the second that of Saint Joseph, the third that of the Patron Saint, and the fourth the husband's night.[33]

A well-known Indian story[34] tells of a king named Pururavas whom Urvashi, an Apsara, married on condition that he embraced her three times each day, but never against her will, and that he did not let her see him undressed. But the Gandharvas, considering that her absence had been long, conspired to get her back. One night, they carried off the two pet lambs that were tied to her bed, and Pururavas leaped out to pursue them. At this they filled the sky with lightning, and Urvashi, seeing her husband naked, vanished. Searching for her in anguish, the king saw a flock of swans on a lake and they revealed themselves to him as Apsaras with Urvashi among them. She took pity upon him and told him to come on the last night of the year (by which time their son would have been born), and he should stay with her one night. He did so and before he left the golden palace where they had met, the Gandharvas offered him a wish. Forewarned by Urvashi, Pururavas replied, 'Let me be one of yourselves,' and, his wish granted, he was transformed into a Gandharva and dwelled with Urvashi evermore. According to another version she returned with him to dwell on earth. Like Urvashi, the

otherworld brides of the heroes of folktales have the peculiarity of becoming approachable at turning points in the year.
The Irish 'Dream of Oengus (the Mac Óc)'[35] offers a close
parallel to the latter part of the Indian story.

Oengus pines for the love of a beautiful maiden who for the
span of a year appears to him at night in his sleep and plays to
him upon a *timpán*. On the advice of a physician he seeks the
help of his mother, Boand, but a year's search for the maiden
proves of no avail. Then his father, the Dagda, is consulted,
and eventually Bodb, king of the *síd* of Munster, whose knowledge is celebrated throughout the whole of Ireland. After a
year's searching, Bodb discovers her at Loch Bél Dracon and
Oengus recognizes her in the midst of a hundred-and-fifty
maidens, every pair joined by a silver chain. She is Caer Ibor-
meith, daughter of Ethal Anbuail from Síd Uamain in Connacht. The Dagda has no power over her, neither has her
father to whom they go to ask for her. The latter tells them that
she spends every other year in the form of a bird and that next
Samain she will be on Loch Bél Dracon with a hundred-and-
fifty swans about her. The Dagda sends his son to the lake on
that day and there he sees the hundred-and-fifty white birds
with their silver chains and golden caps. Oengus, still in
human shape, calls the maiden to him, promising to return
with her into the lake. He puts his arms around her and sleeps
with her in the form of a swan. They circle the lake three times
and then, with Oengus's promise fulfilled, they fly to his *síd*,
where their song lulls the people to sleep for three days. And
the maiden remains there with him.

The equation of the swan-maidens and fairy brides of Celtic
story with the Indian apsaras seems a reasonable one, and
Oengus thus becomes, at least temporarily, a 'Gandharva'.
Scholars have dubbed him the Celtic God of Love, and it is
noteworthy that Kāma, 'the Indian Eros', is also called 'the
Gandharva'.[36]

CHAPTER XIV

Elopements

'To separate us two is to separate children of one home,
it is to separate body from soul . . .'
                              Gráinne's sleep-song for Diarmaid

Irish storytellers had a distinct class of tales known as Elopements (*aitheda*), and another called Loves (*serca*), which portray
the eternal triangle of two men in conflict over one woman,
and the clash between morality and erotic love. The best-
known of these tales are 'The Exile of the Sons of Uisliu' and
'The Pursuit of Diarmaid and Gráinne', while 'Trystan and
Esyllt', an Elopement whose renown rivals that of the Tale of
Troy, stems from Welsh or 'British' tradition. There are in
addition diverse less elaborate variations on the same theme,
both as independent tales and as motifs within other tales, to
which we shall have occasion to refer. But we shall begin with
a resumé of an early recension of 'The Exile of the Sons of
Uisliu',[1] which was already in writing over a thousand years ago.
    One night King Conchobar and the men of Ulster were
feasting at the house of Feidlimid, the king's storyteller, and
the storyteller's wife though pregnant was serving them. As
they were about to retire, the child in the woman's womb
screamed, and Cathbad the druid foretold the birth of Derdriu, a girl of surpassing beauty, who would bring great sorrow
to Ulster. The men of Ulster wished to kill her at birth, but
Conchobar ordered her to be reared as a wife for himself. No
one except her foster-parents and Lebarcham, the woman-
satirist to whom naught could be refused, was admitted to the
house where Derdriu was being brought up, and there, concealed from the eyes of men, she grew into the most beautiful
girl who had ever been seen in Ireland. One winter's day, seeing

her foster-father skinning a calf on the snow and a raven alight-ing to drink the blood, she declared to Lebarcham that beloved would be the man who would have hair as black as the raven, cheeks as red as the blood and a body as white as the snow. Lebarcham replied that Noísiu son of Uisliu was such a man, and from then on Derdriu pined for a glimpse of him.

Noísiu and his two brothers, the three sons of Uisliu, were valiant warriors, equal in prowess to all the other warriors of Ulster combined, and they were so swift that they could run down their quarry on foot. One day Noísiu, alone on the ram-part of Emain, uttered his musical war-cry—a cry which gave pleasure to all who heard it and induced cows to increase the yield of their milk by two-thirds. Derdriu escaped from her confinement and ran past him. 'Fair is the heifer that goes past me,' he cried. 'Well may the heifers be great,' she said, 'in a place where there are no bulls.' 'You have the bull of the whole province, the king of the Ulstermen,' said he. She replied that she preferred a young bull like him, and when he demurred she sprang upon him and, seizing his two ears, cried: 'these will be two ears of shame and of mockery unless you take me away with you.'

On hearing Noísiu's story, his brothers and their men resigned themselves fatalistically to leaving the province with him and Derdriu, though they knew that evil would ensue. For a long time they wandered through Ireland, pursued by Conchobar and the Ulstermen, and then they crossed to Scotland, where after dwelling for a time in the wilderness, they entered the service of the king. Soon, however, their lives were again in danger, for the king of Scotland had designs upon Derdriu. Learning of their plight, the men of Ulster persuaded Concho-bar to allow them to return under his protection, and Fergus, Dubthach, and Conchobar's own son, Cormac, were sent as sureties. On their return, however, the three sureties were side-tracked at the instigation of Conchobar, and Noísiu and his brothers were slain at Emain by Eogan son of Durthacht who had been entrusted to kill them. Derdriu was bound and brought to Conchobar. When Fergus and his two companions heard of the treachery, they perpetrated a great slaughter in Emain and then went into exile to the court of Ailill and Medb in Connacht, whence they harried the Ulstermen for sixteen years.

For a year Derdriu was with Conchobar, but all that time she never smiled. She ate and slept but little and she did not raise her head from her knee. Whenever they brought musicians to her, she replied with memories of the joy of her life in the woods:

> 'Though you find sweet the goodly mead
> That battle-glorious Mac Nessa drinks,
> Before now I often have had on the brink of the sea
> Food that was sweeter.
>
> 'Every time modest Noísiu prepared
> The cooking hearth on the *fian* plain of the forest,
> Always sweeter than any honeyed food
> Was what the sons of Uisliu contrived.
>
> 'Though Conchobar, your king, finds
> Pipers and hornblowers melodious,
> More melodious to me . . .
> Was the strain sung by the sons of Uisliu.'

Conchobar asked her what she hated most, and she replied, 'You yourself and Eogan the son of Durthacht.' 'Then,' said Conchobar, 'you shall be a year with Eogan.' Next day as they were leaving, Derdriu stood behind Eogan in the chariot. 'Well, Derdriu,' said Conchobar, 'it is the eye of a sheep between two rams that you make between me and Eogan!' At this Derdriu shattered her head on a great rock that was in front of them, and so she died.

In the Elopement of Diarmaid and Gráinne the plot is essentially the same. The earliest fragments of this tale date from the tenth century, but complete recensions are available only in late manuscripts and in oral tradition. Since these are long and

complicated stories which lack the restraint of the earlier version of 'Derdriu', we shall have to be content with a mere
enumeration of the points that appear relevant to our theme.[2]

1 At the wedding-feast of Finn and Gráinne daughter of
King Cormac, Gráinne administers a sleeping draught to the
whole gathering with the exception of Diarmaid and three of
his friends. She puts Diarmaid under *gessa* of danger and destruction to elope with her. He is reluctant to break faith with
Finn, but his companions tell him that he has no alternative
but to go, 'for he is a wretched man who violates his *gessa*.'

2 Pursued by Finn and the Fiana, the couple dwell as fugi-
tives in the wood. Diarmaid builds an enclosure with seven
doors of wattles and a bed of rushes and birch-tops for Gráinne.
There they are surrounded by the Fiana, but Oengus of the
Bruig comes to the rescue and bears Gráinne away under his
cloak. Diarmaid leaps clear of the Fiana and follows Oengus
and Gráinne. When Gráinne sees him coming, her heart is in
her mouth for joy.

3 Left to themselves, the two continue to wander, neither
eating where they have cooked nor resting when they have
eaten, and Diarmaid overcomes the Green Fiana whom Finn
sends by sea to slay him.

4 For a long time, though they sleep together, 'there is no sin
between them', and Diarmaid leaves raw meat at their camping-
sites as a token of their continence. Then one day as they are
walking together, water splashes on to Gráinne's leg, and she
says, 'Diarmaid, though your bravery is great in battles and
contests, I think this bold splash is more daring than you are.'
'That is true,' says Diarmaid, 'and although I have kept my-
self from you for fear of Finn, I can endure your reproaches no
longer. It is hard to trust a woman.' And then Diarmaid makes
a wife of Gráinne.

5 Diarmaid gets permission from a one-eyed giant to hunt in
his territory, provided he does not touch the berries of his
magic tree. But Gráinne, who is now pregnant, longs for the
berries, and Diarmaid slays the giant. They climb the tree

and eat the life-giving berries; the berries below are bitter compared with those above. While they are together in the giant's bed on top of the tree, they are again surrounded by Finn and the Fiana, but they escape, Gráinne with the help of Oengus, Diarmaid by leaping.

6 After further encounters, Oengus makes peace between Finn and Diarmaid. Diarmaid and Gráinne are given lands in Connacht, and there they bring up four sons and a daughter.

7 'On the last day of the year,' Diarmaid joins Finn in hunting the Wild Boar of Ben Gulban. (The boar is really Diarmaid's foster-brother by whom he is destined to fall.) Diarmaid slays the boar, but is wounded by one of its poisonous bristles. Only water from the healing hands of Finn can save him. Reluctantly, Finn goes for water, but, remembering Gráinne, he lets it run through his fingers. He does this twice, and when he returns the third time Diarmaid is dead. Oengus comes and bears away the body to the Bruig of the Boyne.

8 The ending varies. In some versions Finn and Gráinne are ultimately reconciled; in others Gráinne mourns Diarmaid as long as she lives.

The oldest extant versions of 'Trystan and Esyllt' are to be found, not in Celtic sources, but in medieval German and French Romance. Yet the similarities between them and the Irish stories we have outlined are so obvious that scholars have long since reached the conclusion that 'Trystan and Esyllt' is derived from Irish prototypes.[3] More recently, Professor Carney has argued the alternative possibility that 'Diarmaid and Gráinne', and even 'Noísiu and Derdriu', are to be traced back to a 'primitive Trystan'.[4] However, the question as to whether the archetype was a primitive 'Trystan', a primitive 'Diarmaid', or a primitive 'Noísiu' does not seriously concern us in this work.

An anomalous Welsh version of 'Trystan',[5] preserved in a sixteenth-century manuscript, reveals a definite seasonal symbolism. Trystan elopes with Esyllt, wife of March ap Meirchion, to the woods of Kelyddon. Trystan's page is Bach

Bychan ('Little Little-one') and Esyllt's maid is Golwg Hafddydd ('Aspect of Summer's Day'). They bring tarts and wine with them and a bed of leaves is made for the lovers. March complains to Arthur, who then goes with him to seek the offender. After setting out to fight March, Trystan passes unharmed through three armies and Kae Hir bears the good news to Esyllt who promises him his beloved Golwg Hafddydd as a bride if the news be true. When March complains again to Arthur, the king advises him to send, first, musicians and poets to mollify Trystan and to sing his praises, and then Gwalchmei ('Hawk of May') as peace-maker. With some persuasion Trystan is thus brought to Arthur's presence and he promises to obey the king. Arthur arranges a compromise: one of the rivals shall have Esyllt while there are leaves on the trees, the other when the trees are leafless, and the husband, March, is given the choice. He chooses the leafless period because the nights are then longer, and Esyllt, overjoyed, sings a stanza saying that the holly, the ivy, and the yew always have leaves. And so March loses Esyllt.[6]

Thus, March, the husband, identifies himself with winter, the leafless period; Trystan, the lover, with the leaves of summer and the open air freedom of the woods. There is ample evidence that this is not an isolated adaptation of the theme.[7] According to the twelfth-century *Vita Gildae*, Arthur's queen, Gwenhwyfar was carried off to the impregnable fortress of Glastonbury, the 'Isle of Glass', by Melwas, king of Summer Land (Somerset). Arthur searched for her for about a year before he discovered her whereabouts, and he was about to give battle to Melwas when St Gildas intervened and persuaded the latter to return the queen.[8] In a medieval Welsh love poem the poet complains that though the night is cold his loved one will not admit him, and he adds: 'Alas! that with a lover's sigh I may not call for the art of Melwas, the robber who, through magic and enchantment took away a woman to the extremity of the world; he, the deceiver, went into the woods among the branched walls of the tree-tops and to-night I

should like to climb on high as he did.'[9] Another poem refers to 'the sleep of Melwas under the green cloak'.[10] A version
of the tradition recorded in the *Vita Gildae* occurs in 'Le
Chevalier de la Charrette' by Chrétien de Troyes. Here
'Meleagant', prince of a land whence no one returns, wins the
queen by combat in a wood on the May festival of Ascension
Day. The final battle, which takes place a year after the challenge is given, is fought in a glade where the herbage is fresh
at all seasons.[11] In Malory's work, the queen and her companions, all dressed in green and bedashed with herbs, moss
and flowers, are a-maying in the woods and fields, when
'Mellyagraunce' and 160 men attack them and carry off the
queen.[12]

The association, in this tale, of abduction with May, the
beginning of the summer half of the year, and with the custom
of maying, is particularly significant, and so is the perennial
May-Day battle inaugurated by the abduction of Creiddylad
daughter of Lludd Llawereint. Creiddylad was affianced to
Gwythyr son of Greidawl* but before he had slept with her
Gwyn ap Nudd (in whom God had set the spirit of the demons
of Annwfn) came and carried her off by force. When Arthur
heard of this he came to the North and commanded Gwyn to
set her free. 'This is the peace that was made: the maiden
should remain in her father's house unmolested by either side,
and there should be battle between Gwyn and Gwythyr each
May-Calends for ever and ever, from that day till doomsday;
and the one of them that shall be the victor on doomsday, let
him have the maiden.'[13]

This idea of an annual combat may account for the inter-
vals of a year which occur between events in a number of other
tales. Pwyll, who in the form of the grey-clad Arawn, Lord
of Annwfn, defeated Hafgan ('Summer White') in what
appears to have been a yearly combat and gained for himself
the title of Head of Annwfn, is invited to wed Rhiannon a

---

* Greidawl: 'Ardent'.

year after he has met her. Gwawl ('Light') appears at the wedding-feast and tricks Pwyll into yielding Rhiannon to him. Rhiannon obtains from Gwawl a year's delay before their nuptials, and at the end of the year Pwyll in turn intrudes upon the wedding-feast, overcomes Gwawl by a humiliating trick and regains his bride.[14] Similarly when Brandubh,* King of Leinster, wins Mongán's wife from him by a trick, she exacts from her new master a year's delay, and at the end of the year Mongán recovers her by another trick.[15] CúRoí mac Dáiri, 'the man in the grey mantle', from Corco Duibne, wins Bláthnat ('Little Flower') from the Ulstermen and carries her to his abode after defeating and humiliating CúChulainn. At the year's end, CúChulainn elopes with Bláthnat after killing CúRoí with her connivance.[16] In this instance, however, the battle takes place at Samain. According to the version we have followed here, Bláthnat had become CúRoí's wife—as Persephone became the wife of Hades—but in another version she belonged first to CúChulainn, and CúRoí came three times to demand her from him, each time at the end of a year.[17] Bláthnat's name connects her with the Welsh Blodeuedd ('Flowers'), the unfaithful wife that was magically made for Lleu Llaw Gyffes from the flowers of the oak and the broom and the meadowsweet.

2

These stories have been correlated with seasonal customs in which a mock-battle is staged between a personification of summer, clad in green or white and crowned with flowers or ribbons, and a personification of winter clad in furs and crowned with holly.[18] But less attention has been given to the fact that the elopers' transgression of marriage ties also finds direct expression in folk-custom. A correlation of freedom and eroticism with summer, particularly with May, the first month

* 'Black-Raven'.

of summer, and especially with the first of May, survives in popular belief. May is the 'merry month', the month of 'may-ing', of dancing and of love-making, 'When merry lads are playing . . . each with his bonny lass.' To Welsh poets of the thirteenth and fourteenth centuries, May was pre-eminently the month of love and of extra-marital relations. One poet closely associates this month with a return to a primeval free-dom in these matters:

'Before there was the law of a pope or his trouble,
Each one made love
Without blame to his loved one.
Free and easy enjoyment will be without blame,
Well has May made houses of the leaves—
There will be two assignations, beneath trees, in concealment,
For me, myself and my dear one.'[19]

Love-poems ascribed to the greatest of these poets, Dafydd ap Gwilym, are replete with praises of May, the three months of summer, the woods, the leaves, the song of birds, and the green bower.

Addressing a nun he has fancied, he or a later poet says:

'Is it true, the girl that I love,
That you do not desire birch, the strong growth of summer?
Be not a nun in spring,
Asceticism is not as good as a bush.
As for the warrant of ring and habit,
A green dress would ordain better.
Come to the spreading birch,
To the religion of the trees and the cuckoo.'[20]

The poems abound with lines associating the birch-tree with love. The lover's bower usually stood beneath a birch-tree or in a birch-bush; wreaths of birch were presented as love-tokens, and in Wales the May-pole was usually a birch-tree.

Dafydd ap Gwilym's most celebrated paramour, Morfudd, 'god-daughter of May', was a married woman ('I love only a girl who has a husband', says another poet). Dafydd sends birds and animals as love-messengers to invite both girls and married women to trysts in his house of leaves, and there is throughout a contempt for chastity and an implication that they should answer the call of May and Summer. The despised husband, styled *Yr Eiddig* ('The Jealous One', the cuckold), does not like summer:

'To hear the song of the little birds of May,
And fresh leaves, wounded him.'[21]

'Winter has been given to men of his age;
Summer belongs to lovers.'[22]

And indeed, the husband seems to be in full possession in winter. January, the black month, 'forbids all to love'. The poet bitterly complains that he is forlorn in the cold and the frost outside the window of his beloved. She is under Eiddig's roof, and when he flees alone to the birch grove he finds nothing but desolation there.[23]

It has not been left to us to connect these ideas of erotic liberty with the elopement tales: poetry and tradition do that for us. Depicting himself outside his beloved's window on a cold night, Dafydd ap Gwilym contrasts his luck with that of Melwas. Although, in various poems, he likens his loved one to several of the beautiful women of Welsh tradition, it is the story of Trystan and Esyllt that fully mirrors his own situation. He compares himself with Trystan and calls his love the 'niece of Esyllt', or 'a second Esyllt', while a poem sometimes attributed to him[24] says that *Eiddig*, 'Esyllt's husband', loves neither play nor nightingale nor cuckoo nor fox nor hound nor bush nor song nor hazel-nuts nor leaves.

Various impressions on rocks and megaliths in Ireland are known as 'Beds of Diarmaid and Gráinne', the beds on which the lovers slept as they eluded Finn and the Fiana. 'Modern travellers report that on asking village girls to accompany them to the localities in question, they found them visibly embarrassed. Further inquiries elicited the information that a girl accompanying a stranger of the opposite sex to one of these

"beds" cannot refuse him any favour that he may ask of her.'[25]
The Beds of Diarmaid and Gráinne also promote fertility. It
is said that if a barren woman goes with her husband to one
of these beds she will be cured.[26] In terms of our interpretation
of Birth Stories, the 'third factor' essential for conception is
present here.

The profanity and laxity of May-Day celebrations in
Britain were condemned by several sixteenth- and seventeenth-
century reformers. It was the custom for large parties of both
sexes to go to the woods on May Eve to spend the night in
pastimes there and return in the morning with branches of
birch and other trees. Stubbes, who castigates the May-pole
as 'this stinking idol', testifies on what he claims to be im-
peccable authority 'that of forty, threescore, or a hundred maids
going to the wood over night, there have scarcely the third part
of them returned home again undefiled.'[27] Of May customs
in France, C. B. Lewis concludes: 'They all go to show that
the May-Day fêtes originally were a festival of love, but I
should add, of love outside the ties of marriage. On this occasion the sexes, both married and unmarried, were exhorted to
indulge freely in love, and many May songs and "Chansons
de mal-mariée" contain an apotheosis of free love together with
scorn and contempt of marriage.' Lewis has correlated these
customs with the idealization of love outside marriage in the
poetry of the Troubadours. Particularly relevant to our argument is his reference to a passage in the Provençal poem *Fla-
menca* which describes May-Day fêtes and in conclusion suggests that if the husband raises objections his wife should say:
'Silence, go away, for in my arms my lover is lying, Kalenda
Maya—the First of May!'[28]

Not without reason has it been believed that it is unlucky to
bring Mayflowers into the home, that it is unlucky to marry
in May or to marry in green, and that 'May cats' bring misfortune, or that they carry snakes into houses.[29] May is the
month of the open air and of love, and for that reason everything connected with it is a threat to home life and conjugal

happiness. In parts of Central Europe it is said that one should not marry in May, when whores and knaves go to church, or when every ass is in love. It is also said that marriages made in May last for only one summer,[30] a saying that accords with a reference in an Irish law-book to Beltaine as the usual time for divorce.[31] Hallowe'en, on the contrary, was the auspicious time for marriage divinations. In the Shetlands and northern Scotland until recent times, winter was the popular marriage season;[32] in Ireland, as in other countries, the period between Christmas and Lent was a great time for match-making and marriages, and at Shrovetide, unmarried adults were subject to mockery.[33] But in May, it was not the unmarried but the unloving that were ridiculed. Thus, in parts of Wales young men used to fix bunches of flowers tied with ribbons to the houses of the girls they loved, but to the door or window of a prude or a girl who had jilted her lover they fixed a horse's skull or the straw effigy of a man.[34] (Esyllt's husband was March, 'Horse'.)[35]

This regime is remarkably similar to the custom in ancient China.[36] There, the season of marriages extended from shortly after the autumn equinox to shortly after the spring equinox, and towards the end of this period young men and women who had remained single for too long were bidden to marry. On the other hand, the idea of love was linked with spring, and with the return of this season young girls and youths assembled and sang songs of love. They entered the woods (south or east of the town) where they gathered flowers, and individual couples went apart and indulged in love-making. But like the *gandharva*-type of marriage in India—'a union between lovers without the consent of mother and father'—[37] such unions were not universally approved, or at least not for all classes.

3

The polarity of summer and winter and of the spring and autumn festivals which inaugurate the two main seasons is correlated in Chinese thought with a whole range of other polarities. The spring festival is a festival of youth as well as of betrothals, the autumn festival a festival of old age as well as the time for setting up house. Women played a leading part in the spring rites (as in European May customs), men in the autumnal ones. 'When the Chinese philosophers wished to build up a theory of love they explained that in springtime the girls were attracted by the boys, and in autumn the boys by the girls, as though each of them in turn feeling his nature to be incomplete was suddenly seized with the irresistible desire to perfect it.'[38]

The 'Elopements' and 'Wooings' of Celtic tradition seem to constitute a similar pair of contraries. In the 'Wooings' man is the suitor while the role of the maiden is largely passive, but in the 'Elopements' it is the woman who chooses the man and compels him to do her will. This difference may account for the origin of the two uses of difficult tasks and riddles in tales which end in marriage. In the one the obstacle is set by the woman or her guardian, in the other by the young man. The polarity of 'husband' and 'lover' in the Elopement tales is also the polarity of age and youth, of jealousy and love. The original marriage is portrayed as a misalliance. The husband is old and has grown-up sons by previous wives. All that Finn wanted was a suitable wife, and it was his followers who suggested that Gráinne would suit him. She had already refused all the kings and champions of Ireland, and to her father's question as to whether she would accept Finn she gave the nonchalant reply: 'If he be a fitting son-in-law for thee, why should he not be a fitting husband and mate for me?'[39]—a marriage of convenience. We have mentioned that in the oldest version of the story she attempted to evade Finn's suit by setting him an 'impossible task'. 'Then in an unlucky hour Gráinne was given to Finn, for they never lived in peace until they separated. Finn was hateful to the maiden and such was her hatred that she sickened of it.'[40] In the medieval German story of Tristan, King March has no wish to marry but his subjects urge him to do so. Like Gráinne he tries to avoid his fate. Two quarrelling sparrows drop a woman's hair from their beaks, and March proclaims that he will marry no woman other than the owner of that hair. Ironically enough, it is Tristan who finds him Isolt whose hair it is[41]—and thus the quarrel of two men over one woman begins. Again, Conchobar's earmarking of Derdriu for himself on the day of her birth was hardly an expression of love, while in the more elaborate recensions his sensual lust contrasts unfavourably with the unselfish devotion of Noísiu. Indeed, the husband in these tales has more in common with the possessive and jealous father than with the young suitor of the 'Wooings'.

The lover, on the other hand, is a dashing young warrior and more than a match for his fellows in manly feats. Yet, he combines valiance with such feminine qualities as beauty, a musical voice, sweet words and charm. Diarmaid is said to have a love-inducing spot on his forehead and he is 'the best lover of women and of maidens in the world'.[42] A fifteenth-century lay refers to the story of his death as a 'tale that makes women sorrowful' and closes with the lament:

> 'Master (?) and charmer of women,
> Son of Ó Duibhne of swift victories,
> Wooing has not lifted her eye
> Since the clay was placed on his cheeks . . .'[43]

In each of our three elopement tales, the lover is related to the wronged husband through the female line: he is a sister's son.[44] We have already noted the ambiguous position of this class of nephew in various societies and the peculiar relationship between him and his mother's brother. In general, the maternal uncle is a kind of female father to a female son—and the latter is often allowed to take great liberties with his uncle and his uncle's possessions.[45]

The lover's connections with the Other World should also be noted. Diarmaid 'son of Donn' hails from West Munster;[46] his foster-father, and the guardian spirit of his elopement with

Gráinne, was the Mac Óc (of Tuatha Dé Danann), foster-son and love-messenger of Étaín's supernatural lover. The ability to cause cows to increase their yield of milk was a gift which Noísiu shared with Tuatha Dé Danann. In continental literature, Tristan is the son of Blanchefleur, as Eros is reputed to be the son of Aphrodite whom the Cretans called 'Flower-lady' (*Anthia*).[47] Blanchefleur died in childbed in a ship at sea and Tristan was cut from her womb. According to a twelfth-century German poem, Lancelot, Queen Gwenever's life-long lover, was borne away when only a year old and reared by the Lady of the Lake in Meidelant, 'The Land of Maidens'.[48] To generalize: the man upon whom the frustrated wife fixes her affections is, by virtue of his nature and other-world associations, a human personification of the super-natural lover—the beautiful Gandharva—who interferes with marriages. He is the feminine man—not an effeminate man in whom the female aspects of the male triumph over the mas-culine—but 'a woman's man'. As Heinrich Zimmer says of Lancelot: 'He represented something very different from the heroic medieval ideals of his companions, something much less timely, more profoundly human and enduring. Sir Lancelot is an incarnation of the ideal of manhood that exists, not in the world of masculine social action, but in the hopes and fancies of the feminine imagination.'[49] Just as the 'Wooings' depict the mythological inversion of marriage from the male standpoint, so the 'Elopements' may be described as the mytho-logical inversion of marriage from the female standpoint.

Such an interpretation explains both the abiding appeal of these tales and the fact that, exalted though he is, the dis-possessed husband commands scarcely more sympathy than does the bride's father in the 'Wooings'. The sympathy rests with the elopers, and great pains are taken to establish the hero's innocence. He is the victim of a destiny which works through such media as an accidentally drunk love-potion, the inadvertent uncovering of the love-spot on his forehead, or the fortuitous concurrence of his colours in a homely winter's scene. With the woman it is different. She is so possessed by the passion that questions of guilt and innocence have no meaning for her. She lays a compulsion on the hero to escape with her, and he is caught between two incompatible obliga-tions, the obligation of loyalty to his kinsman and the obliga-tion of love laid upon him by his kinsman's wife. He will incur shame if he stays; he will incur shame if he goes. He submits the riddle to his friends, and according to their judge-ment rather than his own he can do nothing but accept his fate, come what may. In some popular versions of 'Diarmaid and Gráinne', Diarmaid counters the *gessa* laid upon him by Gráinne by setting her an impossible task. He charges her not to appear before him either by day or by night, clothed or un-clothed, on foot or on horseback, in company or without company. She goes to a fairy woman and procures garments made from mountain down and she comes to him in these gar-ments, riding on a he-goat in the dusk of the evening.[50] There are several variations on this theme: 'I will not take you in soft-ness, and I will not take you in hardness; I will not take you without, and I will not take you within; I will not take you on horseback, and I will not take you on foot,' said he. One morning Gráinne cried to him, 'Are you within Diarmaid?' She was between the two sides of the door on a buck-goat. 'I am not without, I am not within; I am not on foot, and I am not on a horse—you must go with me,' said she.[51] Through this device Diarmaid is ritually absolved of guilt. If he did not take her by day or by night, without or within, and so on, the logical conclusion is that he did not take her at all—he could not possibly have done what he did. It is also a symbolical expres-sion of the nature of Gráinne's love, a love which transcends the ordinary oppositions of contingent existence and is a law unto itself.

Several scholars have drawn attention to the similarities between the May ceremonies of Europe and the spring-rituals connected with various cults of the 'Great Mother' and her youthful, often effeminate, consort, the 'Dying God', which prevailed in Mediterranean lands—rituals in which women played a very prominent part. C. B. Lewis derives the Queen of May and the sexual liberties associated with that month directly from a spread of the cult of the Phrygian goddess Cybele in Europe during Roman times. She was a 'goddess of love, especially of free love, of love outside marriage', and allowing for calendrical adjustments, her great festival, the Hilaria, would fall on Lady Day and on May Day in alternate years.[52] But striking as the resemblances undoubtedly are, it would be rash to attribute all the material discussed in this chapter to a single cultural influence of this kind. With equal cogency, A. H. Krappe has shown the similarity between the story of Diarmaid and Gráinne and that of Adonis and Aphro-dite. Aphrodite, goddess of love and of nature in bloom, fell in love with the beautiful Adonis, as Gráinne did with Diar-maid, and he became her paramour, though in his case as in Diarmaid's there is a different tradition which says that he was innocent of actual congress with her. Aphrodite was the wife of Ares, the god of war, as Gráinne was the wife of the *fian* chief. Suspecting an improper relationship between Adonis and his wife, Ares sent a wild boar, or himself assumed the shape of a wild boar, which fatally wounded Adonis while he was hunting. Similarly Finn was believed to have arranged the boar-hunt to allure Diarmaid to his death at the year's end. Both Adonis and Diarmaid went boar-hunting against his mistress's will. There is a general lament for both. Diarmaid, borne away on the Mac Óc's gilded bier, recalls the annual ritual in which the image of the dead Adonis was borne away, mourned by women bitterly wailing, while the couches on which images of the god and goddess were shown may be compared with the 'Beds of Diarmaid and Gráinne'. At shrines of Aphrodite women gave themselves to strangers, as we are told Irish girls were expected to do at the Beds of Diarmaid and Gráinne.[53]

In India too, devotion to the 'Divine Woman' has expressed

itself in the idealization of adulterous love, witness the Krish-
naist form of Vishnuism which dominated the subcontinent
from the seventh to the eighth century. Disputes in the Ben-
galese Courts of Love between the adherents of love of
'another's wife' and the champions of conjugal love always
ended with the latter as losers. Professor Eliade writes:[54] 'The
exemplary love remained that which bound Rādhā to Kṛṣṇa—
a secret, illegitimate, "antisocial" love, symbolizing the rupture
that every genuine religious experience imposes . . . Rādhā is
conceived as the infinite love that constitutes the very essence
of Kṛṣṇa.' 'Such an abandonment of all social and moral
values as mystical love implies' is echoed in Diarmaid's
plaint:[55] 'I have forsaken all my people . . . I have lost my inheritance and my comrades . . . I have lost the kindness and love
of the men of Erin and all the Fiann. I have lost delight in
music; I have lost the right to my own honor. Erin and all
that are in it have forsaken me on account of thy love and
affection alone.' And so, once more in this study, the most holy,
in its sacrificial aspect, is symbolized by the most disgraceful.

Looked at from this point of view, the return of Gráinne to
Finn after Diarmaid's death, like the reconciliation of Helen
and Menelaus after the death of Paris, cannot but appear to be
an unsatisfactory ending. Nevertheless, it accords with the
seasonal or cyclical nature of the ritual to which we have
referred. In other versions of the tale Gráinne is constant to the
end of her days.[56] Similarly, Tristan and Isolt are buried in
the same grave; a rosebush over the woman and a vine over
the man grow together so that they can in no wise be sundered.[57]
Recently-recorded versions say that Conchobar caused Derdriu
and Noísiu to be buried on opposite sides of the loch, so that
they might not be together in death. Then a young pine grew
out of each grave 'and their branches grew towards each other,
until they entwined one with the other across the loch. And
Conchobar would have cut them down, but the men of
Ulster would not allow this, and they set a watch and protected the trees until King Conchobar died.'[58]

CHAPTER XV

Adventures

VISITS TO A STRANGE LAND and experiences among a strange race constitute a substantial part of Celtic mythology, and, as in modern fiction, a whole class of tales are known as 'adventures'. But whereas the adventures of fiction are concerned with escapades among the natives of distant lands or planets in *this* world, the adventures of mythology are experienced among the mysterious denizens of a supernatural world. In this the Celt is no exception. The prodigies of Asia, Africa, and native America may be sufficient to excite the imagination of modern man, but for the inhabitants of those continents, no less than for the ancient Celts, the adventures worth recording are adventures in another 'dimension', and the only journeys of real significance are journeys between this world and the world beyond.

> 'In Asia, in Polynesia, even in Africa, man's chief intellectual preoccupations and speculations are with spiritual adventure. . . . The lonely pioneering of the soul . . . and the defeat or success of its quest forms the principal theme in the oral literature of the Old World. . . . Our modern fiction is mainly concerned with social life. . . . It is a valuable achievement of oral literature to show that this predominant preoccupation of man with himself—his almost total absorption in his temporary physical life—is a European phenomenon. . . . Directly or indirectly the quest for immortality is the most outstanding motif, both in Asia and in Polynesia.'[1]

Every experience of the Other World is in a sense both an initiation and a marriage, and no clear line can be drawn between 'Adventures' and the tales of youth and courtship which we have already discussed. Indeed, the story of how Art won a wife is called 'The *Adventures* of Art son of Conn and the Courtship of Delbchaem', while CúChulainn's initia‑ tion in the land of Scáthach could well be classified with 'Adventures'. But there are kinds and degrees of initiation. In this chapter we shall deal with Adventures which are not initiations into manhood or into a particular vocation, and with the love of a supernatural woman who can never be brought home as a bride. Our first story is 'The Adventures of Nera'. It is derived from a text written perhaps as early as the eighth century, but this, of course, is no indication of the age of a story which is so obviously pre‑Christian in its inspiration.[2]

One Eve of Samain, Ailill and Medb were in Ráth Crua‑ chan with their whole household. Two captives had been hanged the day before and Ailill now offered any prize he might choose to the man who would put a withe round the foot of either of the captives on the gallows. Great was the terror of Samain Eve; demons would always appear on that night. Every man took up the challenge in turn, but quickly returned to the house. Then Nera declared that he would have the prize and Ailill promised to give him his gold‑hilted sword if he succeeded.

After Nera had thrice failed to fix the withe, the captive on the gallows told him to put a proper peg in it. The task accom‑ plished, the captive said: 'By the truth of thy valour, take me on thy neck, that I may get a drink with thee. I was thirsty when I was hanged.' Nera carried him to the nearest house, but around this house they saw a lake of fire. The captive explained that there was no drink there, for the fire was well covered at night. Around the next house they saw a lake of water, which signified that there was never a washing‑ nor a bath‑tub, nor a slop‑pail in it at night. They found these three vessels in the third house. The captive drank from the first two and squirted the last sip in the faces of the people that were in the house, so that they all died. Hence it is not good to have such water‑ vessels, or an uncovered fire, in a house after sleeping.

Nera then carried the hanged man back to his torture and
returned to Cruachan. There he 'saw something'. Cruachan
was burnt and he saw a heap of its people's heads cut off by
enemies from the fort. He followed the warriors through the
cave of Cruachan and saw the heads being displayed to the
king of the *síd*. The king called Nera to him and after question‐
ing him he directed him to the house of a single woman and
ordered him to bring a burden of firewood daily to the royal
house. The woman welcomed him and, unknown to the king,
she became his wife.

Every day, as he bore his burden of firewood, Nera saw a
blind man with a lame man on his neck coming from the
fort to the well in front of it. At the well, the blind one asked:
'Is it there?', and the lame one replied: 'It is indeed, let us go
away.' Nera asked his wife about this and she explained that
the two men, one of whom had been blinded and the other
lamed, were trusted by the king to visit his golden crown which
was in the well. Then she told him that Cruachan had not
really been destroyed as he imagined, but that the illusion he
had seen would come true next Hallowe'en unless he warned
his people to come and destroy the *síd*. She sent him to them,
telling him that they would still be around the same cauldron
as when he left them, and that he should take fruits of summer
—wild garlic, primrose, and golden fern—from the *síd* to sub‐
stantiate his story. She herself had conceived and would bear
him a son, and Nera should take his family and his cattle from
the *síd* before his people came to destroy it. Finally, she pro‐
phesied that the crown of Brion would be carried off by
Ailill and Medb.

Nera went to his people and told his tale, and he was given
the sword Ailill had promised him. At the end of the year he
returned to the *síd* to fetch his family and cattle to safety. Then
the men of Connacht and the Ulster exiles destroyed the *síd*
and took out what there was in it. 'And then they brought away
the crown of Brion. This crown, the mantle of Loegaire in
Armagh, and the shirt of Dúnlaing in Kildare in Leinster are

the three wonders of Ireland. Nera was left with his people in the *síd*, and has not come out until now, nor will he come till Doom.'[3]

The strange challenge with which this tale begins and the weird affair with the hanged man—a man who is both dead and alive—suggests a Hallowe'en ritual, comparable to visit-ing a graveyard on this night when time and eternity inter-mingle, a ritual by which men made contact with other-world forces. The similarity between the opening episode and the setting of the famous Indian 'Twenty-five Stories of the Spectre in the Corpse' bears witness to its extreme antiquity. In the Indian tale a king, at the behest of a necromancer disguised as a beggar ascetic, goes to the place of execution on the night of the new moon, cuts down from a tree the body of a hanged man and carries it on his back through the eerie cremation ground, while a ghost in the corpse tells him didactic stories 'to shorten the way'. When the twenty-five stories have been told, the dead man warns the king that the necromancer intends to kill him as a sacrifice to enhance his own super-natural powers. And he teaches him how to outwit the necro-mancer and secure the powers for himself.[4]

In the Irish story, Nera's experience with the hanged man is, as we shall explain in a moment, an object lesson in how to withstand the incursions of spirits into the home. Similarly, through the knowledge he subsequently gains in the *síd* he is able to turn the tables on the *síd*-folk who are conspiring to in-vade and to destroy the royal court of Cruachan. Again, Nera's journey in search of water, guided by the superior wisdom of the helpless hanged man, seems to foreshadow the journey of the blind man to the well of the crown of Brion, guided by the eyes of the lame man on his back. He enacts, as though in a ritual, the scene which will eventually lead him to the dis-covery of the other-world crown.

This crown is mentioned in another Hallowe'en tale.[5] A certain prophetess used to visit King Fíngin mac Luchta of

Munster every Samain and used to relate to him 'all the occur-
rences that took place in Ireland on that sacred night and the
results that should issue from them until that night twelve-
months.' On one of these occasions, she told him that among the
wonders of that night would be the revelation of the 'three chief
artifacts' in Ireland. These were the crown of Brion, concealed
from the Morrígan in the well of the hill of Cruachan, the
fidchell of Crimthann which was brought from the secret
recesses of the sea and hidden in the Rath of Uisnech, and the
crown of Loegaire in Síd Findacha in Ulster.

Some of the main features of Nera's initial adventures have
been preserved in a modern Irish folktale, though the hanged
man has been superseded by the Devil, and the pagan practices
are interspersed with Christian ones. The following is a
shortened version of a *schema* drawn up by Professor Delargy
from a detailed examination of thirty-nine variants of this tale
recorded by the Irish Folklore Commission.[6]

A youth is sent by his father, stepfather, or godfather to
fetch some lost object from a field, garden, cairn, church,
churchyard, slab in a churchyard, byre, wood, or cross-roads.
The youth meets with the Devil and agrees to accompany him
or to carry him to a house.

For various reasons the Devil is unable to enter the house. For
example, feet-water has been thrown out and a lake has been
formed by it around the house, or there is feet-water inside the
house, or the fire has been smoored and there is a protecting
wall of fire around the house.

They go to a second house and the Devil fails to enter because of barriers created by saying the Rosary or by having, or
by sprinkling, holy water in the house. Another deterrent is the
presence of a crowing cock in the house.

Finally, the Devil enters the third house, which is occupied
by a quarrelling couple, or a childless or newly-married couple.
The Devil tells his companion that a son will be born to the
couple and will become a 'priest'. As the 'priest' will be the
son of the Devil, those persons will be damned who will be

present at his first Mass or who will be sprinkled with holy
water by him.

Eventually the youth, by cutting off the head or the hand of
the Devil's son or by some other means, prevents him from
performing the rites. The priest is revealed to all as a devil and
he disappears in flames. Or, revealed as the Devil's son, he
seeks to do penance, and God outwits the Devil in a contest
for his soul.

Inasmuch as he is carried by the hero and warns him of
impending danger, the Devil in this tale performs the same
function as the corpse in the Indian story, while the false priest
who would perform holy rites corresponds to the sorcerer who
masquerades as an ascetic. When, at the end of the Indian tale,
the spectre in the corpse offers to grant the king a wish as a
reward for his toils during that strange night, the king asks
that the twenty-five riddle-tales related by the spectre should be
made known over the whole earth and remain eternally famous
among men. The spectre promises that it shall be so, and adds
that the stories will have the virtue of rendering spectres and
demons powerless and that 'even Shiva, the Great God, Over-
lord of all the Spectres and Demons, the Master-Ascetic of the
Gods, will himself do them honour'[7]—a pronouncement which
may well contain a clue to the original status of other Irish
stories which are now obscure and degenerate folktales.

It is clear from the folktale as from 'The Adventures of Nera'
that a covered-up fire and the absence of bath-water (particularly feet-water) and slops in a house, at night, keep the
supernatural outside, and this is considered prudent. Such precautions, however, conflict with the folk-custom of preparing
the house before retiring to rest, especially on Hallowe'en, in
readiness for the nocturnal return of dead relatives and friends.
As we have already mentioned,[8] a good fire was prepared, the
hearth was swept clean, and food and water were left out for the
expected guests. It was also believed that to throw out water,
especially feet-water or dirty water generally, interfered with the
'good people' and prevented the dead from returning. But there

are inconsistences in the folklore evidence itself. For example, a record from one district[9] to the effect that 'no vessel contain-ing dirty water should be left in the kitchen at night' is directly contradicted by a record from another district. The subject needs further investigation, but the explanation would appear to be that the measures mentioned in the stories keep away *all* supernatural beings whether malevolent or otherwise. To dis-pense with these measures involves a risk, as does all traffic with the supernatural, but without such risk the return of the friendly dead must also be suppressed and man must deny himself all 'adventures'.

There are other stories about the Cave of Cruachan, some-times called the Hell's Gate of Ireland. From it came a flock of white birds that withered up everything with their breath, and equally devastating pigs which could not be counted: whenever people tried to count them the count of each person would be different.[10] In one of the *dindsenchas* poems,[11] 'the horrid Morrígan' comes out of this same cave, 'her fit abode', and in 'The Colloquy of the Ancients' the immortal daughter of Bodb son of the Dagda comes from there to converse with Caílte.[12] There were other mysterious caves in Ireland as well as elsewhere in the Celtic lands. The Fenian tale called 'The Dwelling at Céis Chorainn' begins with Finn seated on his hunting-mound. The three mis-shapen daughters of the local chief of Tuatha Dé Danann, seeking vengeance, sat at the mouth of the cave beneath the hill and reeled off bewitched hasps of yarn left-handwise from three wry holly-sticks. On approaching them, Finn and Conán became entangled in the hasps and lost all their strength, whereupon the hags bound them and carried them into the cave. All the Fiana were bound in the same way except Goll son of Morna, who appeared on the scene, slew the hags, released his fellows, and won Finn's daughter for his wife.[13] Thus, caves were entrances to the Other World. The storytellers had a group of tales called 'Caves' (in the Lists), but hardly any of those listed have survived in a complete form. 'The Cave of Ainged', in List A, is believed to be another name for 'The Adventures of Nera'.[14]

Even today, Ireland has what is probably the most famous 'cave' in Europe, St Patrick's Purgatory,[15] which, as its name implies, is an entrance to the Underworld. In it is the very mouth of Hell. This cave is situated on a holy island in Loch Derg. Formerly pilgrims were shut up in it for hours, and there they suffered some of the torments of Purgatory. If they slept, they ran the risk of being transported to Hell by the Devil. The adventures of a certain Knight Owen in this cave comprise one of the most widely known of medieval 'Visions' prior to Dante's. He first encounters demons who show him the horrors of Purgatory and of Hell, and then, after he has crossed a narrow bridge over the River of Hell, two prelates conduct him through Paradise and show him the Gate of Heaven. In modern times, the cave has been closed and the 'purgatory' housed in a chapel. Every year, thousands of barefooted pilgrims continue to perform the penances of Loch Derg, and the climax of the ritual is to spend a sleepless night in prayer at this chapel. A twentieth-century pilgrim describes his experience:[16]

> 'The night shadows had fallen and but for two tapers the Chapel was grimly dark. It was something strange and weird, without counterpart on this earth, to look round at the rows of white haggard faces peering in the fragile candlelight. Generations of Gaels have spent a night there . . . for few of the Irish care to die without a glimpse of what they are coming to. All night we kept vigil in our prison-house, reciting the next day's Stations by advance. . . . With the fall of night the world slipped away. We seemed to stand in a dim place where two worlds meet.'

It is true that Nera finds himself in a different kind of other-world, but St Patrick's Purgatory is undoubtedly a Christianized version of the kind of ritual with which the Adventures of Nera were originally connected. There is nothing specifically Christian about ritual descents into caves as such; similar practices occur in such widely separated initiation rites as those of the Mithraic Mysteries and those of certain Australian aborigines,[17] and everywhere they symbolize a visit to the world beyond. The Siberian shaman in his ritual journey to the Underworld takes his little caravan southward 'over a yellow steppe across which a magpie cannot fly', and then he climbs a high mountain. 'And having climbed, the shaman in his song and ritual dance conducts his caravan down into a hole in the ground, and what do they find? In his chanted pictures we find precisely the paraphernalia of the Buddhist caves which lie under the temples of Tibet where hideous sculptures impress on the faithful the horrors of the Underworld. . . .'[18]

2

In our next Hallowe'en story the hero's adventure is the outcome of a malady brought upon him by otherworld agencies. It is called 'The Wasting Sickness of CúChulainn'.[19]

The Ulstermen are assembled on the Plain of Muirthemne to celebrate the feast of Samain. A flock of beautiful birds settles on the nearby lake, and all the women long to have a pair of them, one for each shoulder. CúChulainn captures the birds, but after he has shared them among the women there is none left for his own wife. She, however, far from displaying anger or jealousy, is so much at one with her husband that she feels as though she herself has distributed the birds among the women. CúChulainn promises her that if more birds come she shall have the two loveliest of them. Soon they see two birds linked by a golden chain on the lake. The birds sing a sleep-inducing song and CúChulainn is warned that there is some power behind them. He fails to catch them, though his spear passes through the wing of one of them, and they go under the lake.

Resting with his back against a pillar-stone, CúChulainn

falls asleep and, in a vision, two women come to him and whip him till he is almost dead. After this experience he lies in silence for a year on a sick-bed. As Samain approaches again, Oengus son of Aed Abrat* from the Other World appears at his bed and invites him to Mag Cruath where he will be healed and where Oengus's sister, Fand,** is longing for him to join her. Then CúChulainn stirs himself and goes again to the pillar-stone, where he meets one of the two women he saw in his vision. She is Lí Ban,† wife of Labraid Luath†† of Mag Mell.‡ The previous year, it was CúChulainn's friend-ship they wished for, and she now brings a message from her husband and from her sister Fand, wife of Manannán mac Lir. If he will fight for one day against Labraid's enemies, he shall have the love of Fand. CúChulainn sends his charioteer with the woman to learn something of her country. They travel in a bronze boat to an island in a lake, where they are welcomed by Labraid and by Fand and her company of women. The charioteer returns and recounts the marvels of the Other World. CúChulainn is then visited by Emer, his wife, who rebukes him for being prostrated by 'woman-love', but after further solicitation by Lí Ban and a further reconnaissance by the charioteer, he goes to the other-world island. There he defeats Labraid's enemies and becomes Fand's lover.

CúChulainn spends a month with Fand, and then takes his leave, promising to meet her again at Ibor Cind Tráchta.‡‡ Emer hears of the tryst, and accompanied by her fifty women, all armed with whetted knives, she surprises the lovers at their trysting-place. CúChulainn protects Fand from the wrath of the women, but the reproaches and taunts of his wife weigh heavily upon him. Emer says that Fand is perhaps no better

---

* 'Light of the Eye'.
** ' Gentle' (explained as an epithet for 'Tear').
† 'Paragon of Women'.
†† Labraid Luathlám ar Claideb: 'Labraid Swift Hand on Sword'.
‡ 'The Plain of Delight'.
‡‡ In Ulster.

than herself, 'but all that glitters is fair, all that is new is bright, all that is lacking is revered, all that is familiar neglected, until all be known. Once you had us in honour together, and we should be so again if you wanted it.' 'By my word,' says CúChulainn, 'I do want you, and I shall want you as long as you live.' 'Leave me then,' says Fand. 'It is more fitting', says Emer, 'that I should be abandoned.' 'No,' says Fand, 'it is I who shall be abandoned.' But her great love for CúChulainn troubles her and lamenting she sings:

'It is I who will go on a journey,
Though I like our adventure best.

Though a man of great fame should come,
I should prefer to stay . . .

'Alas for one who gives love to another
If it be not cherished;
It is better for a person to be cast aside
Unless he is loved as he loves . . .'

Manannán comes from the east to fetch her, and reluctantly she decides to go with him. 'There was a time he was dear to me. . . . Love is a vain thing; it vanishes quickly.' She says that CúChulainn has deserted her, and that, in any case, he has another consort whereas Manannán has none. The disconsolate CúChulainn wanders through the mountains of Munster, taking neither food nor drink, until the druids give him a drink of forgetfulness, a draught of which is also given to Emer so that she may forget her jealousy. And Manannán shakes his cloak between CúChulainn and Fand so that they shall never meet again.

In 'The Adventures of Nera' the initiative in contacting the supernatural comes from the human side. Here, on the contrary, it is the Other World that beckons and it does so for its own purposes. Strife and longing within that strange realm impel it to break in and disturb the everyday world of men. The guise of sea-birds is again the mode of crossing the boundary. Like Pwyll, who as an atonement for the unwitting offence of driving away the dogs of Annwfn, places himself at the service of its king, CúChulainn falls under the power of the *Síd* after he has shown violence to its harbingers. The 'sickness' which overcomes him for a year after his first vision at the pillar/stone may be regarded as the 'this world' aspect of the other/world adventure which follows his further visit to the same pillar on the subsequent Samain. Similarly in 'The Adventures of Nera', the second episode is, so to speak, the esoteric aspect of the first.

Strange as it is, the appeal for the aid of a mortal to settle differences in the supernatural world is not uncommon in Celtic story. For example, 'The Adventures of Loegaire'[20] begins with the men of Connacht at an assembly at Énloch ('Bird/lake'), on an unspecified occasion in the time of King Crimthann. Early in the morning, they see a man approaching through the mist. He is Fiachna mac Rétach from the *Síd* and he has come for help. His wife has been abducted, and though he has killed the abductor she now dwells with the latter's nephew, Goll son of Dolb, king of the fort of Mag Mell, who has defeated Fiachna in seven battles. Another battle is to be fought this day and Fiachna offers silver and gold to all who will aid him. Loegaire son of Crimthann goes with fifty men. He slays Goll and demands the return of Fiachna's wife, who then comes lamenting the death of her two paramours. Fiachna gives his daughter, Dér Gréine,* to Loegaire, and he remains in the *Síd*.

Far from being mutually exclusive entities, the natural and supernatural worlds thus intrude upon one another in a variety of ways. They can help and they can harm one another; they can rob and they can enrich one another. Through his services to the otherworld king, Loegaire becomes joint ruler in the *Síd*; Pwyll, after resolving a conflict in Annwfn, is known as its 'Head'. Between the two worlds is an interaction which is

---

* 'Sun/tear'.

similar in many ways to the interaction between the 'conscious' and 'unconscious' mind as described by modern psychologists.

The otherworld mistress is for man the counterpart of the otherworld lover of woman, and she must be distinguished from the otherworld bride of the marriage quests. Whereas the bride must be abducted from a hostile masculine world, the supernatural mistress entices the hero to a friendly feminine world like that where the suitor is sometimes instructed by a woman or his maternal kinsmen on his way to the perilous terrain of the bride. In the Adventures of Bran and of Conle it is a veritable 'Land of Women'. Conle is consumed with longing after seeing the beautiful fairy woman and hearing her song about this 'Land of the Living', this 'Plain of Delights', and when she appears to him a second time he springs into her ship of glass and 'from that day forward they were never seen again.'[21] When Loegaire returns from the *Síd* on a farewell visit to his people, his father offers him the kingdom of the Three Connachts if he will stay. But he refuses, saying how he loves

'The noble plaintive music of the *Síd*,
Going from kingdom to kingdom,
Drinking from burnished cups,
Conversing with the loved one.

'My own wife
Is Fiachna's daughter, Dér Gréine;
Also, as I may tell you,
(There is) a wife for every man of my fifty . . .

'One night of the nights of the *Síd*
I would not give for your kingdom.'[22]

And so he re-enters the *Síd*, 'and he has not come out yet.'

Those who succumb altogether to the fascination of the mysterious otherworld woman are thus lost for ever to the world of men. But it may be said of these, even more than of the heroes of the Elopement Tales, whom they resemble, that they are the lesser figures of Celtic story. Like CúChulainn, Conle finds himself on the horns of a dilemma: 'It is not easy for me, for I love my people, but a longing for the woman has come upon me.' But his choice is different from CúChulainn's, and it may not be insignificant that for the storyteller the whole purpose of telling the tale is to explain why the father he left behind is known as 'Art the Lone One'. These supernatural mistresses bear a close resemblance to the 'celestial bride' who instructs and helps the Siberian shaman in his art. Desiring to keep him for herself, she too is prone to hinder her lover's further spiritual progress.[23]

3

This is how Cormac's cup of gold was found.[24] Early one May morning, Cormac was alone on the rampart of Tara when a splendidly-clad warrior approached, bearing on his shoulder a silver branch with three golden apples on it. So delightful was the music of the branch that the sick, the wounded, and women in childbed would fall asleep when they heard it. The warrior hailed from a land where there was nothing but truth, a land where there was neither age nor decay nor gloom nor sadness nor envy nor jealousy nor hatred nor arrogance. They avowed friendship, and Cormac asked for the branch. The warrior gave it to him on condition that he should be granted three wishes, in Tara, and then he disappeared. Cormac went back to his palace. When he shook the branch, the household was lulled to sleep until the next day.

At the end of the year, the warrior came again and demanded Cormac's daughter as his first wish. Cormac gave her to him, dispelling the sorrow of the women of Tara by shaking the sleep-inducing branch. A month later the warrior reappeared and took away Cormac's son, and the third time he claimed Cormac's wife. This was more than Cormac could endure. He set out with his followers in pursuit. A great mist fell upon them and Cormac found himself alone on a great plain. There he saw a large fortress surrounded by a wall of bronze. Inside was a house of silver, half thatched with white bird feathers.

There were men at work with lapfuls of bird feathers, but as they laid on the thatch, a gust of wind would come and blow it all away. He saw a man kindling a fire and throwing a great great tree on it, root and branch, but by the time he came back with another tree the first was completely burnt. Then he saw another royal fortress with four houses in it, and a bright well with nine ancient hazels growing over it. In the well, there were five salmon and they ate the nuts that dropped from the purple hazels, and sent the husks floating down the five streams that flowed therefrom. The sound of the streams was the sweetest music.

In the palace awaiting him was a couple—a noble warrior and a beautiful woman. He bathed in water heated by stones that came and went of themselves. Then a man came in with an axe in his right hand, a club in his left, and a pig behind him. He killed the pig, cleft the log, and cast the pig into the cauldron, but it would never be cooked until a truth were uttered for each quarter of it. The man with the axe, the warrior, and the woman each told a tale, miraculous but true, and three quarters were cooked. Cormac then told of the disappearance of his wife and family, and this completed the cooking. When Cormac's portion was served, he protested that he never ate a meal without fifty in his company. The warrior sang him to sleep, and when he awoke there were fifty warriors around him, together with his wife, his son and his daughter.

As they feasted, Cormac marvelled at the beauty of his host's golden cup. 'There is something more marvellous about it,' said the warrior. 'Let three lies be told under it, and it will break into three, but three truths will make it whole again.' The warrior told three lies and the cup broke, but when he said that neither Cormac's wife nor his daughter had seen a man, nor his son a woman, since they left Tara, it became whole again.

Then the warrior revealed himself as Manannán mac Lir, and told Cormac that he had brought him there to see the Land of Promise. He gave him the cup to distinguish truth from falsehood, and the branch for his delight. He explained that those he had seen thatching in vain were the poets of Ireland, who amassed perishable wealth; the man kindling the fire was a thriftless young lord; the spring was the Well of Knowledge, and the five streams the five senses through which knowledge is obtained. 'And no one will have knowledge who drinks not a draught out of the well itself and out of the streams. The folk of many arts are those that drink of them both.'

When Cormac arose in the morning, he was on the green of Tara with his family, and he also had the branch and the cup.

The other 'Adventures' make passing references to the absence of falsehood in the Other World, but only in Cormac's does truth appear as its central principle. Cormac, by giving his all for a branch of the otherworld tree, recovers what he has given and wins the talisman of truth. Above all he sees the Land of Promise and this is Manannán's purpose in bringing him there. He discovers that the source of knowledge and of art lies in the Other World, and in little dramatic parables, which anticipate the adventures of the Voyagers discussed in the next chapter, he is shown how human attitudes and behaviour appear in the Other World.

In this Adventure, the storyteller's expressed purpose is to explain the supernatural origin of Cormac's Cup of Truth. Similar miraculous objects figure as subsidiary motifs in other tales. We have already come across the crowns secured by Nera and Loegaire, and Crimthann's *fidchell*. Again, Conn with his druids and poets loses his way in a mist, and in a house near a golden tree he sees Lug and with him Sovereignty seated in a chair of crystal, with a silver vat, a vessel of gold, and a golden cup before her. The girl serves Conn with meat, and with red ale (*derg flaith*) in the cup, and Lug foretells the names of every prince from the time of Conn onwards. A druid records the names on staves of yew. Then the vision vanishes, but the vat, the vessel, and the staves are left with Conn.[25] Other wonderful vessels are the Dagda's 'undry' cauldron, from which no company ever went unthankful, Cormac's cauldron and Gwyddneu Garanhir's hamper, which gave to each his proper food, the cup which Tadg obtained in the land of the Immortals and which turned water into wine, the cauldron of the head of Annwfn (described in the early Welsh poem, 'The Spoils of Annwfn'), which would not boil food for a coward, the cauldron of Ceridwen, which after boiling for a year and a day produced three drops of grace and inspiration, and the Cauldron of Rebirth (brought from a lake in Ireland), which restored the dead to life.[26] These vessels of life and plenty may be classed with the Holy Grail of medieval romance. Everlasting foods, bottles that cannot be drained, and the Water of Life, which revives the dead, also figure among the objects of the hero's otherworld quest in Celtic folktales.

As symbols in myth, and probably as insignia and utensils in pre-Christian rites, such sacred relics enshrined eternity in the world of mortal existence. They also enhanced the meaning of their counterparts in ordinary life. In some measure, the cauldron and cup of every generous host partook of the nature of the archetypal vessels of plenty, every crown and every sword reflected a little of the brilliance of the eternal diadem and of the 'Sword of Light'.

CHAPTER XVI

Voyages

'Oh build your ship of death. Oh build it! for you will need it.
For the voyage of oblivion awaits you.'

D. H. LAWRENCE

The Irish storytellers distinguished between 'adventures' (*echtrai*) and 'voyages' (*immrama*), the latter involving visits to a number of otherworld islands. The distinction between the two types of stories is not absolute; the famous Voyage of Bran son of Febal is classified as an *echtra* in the Lists, but is called an *immram* in the text itself. Apart from the story of Bran, the Lists name seven *immrama*, only three of which have been preserved: 'The Voyage of Maeldúin', 'The Voyage of the Uí Chorra', and 'The Voyage of Snédgus and Mac Riagla'. The theme of the otherworld voyage is one of the most distinctive in Celtic tradition, and through the celebrated 'Voyage of St Brendan' it exercised the imagination of medieval Christendom and helped to arouse the spirit of adventure which prompted the great voyages of the fifteenth and sixteenth centuries. But the discovery of new lands has proved a constrictive substitute for the endless marvels of the otherworld ocean.

One day, as Bran son of Febal walks near his royal house, he hears sweet music behind him. The music lulls him to sleep and when he wakes there is a branch of silver beside him with white blossom on it. Bran takes the branch to the house and when all the hosts are assembled behind closed ramparts they see a woman in strange raiment in the middle of the house. To Bran she sings a long lay which all can hear, describing the splendour and delight of the world beyond the sea, with its

thrice fifty islands, each of them larger than Ireland, its thousands of women and its sweet music, a world where treachery,
sorrow, sickness and death are not known. She ends the lay:

'Not to all of you is my speech,
Though its great marvel has been made known.
Let Bran hear from the crowd of the world
What of wisdom has been told to him.

'Do not fall on a bed of sloth,
Let not intoxication overcome you,
Begin a voyage across the clear sea,
If perchance you may reach the Land of the Women.'

As she departs, the silver branch—'a branch of the apple-
tree from Emain Ablach'—springs from Bran's hand to hers.

Next day Bran goes to sea with three companies of nine,
each headed by one of his foster-brothers. After two days and
two nights, he meets Manannán mac Lir riding in his two-
wheeled chariot over the sea. In a long poem Manannán tells
Bran that to him the sea is solid earth, a many-flowered Plain
of Delight:

'Speckled salmon leap from the womb
Of the white sea, on which you look:
They are calves, they are coloured lambs
With friendliness, without mutual slaughter.

'Though you see but one chariot-rider
In Mag Mell of the many flowers,
There are many steeds on its surface,
Though you do not see them.

'Along the top of a wood
Your coracle has sailed, over ridges,
There is a wood of beautiful fruit
Under the prow of your little skiff . . . '

Manannán is on his way to Ireland where he will beget Mongán upon the wife of Fiachna, and he prophesies the coming
of Christ to save the world from the sin of Adam.

'Steadily then let Bran row,
It is not far to the Land of the Women,
Emne* with its many hues of hospitality
You will reach before the setting of the sun!'

Bran goes his way and comes to the Island of Joy, where he sees a large crowd of people all laughing and gaping. He sends a man ashore and the man begins to gape with the others, heedless of the calls of his comrades. So they leave him there.

Before long they reach the Land of the Women. The leading woman greets him: 'Come hither on land, O Bran son of Febal. Welcome is your coming.' She throws a ball of thread which cleaves to Bran's hand, and she pulls the boat ashore by the thread. They enter a large house where there is a bed for every couple, even thrice nine beds, and the food that is put before them does not diminish. 'It seemed a year to them that they were there; it was really many years.' Then one of the company becomes homesick, and Bran is persuaded to depart. The woman says they will regret it, warns them not to touch land, and directs them to pick up the man left on the Island of Joy.

They approach the land of Ireland at Srúb Brain, where there is an assembly of people. Bran tells the assembly that he is Bran son of Febal, but they know no such man, though the Voyage of Bran is in their ancient stories. The homesick man jumps ashore, but as he touches the ground he becomes a heap of ashes, as though he had been dead for many hundreds of years. Bran tells the assembled people all his wanderings and he writes the verses in ogam. Then he bids them farewell. 'And from that hour his wanderings are not known.'[1]

Unlike the Voyage of Bran, the three other extant Voyages are set in Christian times; neither magic branch nor fairy damsel entices the voyagers to sea. Two of them are pilgrimages directly or indirectly connected with the expiation of crimes.

* Emain Ablach.

The Uí Chorra[2] were three brothers who, in the service of the Devil, had plundered the churches of Connacht. After the eldest had seen a vision of Heaven and Hell they repented and restored the churches. Then they set out in a three-skinned boat, drawing in their oars and committing their destiny to the wind. The story of the Voyage of Snédgus and Mac Riagla[3] opens with the assassination of a tyrannical king by the Men of Ross. The king's brother imprisoned them all in one house to burn them alive, but on second thoughts he sought the advice of St Colum Cille of Iona. Two of the saint's clerics, Snedgus and Mac Riagla, brought the counsel that sixty couples of the Men of Ross be cast on the sea in small boats: God would pass judgement upon them. This was done and the two clerics embarked for home. As they were in their coracle, they decided to go voluntarily on the same pilgrimage as the sixty couples had undertaken involuntarily, and after three days they, like the Uí Chorra, shipped their oars and the sea carried them to many marvellous islands. On the sixth island they found the sixty couples dwelling without sin, until Doom, in the neighbourhood of Enoch and Elijah (who, like them, had left the earth without tasting death).

The beginning of the Voyage of the Uí Chorra corresponds closely with a reference in the Tripartite Life of St Patrick to a repentant tyrant who tried to kill St Patrick and was ordered by the saint to go to the sea-shore, scantily clad and bearing no food or drink, and, his feet fettered and the key of the fetter thrown into the sea, to be set adrift in a boat of a single hide without oar or rudder, to go wherever Providence might bring him. Other references in Irish texts show that setting adrift was a recognized method of punishment, but it seems to have been customary to show a little more mercy than St Patrick did. The victim was equipped with gruel and water for one night, a single paddle, and a hammer-shaped 'wedge' to keep off large sea-birds. He was abandoned as far out as a white shield is clearly visible on the sea. This indeterminate kind of penalty—a death penalty which is not a death penalty—was deemed appropriate for transgressors whose guilt likewise was not un/qualified[4]—those whose crimes were unintentional and, if we accept the evidence of the *immrama*, those who had acted under extreme provocation and those who had tried to make amends. It was also considered appropriate for women who had com/mitted murder or a crime deserving the death penalty, while the *Senchus Mór* speaks of 'a hermit condemned to the sea and the wind'.[5]

We have already noted the correspondence between the practice of setting infants born of incest adrift and the myth of the committal of the infant hero to the sea, an act which sym/bolizes his return to the OtherWorld. Here we have a similar correlation between setting an offender adrift and the voyages of mythological heroes to the world beyond. In its origin the custom undoubtedly springs from the same complex of beliefs in an Other World across the sea as gave rise to boat burials and the placing of little boats in tombs, the setting of the great adrift in burning ships in Norse myth and ritual,[6] and the story of the voyage of the mortally wounded King Arthur to Afallon for the healing of his wounds.[7] This belief in a voyage of death is perhaps echoed in the ribald games dramatizing 'The Building of the Ship' which were played at wakes for the dead, in Ireland, until recent times.[8]

2

In her lay to Bran, the fairy woman speaks of thrice fifty distant islands, but he brings back tidings of only two, the Island of Joy and the Island of the Women. After that his wanderings are not known. Many other islands appear in the two voyages we have referred to, but it is in the Voyage of Maeldúin[9] that we encounter the widest range of islands—thirty/one in all, together with two wonders beheld at sea. It is a long tale, said to have been arranged in its present form by Aed Finn, chief sage of Ireland, 'for the elation of the mind and for the people of Ireland after him.' The following is a bald summary.

On the advice of a druid, Maeldúin builds a three-skin boat in which to seek out his father's slayer. The druid fixes the day on which he shall start making his boat, and the day on which he shall start out, and he tells him to take no more and no less than seventeen men with him. Diurán the Rhymer is one of the crew. After Maeldúin has set sail, his three foster-brothers swim out to him and they are reluctantly taken into the boat despite the prohibition. The voyagers first come to two small islands, on each of them a fort from which comes the noise of carousal and contest. One warrior boasts to another that he slew Ailill, Maeldúin's father, and Maeldúin is about to land when a great wind blows his craft out to sea. They cease rowing and submit their course to God's guidance. These are the islands they come to:

1 An Island of Enormous Ants, each as large as a foal.
2 An Island of Great Birds.
3 An Island with a Fierce Beast, like a horse but with clawed feet like a hound's.
4 An Island of Giant Horses, with a demon horse-race in progress.
5 An Island where the sea hurls salmon through a stone valve into a house.
6 An Island of Trees. Maeldúin cuts a rod and each of the three apples which appear on it sustains him for forty nights.
7 An Island with a Wondrous Beast, which can turn its body round inside its skin and revolve its skin round its body.
8 An Island of Beasts like Horses, tearing the flesh from one another's sides until the island runs with blood.
9 An Island of Fiery Swine, which feed by day on the fruit of golden apple-trees and sleep by night in caverns while sea-birds come to eat the apples.
10 The Island of the Little Cat. Here they enter a deserted white house, full of treasure, four stone pillars in the middle of it and a small cat leaping from one pillar to the next. They partake of the food and drink they find there, and then they sleep.

Before they leave, one of Maeldúin's foster-brothers takes a necklace from the wall. The cat leaps through him like an arrow and he falls a heap of ashes. Maeldúin, who has forbidden theft, replaces the necklace.

11 The Island of Black and White. This is divided into two by a brass palisade, black sheep on one side, white sheep on the other. Tending them is a big man who sometimes puts a black sheep among the white or a white among the black. Immediately it changes colour. Maeldúin throws a peeled white wand into the black section and it turns black.

12 An Island of Giant Cattle and Huge Swine, separated by a river that burns like fire.

13 The Island of the Mill and the Giant Miller. 'Half the corn of your country,' he says, 'is ground here. Here comes to be ground all that men begrudge to one another.'

14 An Island of Black Mourners, all weeping and wailing. One of Maeldúin's foster-brothers joins them. He too weeps and, no longer recognizable, he is left behind.

15 An Island with Four Fences—of gold, silver, brass, and crystal—which divide it into four parts, containing kings, queens, warriors, and maidens, respectively.

16 An Island with a Great Fortress approached by a Glass Bridge. The bridge throws back those who seek to cross it. There is a beautiful maiden who thrice rebuffs the voyagers and then welcomes each by his name, saying that their coming has long been a matter of established knowledge. His men try to woo the maiden for Maeldúin, but she replies that she has never known sin. They ask her again and she promises them an answer on the morrow. When they awake they find themselves at sea in their boat and there is no sign of the island.

17 An Island of Shouting Birds.

18 An Island of Birds and One Solitary Anchorite, clothed only in his long hair. He had come there standing on a sod of his native land, and God had made an island of it, adding a foot's breadth and one tree to it every year. The birds are the souls of his children and his kindred who are awaiting Dooms-

day. They are all fed by angels. He prophesies that Maeldúin's company shall all reach their country, except one man.

19 An Island with a Wondrous Fountain, which yields water and whey on Fridays and Wednesdays, milk on Sundays and on some feast-days, and ale and wine on other feast-days.

20 An Island with a Great Forge worked by a Giant Smith.

21 A Sea like Glass. 'Great was its splendour and its beauty.'

22 A Thin Sea, like a transparent cloud, and beneath it a fair land where they see a monstrous beast in a tree surrounded by cattle. In spite of the vigilance of an armed man, the beast stretches down its neck and devours the largest ox of the herd.

23 An Island whose People Shout 'It is they!' at the voyagers, as though they knew of their coming and feared them.

24 An Island with an Arch of Water, like a rainbow full of salmon, rising on one side of it and falling on the other.

25 A great Square Silver Column rising from the sea, its top out of sight, but with a silver net stretching from it away into the sea. Diurán hacks away a piece of the net as they go under it. (On his return to Ireland, he offers it at the high altar at Armagh.) A voice speaks in a strange tongue from the summit of the pillar.

26 An Island on a Single Pedestal, a door in its base.

27 An Island of Women. Here Maeldúin and his seventeen men are received by a queen and her seventeen daughters. The women feast them, consort with them and try to induce them to remain there to live a life of perpetual pleasure and eternal youth. They stay for three months of winter which seem like three years, and the men weary of it. When they embark, the queen throws a ball of thread which clings to Maeldúin's hand and she hauls in the boat. She does this three times, and after each attempt to leave they stay another three months. The next time Maeldúin lets one of his men catch the ball and again it clings to the hand, but Diurán strikes off the man's hand and they escape.

28 An Island with Trees bearing Great Berries which yield intoxicating and slumber-inducing juice.

29 The Island of the Hermit and the Ancient Eagle. A great bird alights on a hill above a lake and eats great red berries, fragments of which fall into the lake and redden it. The bird's plumage is decayed, but two eagles come and pick off the vermin and old feathers. Next day the great bird plunges into the lake, and it is further groomed until its feathers are glossy and its flight becomes swift and strong. Watching it they apprehend the words of the prophet: 'Thy youth is renewed like the eagle's.' Diurán bathes in the lake, and so long as he lives he loses not a tooth nor a hair, nor suffers illness or infirmity.

30 The Island of Laughter. The last of Maeldúin's foster-brothers lands, laughs with the multitude there and has to be abandoned.

31 The Island with a Revolving Rampart of Fire. When the doorway comes opposite them they see, inside, handsome, luxuriously-clothed people bearing vessels of gold, and the air is filled with music.[10]

32 The Island of the Monk of Torach, who had robbed the church and put to sea with his treasures. On the instructions of a supernatural personage he had thrown his possessions overboard and let go his oars and his rudder. Eventually he had landed on this rock where he was miraculously fed. He counsels Maeldúin to forgive his father's slayer because God has preserved him and his men through manifold perils.

33 An Island on which they see a Falcon like the falcons of Ireland. Following it, they row until they sight their native land. They are welcomed on the island of the slayer, where Maeldúin's coming is even then the subject of conversation.

We have burdened the reader with this catalogue of islands in order to show that the Other World of the Voyages is different from the Other World of the Adventures. When Bran has passed through the paradoxical zone where sea and dry land are one and the same, and where men and women enjoy the pleasures of normal life without the attendant griefs, he enters a world where our world as we know it seems to resolve itself into its components. The people of the Island of Joy are not enjoying any particular pleasure; they are not laugh, ing *at* anything. The island symbolizes joy in its elemental iso, lation. The Island of the Women is likewise the quintessence of femininity and erotic pleasure, separated from everything with which it is intermingled in normal experience. The longer Voyage of Maeldúin continues the process of disentangling the constituent elements. The separation of animals into species and natures is particularly striking—ants, birds, shout, ing birds, race-horses, biting horses, salmon, pigs, sheep, cattle, all have their appointed places. Again forms, such as pillar, pedestal, arch, are singled out, and so are the contrasting attri, butes of 'blackness' and 'whiteness'. In 'Snédgus' there is an island with two lakes in it, one of water, the other of fire. But for the prayers of the saints these two elements would have overwhelmed Ireland.[11]

Again, mankind is segregated into four classes, with kings, queens, warriors, and maidens in separate compartments. On a similar island in 'The Voyage of Uí Chorra' they are classified differently into 'sedate people', lords, young men, and servants (the four functions?).[12] In 'The Voyage of Maeldúin' there is again a land of Women; Brendan saw an Island of Strong Men divided into three age-groups—boys, young men, and old men[13]—and the Uí Chorra came to an island where Living Men and Dead Men were in separate parts.[14] To the Island of Laughter is added its opposite, an island of spontaneous and causeless grief. As things turned black or white in the con, trasting halves of another island, so here everyone who landed wept irrespective of cause. The metaphysical implication would appear to be that Whiteness, Blackness, Fire, Water, Joy, Sor, row, Femininity, Masculinity, Youth, Age, Life, Death, and so on, exist as abstract principles over and above the objects or people in which they are manifested. (The doctrines of primeval elements and of archetypal ideas have, of course, a far wider provenance and a much greater antiquity than their particular formulations by Greek philosophers.) As though to emphasize further the detachment of principles from their usual vehicles in the manifest world, they are sometimes represented in com-binations which have no earthly counterparts—a horse with dog-claws, in 'Maeldúin,' and three islands inhabited, respect-ively, by cat-headed men, pig-headed men, and men with dog heads and bovine manes, in 'Snédgus'. Like the animal-masked mummers of seasonal rites and the hobby-horses (which can move round inside their skins), these monstrosities show that the principial ideas might have been combined to make quite a different world from the one we know.

In addition to the elements that constitute the corporeal world, human attitudes and behaviour also are depicted in the islands. There is an island symbolizing the true nature of niggardliness, another the sanctity of property and the sin of theft. The Island of the Bridge of Glass may represent Chastity, and there is no doubt that many of the other tableaux have parabolic meanings which elude us. In the more thoroughly Christian 'Voyages', islands of mice, of birds, of fruit-trees, and so on are intermingled with others depicting one by one the tortures which fit individual sins.

Little has been said in this book about the Celtic doctrine concerning life after death, because native sources are strangely silent on the subject. The only future world of which the texts speak is the Christian one. In this respect the native literature presents a striking contrast to the testimony of classical writers who assert that the druids believed that the souls of men are immortal. So strong was the belief that, according to Valerius Maximus,[15] even the payment of debts could be deferred to the next world. Along with the belief in immortality went a doctrine of reincarnation. However much Classical observers may have misunderstood the religious beliefs of the Celts, it is hardly possible that they were completely mistaken about this, and it is not by accident that the earliest and most vivid 'visions' of a Christian Other World recorded in medieval Europe appeared in the Celtic West, 'visions' in which there is a wealth of imagery not easily traced to other Christian sources.

In the religious systems of Egypt, India, and many other parts of the world, the priests have been the custodians of a body of doctrine concerning the progress of the soul after death. It was imperative that those at death's door should be conver' sant with the doctrine, and measures were taken to remind them of it. Even medieval Christendom produced its 'Book of the Craft of Dying'. 'The Tibetan Book of the Dead', in particular, casts a glimmer of light on our Voyages. This book portrays the succession of states through which the spirit passes after death, states in which thoughts become things, and atti' tudes take form as objective entities. 'The deceased human being becomes the sole spectator of a marvellous panorama of hallucinatory visions. . . . At first, the happy and glorious visions born of the seeds of the impulses and aspirations of the higher or divine nature awe the uninitiated; then, as they merge into the visions born of the corresponding mental ele' ments of the lower or animal nature, they terrify him, and he wishes to flee from them'[16]—as did the Irish Voyagers from some of the islands they saw. Among the manifold connota' tions of the long succession of symbols in the Tibetan book, are the four elements (fire, water, earth, and air), the four colours, and other sets of four 'orders' (each set making *five* in its totality and union). There are 'Peaceful Deities', and 'Wrathful Deities' with frightful beastly heads, whose aspect and behaviour recall the torture scenes in 'Uí Chorra'.

In the 'Voyages', we submit, have been preserved the tat' tered remnants of an oral Celtic 'book' of the dead, which proclaimed that the mysteries of the world beyond death had been at least partially explored and the stations of the soul's pilgrimage charted. The Plain of Delight and the Land of the Women are but stages on the way. In Maeldúin's Voyage there are thirty'three wonders to be seen, and the number may not be accidental. Thus, like the other types of tales we have des' cribed, the *immram* has its own function. It is to teach the 'craft' of dying and to pilot the departing spirit on a sea of perils and of wonders.

CHAPTER XVII

Deaths

THE CIRCUMSTANCES of the hero's death have been fore⁄told by druids or seers and in many cases he goes through life knowing precisely what his end will be. So fully are the inci⁄dents which culminate in the Destruction of Da Derga's Hostel and the death of Conaire prefigured by the wizards of the attackers that relatively few words are necessary to tell the story of the actual battle. This is no more than a repetition or a materialization of a story which has its origin and being in a world outside the limitations of here and now. One is re⁄minded of the relationship between a sentence of death and an execution. The sentence has prescribed the form of death and nothing remains but to carry it out.

CúChulainn's journey to his last battle[1] is a veritable 'death ride'. Before he sets forth, a number of omens warn him of impending doom. Weapons fall from their racks, and as he throws on his mantle the brooch falls and pierces his foot. The Morrígan has broken his chariot during the night to hinder his departure. The Grey of Macha resists being har⁄nessed to the chariot; he turns his left side to his master and when reproached he weeps tears of blood. As the hero departs, Lebarcham the female satirist beseeches him not to go and thrice fifty queens who love him give a scream of wailing and lamentation and smite their hands, for they know that he will not come to them again. On his way he calls for a drink at the house of his foster⁄mother as was his wont, and he bids her farewell. According to some versions, the cupful of milk he is given to drink becomes a cupful of blood, and his path takes him past two beautiful maidens in grief and tribulation wash⁄ing a bloody garment at a ford. It is his garment that they are washing.[2] He also encounters three crones, blind in the left eye, who with poisons and spells have cooked a dog on spits of rowan. The hero is thereby placed in a quandary: it is *geis* ('a prohibited thing') for him to eat his namesake, the dog, and it is *geis* for him to pass a cooking-hearth without partaking of the fare. At first he refuses the invitation extended by one of the crones, but when she reproaches him for disdaining their humble meal he submits. With her left hand she gives him one of the shoulder-blades of the hound, and he eats it out of his hand and places it under his left thigh. The hand and the thigh lose their strength.

The violation of *gessa* is such a sure omen of approaching death that it might almost be inferred that a hero is safe from harm while his *gessa* remain inviolate. Then, as his time approaches its end, he finds himself in situations where he cannot avoid breaking them, just as Greek heroes unwittingly work their own undoing when their fated hour has come and their divine guardians have forsaken them. Nowhere is this process so dramatically depicted as in 'The Destruction of Da Derga's Hostel'[3], where in the course of the events which lead up to his death Conaire violates one after another the *gessa* laid upon him, by the King of the Birds, before he was installed King of Ireland. These *gessa* were:

1 Thou shalt not go right-handwise round Tara and left-handwise round Brega.

2 The crooked beasts of Cerna must not be hunted by thee.

3 Thou shalt not be away from Tara for nine nights in succession.

4 Thou shalt not stay a night in a house from which fire-light can be seen after sunset and into which one can see from outside.

5 Three Reds shall not go before thee to the house of Red.

6 No plunder shall be taken in thy reign.

7 After sunset a company of one woman or one man shall not enter the house in which thou art.

8 Thou shalt not settle the quarrel of two of thy serfs.

The beginning of Conaire's undoing is the leniency he shows towards his foster-brothers, the Sons of Donn Désa who, resenting the peace of his reign, have taken to marauding (_geis_ 6). First he spares these foster-brothers while condemning their fellow-offenders to death. Then he revokes this judgement —'the judgement I have given is no extension of life to me'— and sends them all to wreak their rapine on the men of Alba. During their voyage they meet Ingcél the One Eyed, son of the king of the Britons, and his men, and they join forces with him. To begin with, they slay Ingcél's father and mother and his seven brothers, and then they sail for Ireland where Ingcél is entitled to a reciprocal plunder.

In the meantime Conaire has gone to Munster to settle a quarrel between the two Corpres, foster-brothers of his (_geis_ 8), and has stayed five nights with each of them (_geis_ 3). On the return journey the king and his company see warbands and stark-naked men and the land around Tara in a cloud of fire. This is a sign that the king's law has collapsed. Conaire and his entourage go right-handwise round Tara and left-handwise round Brega (_geis_ 3), and the king hunts the crooked beasts of Cerna (_geis_ 2) without knowing what he is doing until the chase is over. Then they follow the coast southward and decide to spend the night at Da Derga's Hostel. Mac Cécht, the champion, goes ahead to kindle a fire for the king at the hostel, a building with seven doorways but only one door, which is moved around to close the doorway where the wind is blowing.

Conaire sees three horsemen riding before him towards the hostel. They are all red, both body and hair and raiment, both horses and men, and they are going to the house of a Red* (_geis_ 5). In vain does Conaire send his son to call them back. They reply only with forebodings of impending tragedy. 'Lo, my son, great news. Weary are the steeds we ride. We ride the steeds of Donn Desscorach from the _síde_. Though we are alive we are dead. Great (will be) the cuttings off of lives. Sating of

---

* Derg: 'Red' (Da Derga).

ravens. Feeding of crows. Strife of slaughter. Whetting of sword-edge. Shields with broken bosses (?) in the hours after sundown. Lo.' Then the company is overtaken by a mon-strous black man, who has only one eye, one hand, and one foot, and his huge loathsome wife. He is Fer Caille ('Man of the Wood') and he welcomes Conaire: 'Long has your coming here been known.' On his back he carries to the hostel a squealing black pig for Conaire to consume. (This too is a *geis*, though it has not been mentioned before.)

Conaire goes into the hostel; all take their seats, both *geis* and non-*geis*, and Da Derga gives them a welcome. Then a lone woman in a grey cloak comes to the door after sunset asking to be let in. Her shins are as long as a weaver's beam and as black as a stag beetle. Her pubic hair reaches to her knee and her lips are in the side of her head. Leaning against the door-post she casts an evil eye on the king and his company and prophesies that neither his skin nor his flesh will escape from that house save what the birds carry away in their claws. 'What do you want?' says Conaire. 'Whatever you want,' she replies. 'It is a *geis* of mine,' says Conaire, 'to receive the com-pany of one woman after sunset.' *Geis* or not, she refuses to go away and reproaches the king for his lack of hospitality. 'Savage is the answer,' says Conaire. 'Let her in, though it is a *geis* of mine.' And great loathing and ill-foreboding falls upon the gathering.

In the meantime, the marauders led by Ingcél and the sons of Donn Désa have landed, and as their boats struck land the Hostel shook so that the weapons fell from their racks. The irony of the situation is fully exploited in the narrative. Asked to explain the noise of the landing, Conaire says: 'I do not know what it is unless it be the earth that has been rent, or the Leviathan encircling the earth that is striking with its tail to overturn the world, or the boat of the Sons of Donn Désa that has come to land. Alas that it is not they! They were our be-loved foster-brothers. Dear was the warrior band. We should not fear them tonight.' And in the landing party one of Donn

Désa's sons says of Conaire: 'His rule was good.' Peace, good-will, and prosperity mark his reign. 'May God not bring that man here tonight. . . . 'Tis grievous that his life should be short.'

Through the wheels of the seventeen chariots that stand at each doorway of the hostel, the invaders can see the great fire kindled for the king (*geis* 4). Ingcél goes forward to spy, and there follows a long colloquy in which he describes the orderly arrangement of the rooms of the hostel and the people in them. His Irish accomplices identify each one from Ingcél's description, and, in an endeavour to deflect him from his determination to sack the hostel, they foretell the mighty deeds that each one will perform in the impending battle, as though they were rehearsing the course of a pre-ordained ritual.

During the attack the hostel is thrice set on fire, and thrice the flames are extinguished. Conaire kills six hundred before reaching for his weapons and another six hundred afterwards. But the druids of the attackers inflict a magic thirst upon him and they take away the water of all the rivers and lakes in Ireland. Conaire calls for a drink and Mac Cécht sets out in search of water, for the water that was in the hostel has been used in quenching the fires. He fails to find any until he comes to Uarán Garaid on the plain around Cruachan, where the water cannot hide itself from him. On his return he finds two men striking off Conaire's head. He kills them and then spills the water into Conaire's gullet and neck. The severed head says: 'A good man Mac Cécht! An excellent man Mac Cécht!' Then the champion follows the routed foe. Only nine of the defenders have fallen; only five of the attackers have escaped.

When Conall Cernach comes back to Tailtiu from the battle, his father reproaches him for returning alive leaving his lord dead among his enemies. Conall shows him his wounds. 'That arm fought tonight, son,' says the father. 'That is true, old warrior,' says Conall. 'Many a man got his drink of death from it tonight in front of the hostel.'

Conaire's *gessa* are a formulation of his fate in a series of 'Thou shalt nots.' All these things must be avoided, but they must all come to pass before he dies. The king need not have spared the sons of Donn Désa, nor need he have settled the quarrel of the two serfs, but after he has taken these first false steps events take their own course with gathering momentum. He is overcome by his *gessa*, and there is nothing he can do to arrest such precursors of doom as the Three Reds and Fer Caille with the squealing pig. When faced with the lone woman at the door, he is caught *between* his kingly obligation to be hospitable and one of his personal *gessa*. And it is of the nature of personal *gessa* that they have a proclivity to trap their victim between themselves and the more general prohibitions of etiquette and propriety. Alternatively, the victim is check-mated by two of his own *gessa*, as CúChulainn was when the *geis* that he should not eat dog and the *geis* that he should not pass a cooking-hearth without sharing the repast intersected. No longer can he choose between right on the one hand and wrong on the other. He is already in a world where right and wrong have merged. To encompass the death of the invincible hero, the enemies of CúChulainn had already had recourse to that world where all things are possible. The Sons of Calatín had been learning wizardry for seventeen years and they had been mutilated: the right foot and the left hand of the sons had been cut off and the daughters had been blinded in the left eye.[4] In short they had been given a Fomorian aspect.

As CúChulainn, after his encounter with the three hags,[5] enters the field of battle single-handed, with the light of valour shining over him, his enemies make a fence of their linked shields, and at each corner Erc son of Cairpre makes them place two of their bravest men feigning to fight each other, and a satirist with each of these pairs to ask CúChulainn for his spear—for the Sons of Calatín have prophesied that a king will fall by that spear. CúChulainn attacks, wreaking great carnage upon his foes. Then he sees one of the pairs of contending warriors and, entreated by the satirist, he intervenes and dashes out their brains. 'That spear to me,' says the satirist. 'I swear what my people swear,' says CúChulainn, 'you do not need it more than I do . . .' 'I shall revile you if you do not give it,' says the satirist. 'I have never yet been reviled for my niggardliness or my churlishness,' says CúChulainn, and he flings the spear at him handle foremost so that it passes through his head and kills nine men beyond him. Lugaid son of CúRoí gets the spear. 'Who will fall by this spear, O sons of Calatín?' he asks, and they answer: 'A king will fall by that spear.' Lugaid casts the spear and kills Loeg, CúChulainn's charioteer.

CúChulainn recovers the spear. He sees the second pair of sham fighters, and the drama that led up to the death of Loeg, 'king of charioteers', is repeated. Lest Ulster be reviled, he again yields his spear and with it Erc strikes the Grey of Macha, 'king of steeds'. Then CúChulainn sees the third pair contending, and this time he yields his spear because the satirist threatens to revile his race. Lugaid flings the spear and it strikes CúChulainn so that his bowels come forth on the cushion of his chariot. With his enemies' consent he gathers up his bowels to his breast and goes to the loch and there he drinks and washes himself. The extended version of the story says that an otter—the Irish word means 'water-dog'—comes to drink the blood. CúChulainn casts a stone at it and kills it. Now he knows that he must die, for it has been prophesied that his last heroic deed, like his first, will be the killing of a dog.[6] He turns back, calling his enemies to meet him. With his breast girdle he fastens himself to a pillar-stone so that he may die standing up, and while his soul remains in his body and the hero's light over his head the wounded Grey of Macha defends him, making three 'red routs' in which it kills fifty men with its teeth and thirty with its hoofs. Eventually the birds descend on CúChulainn's shoulder, and Lugaid ventures forward to arrange his hair and to cut off his head. As the sword falls from the dead hero's hand it severs Lugaid's right hand. CúChulainn's right hand is cut off in revenge and it is buried with his head in Tara.

In this fantastic battle CúChulainn is once more placed between the devil and the deep blue sea. He has either to make the foolhardy gesture of presenting his enemies with his weapon, or he has to suffer the ignominy of being reviled for behaviour unbecoming of a warrior, and that in a society in which satire too can be a death-dealing weapon. And so CúChulainn is brought to his death by being placed in a series of ambiguous situations where heroism is of no avail.

2

This meeting of opposites is symbolized in a different way in the death of the Welsh Lleu Llaw Gyffes.[7] It is said that Lleu could not be slain within a house nor outside, on horseback nor on foot, and, judging by the conditions under which he was eventually rendered vulnerable, he could also not be killed in water nor on land, clothed nor unclothed. As if to put a fine point on it, he could be killed only with a spear which had taken a year to make and which had been worked on only when people were at Mass on Sunday, that is during sacred 'intemporal' moments when eternity impinges upon the world of time. He was in fact smitten in circumstances where all the opposites we have mentioned met. The same motif is to be found in Indian stories. Thus the demon Namuci once got the better of Indra but released him on condition that he agreed not to slay him by day or by night, with a staff or a bow, with the flat of the hand or with fists, with anything wet or dry. Eventually, Indra slays him in the twilight with the foam of the waters.[8]

These 'betwixts and betweens'[9] are mid-points or the mid-way-line between opposites; they are neither this nor that. Or they may be regarded as a union of opposites, both this and that. Conceived of in this latter way, betwixts-and-betweens shed a ray of light on the significance of the 'multiple death', which is another characteristic motif of Irish death tales. King Diarmait (son of Fergus) had caused the house of Flann son

of Dima to be burnt and its owner, sorely wounded and seeking to avoid the flames, had got into a bathing vat and had
expired there. And St Ciarán had prophesied that Diarmait
himself would suffer the same death, 'to be wounded, and
drowned, and burnt'. Later on, Bec, the best seer of his time,
prophesied that the king would be killed by Aed Dub ('Black
Aed') in the house of Banbán,* the hospitaller, where the
ridge-pole would fall on his head. The seer also foretold the
paradoxical circumstances of the king's end, and although Aed
was immediately banished these were confirmed when Diarmait enquired of his druids what death he was to die.
'Slaughter,' said the first druid, 'and 'tis a shirt grown from a
single flax-seed, with a mantle of one sheep's wool, that you
will wear on the night of your death.' 'It is easy for me to evade
that,' Dairmait said. 'Drowning,' said the second druid, 'and
it is ale brewed from one grain of corn that you shall despatch
that night.' 'Burning,' said the third druid, 'and bacon of
swine that never were farrowed—that shall be on your dish.'
'That is unlikely,' said Diarmait.

His death was eventually encompassed in circumstances
which reconciled all these contradictions. Banbán invited the
king to a night's entertainment. Mugain, the king's wife, refused to go with him and warned him that to go upon an invitation was destined to have evil consequences for him.
Nevertheless Diarmait went with Banbán and when they had
settled down in the house, a graceful young woman in fine
raiment entered. 'Whence the woman?' asked Diarmait. 'She
is a daughter of mine,' replied Banbán, 'and, to spite Mugain
because she came not with me, the girl shall this night be your
wife.' 'I am well pleased,' said the king. A bed was made
ready for them. Then Banbán said: 'Well girl, have you
brought raiment for the king?' She handed a shirt and a mantle
to Diarmait and he put them on. "Tis a good shirt,' said all.
'It befits you,' said Banbán, 'the shirt of one flax-seed—she is

* Little Pig'.

a fanciful girl and it is she that sowed a single seed of flax and made a strike of it which then became a ridgeful.' "Tis a good mantle,' cried all. 'It is good,' said Banbán, 'it is made of a single sheep's wool.' Then food and drink was brought them. 'The bacon that was never farrowed is good,' said Banbán, and he explained that the piglings were cut, with knives, from their mothers and afterwards fattened. "Tis good ale!' said all. 'It is good,' said Banbán, 'ale brewed of a single grain of corn.' The grain had been found in the crop of a ringdove; it had been sown and its yield sown again and from the second harvest the ale had been made.

Diarmait looked up and observed that whereas the lower part of the house was new, the upper-work was older. Banbán explained that the ridge-beam had been found floating towards himself and his companions while they were fishing. 'Truthfully uttered was the prophecy of Bec and the druids,' said Diarmait, and he sprang to get out. 'This is the way,' said Aed Dub at the doorway, planting in the king's breast a spear which broke his spine. Then Diarmait turned back into the house. Ulster-men surrounded the dwelling and burned it upon those that were in it. Diarmait, seeking to avoid the flames, entered the ale vat, whereupon the roof-tree fell on his head, and so he died.[10]

To the question: 'What was the cause of Diarmait's death?', there are four different answers, each of which is both true *and* untrue. He was speared: no, he was drowned: no, he was burnt: no, it was the roof-tree that fell on his head! In a world of 'either/or' or 'nothing but' he could not have died at all.

3

The Death of Diarmait brings into prominence the fatal feast, the hero's last supper before his death, which has already appeared in a less pronounced manner in the stories of Cú-Chulainn and Conaire. The supernatural character of this meal is expressed in different ways. By eating his namesake CúChulainn partakes of himself: the opposition of eater and eaten, of subject and object, is superseded. The squealing pig which Conaire is destined to consume is carried by a one-eyed, one-armed, one-footed man, a being like the Sons of Calatín whose bodies are free from the duality which is inherent in the human frame. And the transcendence of multiplicity is symbolized in the derivation of Diarmait's death drink and death clothes from unitary origins, while his repast consisted of the flesh of pigs that had never been born. We would suggest that Conaire in acting as a go-between in the quarrel of the two serfs, and CúChulainn in his repeated slaughter of pairs of contending warriors, were placing themselves on that supernatural level which is above opposites. In Norse stories of journeys to the land of the dead, two armies engaged in unending conflict are among the wonders encountered on the way.[11] There is an analogous motif in the story of the feast which precedes the sequence of events that lead to the death of Finn. The two cupbearers who carry Finn's magic drinking-horn engage in a quarrel. Neither is the victor, for each kills the other in the presence of the Fiana. 'That deed weighed heavily on Finn's mind, so that for a long time he was silent, without drink or food, or delight of mind. . . . "I regret those two", said Finn; "but I am not so much troubled about their death as about that which gave rise to it".' And he told the story of how he had received the cup from Cronánach of Síd ar Femuin. 'Thereupon with great sadness Finn put the horn from him and thenceforth they ceased from that conversation.'[12]

Another curious feature of the hero's death is its connection with an incident of a sexual nature. Conchobar is fatally wounded by Cet when the women of Connacht have persuaded him to turn aside 'that they might see his shape',[13] and Niall of the Nine Hostages is slain in similar circumstances.[14] At the instigation of Ailill, the blind Lugaid unwittingly slew Fergus mac Roich with a spearcast when the warrior was swimming in a lake with Medb on his breast, her legs entwined around him.[15] Conall Cernach, prompted by a jealous Medb, slew Ailill in his turn when the latter was behind a hazel-bush, consorting with a woman, on the morning of May Day.[16] On the eve of the battle at which he was doomed to die, Eogan son of Ailill slept with his host's daughter at her father's request, as, in a like situation, did Art the father of Cormac.[17] CúRoí's abduction of Bláthnat led to his being killed with her connivance as he slept with his head in her lap.[18] It is told that Cumall, chief of the Fiana, could be killed only when he lay in the arms of his wife and then only with his own sword. His enemies brought the daughter of the king of Lochlann to be his wife, and they took the bridal couple through seven doors and seven rooms and left them there, locking each of the seven doors as they retired. A traitor, Arca Dubh,* the king's fisher, was hidden in the inner room and he slew Cumall with the fatal sword.[19] Or, according to another version,[20] a beautiful woman is placed on an islet; Cumall swims to her and is killed by Arca Dubh who hides in the grass.

In the tales we have told in this chapter, the mysterious woman with whom the hero consorts helps to seal his fate. Diarmait lies with Banbán's daughter who then regales him with the food and raiment of his death. It is from among a company of women that CúChulainn sets out to his last battle. In the version of the story which we have followed, the Mórrigan (Badb), acting like a friend, breaks the chariot to impede his going to the battle. According to the longer version,[21] his closest companion during his last days is his mistress, Niam,** wife of Conall, the woman whose requests he finds it most difficult to refuse. With her he goes to a feast in Glenn na mBodar to which Cathbad the druid has invited him and a company of noble ladies, while Emer, his wife, remains behind. The noise of fighting cannot be heard from this glen, and Niam's purpose is to dissuade CúChulainn from joining battle, but 'Calatín's daughter', Badb, presents herself to him *in the form of Niam* and exhorts him to go. Niam

* 'Black Arca'.
** 'Brightness', 'Beauty'.

and the Badb seem to be personifications of the two-fold character of the woman who befriends the hero at the time of his death. She is both his friend and the feminine personification of his doom.

Transgressing his *gessa* Conaire admits the lone woman, Cailb, into Da Derga's Hostel. The description of her monstrous form includes an allusion to her sexual parts, as does the description of her double who accompanies the black man with the squealing pig, and she answers Conaire saying that she desires what he also desires. In the obscure roll of thirty-two (?) names which she chants on one foot and with one breath, when she is neither in the house nor outside it, are Samain, Ugliness, Oblivion, Crime, Conflict, Fray, Crash, Noise (?) and Amazement (?) as well as Nemain (or Macha), the name of the goddess of war, and Badb, that of the ominous crow of the battlefield.[22] Thus Cailb, like the Indian Kālī, is the personification of death, woe, and destruction, and she invites the reluctant hero to make her his ultimate bride.

4

We will now relate the story of the Death of Muirchertach[23] which embodies in still another way the motifs of the bride of the victim, the fatal feast, the contending warriors, a Fomorian-like killer, and a body shared between fire and water in death.

One day when Muirchertach, King of Ireland, is seated alone on his hunting-mound, a beautiful girl in a green mantle appears beside him and he is so filled with love for her that he would give the whole of Ireland if he could have her for one night. She describes herself as 'the paramour of Muirchertach' and declares that, being skilled in places more secret than this, she already knows him and the other men of Ireland. 'I will give you power over me, O damsel,' says he, and she offers herself to him on condition that he never utters her name, that the mother of his children shall not be in her sight, and that clerics shall never be in the same house as herself. The king accepts these conditions and asks her what her name is, so that he may avoid uttering it. Beautiful though she is, she utters a string of names similar to those of the loathsome Cailb—'Sigh, Sough, Storm, Rough Wind, Winter-night, Cry, Wail, Groan.'

To please her, the queen and her children are turned out of the house of Cletech, and practitioners of every craft and art in Ireland together with their wives are brought into the drinking-hall. St Cairnech is so incensed by the expulsion of the queen that he curses the steading and digs a grave for the king, saying, 'He whose grave this is has finished, and truly it is an end of his realm and his princedom.' The king sits on the throne with the girl on his right, and feeling that she is 'a goddess of great power' he asks her what kind of power she has. She replies that she believes in God; she is of the race of Adam and Eve, yet she can work great wonders. Muirchertach asks her to perform miracles. She makes wine of the water of the Boyne and enchanted pigs of ferns, and this magic repast saps the strength of the king and his host. She conjures up illusions, among which are two battalions of equal strength slaughtering each other, the one blue and the other headless. Muirchertach exhausts himself in battling against these shadows which are really nothing but stones, ferns and sods. Then on the seventh night, the eve of Wednesday after Samain, a storm arises. 'This is the sigh of a winter night,' says the king. The girl replies: ''Tis I am the Rough Wind . . . Winter night is my name . . . Sigh and Wind, Winter-night.' When he again speaks of the storm (*sín*) that is raging she asks him: 'Why do you utter my name, O man?' and tells him that he is doomed. 'That is true, O damsel . . . for it was foretold that my death and the death of my grandfather would be alike.' Muirchertach had burned his grandfather in his house. Visions of burning and drowning[24] now disturb his enchanted sleep. Sín sets the house on fire and arrays around it phantom attackers said to be Tuathal Maelgarb*[25] son of Cormac the One-Eyed and his armies seeking revenge. Muirchertach gets into a cask of wine and is drowned while fire falls on his head and burns the upper part of his body.

Like the feast of Samain at Emain Macha, the story of Muirchertach's death extends over seven days, with Samain Eve presumably in the middle, and it was indeed a time of 'mischief and confusion'. CúRoí, Crimthann, CúChulainn, and Conaire are all said to have died at Samain, while Ailill and Flann died at Beltaine.[26] Thus, just as the incidents preceding the death of the hero symbolize in various ways the convergence of opposites, so the time of his death is a time when pairs of worlds which are normally in contradistinction —summer and winter, natural and supernatural, the living and the dead—fuse together and intermingle.

The Irish death-tales are called *Oitte*, 'violent (or tragic) deaths'. For CúChulainn, and for champions generally, to die of disease or old age would be an anti-climax. It is essential to the ethos of a warrior caste that death in battle should be the most glorious of all deaths, the death which ensures admission to paradise. Lucan says that the Celtic warrior had no fear of death, for 'death . . . is but the centre of a long life.' Most of the Irish kings mentioned in the official annals also died violently, many of them at the hands of their successors. In the stories we have told, however, it is not merely a case of the strong ousting the weak from the throne. The festive occasion, the fateful bride and the elaborate predetermined circumstances of the deaths of Conaire, Diarmait, Muirchertach—and of CúChulainn too—recall the ceremonial 'killing of the king', when his powers failed or when he had ruled for a prescribed term, which was once the custom over a large part of Africa and of which there are traces in other parts of the world.[27]

Nevertheless, if the interpretation put forward in the previous chapters is valid, the myths have a bearing on the meaning of

* 'Rough-head'.

death itself. They proclaim that death, however peaceful it may appear to be, is a work of violence, a cutting down. The myths do not mitigate the impact of death with soothing words; they present it in its grimmest brutality. And yet, the declamation of such stories at Samain, perhaps, and at wakes for the dead, had its proper function. They elevated death to the plane of the tragic and the heroic. From a human standpoint deaths may be dismissed as due to natural causes: accidents, diseases, and so on; some are expected, others are 'premature'. But mythologically speaking no death is natural, nothing is ever premature and there is no such thing as accident. Deaths are preordained; and the contingent causes are but the agents of pre-existent and precognizable destinies. It is noteworthy that folk-belief is in agreement with the myths. However 'sudden' the death, there will have been omens. An apple-tree will have blossomed out of season, a hen will have crowed like a cock, or a dog will have howled at night. Someone will have seen a corpse-candle or a phantom-funeral or there will have been a premonitory dream or an inexplicable uneasiness. These portents accentuate the eeriness and mystery of death; they enhance its meaning. It is a reality of whose imminence the natural and supernatural worlds are aware and of which they take cognisance. Unlike such contemporary banalities as 'Well, he had a happy life' or 'He did not suffer much' or 'He is better out of his misery', myth and folk-belief do not strip death of its significance and so do not depreciate the nobility of human beings.

CHAPTER XVIII

Epilogue

'Whatever is here, that is there; what is there, the same is here.
He who seeth here as different, meeteth death after death.'

KATHA UPANISHAD

'And for this cause it were right for thee to buy the poems of the
poets, and to keep the poets in Ireland, and since all the world is
but a story, it were well for thee to buy the more enduring story,
rather than the story that is less enduring.'

JUDGEMENT OF ST COLUM CILLE

In diverse ways myth and ritual loosen the grip of the temporal
world upon the human spirit. Under the spell of the storyteller's art, the range of what is possible in this world is trans-
cended: the world of magic becomes a present reality and the
world of every-day is deprived of its uniqueness and universality. The storyteller, like the juggler and the illusionist, by
convincingly actualizing the impossible, renders the actual
world less real. When the spell is over, the hearer 'comes back
to earth', but the earth now is not quite so solid as it was before,
the cadence of its time is less oppressive and its laws have only
a relative validity.

> 'If poets' verses be but stories,
> So be food and raiment stories;
> So is all the world a story;
> So is man of dust a story.'[1]

As myth and ritual are realized, the present world becomes a
stage and ordinary life a play.

Not only is myth not bounded by the laws of nature, it
transcends the limitations of common sense. To the questions:
'Where is the Other World?', 'Is it one or many?', the answers
furnished by myth are contradictory. It is the 'lower' half of

Ireland, the land under the earth or the *síd*/mounds. It is also 'the land under the wave', an island, or a whole series of islands beyond the sea. Yet it can manifest itself in other places. A mist falls upon us in an open plain, and lo, we are there witnessing its wonders. We go to sleep in the enchanted land and by morning all has disappeared, or we have been mysteriously re/transported to our own homes. The limits of such a world cannot be 'defined' in terms of distance or direction. Situated far beyond the horizon, it is the goal of the most perilous journey in the world; present unseen all round us, it can break in upon us 'in the twinkling of an eye'.

Stranger still, it can be two things at once. In the Adventure of Bran, even the opposition of land and water is effaced in the Plain of Delight. Again, it is a land of truth, peace, and ever/lasting life—

> 'Unknown is wailing and treachery
> In the familiar cultivated land,
> There is nothing rough or harsh,
> But sweet music striking on the ear.
>
> Without grief, without sorrow, without death,
> Without sickness, without debility . . .'[2]

—and yet, some of the tales tell of battles, abductions, and slaughter in this delightful land. The same ambivalence char/acterizes its inhabitants; they are either 'good people' or they are the most horrible monstrosities conceivable. Its women are either divinely beautiful or they are fiendish hags. It is a world of superlatives.

Defying definition in space, the Other World also transcends mundane time. Characteristically, this is expressed in the stories in two opposite ways. On the one hand, a very short time in the Other World corresponds with a very long time in this world. Many are the stories in medieval texts and in modern folklore which tell of a man who returns after a seemingly brief sojourn in that enchanted world and finds that his contemporaries are dead and that his own name is but a memory. When he touches the ground or embraces a venerable grand-nephew or tastes the food of mortals, he moulders into a little heap of dust as though he had been dead for ages.[3] On the other hand, a long time in the Other World sometimes transpires to have been but an instant in this world. Nera, after three days in the *síd* returns to find his companions at the same meal as they were preparing when he left them. Similarly, Becfola, who goes out early one Sunday morning, leaving her husband, King Diarmait, in bed, and spends a day and a night on an otherworld island in a lake, finds on her return that it is still the same Sunday morning and that her husband is just getting out of bed.[4] Thus otherworld 'time' is *both* longer *and* shorter than the time of our world. The same paradox appears in the Second Epistle of St Peter: 'one day is with the Lord as a thousand years, and a thousand years is as one day.'

'The wall of Paradise,' says Nicholas of Cusa, 'is built of contraries, nor is there any way to enter but for one who has overcome the highest spirit of reason who guards the gate.'[5] It is a function of mythology to confound this guardian spirit of reason so that finite man may glimpse the infinity which lies beyond the confines of the cosmos. Coincidences of opposites and of other irreconcilables give a shock to the understanding and transport the spirit to the gateway of the Other World. In the Welsh story of Llyn y Fan,[6] a youth sees a supernatural woman on the surface of the lake. The gulf that separates him from her is bridged when he offers her a symbol of the union of opposites, bread which is both baked and unbaked, and when he performs the further feat of drawing a distinction between identities by recognizing her beside a sister who is exactly like herself. She abides with him until he has given her 'three causeless blows', and the circumstances in which these blows are given reveal his failure to apprehend the universality of the paradox by which he has won her. The first arises out of his misunderstanding of her reluctance to attend a christening ceremony—a rite which separates a human being from his supernatural associations. The second blow is given when she weeps at a wedding, and the third when she laughs at a funeral. The revelation that seen through supernatural eyes joy and sorrow coincide both at weddings and at funerals comes as a shock to him, and instead of letting this truth loosen the bonds of his spirit he tries to suppress it and to impose upon his god-dess his own one-sided view.

The thin line between opposites has essentially the same signi-ficance as the dangerous bridges that lead to the citadels of the OtherWorld, the narrow bridge, the razor-edge bridge, or the see-saw bridge which can only be negotiated by leaping on to its *middle*. It is the space between the blades that rise from the threshold and those that depend from the lintel of the door to the giant's castle, it is the middle course between Scylla and Charybdis.[7] Irish poets deemed that the brink of water was always a place where *éicse*—'wisdom', 'poetry', 'knowledge' —was revealed.[8] Such lines without breadth symbolize the supernatural in the realm of space, and in modern folklore banished spirits can be confined in such spaceless places as 'between the froth and the water' or 'between the bark and the tree'.[9] Temporally, the same phenomenon is represented as the juncture between two years or between two seasons, or it is 'to-day', that which never was and never will be, and yet *is*.[10]

Similarly, objects which can be regarded as 'neither this nor that' have a mysterious supernatural virtue. The efficacy of dew (washed in at dawn, when it is neither day nor night, on May morn when it is neither winter nor summer)[11] no doubt derives from its being neither rain nor sea water, river nor well water. It appears to come neither from above nor from below. So too, the mistletoe is neither a shrub nor a tree. As a plant which does not grow from the ground, it falls into the same intermediate category as 'a man not born of woman' or of 'pigs that never were farrowed'. It defies classification, and is therefore free from the limitations that are inherent in a definition. Though all the plants of the earth had sworn not to hurt Balder, the mistletoe was exempt from this oath and could still be used to slay the god.[12] In popular custom a person who stands beneath a bough of this tree which is not a tree frees himself from the restrictions of convention: he can take liberties. Conversely, he places himself outside the protection of normal conventions, and forfeits which he cannot refuse can be exacted from him. We have suggested that the reason why CúChulainn's spear could be demanded from him every time he intervened in the feigned quarrel of two warriors is that by intervening he placed himself in that free but vulnerable position between contraries, where no boon can be refused. All things are possible in this sacred state between being and non-being. The individual who dares to enter it in defiance of the spirit of reason places himself within reach of salvation, but he also exposes himself to the dangers of annihilation in the river of death that lies under the sword-edge bridge.

Much has been written during the past three decades about the ritual significance of mazes, both as a protection against supernatural powers and as a path which the dead must follow on their way to the world of the spirits.[13] Here we will simply note that mazes are in relation to directions what betwixts-and-betweens are in relation to opposites. In passing through a maze one is not going in any particular direction, and by so doing one reaches a destination which cannot be located by reference to the points of the compass. According to Irish folk-belief, fairies and other supernatural beings can cause a man to lose his bearings (just as they can upset his sense of time); he can also lose them by stepping on a 'stray sod' beneath which a foetus or an unbaptized infant has been buried.[14] Conversely, in some of the 'Voyages' it is when the voyagers have lost their course and shipped their oars—when they are not going anywhere—that they arrive in the wondrous isles.

Whereas the union of two opposites is symbolized by the *line* along which they impinge upon one another, the reconciliation of three or more independent entities involves the discovery of the *point* at which they coincide. The former corres⁄ponds to a territorial boundary, the latter to 'The Meeting of the Three Waters', the meeting of three townlands, or the centre of Ireland where all the provinces meet and fuse together. Uisnech is in all the four provinces, and in none of them. Analogically, the multiple deaths we have discussed are points where three or more independent deeds meet in one deed. An effect should have a sufficient cause, but in these tales the effect is produced by several sufficient causes, with the result that a common⁄place explicable event is transmuted into an enigma which is an affront to the principle of causality. For an event to have three or more adequate causes is tantamount to its having no cause at all. The spearing, drowning, and burning of Diarmait are not factors in an integrated process; they are incompatibles between which there is no relation other than coincidence.

The discovery of points where unrelated things coincide is one of the great arts of seers and magicians. It is said of the seer Bec mac Dé that he could speak with nine persons at once, and that with one answer he could resolve the nine separate questions addressed to him. Three men once asked him three disconnected questions: (1) How long will there be dwellers in the fort? (2) What is the river's depth? (3) What is the thick⁄ness of bacon⁄fat this year? '*Pas go tóin amárach*. A short measure (3) to the bottom (2) tomorrow (1),' said Bec, answering the three questions in the reverse order.[15] Here we have · the compression of three unrelated answers into one sentence, just as two or more unrelated meanings are composed in a pun.

The enigmatic quality of certain situations, things, char⁄acters, deeds and events is bound up with coincidences which are essentially the same as those found in puns—coincidences which cannot but baffle those who follow the dictates of common sense. Mongán stands with one foot on a sod from Ireland and the other on a sod from Scotland. The wizards of the king of Leinster divine that he has one foot in Ireland and the other in Scotland, and the king concludes that so long as he is like that he is harmless.[16] When Diarmaid and Gráinne are in the forest, Gráinne sleeps on a bed of rushes while Diarmaid sits on a bag of sea sand. By chewing his thumb of knowledge Finn learns that Gráinne is on the rushes and Diarmaid on the sands of the sea, and he pursues both in vain.[17] A multiple death is of the same order as a pun, and so is an incestuous birth through which a man can be both the son and the grandson of the same woman, or his own mother's brother. They are abnormalities which demonstrate the ultimate inadequacy of logical cate-gories, just as the coincidence of conflicting *gessa* shows the limitations of moral precepts.

Punning is an ancient art and recent studies have shown that it was not indulged in merely for fun. Among the Egyp-tians punning was not only an 'inveterate habit'; theological and cosmological concepts were inextricably bound up with it.[18] The same 'insidious habit' 'moulds much Hindu ritual'.[19] The recognition of puns in early Celtic literature will no doubt increase as the texts are studied in more detail. It may well be that the philological uncertainty which haunts the interpreta-tion of so many names in Celtic and other early literatures is partly due to their being puns the clues to which have long been forgotten. The Irish *Cóir Anmann* and the *Dindšenchas* very often give two or three alternative explanations of the names of persons and places, but unlike the modern etymologist they do not single out one of these explanations as the true one. One wonders whether these alternatives can be dismissed as mere fragments of unrelated lore gathered together and recorded for the sake of completeness, as in a modern folk-lore collection, or whether it was considered fitting that the meaning of sig-nificant names should be complex and enigmatic.

Just as several meanings can meet in the same name, so can several names meet in the same person. We have mentioned the fateful Cailb who expresses unity through her posture and multiplicity through her numerous names. Sín also gives her-self a number of names which she utters together, while her insistence that her name must not be spoken by Muirchertach indicates a refusal to be identified with, or contained in, one word or idea. It will be recalled that the wizard Amairgen describes himself as wind, wave, roar, bull, vulture, dew-drop, flower, boar, salmon, lake, mountain, word of skill, point of weapon, god. Lug is a craftsman of consummate skill, but his art cannot be defined as that of any one category of crafts-man. Master of every art, he is the concurrence and synchrony of what can only appear as many in the world of ordinary experience.

To summarize: there is in the concepts of the boundary, the centre, intercalary time, 'to-day', betwixts-and-betweens, in-cestuous births, Caesarian births, multiple deaths, multiple names, multiple skills, puns and, we may add, metaphors, an ambiguity, or a multiplication or concentration of meaning which makes them fitting symbols of the unmanifest, which is itself the world of chaos and at the same time the ground of all being. They can all be formulated as paradoxical riddles and this may well be the reason why riddles play such an important part in all traditional cultures. The master poets of ancient Ireland had their riddling contests, and according to Marbán the Swineherd, 'chief prophet of heaven and earth', such disputa-tions first arose from the knowledge-bearing nuts of the nine hazels of wisdom that grew over the mysterious well of Segais. In a contest between Marbán and Dael Duiled, the *ollam* of Leinster, the riddles for the most part involve such 'irishisms' as:

What good did Man find on earth that God did not find?
Answer: A worthy master.

What beast lives in the sea and is drowned when it is taken out of it?
Answer: *Gním Abraein.*

What animal lives in fire and is burnt when taken out of it?
Answer: *Tegillus* (Salamander).

When Dael Duiled loses the contest, he throws himself upon
the protection of Marbán.[20] Widespread stories could be quoted
in which people who cannot find the answer to a riddle die or
are carried away by demons, and others in which men save
their lives by posing riddles which their judges cannot answer.[21]

Several kinds of riddles figure in marriage stories and rituals,
as means of bringing opposites together. In 'The Wooing of
Ailbe' there are many of the kind which requires finding a
degree beyond the superlative:[22]

> What is sweeter than mead?—Intimate conversation.
> What is blacker than the raven?—Death.
> What is whiter than snow?—Truth.
> What is swifter than the wind?—Thought.
> What is sharper than the sword?—Understanding.
> What is lighter than a spark?—The mind of a woman
> between two men.

Each answer involves a metaphorical transmutation of the
adjective in the question. There are other riddles in which
merely numerical questions are answered in terms of the duality
of things:

> How many horses came to Tailtiu?—Two horses, mare
> and stallion.[23]
> How many trees are in Assal?—Two trees, the green and
> the withered.

It need hardly be added that with these, as with the other arti-
fices we have mentioned, the answer can be found only by
juggling with the normally accepted categories of thought.

If we fail to discern a deep profundity in such subtleties and
satisfy ourselves that punning is 'the lowest form of wit', we
might well remember that our minds are so conditioned that
we do not see much in myths either. We have relegated both
riddles and myths to the kindergarten, and it is disconcerting
to find that for the seers and sages of old they enshrined the
deepest wisdom. Vishnu, the supreme Hindu god, is known
as the 'Cosmic Juggler',[24] while the very word *bráhman*

(neuter) signifies the 'cosmic enigma'. 'Expressed in and by the liturgy, the enigma contains the sum of the correlations by which the hidden architecture of the universe is revealed. . . . Through the play of riddles, the great connections and the major equivalences are discovered; it is a subterfuge designed to admit the ineffable into human discourse.'[25]

And is not the mercurial, shape-shifting, enigmatic magic which we have described the essence of all art? However exact a likeness a sculptor may carve, he is defeating his purpose if the work lacks perfection of form and rhythm, or if the fact that it is also stone is obscured. A poem, likewise, is a synchronization and synthesis of many things, related and unrelated to one another. There are ideas, often superimposed upon one another in metaphors conveying a concentration of meaning; there is rhythm which may bear no relation to the syntax; there is rhyme which ties together in near-puns words which do not otherwise belong together, and there is alliteration or assonance which establishes further connections where reason would find none.

From a mythological standpoint, such correspondences are neither accidents nor inventions. They are discoveries, their validity grounded in the inexhaustible analogical riches of the universe. Their magic has delighted and sustained the spirit of man throughout the ages, for it has the power to breach the constraining boundaries of the finite so that the light of eternity may transubstantiate that which is commonplace and fill it with mystery. And strange as these paradoxes may appear, they do not lack points of contact with our own tradition, in which God is both One and Three, in which the Saviour is both God and Man, and in which the central rite is to partake of bread which is not bread, and wine which is not wine.

ABBREVIATIONS

C	Cardiff	L	London
Cb	Cambridge	NY	New York
D	Dublin	O	Oxford
E	Edinburgh	P	Paris

ACL   *Archiv für celtische Lexicographie*, ed. W. Stokes and K. Meyer (Halle a S., 1900–7).

AER   H. Frankfort, *Ancient Egyptian Religion* (NY, 1948).

AESC   *Annales Économies Sociétés Civilisations.*

AIM   *Anecdota from Irish Manuscripts,* ed. O. J. Bergin and others (Halle a S., 1907–13).

AKI   *Annals of the Kingdom of Ireland,*[2] ed. and tr. J. O'Donovan (D, 1856).

AKSG   *Der Abhandlungen der philologish-historischen Klasse der königlish Sächsischen Gesellschaft der Wissenschaften.*

ALI   *Ancient Laws of Ireland* (D, 1865–1901).

ALW   *Ancient Laws of Wales* (L, 1841).

AS   Acallamh na Senórach, ed. W. Stokes, *IT,* IV (1900).

ASt   *Aberystwyth Studies.*

ATC   R. S. Loomis, *Arthurian Tradition and Chrétien de Troyes* (NY, 1949).

AW   *African Worlds*, ed. D. Forde (L, 1954).

BBC   *The Black Book of Carmarthen*, ed. J. G. Evans (Pwllheli, 1906).

BBCS   *Bulletin of the Board of Celtic Studies.*

BCCS   M. M. Banks, *British Calendar Customs: Scotland* (L, 1937–41).

BDBM   *The Banquet of Dún na nGéd and the Battle of Mag Rath*, ed. and tr. J. O'Donovan (D, 1842).

Bdd   E. Conze, *Buddhism* (O, 1959).

BDL   P. Mac Cana, *Branwen Daughter of Llŷr* (C, 1958).

BEE   A. H. Krappe, *Balor with the Evil Eye* (NY, 1927).

BL   *The Book of Leinster*, ed. R. Atkinson (O, 1880).

BLt   A. K. Coomaraswamy, *The Bugbear of Literacy* (L, 1949).

BT   *The Book of Taliesin*, ed. J. G. Evans (Llanbedrog, 1910).

CA   Cóir Anmann, ed. and tr. W. Stokes, *IT,* III (1897).

CC   A. H. Allcroft, *The Circle and the Cross* (L, 1927).

CCC	*Compert Con Culainn*, ed. A. G. van Hamel (D, 1933).
CF	J. Rhys, *Celtic Folklore* (O, 1901).
CFt	*Cath Finntrága*, ed. and tr. K. Meyer (D, 1885).
CG	*Críth Gablach*, ed. D. A. Binchy (D, 1941).
CGd	*Carmina Gadelica*, ed. and tr. A. Carmichael (E, 1928–).
CGl	*Cormac's Glossary*, tr. J. O'Donovan, ed. W. Stokes (Calcutta, 1868).
CGt	W. F. J. Knight, *Cumaean Gates* (O, 1936).
Chm	M. Eliade, *Le Chamanisme* (P, 1951).
CI	E. MacNeill, *Celtic Ireland* (D, 1921).
CIL	K. Meyer, *Contributions to Irish Lexicography* (Halle a S., 1906).
CJS	*Ceylon Journal of Science*.
CK	M. Dillon, *The Cycles of the Kings* (Cb, 1946).
Cm	*Y Cymmrodor*.
CMT	Cath Maighe Tuireadh, ed. and tr. W. Stokes, *RC*, XII (1891).
CMT(C)	*Cath Muighe Tuireadh*, ed. B. Ó Cuív (D, 1945).
CR	*The Celtic Review*.
CS	*The Cuchullin Saga in Irish Literature*, ed. E. Hull (L, 1898).
CsI	J. H. Hutton, *Caste in India* (Cb, 1946).
CSS	G. H. Doble, Cornish Saints Series: III *Saint Budoc*[2] (1937), XIII *Saint Melor* (1927), XV *S. Senan* (Long Compton, 1928).
Cst	A. M. Hocart, *Caste* (L, 1950; first published in French, 1938).
CT	I. Williams, *Chwedl Taliesin* (C, 1957).
CTGV	A. Varagnac, *Civilisation traditionnelle et genres de vie* (P, 1948).
DF	*Duanaire Finn*, ed. and tr. E. MacNeill (I) and G. Murphy (II-III) (L, 1908, '33; D, 1953).
DH	M. Deren, *Divine Horsemen* (L, 1953).
DIL	*Dictionary of the Irish Language* (Royal Irish Academy, D, 1913–).
DIL(C)	*Contributions to a Dictionary of the Irish Language* (Royal Irish Academy).
DT	*The Death Tales of the Ulster Heroes*, ed. and tr. K. Meyer (D, 1906).
ÉC	*Études Celtiques*.

ECNE   *Early Cultures of North-West Europe*, ed. C. Fox and B. Dickins (Cb, 1950).

EHR   R. Pettazzoni, *Essays on the History of Religions* (tr., Leiden, 1954).

EIHM   T. F. O'Rahilly, *Early Irish History and Mythology* (D, 1946).

EIL   M. Dillon, *Early Irish Literature* (Chicago, 1948).

EILI   E. MacNeill, *Early Irish Laws and Institutions* (D, n.d.).

ERE   *Encyclopaedia of Religion and Ethics*, ed. J. Hastings (E, 1908–1926).

ESC   M. Granet, *Études sociologiques sur la Chine* (P, 1953).

ESM   *Essays and Studies presented to Professor Eoin MacNeill*, ed. J. Ryan (D, 1940).

FB   *Fled Bricrend*, ed. and tr. G. Henderson (L, 1899).

FBI   E. Hull, *Folklore of the British Isles* (L, 1928).

FD   J. G. Frazer, *The Fear of the Dead in Primitive Religion* (L, 1933–6).

FESB   L. C. Wimberly, *Folklore in the English and Scottish Ballads* (NY, 1928).

FF   *Forus Feasa ár Éirinn, The History of Ireland* by Geoffrey Keating, ed. and tr. D. Comyn (I) and P. Dinneen (II-IV) (L, 1902–14).

FI   G. Dumézil, *Le Festin d'Immortalité* (P, 1924).

FL   *Folk-Lore.*

Fn   *Fianaigecht*, ed. and tr. K. Meyer (D, 1910).

Fns   *The Fians*, collected by J. G. Campbell (L, 1891).

FOT   J. G. Frazer, *Folklore in the Old Testament* (L, 1918–19).

GB   J. G. Frazer, *The Golden Bough*[3] (L, 1911–15). Vols. numbered as in General Index.

GDG   *Gwaith Dafydd ap Gwilym*, ed. T. Parry (C, 1952).

GHC   M. L. Sjoestedt, *Gods and Heroes of the Celts* (tr., L, 1949).

GL   H. M. Chadwick and N. K. Chadwick, *The Growth of Literature* (Cb, 1932–40).

GPC   *Geiriadur Prifysgol Cymru*, ed. R. J. Thomas (C, 1950–).

GT   *Genealogical Tracts,* I, ed. and tr. T. Ó Raithbheartagih (D, 1932).

HB   Historia Brittonum (Nennius's), *Chronica Minora*, ed. T. Mommsen, III (Berlin, 1898). Refs. are to paragraphs.

HDA   *Handwörterbuch des Deutschen Aberglaubens*, ed. H. Bächtold-Stäubli (Berlin, 1927–42).

HGS   *Homage to George Sarton* (NY, 1947).

HHM	E. Westermarck, *History of Human Marriage*[5] (L, 1921).
HIF	S. Ó Súilleabháin, *A Handbook of Irish Folklore* (D, 1942).
HL	J. Rhys, (The Hibbert Lectures, 1886) *Lectures on the Origin and Growth of Religion as illustrated by Celtic Heathendom*[3] (L, 1898).
HLt	W. E. Soothill, *The Hall of Light* (L, 1951).
HM	*Hibernica Minora*, ed. and tr. K. Meyer (O, 1894).
HRB	*Historia Regum Britanniae* (Geoffrey of Monmouth), ed. A. Griscom (NY, 1929).
HRI	*Heroic Romances of Ireland*, tr. A. H. Leahy (L, 1905–6).
HS	R. Caillois, *L'homme et le sacré*[4] (P, 1950).
HTI	*Hero Tales of Ireland*, ed. J. Curtin (L, 1894).
HW	J. E. Lloyd, *A History of Wales*[3] (L, 1939).
HWI	P. D. Hardy, *The Holy Wells of Ireland* (D, 1836).
ID	T. F. O'Rahilly, *Irish Dialects* (D, 1932).
IED	P. S. Dinneen, *Foclóir Gaedilge agus Béarla*, An Irish-English Dictionary (D, 1927).
IEW	J. Pokorny, *Indogermanisches Etymologisches Wörterbuch* (Bern, 1949–59).
IF	*Iomarbág na bFilead*, ed. and tr. L. McKenna (L, 1918).
IHK	R. Thurneysen, *Die Irische Helden- und Königsage* (Halle, 1921).
IMC	H. D'Arbois de Jubainville, *The Irish Mythological Cycle* (tr., D, 1903).
IT	*Irische Texte*, ed. W. Stokes and E. Windisch (Leipzig).
ITI	G. Dumézil, *L'idéologie tripartie des Indo-Européens* (Bruxelles, 1958).
ITr	R. Flower, *The Irish Tradition* (O, 1947).
IVHB	*The Irish Version of the Historia Britonum of Nennius*, ed. and tr. J. H. Todd (D, 1848).
JAOS	*Journal of the American Oriental Society*.
JCS	*The Journal of Celtic Studies*.
JHS	*Journal of the Hellenic Society*.
JMQ	G. Dumézil, *Jupiter Mars Quirinus* (P, 1941).
JRS	*The Journal of Roman Studies*.
JRSA	*Journal of the Royal Society of the Antiquaries of Ireland*.
KC	A. M. Hocart, *Kings and Councillors* (Cairo, 1936).
KCp	H. Zimmer, *The King and the Corpse*[2] (NY, 1956).
Kng	A. M. Hocart, *Kingship* (O, 1927).
KP	J. Abbott, *The Keys of Power* (L, 1932).

LBS   S. Baring-Gould and J. Fisher, *The Lives of the British Saints* (L, 1907–13).

LF   *Legendary Fictions of the Irish Celts*, collected by P. Kennedy (L, 1891).

LG   *Lebor Gabála Érenn*, ed. and tr. R. A. S. Macalister (D, 1938–56).

LGSG   J. Jones, *Llên Gwerin Sir Gaernarfon* (Caernarfon, n.d.).

LIS   *Lives of Irish Saints*, ed. and tr. C. Plummer (O, 1922).

LMM   E. O'Curry, *Lectures on the Manuscript Materials of Ancient Irish History* (D, 1878).

LMU   *Longes Mac n-Uislenn*, ed. and tr. V. Hull (NY, 1949).

LP   E. S. Hartland, *The Legend of Perseus* (L, 1894–6).

LSC   *Leabhar Sheáin Í Chonaill*, ed. S. Ó Duilearga (D, 1948).

MA   *The Myvyrian Archaiology of Wales,*[2] ed. O. Jones (and others) (Denbigh, 1870).

Mb   *The Mabinogion*, tr. G. Jones and T. Jones (L, 1949).

MC   E. O'Curry, *On the Manners and Customs of the Ancient Irish* (L, 1873).

MD   *The Metrical Dindshenchas*, ed. and tr. E. Gwynn (D, 1903–35).

MDG   G. Dumézil, *Mythes et dieux des Germains* (P, 1939).

MER   M. Eliade, *The Myth of the Eternal Return* (tr., L, 1955).

MM   W. J. Gruffydd, *Math vab Mathonwy* (C, 1928).

MP   *Modern Philology*.

MS   H. Zimmer, *Myths and Symbols in Indian Art and Civilization* (NY, 1946).

MSL   *Medieval Studies in Memory of Gertrude Schoepperle Loomis* (P, 1927).

Mth   R. Briffault, *The Mothers* (L, 1927).

MU   *Mesca Ulad*, ed. J. C. Watson (D, 1941).

MV   G. Dumézil, *Mitra-Varuna*[3] (P, 1948).

MWHT   *More West Highland Tales*, ed. J. G. McKay and others (E, 1940).

NM   M. Eliade, *Naissances mystiques*[3] (P, 1959).

NSF   A. M. Hocart, *The Northern States of Fiji* (L, 1952).

OLRT   G. Murphy, *The Ossianic Lore and Romantic Tales of Medieval Ireland* (D, 1955).

OS   *The Ocean of Story*, tr. C. H. Tawney, ed. N. M. Penzer (L, 1924–8).

OST   *Ossianic Society Transactions*.

PBA	*Proceedings of the British Academy.*
PC	G. Dumézil, *Le problème des Centaurs* (P, 1929).
PCR	M. Eliade, *Patterns in Comparative Religion* (tr., L, 1958).
PE	*The Prose Edda*, tr. J. I. Young (Cb, 1954).
PKM	*Pedeir Keinc y Mabinogi*, ed. I. Williams (C, 1930).
PLGI	D. Deeney, *Peasant Lore from Gaelic Ireland* (L, 1901).
PMLA	*Publications of the Modern Language Association of America.*
PP	N. K. Chadwick, *Poetry and Prophecy* (Cb, 1942).
PRIA	*Proceedings of the Royal Irish Academy.*
PTWH	*Popular Tales of the West Highlands*, ed. and tr. J. F. Campbell (E, 1860–2).
QJMS	*The Quarterly Journal of the Mythical Society* (Bangalore).
RAC	J. A. MacCulloch, *The Religion of the Ancient Celts* (E, 1911).
RC	*Revue Celtique.*
RH	H. R. Ellis, *The Road to Hel* (Cb, 1943).
Rhn	W. J. Gruffydd, *Rhiannon* (C, 1953).
RIR	G. Dumézil, *Rituels Indo-Européens à Rome* (P, 1954).
RIC	J. Vendryes, La religion des Celtes, *Les religions de l'Europe Ancienne* (P, 1948).
RVAV	U. Harva, *Die Religiösen Vorstellungen der Altaischen Völker*, (Helsinki, 1938).
RVL	A. K. Coomaraswamy, *The Ṛg Veda as Land-Náma-Bók* (L, 1935).
SAI	R. S. Shamra, *Śūdras in Ancient India* (Delhi, 1958).
SAL	J. Rhys, *Studies in the Arthurian Legend* (O, 1891).
SBE	*The Sacred Books of the East.* General Editor: F. Max Müller (O, 1879–94).
SC	*Serglige Con Culainn*, ed. M. Dillon (D, 1953).
SEIL	R. Thurneysen and others, *Studies in Early Irish Law* (D, 1936).
SF	G. Dumézil, *Servius et la Fortune* (P, 1943).
SFT	E. S. Hartland, *The Science of Fairy Tales* (L, 1891).
SG	*Silva Gadelica*, ed. and tr. S. H. O'Grady (L, 1892).
SGS	*Scottish Gaelic Studies.*
SHI	P. W. Joyce, *A Social History of Ancient Ireland*[2] (D, 1913).
SILH	J. Carney, *Studies in Irish Literature and History* (D, 1955).
SM	G. Murphy, *Saga and Myth in Ancient Ireland* (D, 1955).
SMMD	*Scéla Mucce Meic Dathó*, ed. R. Thurneysen (D, 1935).
SnC	*Sean-focla Connact*, ed. T. S. ÓMáille (D, 1948, '52).

TBC   *Die altirische Heldensage Táin Bó Cúalnge*, ed. (and tr.) E. Windisch (Leipzig, 1905).

TBC(D)   *The Ancient Irish Epic Tale Táin Bó Cúalnge*, tr. J. Dunn (L, 1914).

TBD   *Togail Bruidne Da Derga*, ed. E. Knott (D, 1936).

TBDd   *The Tibetan Book of the Dead*,[2] ed. W. Y. Evans-Wentz (O, 1949).

TÉ   *Tochmarc Étaíne*, ed. and tr. O. Bergin and R. I. Best (D, 1938).

TEF   W. G. Wood-Martin, *Traces of the Elder Faiths of Ireland* (L, 1902).

TG   A. B. Gomme, *Traditional Games of England, Scotland and Ireland* (L, 1894).

THSC   *Transactions of the Honourable Society of Cymmrodorion.*

TI   G. Schoepperle, *Tristan and Isolt* (Frankfort, 1913).

TIG   *Three Irish Glossaries*, ed. W. Stokes (L, 1862).

TKI   'The Taboos of the Kings of Ireland', ed. and tr. M. Dillon, *PRIA*, LIV (1951).

TLM   G. J. Williams, *Traddodiad Llenyddol Morgannwg* (C, 1948).

TLP   *The Tripartite Life of Patrick*, ed. and tr. W. Stokes (L, 1887).

Trp   G. Dumézil, *Tarpeia* (P, 1947).

TS   G. Dumézil, *Le troisième Souverain* (P, 1949).

UF   J. C. Foster, *Ulster Folklore* (Belfast, 1951).

VB   *The Voyage of Bran*, ed. and tr. K. Meyer with an Essay by A. Nutt (L, 1895).

VM   A. A. Macdonell, *Vedic Mythology* (Strasburg, 1897).

VSB   *Vitae Sanctorum Britanniae*, ed. and tr. A. W. Wade-Evans (C, 1944).

VSH   *Vitae Sanctorum Hiberniae*, ed. and tr. C. Plummer (O, 1910).

WAL   R. S. Loomis, *Wales and the Arthurian Legend* (C, 1956).

WBM   *The White Book Mabinogion*, ed. J. G. Evans (Pwllheli, 1907).

WFC   T. M. Owen, *Welsh Folk Customs*, (C, 1959).

WFFC   T. Gwynn Jones, *Welsh Folklore and Folk-Custom* (L, 1930).

WTL   T. P. Ellis, *Welsh Tribal Law and Custom* (O, 1926).

Yg   M. Eliade, *Yoga* (tr., L, 1958).

ZCP   *Zeitschrift für celtische Philologie.*

NOTES

CHAPTER I INTRODUCTION

1 Seán Ó Súilleabháin in *Four Symposia on Folklore*, ed. Stith Thomp-son (Bloomington, 1953), 5.

2 *CGd*, I, xxii f.

3 'The Gaelic Storyteller', *PBA*, XXXI (1945), 183 ff.

4 The information in this paragraph is derived from Delargy, op. cit., 181–96. C. I. Maclean tells of a storyteller who took from seven to nine hours to narrate some of his tales ('Hebridean Traditions', *Gwerin*, I (1957), 30). In Co. Kerry, Delargy heard of a beggar-man who took seven nights to tell a story, while a story current in Scotland was in twenty-four parts, each occupying a night in telling (Car-michael, loc. cit. Cf. *Transactions of the Gaelic Society of Inverness*, XXV, 179).

5 Delargy, op. cit., 181, Maclean, op. cit., 32.

6 Delargy, op. cit., 194 ff.

7 Maclean, op. cit., 31, 29. In his youth Seán Ó Conaill twice heard the first twenty-five pages of an old story read from a book at a fire-side gathering. Fifty years later he was heard to tell that portion of the tale almost word for word as it is found in the printed book (Delargy, op. cit., 201). Nevertheless, the storytellers do not seem to regard verbal accuracy as essential. 'The incidents', says Douglas Hyde, 'and not the language were the things to be remembered.' (*Beside the Fire* (L, 1890), xxiv.) On the memorized learning of other illiterate peoples, see Coomaraswamy, *BLt*, 25–41.

8 *PKM*, 69.

9 *VB*, I, 46, 49; Delargy, op. cit., 196.

10 H. Webster, *Taboo* (L, 1942), 299 f., 309; *EHR*, 14 f.

11 *AER*, 140 ff. (where the verse sequences translated are very similar in form and mood to Welsh three-line stanzas dated to the ninth century), M. Dillon, 'The Archaism of Irish Tradition', *PBA*, XXXIII (1947), 253 ff.

12 'Mittelirische Verslehren', ed. R. Thurneysen, *IT*, III (1891), 50. These metrical tracts indicate what was to be learned during a twelve years' course of study. In the *Memoirs* (1722) of the Marquis of Clan-ricarde (quoted by O. Bergin in the *Journal of the Ivernian Society*, V, 157) the poet's training is said to take 'six or seven years'.

13 Sylvain Lévi, quoted by Dillon, op. cit., 259, where he discusses the relation of the Celtic learned class to the Indian, a subject also dealt with in Dumézil, *SF* (1943).

14 Chadwick, *PP*, 58.

15 *TBC*, 911.

16 *The Triads of Ireland*, ed. and tr. K. Meyer (D, 1906), 9.

17 Ed. and tr. Lilian Duncan, *Ériu*, XI, 224. (We quote Miss Duncan's translation.) The injunction that the tale should be told only to a few good people accords with the practice, found in some other parts of the world, of entrusting the custody of certain kinds of tales to a few initiates who tell them to small gatherings or only to one sex.

18 Op. cit., 248 f.

19 A. M. Hocart, *The Life-giving Myth* (L, 1952), 16.

20 *The Rámáyan of Válmíki*, ed. and tr. R. T. H. Griffith (L, 1874), V, 314, n., I, 17.

21 Dillon, op. cit., 249.

22 *ESM*, 526. There are also peoples who believe that the evocative power of stories can be dangerous as well as beneficial and those who have been present at a night's storytelling are enjoined to engage in shaking, washing or blood-letting rituals, next morning, to free themselves from the uncanny influence (Pettazzoni, *EHR*, 16 f.).

23 Zimmer, *KCp*, 215 f.

24 *PTWH*, I, xiii.

25 Op. cit., 182.

26 Ibid., 186.

27 *GB*, V, vii.

28 *GB*, XI, 304.

29 B. Malinowski, *Myth in Primitive Psychology* (L. 1926), 39.

30 C. G. Jung, *Collected Works*, XII (L, 1953), 32 f.

31 A. K. Coomaraswamy, *Christian and Oriental Philosophy of Art* (NY, 1956), 139 f. 'What has really been preserved in folk and fairy tales and in popular peasant art is, then, by no means a body of merely childish or entertaining fables or of crude decorative art, but a series of what are really esoteric doctrines and symbols. . . . It is not at all shocking that this material should have been transmitted by peasants for whom it forms a part of their lives, a nourishment of their very constitution, but who cannot explain; it is not at all shocking that the folk material can be described as a body of "superstition", since

it is really a body of custom and belief that "stands over" (*superstat*) from a time when its meanings were understood.'

32 *TBC*, 911.

CHAPTER II BRANCHES OF THE TRADITION

1 Surveys or summaries are available in Dillon, *EIL* and *CK*; D'Arbois de Jubainville, *IMC*; Thurneysen, *IHK*; *DF*, III (G. Murphy). For further references see R. I. Best, *Bibliography of Irish Philology and of Printed Irish Literature* (D, 1913), *Bibliography of Irish Philology and Manuscript Literature* (D, 1942).

2 There are English translations of *LG* (Macalister), Cormac's Glossary (*CGl*, O'Donovan), the *dindšenchas* (*MD*, Gwynn. Prose: *RC*, XV, 272, 418, XVI, 31, 135, 269, *FL*, III, 467, IV, 471, Stokes), *CA* (Stokes). Irish scholars argue that most of these works were compiled in the eleventh century; cf. *Celtica*, IV (1958), 249 (M. Dillon).

3 The principal prose texts are translated in *Mb* (G. Jones and T. Jones). The early poems, genealogies, etc. are surveyed in Chadwick, *GL*, I, and Ifor Williams, *Lectures on Early Welsh Poetry* (D, 1944).

4 'The First Battle of Moytura', ed. and tr. J. Fraser, *Ériu*, VIII, 1. Except where otherwise noted, our account here and in the next paragraph follows *LG*. Some Celtic scholars have been loath to accept as authentic tradition the references to *two* Battles of Mag Tuired. The account of each of the battles in turn has been dismissed as a later fiction; cf. G. Murphy, 'Notes on Cath Maige Tuired,' *Éigse*, VII, 191. For arguments from comparative mythology in support of the two battles see Dumézil, *MV*, 180 ff.

5 *Ériu*, VIII, 21. J. Fraser's translation is quoted.

6 The sources quoted in this paragraph are *VB*, II, 291, 300, E. MacNeill, *Phases of Irish History* (D, 1913), 85 f., *LG*, IV, 219.

7 *LG*, IV, 163, 135.

8 *DIL*, Fasc. I, 82.

9 *RC*, XII, 82; *CA*, 354 ff.; *AIM*, IV, 98; *MSL*, 402.

10 *TIG*, xxxiii ff.; *AIM*, IV, 15, 36, 82, 78. J. Vendryes argued that *mac lir* 'sea-farer' has been misinterpreted as a patronymic; *ÉC*, VI, 248.

11 Rhys, *HL*, 125 ff., 75, 419 ff. The evidence of the inscriptions is surveyed in Vendryes, RIC.

12 What is stated in some versions is that the battle was fought on single legs and with single arms and single eyes, *LG*, III, 13. Macalister (*LG*, I, 260) refers to one-armed, one-legged, one-eyed demons who are a source of terror to the inhabitants of the neigh-bourhood of Mombasa and Zanzibar. His authority is W. Hichens in *Discovery*, XVII (1936), 185. In the sacred drum rituals and annual harvest ceremony of the Lovedu of the Transvaal weird whistling ancestor spirits of royal lineage come to earth in the guise, it is said, of half men with one eye, one arm, and one leg. 'They are in fact, as is known to those initiated in the *gomana*, old men mas-querading as spirits. They appear in the bush near the village and join in the singing of *lesugu* songs, which are sung on these occasions through specially constructed secret whistles.' (J. D. and E. J. Krige, in *AW*, 67.) On the use of only one eye, one arm and one leg in certain Irish rituals see *ACL*, II, 257, and *infra*, p. 37.

13 *LG*, III, 13.

14 Our summary and quotations from here to p. 38 follow CMT (tr. W. Stokes, except for a few insignificant changes).

15 *SILH*, 103 f. Cf. *LG*, I, 136. For two hundred years before the coming of Partholón, the Fomoire had subsisted by fowling and fishing.

16 The same qualification is said to have been required for admission to the court at Emain Macha (*ZCP*, XVIII, 298), to Arthur's hall and to the fort of the giant Wrnach in the Welsh 'Kulhwch and Olwen' (*Mb*, 97, 121) and to Utgarð in Snorri's *Edda* (*PE*, 73). Cf. *The Early English Carols*, ed. R. L. Greene (O, 1935), 9:

> 'Lett no man cum into this hall
> Grome, page, nor yet marshall,
> But that sum sport he bryng withall,
> For now ys the tyme of Crystmas.'

17 See W. M. Hennessy, 'The Ancient Irish Goddess of War', *RC*, I, 32. The Morrígan appears sometimes as a bird—a hooded crow—sometimes as a hag (*caillech*). Nirṛti, the Vedic goddess of dissolution, is likewise assimilated to a black bird and to a sterile woman. Refer-ences to Nirṛti are discussed in G. Dumézil, *Déesses latines et mythes védiques* (P, 1956), 108 ff.

18 Cf. *LG*, IV, 132, 158.

19 Cf. *CMT*(*C*), 6.

20 M. M. Banks, 'Na Tri Mairt . . .', *ÉC*, III, 131.

21 *MD*, III, 218 ff., *RC*, XV, 439.

22 Tr. J. C. Watson in *SGS*, V, 2, (*MU*, 1).

23 *IVHB*, 250; 'De Gabáil in t–Sída', ed. and tr. V. Hull, *ZCP*, XIX, 57.

24 'Altram Tige Dá Medar', ed. and tr. L. Duncan, *Ériu*, XI, 184.

25 *VB*, I, 19; *CCC*, 26, 35.

26 Cf. the Indian belief: 'A person blind in one eye is a destroyer of the world; a person lame in one leg is the bane of all men' (*KP*, 284). In Egypt, 'A one–eyed person is regarded as of evil omen, and especially one who is blind of the left eye' (E. W. Lane, *Manners and Customs of the Modern Egyptians* (L, 1896 edn.), 272. Cf. *infra*. Index, under 'One–eyed personages'.

27 See A. R. Radcliffe–Brown, 'On Joking Relationships', *Africa*, XIII (1940), 195 (cf. also *Africa*, II, 244; XII, 433; XIV, 386; XIX, 133); A. M. Hocart, *The Progress of Man* (L, 1933), 241 ff., *NSF*, 43 ff.; *The Social Anthropology of North American Tribes*, ed. F. Eggan (Chicago, 1937), 75 ff.; Dumézil, *FI*, 272 ff.

28 *CF*, 661, 671, *FBI*, 59. Cf. *MWHT*, 503, 209. Note also the pro– minence of the Matres or Matronae in dedications and images of the Roman period throughout the Celtic world (RIC, 275 ff.). In Brittany, the fairies are known as 'Good Ladies' and 'Good Mothers'—H.–F. Buffet, *En Haute Bretagne* (P, 1954), 259. In Jersey, too, they are called 'Dames' (J. H. L'Amy, *Jersey Folklore* (L, 1927), 26).

29 See Dumézil, *FI* and *JMQ*.

30 A. K. Coomaraswamy in *Speculum*, XIX, 106. D'Arbois de Jubainville compared the conflict between the Tuatha and the Fomoire with that between the Devas and the Asuras, *IMC*, 9.

31 *VM*, 156.

32 A. K. Coomaraswamy, 'Angel and Titan', *JAOS*, LV, 394 n., 374. On the kinship of Asuras and Devas, cf. Dumézil, *FI*, 32, 165; *infra*, pp. 78 f.

33 *PKM*; *Mb*, 1–75.

34 *PKM*, 99 ff., Loomis, *WAT*, 137 ff.

35 *WBM*, 241, *Mb*, 115. For Irish parallels see Mac Cana, *BDL*, 103 ff.

36 Vendryes, RIC, 268 f. On the relation of Rhiannon to Epona: H. Hubert, 'Le mythe d'Epona', in *Mélanges linguistiques offerts à M. J. Vendryes* (P. 1925), 187; Dumézil, *PC*, 264; Gruffydd,

Rhŵ, 103 f., 68 n.; J. Gricourt, 'Epona-Rhiannon-Macha', *Ogam*,
VI, 25, 75, 165. On Epona: R. Magnen, *Épona* (Bordeaux, 1953),
F. Benoit, *Les mythes de l'outre-tombe* (Bruxelles, 1950), id., *L'héroisation
équestre* (Aix-en-Provence, 1954). Cf. *SBE*, XLIV, 465 f.
(*Śatapatha Brāhmaṇa*): the earth as mare.

37 *Cyfranc Lludd a Llevelys*, ed. I. Williams (Bangor, 1922); *Mb*, 89 ff.
(quoted).

38 Rhys, *HL*, 125.

39 *HIF*, 334 ff.

40 The Irish affinities of the Second Branch are studied in Mac Cana,
BDL.

41 *BT*, 54, 33. Cf. W. J. Gruffydd, *Folklore and Myth in the Mabinogion* (C, 1958), 16 ff., Rhys, *SAL*, 10. The Other World is a land
across the water. It appears that for the Celts of Gaul it was in
Britain (Procopius, *De Bello Gothico*, vi, 20, cited in *IMC*, 130.
Cf. *Beáloideas*, XVIII, 150).

42 *The Fate of the Children of Lir*, ed. and tr. R. J. O'Duffy (D, 1883).
Dr Mac Cana does not consider this tale relevant to his theme;
BDL, 122 n.

43 On the conflicting views concerning their relationship see Mac
Cana, *BDL*, 122 ff.

44 *VB*, I, 17; *RC*, XVI, 142. In *MD*, III, 424, the name is Brón.

45 *Mb*, 73; the translation involves two emendations.

46 *RC*, XXXVI, 353 (C. Marstrander). For references to Math, Lleu
etc. in Welsh poems see *MM*, 55 ff., 165 ff., 187 ff.

47 *DF*, III, lxxxii ff.

48 Rhys, *HL*, 387 f., Gruffydd, *MM*, 218 ff. (See also *IED*, s.v. *ruadán*.)
Cf. *Revue des études latines*, XXXVI, 121 ff. on the offering of
fishes to *Vulcan*.

49. *MSL*, 399 ff., *MD*, IV, 278.

50 *AS*, 19, *SG*, II, 117; *IHK*, 431 ff., Gruffydd, *MM*, 263 ff.

51 Cf. K. Jackson, *Language and History in Early Britain* (Edinburgh,
1953), 382, M. Förster, *Der Flussname Themse und seine Sippe*
(München, 1941), 814. (One would expect *Dawn* as in the name
Cair Daun which occurs in Nennius.) *Dono*, which occurs instead
of *Dôn* in one or two contexts, may be a variant of *Donwy*; see
W. J. Gruffydd's note in *BBCS*, VII (1935), 1, where he relates
these names to *Danann* and *Danuvios*. (Cf. also Rhŷs, *CF*, 441,
544.)

52 *BBCS*, V, 134; *MA*, 25.

53 *VM*, 158. In modern texts the Children of Dôn have associations with the firmament: *WFFC*, 16, *CF*, 645, *GPC*, s.v. *caer*.

54 Förster, op. cit., 141 ff.; Pokorny, *IEW*, 175.

55 A. K. Coomaraswamy in *JAOS*, LV, 393 n., citing *Rig Veda*, I, 136 (3), II, 41 (6). He notes that Dānu is also named as the consort of the Aśvins; *Rig Veda*, VIII, 8 (16).

56 A similar ambiguity occurs in the case of Beli. A triad describes Aranrhod as the daughter of Beli who is thus, perhaps, to be regarded as the consort of Dôn. In the *Mabinogi*, Beli is the maternal grandfather of the Children of Llŷr and also the father of Caswallawn who dispossesses them of their dominion. The father of Lludd and Llefelys again was Beli, but in the 'Stanzas of the Graves' Beli is the son of Benlli the Giant who in modern folklore is an ogre classed with the Coraniaid who plagued the kingdom of Lludd. For references see *MM*, 173 ff.

57 *RC*, XII, 82; *TÉ*, 23.

58 *MU*, 28, *RC*, XII, 77 (Ethliu is a variant form).

59 *MD*, III, 29. Here, at the close of this section, we would pose a question of 'the fitness of names': can the similarity, and interrelationship, of the names in the following paragraph be dismissed as 'mere' co-incidence?—

The Irish Tuatha Dé *Danann* are obliged to come to terms first with the Men of *Bolg*, finally with the descendants of *Bile* (father of Míl), and in their greatest battle their chief adversary is *Balor*, giant champion of the Síd. The father of Aranrhod, *Beli*, who appears as the progenitor of several Welsh dynasties, is perhaps the consort of *Dôn*, while there is some evidence to suggest that the *Bellerus* whose story (according to Milton) was linked with the Cornish St Michael's Mount, was, like the Balor of folk-tales, a one-eyed thieving giant. *Belenus*, whose name occurs more frequently than any other Celtic god-name in the inscriptions of the Roman period, is described as the patron of the *Danubian* province of Noricum; the giant or dragon of modern Roumanian folklore is *Balaur*. In Greek mythology, *Belus* is the father of *Danaus* and grandfather of the Danaids who kill their cousin-husbands, grandsons of Belus, and furthermore the Medusa is killed by the son of *Danae*, the Chimaera by *Bellerophon* (? 'The Slayer of Belleros'). Lastly, the Indian *Bali*, mighty king of the Asuras, and Sovereign of Patala, an underworld realm of riches, beauty and pleasure comparable with the Síd and Annwfn, conquers Indra and the gods—Indra who is born to be the slayer of the son of *Dānu*. No two of these names—Beli, Bile, Bali, Bolg, Belus, Balor, Balaur, Bellerus, Bellerophon, Belenus—have been convincingly related to one another philologically. But to disprove etymological relationship throughout would not necessarily be to dispose of our question. (References: *Bellerus*: MM, 183 f.; *Belenus*: RIC, 268 f.; *Balaur*: *Ogam*, VIII, 268; *Belus* (and *Danaus*): C. Bonner, 'A Study of the Danaid Myth', *Harvard Studies in Classical Philology*, XIII, 129; *Bellerophon*: IMC. 115; *Bali*: *infra*, p. 77.)

60 *SMMD*, 6. Festive contests in boasting and raillery are briefly discussed (with references to parallels from other lands) in J. Huizinga *Homo Ludens* (tr., L, 1939), 65 ff., and Dumézil, *MDG*, 122 ff.

61 *Ériu*, II, 176.

62 *SMMD*; tr. in *HM*, 57 (Kuno Meyer), *HRI*, I, 37 (Leahy), and N. K. Chadwick, *An Early Irish Reader* (Cb, 1927), 16. Cf. also Murphy, *SM*, 37.

63 *DT*, 36.

64 *FB*. We quote from G. Henderson's translation.

65 *RC*, XIV, 396.

66 *TBC*; tr. *TBC(D)*.

67 See Thurneysen, *IHK*, 248 ff.

68 As to the meanings of *noínden* see *DIL(C)*, s.v. 'Stokes compares the Latin *nundinae* 'market-day' (< novem); if the meaning *assembly* be right, its original meaning may have been the time occupied by a warlike assembly or muster.' On the confinement of warriors, see Hocart, *NSF*, 53.

69 *TBC*, 881, *Ériu*, I, 126.

70 Ed. by E. Windisch, *IT*, III, 230; K. Meyer's tr. in *VB*, II, 58. The story has some points of similarity with accounts of shaman contests.

71 *MU*, 24.

72 *GHC*, 67.

73 *TBC(D)*, 144.

74 *MU*, 28.

75 Cf. B. S. Phillpotts, 'Wyrd and Providence in Anglo-Saxon Thought', *Essays and Studies by Members of the English Association*, XIII (1928), 8 ff.

76 Ed. and tr. K. Meyer, *Ériu*, I, 114. A recent comparative study:

J. de Vries, 'Le combat du père et du fils ...', *Ogam*, IX (1957), 122.

77 The meanings of *fían* (except 'pieces of inferior status') and *óc féne* are given from *DIL*, Fasc. III, 118.

78 *ZCP*, XV (1925), 262.

79 Cf. *DF*, I, xxxiv (E. MacNeill).

80 *CG* (D. A. Binchy), 101.

81 *The Oxford Dictionary*, s.v.

82 *SG*, II, 118.

83 Ibid., 99 (I, 92). S. H. O'Grady's translation is given.

84 *Fn* (K. Meyer), ix.

85 *FF*, II, 326.

86 'The Battle of Gabhra', *OST*, I, 135 ff.; *CFt*, 29.

87 See e.g. K. R. V. Wickman, 'Die Einleitung der Ehe . . .', *Acta Academiae Aboensis*, XI (Abo, 1937), A. D. Rees, *Life in a Welsh Countryside* (C, 1950), 82 ff., Varagnac, *CTGV*, Ch. V.

88 *SG*, II, 165.

89 Ibid., 260.

90 *DIL*, Fasc. III, 118.

91 *PRIA*, XXXVI, C, 81 n.; *CFt*, 14.

92 Ed. by K. Meyer, *RC*, XXV, 344; tr. Murphy, *OLRT*, 9.

93 *EIHM*, 278; *DF*, III, lxiii ff.

94 *DF*, III, Appendix G (I. Ll. Foster), lxxvi ff., 446.

95 *DF*, III, civ.

96 Ibid., xli.

97 Murphy, *OLRT*, 11.

98 Ed. and tr. *SG*; *AS* (with tr. of parts omitted from O'Grady's translation).

99 *AS*, 10. The translation follows renderings in S. H. O'Grady, *SG*, II, 109, K. Meyer, *Selections from Ancient Irish Poetry* (L, 1911), 59, and K. Jackson, *A Celtic Miscellany* (L, 1951), 74.

100 *IT*, II, Pt. ii, 127, 158, *LMU*, 48, 66.

101 These words are used by Gerard Murphy in his description of certain Fenian poems, *DF*, III, ciii. As to the 'heroic' and 'romantic' character of the Cycles, cf. Flower, *ITr*, 101.

102 K. Jackson, *Studies in Early Celtic Nature Poetry* (Cb, 1935), 174 and Ch. II.

103 *VB*, II (A. Nutt), 22 ff.; *PBA*, XX (1934), 231 ff. (A. G. van Hamel.)

104 HB, 56. There are references to an Arthur of renown in two Welsh poems which are probably earlier; *Canu Aneirin*, ed. Ifor Williams (C, 1937), 49, *BBCS*, VI, 136.

105 *PBA*, XX, 247. As to the translation, 'leader of troops', cf. *BBCS*, XVII, 242 (Thomas Jones).

106 *HB*, 73; *WBM*, 242 f., 249 ff., *Mb*, 117 ff.

107 On the cult of Maponus (Mabon): I. A. Richmond's contribution to *Dark Age Britain*, ed. D. B. Harden (L, 1956), 11; Rhys, *HL*, 21, 29, etc.

108 The three texts quoted: *LG*, IV, 122, 132, 158; *RC*, XV, 27; AIM, IV, 86 f., *CGl*, 129. (Cf. also *CCC*, 38.) (In *CR*, I (1904–5), 384, mention is made of a 'Troit Fair' held at Alyth, Perthshire, about Christmas.)

109 *DF*, III (G. Murphy), lxxvi.

110 'The Pursuit of Diarmaid and Gráinne', ed. and tr. S. H. O'Grady, *OST*, III, 36.

111 *WAL*, 183, 186.

112 E. K. Chambers, *Arthur of Britain* (L, 1927), 17 f., 46, 107 ff., 123 f.; *BBC*, 67.

113 Chambers, op. cit., 221 f., 249; Loomis, *WAL*, Ch. V.

114 *Breudwyt Ronabwy*, ed. M. Richards (C, 1948), *Mb*, 137.

115 G. Cohen, *Histoire de la chevalerie en France au moyen age* (P, 1949), 11 ff.

116 For discussion and references see J. D. Bruce, *The Evolution of Arthurian Romance* (Baltimore, 1923), II, 59; Loomis, *ATC*, 33; R. M. Jones, 'Y Rhamantau Cymraeg . . . ', *Llên Cymru*, IV (1956–7), 208.

117 There are studies of this theme by T. ÓMáille in *ZCP*, XVII (1928), 129, A. H. Krappe in *Journal of American Philology*, LXIII (1942), 444, J. Weisweiler, *Heimat und Herrschaft* (Halle, 1943), A. K. Coomaraswamy in *Speculum*, XX (1945), 391, T. F. O'Rahilly in *Ériu*, XIV (1946), 14, G. Dumézil in *Ogam*, VI (1954), 3, and P. Mac Cana in *ÉC*, VII (1955), 76. For the story of Niall, see *SG*, I, 328, II, 370, *RC*, XXIV, 190 (ed. and tr. W. Stokes), *Ériu*, IV, 91, and for the story of Lugaid, *CA*, 323. (Cf. *MD*, IV, 135.)

118 Krappe, loc. cit., 446 ff., cites parallels to show that the fawn symbolizes the kingship.

119 *Ériu*, IV, 105. In other texts her mantle is purple.

120 Dumézil, loc. cit.

121 *Revue d'assyriologie*, XLIV (1950), 67.

122 Our source, in this paragraph, is Ó Máille's study, loc. cit. For a reference to Medb's nine husbands, see *GT*, 148. In the *dindṡenchas* (*MD*, III, 366 f.) Macha (who in one story overpowers five brothers), Medb of Connacht and Medb Lethderg are named together as three queens 'of fiery force who had right comely consorts'.

123 J. C. De in *The Cultural Heritage of India* (1937), III, 258, quoted by A. K. Coomaraswamy in *Speculum*, XX, 393. Cf. Krappe, loc. cit., 450.

124 *Speculum*, XX, 400.

125 *ZCP*, XVII, 145.

126 *Ériu*, IV, 107.

127 *RC*, XXVII, 266 ff. (ed. and tr. W. Stokes).

128 On Suibne and Myrddin, see *BBCS*, I (1923), 228 (I. Williams), IX (1939), 8 (A. O. H. Jarman), *ESM*, 535 (K. Jackson), Carney, *SILH*, Ch. IV.

129 Hocart, *Kng*, 215. The black heifer, the surprisingly small reward the Dagda asks of the Fomorian Bres, recalls all the cattle of Ireland. *Supra*, p. 38.

130 Cf. *Man*, XLV (1945), 118 (A. D. Rees).

131 *Kng*, 216 ff.

132 Ibid., 219.

133 *Cm*, XXIV, 10 f.

134 *TLP*, I, 40 ff.

PART TWO

CHAPTER III DARKNESS AND LIGHT

1 *WFFC*, 196.

2 *PLGI*, 5 f.; *Béaloideas*, XXIV, 27, 'The day is yours, the night is ours (the dead).' Cf. Anatole le Braz, *La légende de la morte* (P, 1945), II, 69.

3 On the division of the year into two parts in various parts of the world, see M. P. Nilsson, *Primitive Time Reckoning* (Cb, 1920), 55–75.

4 *Infra*, Ch. XVI.

5 *BBCS*, IX, 40, XIII, 204; *BCCS*, II, 16, III, 107.

6 *BCCS*, II, 17.

7 J. Loth in *RC*, XXV, 130; J. Rhŷs in *PBA*, 1909–10, 207 ff.;
   E. MacNeill in *Ériu*, X (1926–8), 38, 41.

8 Cf. C. Lainé-Kerjean, 'Le Calendrier Celtique', *ZCP*, XXIII
   (1943), 257 ff., F. Le Roux in *Ogam*, IX (1957), 338.

9 *De Bello Gallico*, vi, 18. On reckoning by nights see M. P. Nilsson,
   op. cit., 14 ff. Cf. J. Layard, *Stone Men of Malekula* (L, 1942), 290 f.

10 The six *ANM* months include *Eqvos* which probably had 30 and
   28 days, respectively, in alternate years—an average of 29. (*ZCP*,
   XXIII, 253.)

11 *ERE*, s.v. Calendar. Cf. *RC*, XXV, 124.

12 See E. MacNeill, loc. cit., 13 f. The phrasing has also been con-
   strued to mean no more than 'that the moon was that by which
   months and years were measured'. (*RAC*, 175 n. 4.)

13 *Encyclopaedia Britannica*, s.v. Calendar.

14 *ZCP*, XIX, 55. Cf. *TÉ*, 15.

15 *Ériu*, IV, 25.

16 *TÉ*, 10.

17 *HIF*, 317.

18 *WFFC*, 151.

19 *TEF*, II, 266 f., *BCCS*, III, 108 f., 168; *UF*, 27–30, 86. Cf.
   WFFC, 151; *WFC*, 123 f.; *infra*, p. 298. Cf. the opening of the Gates
   of the Apsu (underworld) during the New Year season in Babylonia. (See *The Labyrinth*, ed. S. H. Hooke (L, 1935), 55 f.)

20 *WFFC*, 152. Cf. *HIF*, 345.

21 *FBI*, 282.

22 *BCCS*, III, 160 f.; *HIF*, 345; *WFC*, 133.

23 Eliade, *MER*, 51 f.

24 On the divisions of the day see *HIF*, 317; on the fourfold division of
   the year, see, for example, G. Lehmacher, 'The Ancient Celtic
   Year', *JCS*, I (1949–50), 144 ff., Joyce, *SHI*, II, 387, f.

25 *HIF*, 344.

26 *BCCS*, II, 19 ff.

27 *BCCS*, III, 244; *HIF*, 363, 349.

28 *WFFC*, 145 f., *RC*, XXV, 118 f. There are variations in the dates
   of the twelve omen days. These days have been compared with the
   Zwölften of Germany and with the sacred 12 nights of India; Loth
   in *RC*, XXIV, 311, Dumézil, *PC*, 38 f.

29 *ZCP*, XXIII, 251, 263 (C. Lainé-Kerjean).

30 *Ibid.*, 251 f.

31 *HIF*, 364 f.

32 *Proceedings of the American Philosophical Society*, XXVI (1889), 398 (J. Mooney).

33 *FBI*, 78 ff.

CHAPTER IV COMING INTO EXISTENCE

1 Gomer son of Japheth had been named as the ancestor of the Gauls, since the time of Josephus (Lloyd, *HW*, I, 191).

2 *LG*, V. In writing *Míl* rather than *Mílid*, the form normally found in the texts, we follow the practice of modern scholars.

3 *MD*, IV, 311

4 *IVHB*, 248; K. Müller-Lisowski, 'Contributions to a Study in Irish Folklore', *Béaloideas*, XVIII, 148. (Cf. also *ÉC*, VI, 24).

5 *Béaloideas*, XVIII, 149.

6 Charles O'Conor quoted in *HWI*, 57. Later writers (e.g. D. D. C. Mould, *Irish Pilgrimage* (D, 1955), 113) give the correct height as about 700 feet.

7 *LG*, V, 110–13.

8 Tr. S. Prabhavananda and C. Isherwood (L, 1947), 114 ff.

9 *Matsya Purána*, CLXVII, 13–25, quoted by H. Zimmer, *MS*, 35 ff.

10 *LG*, V, 114–17. We quote R. A. S. Macalister's translation.

11 *EIHM*, 197.

12 *LG*, V, 46, 68, 94.

13 *MD*, IV, 261; *LG*, V, 160, 420.

14 *LG*, V, 419; MacNeill, *CI*, Ch. VIII.

15 *LG*, V, 416 ff.

16 For references to the traditions concerning Conn and Mug Nuadat, see O'Rahilly, *EIHM*, Ch. X. On the names: ibid., 282, MacNeill, *CI*, 61. Cf. *Mug* and *Servius* (derived from *servus* 'slave'), the name of the first Roman king to be chosen on account of his services, and see further, Dumézil, *SF*, Ch. II.

17 *FF*, II, 265. (P.S. Dinneen's translation.)

18 Hocart, *KC*, Chs. XX, XXI; 84 f., 116, 246 f., 277 etc.

19 *LG*, II, 183.

20 'As far as there is form and name, so far, indeed, extends this whole (universe)' (*Satapatha Bráhmaṇa*), *SBE*, XLIV, 28; 'for whatever is not, that is unmarked (by characteristics)', ibid., XLI, 320.

21 *LG*, IV, 13, 27, 39.

22 'The Settling of the Manor of Tara', ed. and tr. R. I. Best, *Ériu*, IV, 147.

23 *CGd*, I, 57, 239, II, 71 (A. Carmichael's translation).

24 Eliade, *MER*, 34.

25 *LG*, III, 69-73, 39 (R. A. S. Macalister's translation).

26 *SBE*, XXV, 309; cf. XIV, 101.

27 See Coomaraswamy, *RVL*, 5 *et passim*.

28 Ibid., 11, quoting *Rig Veda*, X, 53.

29 Dumézil, *TS*, Ch. 16; retracted in *ITI*, 94. The births of the Sons of Míl, like those of the Ādityas, are grouped in pairs; *LG*, II, 125, *RIR*, 34. Their number varies between three and eight, in different contexts.

30 Macdonell, *VM*, 170; Dumézil, *RIR*, 34-7 (on Vivasvat and Yama).

31 *LG*, IV, 11, 21.

32 Ibid., 33, 51.

33 *Ériu*, VIII, 5.

34 Macalister in *LG*, III, 115.

35 *PRIA*, XXXVI, C, 266.

36 *MD*, III, 418 (in a poem).

37 *LG*, III, 27, II, 273. The king's villeins, in medieval Wales, were required to build houses for the king. Moreover, they were required to receive the queen and her retinue, when she made her annual progress, and also various court officers on similar occasions (*ALW*, I, 486.)

38 Cf. *bothach*, 'cottier, crofter', (from *both* 'hut') and *sen-chléithe* 'hereditary serf', literally 'ancient house' (*CG*, 78, 105),

39 *RC*, L, 231 (A. G. van Hamel); *UF*, 134, *LSC*, 449, on the harvest *cailleach*; *HIF*, 344.

40 *IEW*, 1112.

41 *CG* (D. A. Binchy), 69. The *óc-aire* (v. supra, p. 62) is in some texts the same as the *bó-aire*; *tánaise* in others, he is 'an off-shoot of the *bóaire*' (ibid., 101 f.). Cf. Modern Irish *buachaill* 'a boy, a herd-boy, an unmarried young man', and English *bachelor*, said to be derived from Latin *vacca*, 'cow'.

42 Cf. L. Gerschel, 'Varron logicien', *Latomus*, XVII (1958), 71. *Mruigfer*, 'land-man', seems to be similar in meaning to *bó-aire*, or identical with it (*CG*, 77 f.).

43 *Supra*, p. 32.

44 *MD*, I, 3; *LG*, V, 83.

45 *JMQ* (1941). The people of Nemed were the ancestors of the two peoples who succeeded them. Similarly, in India the clansmen (or third estate) are equated with the Fathers (*SBE*, XLI, 299).

46 *ITI* (1958) (p. 19)—a book which provides references to his earlier publications and to the work of other scholars in the same field.

47 Hocart, *Cst*, 41 f. Further details are now given in Sharma, *SAI*.

48 Discussed by L. Gerschel, loc. cit.

49 *PRIA*, XXXVI, C, 280. The third estate is referred to as 'classes of worth' (ibid., 276; cf. Varro's characterization of them).

50 MacNeill, *EILI*, 94 f. Cf. *PRIA*, XXXVI, C, 273, 278 ff.

51 *Vedânta-Sûtrâs*, *SBE*, XXXIV, 261 f., Hocart, *Cst*, 5 f.

52 *LG*, II, 176 ff.

53 *LG*, III, 139.

54 *LG*, II, 177, 185, 197, V, 35.

55 See, for example, H. Frankfort, *AER*, 21, 154, id., *Kingship and the Gods* (Chicago, 1948), 151 ff.

56 *LG*, II, 194.

57 *LG*, IV, 107, 15, III, 9.

58 *LG*, II, 188 f.

59 *LG*, I, 155, 167; *GT*, 37, 44.

60 Hocart in *CJS*, G, I (1925), 67, *Cst*, 41. We have added the aborigines to Hocart's scheme.

CHAPTER V A HIERARCHY OF PROVINCES

1 *LG*, IV, 13, 27, 61 f., 73 f.

2 For detailed references, see O'Rahilly, *EIHM*, 154-72.

3 Ed. and tr. R. I. Best, *Ériu*, IV (1910), 121. We quote (Fintan's words) from R. I. Best's translation, 145, 147 ff., 153, 155.

4 A different meaning is perhaps to be preferred. When Cormac mac Airt was born, his maternal grandfather, a wizard smith, made five protecting *essa* 'against wounding, drowning . . . and every ill' (*ZCP*, VIII, 310).

5 In the *dindsenchas*, Cruachan is referred to as the burying-ground of Tuatha Dé Danann (*MD*, III, 432).

6 *VB*, II, 24 (A. Nutt); Dillon, *EIL*, 34. We have noted (*supra*,

p. 63) that the Ulster warriors, unlike the Fiana, fight in chariots. In ancient India and Persia, members of the warrior class were known as 'chariot men'. (*AESC*, IV, 718). It may be noteworthy too that in the *Rig Veda* most of the princes, at least in the earlier phases, belong to the Punjab, and there are numerous references to the Indus and the Sarasvati; the scene of the epic *Mahābhārata* is laid in the kingdoms of the Ganges and Jumna basins (*GL*, II, 485, III, 737), while the scene of the later *Rāmāyana*, in which the main action is centred on the abduction of a woman by a demon, is south India. Cf. *SAI*, 87; information gleaned from the Dhar-masūtras which emphasize the supremacy of the *brāhmanas* is generally limited to northern India, that from Buddhist and Jain sources which emphasize the primacy of the *Ksatriyas* is generally limited to north-eastern India. Cf. *infra*, pp. 383, 392.

7 *Ériu*, II, 176 ff.

8 Dumézil, *Trp*, 117 ff.

9 *SG*, I, 359, II, 401; *RC*, XIII, 36 (ed. and tr. W. Stokes). On the name *Bórama*: *Ériu*, IV, 171 (K. Meyer).

10 Quoted in Hocart, *Cst*, 40.

11 *Supra*, p. 54; *infra*, p. 328.

12 Ed. and tr. W. Stokes, *RC*, XXV, 20. (Cf. *ZCP*, VIII, 261.)

13 *MD*, IV, 190.

14 *RC*, XXV, 31. In *LG*, guesting is instituted by Partholón's people; according to the earliest law tracts, a servile client (*céle giallnai*) was required to provide a night's entertainment for his lord during the 'coshering season'—between New Year and Shrovetide—in addition to ordinary food-rents and services (*CG*, 81). But the *briugu* 'hospitaller', 'rich landowner', dispensed unlimited hospitality to all persons (ibid., 79). In Wales, food-rents were due to the king from both freemen and villeins, and the entertainment of royal officers was also incumbent upon freemen and upon the king's villeins, though not, apparently, to the same degree. But it is the *breyr* or *uchelwr*, 'freeman in authority', who is celebrated for his hospitality and 'householding'.

15 *CI*, 59, *PRIA*, XXIX, C, 95.

16 *EIHM*, 186. Mug son of Míl is the eponym of a people who occupied land (including Corco Duibne) in Munster (*GT*, 117). Cf., again, Mug Corb, King of the two Munsters (ibid., 96, but in other con-texts King of the Leinstermen—*EIHM*, 134).

17 By Dr P. Mac Cana in *ÉC*, VII, 91 ff. He suggests that 'Mugain was an old district-name ... and that it was closely associated with the province of Munster in such a way that the two names might be regarded in certain contexts as interchangeable.' (p. 101.)

18 Ed. and tr. K. Meyer, *Cm*, XIV, 105.

19 *VM*, 157.

20 *Supra*, p. 113. Irish *cerd* and Welsh *cerdd* signify both 'craft' and 'music'.

21 *PRIA*, XXXVI, 280.

22 Ibid., *CIL*, s.v. *crónán*. Cf., perhaps, *An Chrón*, 'Hell or a dread female resident there' (*DF*, III, 397).

23 The first (only) is thought to be derived from Irish *cléir* 'band (of poets etc.)' (? Cf. *Caiseal na cliar*). It is used (a) of poets in general and (b) in contemptuous references to low-grade entertainers. Monks chanting, before dawn, on the grave of an abbot, and angels singing on the grave of a saint, are referred to as *clér*. See *GPC*, s.v., *GDG*, 438 ff.

24 Ed. by K. Meyer, *ZCP*, XII, 290 f.

25 *ALI*, III, 25; cf. *RC*, XXVIII, 318.

26 *FI*, 34, *Cst*, 19 (*śūdra* = *asura*).

27 *GT*, 189. The people of Ulster are likened to bulls (cf. *supra*, p. 124), the people of Leinster to dung-hill dogs', and the people of Con-nacht—if the editor's suggestion is accepted—to foxes.

28 *HDA*, s.v. *fliege*; R. Karsten, *The Civilisation of the South American Indians* (L, 1926), 292

29 *Kng*, 124; *OS*, II, 264, III, 84; *CJS*, I, 77; *Numen*, III, 122. Cf. 'a tail (-whisk) for turning away evil' (*Śatapatha Brāhmaṇa*, *SBE*, XLIV, 220).

30 Represented by 'charioteership'.

31 MacNeill, *EILI*, 97. Cf. G. Dumézil's account of the relations of the Roman king to the 'functions', in *The Sacral Kingship* (Leiden, 1959), 410 ff. Mael Mura speaks of the Sons of Míl making alliances with the Children of Nemed, Fir Bolg, and Tuatha Dé Danann—without mentioning Partholón and Cessair (*IVHB*, 250). On the other hand, the fourth caste was represented among the Indian king's *ratnins* ('high functionaries of state')—*SAI*, 49.

32 *Kng*, Chs. III, IV, V.

33 *SG*, I, 90 f., II, 96 f.

34 'The Hindu Act of Truth in Celtic Tradition', *MP*, XLIV, 140.

35 Ibid. (Ed. by R. Thurneysen, *ZCP*, XI, 81 f.)

36 *BBC*, 56.

37 *SG*, II, 288.

38 *AKI*, I, 95 f.

39 *Ériu*, III, 155.

40 'Advice to a Prince', *Ériu*, IX, 54 (tr. Tadhg O'Donoghue).

41 *TBC*, 7; *Ériu*, II, 183. Cf. Dumézil, *JMQ*, 115.

42 A. K. Coomaraswamy, *The Dance of Shiva* (Calcutta, 1946), 34.

43 *MD*, III, 20.

44 *IVHB*, 250 ff. On the attributes of Connacht cf. *Ériu*, V, 235, 'noble ancient lore . . . triumphs . . . judgements'. Cf., further, the two quatrains given in *Búrdúin Bheaga*, ed. Tomás Ó Rathile (D, 1925), 10: (1) Connacht: 'eloquent, musical, the glory of the company'; Ulster: 'staunch in time of fighting'; Leinster: 'cheerful, bright, glad, pleasant'; Munster; 'in deeds and words clearly renowned'. (2) In the same order, 'talkative, worthless', 'covetous, given to envy and hatred', 'prosperously capable', 'vainly boastful'. For other modern versions of these characterizations see *The Gaelic Journal*, XIV, 475; *Seanfocla Ulad*, ed. Énrí Ó Muirġeasa (1936), 7, *SnC*, 246, *TEF*, II, 280.

The association of a particular colour with each of the four cardinal points is a very widespread phenomenon. In ancient times the three 'functions' (*supra*, p. 112) of Indo-European traditions were symbolized by the colours white, red, and blue (or green)—Dumézil, *RIR*, Chs. III and IV, *ITI*, 26 f., where slight indications of white as the druid colour and red as the warrior colour in Irish tradition are noticed. To these we may add (1) Laigne *Lethan-glas* (Broad-blue/green') as the eponym of the Leinstermen, 'green spotted (? cloth)' (*brecc glas*) amongst the attributes of Leinster (*supra*, p. 123), and *UíEnechglais* ('Blue/Green-face') the name of an ancient Leinster people (*EIHM*, 30); (2) the jet-black colour of the *crossáin*. The colour of the Indian fourth caste was black.

45 *Kauṭilya's Arthaśāstra*, trans. by R. Shamasastry (Bangalore, 1915), 61 f. On the symbolism of the world quarters and the division of society accordingly, see further *L'année sociologique*, Ser. i, VI, 34 ff., 60, etc. (E. Durkheim and M. Mauss), *AW*, 224 f., 86, 89. In Zuñi society, priests are associated with the West, warriors with the North, dancers with the East, and farmers and doctors with the South (*HS*, 113). If the order of the last two were reversed, the scheme would correspond closely with the Irish one.

46 In India different arrangements were stipulated for various rites. See *CJS*, G, I, 105 ff. (references to Śatapatha Brāhmana).

47 Cf. *Ériu*, XVIII (1958), 51 (D. A. Binchy); cf. *IF*, 45 (a seven‑teenth‑century poem).

48 *Ériu*, II, 49; *FF*, I, 126 f.

49 *VB*, I, 47, 50.

50 *RC*, XI, 43 f.

51 *PRIA*, XXVII, C, 330. In later tradition Gleann‑na‑nGealt in Corco Duibne is famous as the resort of 'wild men' (*Trioca‑céad Corca Duibne*, ed. An Seabac (D, 1939), 284 f.). In the early litera‑ture, Mór, Mis, and during a period of mental derangement, Cú‑Chulainn, are associated with Munster (*SILH*, 147; *Celtica*, I, 382). The story of Suibne Geilt is linked with Moling of Munster.

52 On the persons named see *Ériu*, XIV, 3 ff., *EIHM*, 288, *SG*, II, 576.

53 *MWHT*, xvii (J. G. McKay).

54 *ZCP*, XIX, 176.

55 *PRIA* (C), LV, 83 f. Cf. *FBI*, 50 f., *ÉC*, I, 292 (A. H. Krappe), *LSC*, 428.

56 *EIHM*, 491, 519.

57 *Ériu*, II, 25, XIII, 167; *GT*, 180; *SMMD*, 26; *MD*, III, 255, 243. (We do not wish to imply that no personage with a *Sen* name is *ever* located outside Munster.) Fintan, whose abode was said to be in Munster, is referred to as 'Fintan from the hazel woods' (*SG*, II, 151). Many a sacred site was 'originally' a hazel wood (*FBI*, 128; *SG*, II, 576; *supra*, p. 111). In two versions of a tale in which the provinces of Ireland are figuratively (and abusively) characterized, it is the people of Munster and those of Meath and Tara, respectively, who are described as 'a hedge of white hazel' in battle (*Ériu*, V, 239; *BDBM*, 125). Cf. *infra*, pp. 161, 311.

58 *EIHM*, 82.

59 *Ériu*, XIV, 7 f. O'Rahilly here rejects (Professor) M. Ó Briain's suggestion (*ZCP*, XIV (1923), 327) that *Érainn* is derived from *eks‑rannī*, 'those living in the outer division' or 'those outside the division'.—It may be added here that in the *Śatapatha Brāhmana* the Fathers are distinguished from the three sacrificial castes (*SBE*, XII, 289 f., 420) despite what is noted *supra*, Ch. IV, n. 45.

60 *HM*, 65 (ed. and tr. K. Meyer). .

61 *GT*, 189; *ALW*, I, 738; cf. telling the bees about a death. Cf.

H. M. Ransome, *The Sacred Bee* (L, 1937), 189 ff. In a variant ver‑
sion of 'The Settling of the Manor of Tara' (*Ériu*, IV, 162) honey is
listed among the attributes of Munster. In Vedic mythology the
Aśvins, twin gods of the third and fourth functions (*RIR*, 57; *SAI*
74 f.), were of all the gods the most closely connected with honey.
They gave honey to the bees and they themselves were compared
with bees (VM, 49 f.).

62 *ÉC*, VII, 91 ff., 78, 89 (P. Mac Cana).

63 *Fn*, 58 ff. A story in Cormac's *Glossary* is about an old poetess of the
Múscraige of Munster. Her condition is wretched when she is dis‑
covered in Man, and her identity is revealed by an unknown black‑
faced youth, most foul and hideous in appearance, who is able to
complete the half‑quatrains she recites. Thereafter, noble raiment is
put upon her, and the youth appears as 'a young hero, kingly,
radiant . . . fairer than the men of the world'. He is said to be the
spirit of poetry. (*CGl*, 135; *AIM*, IV, viii).

64 See Dumézil, *MV*, 42, 45.

65 *JAOS*, LX, 65.

66 *HLt*, 223, 221 (quoting the Book of Rites). Cf. '*Rik* is *Saman*', *SBE*,
I, 8.

67 *EIHM*, 175, 177, 179.

68 *MD*, III, 338; *AIM*, I, 27; *LG*, II, 265; *ZCP*, XIV, 155 ff.,
TBD, 42; *AS*, 170 ff., 239 ff. (tr. W. Stokes).

69 *Supra*, pp. 55 ff.; cf. *ATC*, 285 ff.

70 *MU*, 20.

71 *FB*, 103 (G. Henderson's tr.).

72 *ZCP*, III, 38 (in a poem).

73 *FB*, 101.

74 *SGS*, V, 15; *MU*, 21. In an eleventh‑century poem which des‑
cribes him as a blazing lion, he appears as a conqueror who des‑
troyed the south of the world (*ZCP*, III, 38). A Welsh poem de‑
voted to him says that 'he held (the) helm on (the) southern sea'
(*BT*, 66).

75 *VM*, 35 ff.; *ITI*, 35, *SBE*, XII, 53, 210, XLIII, 195.

76 See *IHK*, 431 ff. CúRoí is said to have shaved CúChulainn's hair
with his sword and then smeared his head with cow‑dung (*ZCP*,
IX, 198). In India, when a child was given his tonsure, the follow‑
ing words were spoken as the left side of the head was being shaved:
'The razor with which Pusan has shaved (the beard) of Brihaspati,

of Agni, of Indra, for the sake of long life, with that I shave thy head.' The hair was then cast on bull's dung or buried in a cow, shed. (*The Grihya-Sûtras*, SBE, XXX, 217, 61.)

77 'Gawain and the Green Knight: Indra and Namuci', *Speculum*, XIX (1944), 105. On the ambivalence of the sun, the *asura* priest of all the *devas*, cf. Eliade, *PCR*, 143 ff.

78 *PRIA*, XXXVI (C), 281. Professor Binchy (*Ériu*, XVIII, 49) translates *ollam* as 'supreme' or 'most transcendent' and notes that the word is used, in the oldest law tracts, for the highest grade in every hierarchy.

79 So among the Sons of Míl, Donn was the king until they took pos, session of Ireland.

CHAPTER VI INVOLUTIONS

1 *LG*, V, 267 ff. In the Fenian literature the fighting forces of Ireland are comprised of twenty-five 'battles' (*PRIA*, XXXVIII (C), 174 n.). On the twenty-five dioceses of Ireland, see Keating, *FF*, III, 298.

2 *SBE*, XXXIV, 257 ff. The commentators differ in their inter, pretation.

3 These classes are discussed in Chadwick, *GL*, I, 607 ff., and more recently in G. Murphy, 'Bards and Filidh', *Éigse*, II, 202 ff. With regard to the distinction between *vates* and druids, cf. P. Arnold, 'Augures et flamines', *Ogam*, IX (1957), 139.

4 *BBCS*, XI, 138 (D. M. Jones).

5 For a study of the power and significance of praise-poems, see Dumézil, *SF*.

6 *PRIA*, XXXVI (C), 277, 273.

7 Murphy, loc. cit.

8 *LG*, III, 23, V, 45, 91.

9 *MD*, IV, 300. In India, the Aśvins, gods of the third estate, are 'the physicians of the gods'.—'Sláinghe of the (guesting) companies', *GT*, 83. (*Slánga* is another variant of the name.)

10 *Supra*, pp. 35 ff. Like Sláine (the first king of Fir Bolg), Nuadu, the first king of the Tuatha and the ancestor of all the Irish (*EIHM*, 467 n.), seems to belong to the province of the ancestors, the third estate.

11 *The Fate of the Children of Tuireann*, ed. and tr. R. J. O'Duffy (D, 1901), 4; cf. *Celtica*, II, 64.

12 *PRIA*, XXXVI (C), 280. In Welsh tradition, the successive des/ tinies which Aranrhod swears upon Lleu bar him from having a name (Function I), arms (Function II) and a wife (Function III), but each of these destinies is circumvented (*supra*, p. 50); cf. *ÉC*, VIII, 283 n. (G. Dumézil). Cf. CúChulainn's three wishes, p. 56.

13 J. G. Frazer, *GB*, IV, Ch. V, *Aftermath* (L, 1936), Ch. XXVI.

14 *LG*, IV, 128, 161, 197.

15 Dumézil, *MV*, 179 ff. Cf. *Ogam*, X, 278 (J. de Vries). A. K. Coomaraswamy observes that there is 'good reason to suppose' that the great seasonal festivals of India were primarily offered to Varuṇa (*Yakṣas*, II (Washington, 1931), 30).

16 *De Bello Gallico*, VI, 17.

17 *Naissance de Rome*[2] (P, 1944), 22 ff. (*MDG*, 9). Among the Indian king's 'jewels' (*ratnins*), Varuṇa is represented by the *sūta*, 'poet, herald, physician, sacrosanct charioteer' (*Numen*, III, 125). The word *sūta* also denotes a low caste comprising the offspring of marriages between members of the *brahman* and *kṣatriya* castes (*SF*, 53).

18 *Germania*, Ch. IX; *EHR*, 138.

19 *MDG*, Ch. II.

20 *RC*, XIV, 426. Conall Cernach and Cet, the protagonists in *SMMD* (*supra*, p. 55), are related to one another in the same way.

21 *DIL*(C), s.vv. *gor* (2), *nia, gnia*.

22 *Germania*, Ch. XX. See, further, W. O. Farnsworth, *Uncle and Nephew in the Old French Chansons de Geste* (*Columbia University Studies in Romance Philology and Literature*, 1913); C. H. Bell, *The Sister's Son in the Medieval German Epic* (*University of California Publications in Modern Philology*, X, 1920–5).

23 On the role of the cross/cousin and the uterine nephew in ritual and myth see A. M. Hocart, *Man*, XXIII, 10 f., XXIV, 103 f., XXVI, 205 f., *The Indian Antiquary*, LII, (1923), 267 f., LIV (1925), 16 f., and A. R. Radcliffe/Brown, *Structure and Function in Primitive Society* (L, 1952), 15 ff., 97 ff.

24 *The Indian Antiquary*, LIV, 18; *DIL*(C), s.v. *gor*, 2; *AIM*, IV, 81; *CGl*, 121.

25 Legendary families outside the Mythological Cycle include sons symbolizing the social functions. Thus the destinies of the five sons of Eochu Muigmedón are revealed in a dream: Brian and Fiachu will be rivals and the kingship will alternate between their descendants

before the line of Brian prevails. Ailill will strive for territory and will gain an abode from his brothers, while Fergus will only beget a sorrowful peasant and his kin will be almost unknown. Niall the son of a secondary wife treated as a slave, becomes high-king (*RC*, XXIV, 174). Again, Artchorp, king of the Déssi, had four sons: Brecc, whose two sons became kings; Oengus, a champion who had the strength of fifty and wielded a terrible spear—he promised that his children should be the first to go to battle and to go across the border, the last to come out of the enemy's land; Eochaid, who like the third group of the Nemedians settled abroad, and lastly Forad who was the son of a bond maid and who, like Donn the son of Míl, though he was the eldest did not get any land. (*Cm*, XIV, 104 ff.; *forad* = 'throne-mound'—cf. *infra*, pp. 183 f.)—'Five generations from king to spade' (*CI*, 125).

26 So too in India, the Maruts, gods of the third estate, act as the body-guard of Indra, the chief god of the second function (*CJS (G)*, I, 67; *SBE*, XII, xvii, 387, 393 f., 398 ff.).

27 *Supra*, p. 124; *EIHM*, 276 f.

28 *Fn*, 61. Cf. *DF*, I, xxxi, xxxvii, where MacNeill asserts that in the folklore of Connacht and Donegal 'Goll is the chief popular hero of the Fiana, the paragon of valour.' It is said that Clanna Baoisgne, Finn's own kindred, supported the claims of the line of Éber (who took the South of Ireland), whereas Clanna Morna, their rivals, supported the line of Éremón (who took the North), *OST*, I, 57—though, in one poem (*DF*, II, 354), Finn is said to be of the race of Éremón.

29 On Arthur as the king of an underworld realm, the southern hemisphere, or the Antipodes, see *WAL*, Ch. V. Cf. Pwyll, lord of a southern territory and the Head of Annwfn, and CúRoí, King of Munster, the 'southern province', and conqueror of the South of the world (*supra*, Ch. V, n. 74). Irish *alltar* denotes 'yon side (of the country), the wilder parts, . . . the other world, the world beyond the grave' (*IED*, 35).

30 *Yg*, 362. Cf. *Encyclopaedia of Social Science*, under 'Death Customs' (A. M. Hocart); also Caillois, *HS*, 161 f., on inversion during festivals.

31 C. C. Miller, *Black Borneo* (L, 1946), 204 f.

32 An identification of 'north' with 'left' and 'south' with 'right' is to be found in several languages. In Irish, not only is this the case, but

the word for 'east' means 'in front' and the world for 'west' 'behind', thus denoting the directions from the standpoint of a person who faces east, as the king of Tara does in stories we shall refer to in the next chapter. One Irish word for 'north' and 'the North of Ireland' in particular (*fochla*, a compound of *clé* 'left') denotes the seat of honour in the hall of a king or lord and the warror's seat on the left side of the war-chariot—the charioteer sat on the right. A law-tract makes it clear that in the house of a *bó-aire*, the man of the house always sat in the north end, facing south. *MC*, III, 29. (In Iceland too, the seat of honour was always on the northern side of the hall, facing south. It is said that the Roman king Numa faced south on the occasion of his inauguration—*RIR*, 41. As for ancient China, 'what did he [the Sovereign] do? Nothing but reverently conduct himself with his face directed to the South.'—*HLt*, 1, from the Analects of Confucius.) According to Irish folk-belief, a new house should always be built to the north of the old house. With regard to the burial of *the dead*, on the other hand, the northern side of a church or the left-hand side of a graveyard is set apart for unbaptised children, suicides, or strangers (*HIF*, 266). Furthermore, one word for 'south' (*dess*) means 'just', 'well-arranged'; *thuas* 'in the south' is derived from *uas*, 'high'; 'the upper part (*uachtar*) of Ireland' and 'the top (*ceann*) of Ireland' are synonyms for 'the *South* of Ireland' (*IED*, 1281), while the usual word for 'north' (*tuath*) means 'evil'—and similar semantic associations occur in other languages. (See H. Pedersen's contribu-tion to *Donum natalicium Schrijnen* (Nijmegen—Utrecht, 1929), 423, *RC*, XLVII, 254 n.) Whereas in India the gods were said to be in the North (as in the belief of the Romans, according to Varro) and the ancestors (and the demons) in the South (*SBE*, XII, 289, *JRS*, XXXVI, 119 ff.), for the ancient Scandinavians the North was the direction of Hel and for the Persians it was the abode of demons. (In Persia, the relation of *daeva* to *ahura* is inverse to the usual rela-tion of (Indian) *deva* to *asura*). The statement referred to above, that in Ireland the man of the house always sat in the north end of the house, occurs in an explanation which is offered of the fact that a fine of a sheep was imposed for disfiguring the south door-post of the house of a *bó-aire*, but only a fine of a lamb for disfiguring the north door-post. 'Why is *the south side more noble*? Answer. Because it is that is in the view of the good man (of the house). . . .' Such subtleties and inversions have their counterparts in the complex symbolism of 'left' and 'right' in ancient China (on which see Granet, *ESC*, 261–78).

It may be added that in Ireland, as in many other parts of the world, the sun-wise or right-hand-wise turn is generally considered pro-pitious and proper, whereas to turn withershins is considered wrong and unlucky, but suitable for sorcery and cursing. Apart from the latter qualification, all actions should be performed right-hand-wise 'with the exception of turning a plough-team at the end of the furrow' (*HIF*, 373). It will be recalled that ploughmen and labourers figure prominently in Partholón's company, and it is the same class of people (*in t-aes trebtha*), among Tuatha Dé Danann, who are accounted *andée* ('non-gods'). In India, some of the features of the left-handed' Tantra are the worship of female deities, the belief that deities exist in a benign and in a terrible form, the inclusion of various forms of 'immoral conduct' among the practices that conduce to salvation, and an elaborate ritual connected with the burial ground. The Prajñaparamita texts (of the left-handed Tantra) originated in the South of India. (*Bdd*, 177, 191 ff. On (artisan) *castes* of the Left Hand in south India, see Hutton, *CsI*, 9, 59 ff.)

Initiation involves doing the exact opposite of what is usually considered proper (*Yg*, 362; cf. *infra*, p. 258). A. K. Coomara-swamy cites the Acts of St Peter: '. . . the Lord saith in a mystery: Unless ye make the things of the right hand as those of the left, and those of the left as those of the right, and those that are above as those below, and those that are behind as those that are before, ye shall not have knowledge of the kingdom.' ('The Inverted Tree', *QJMS*, XXIX, 142 f.)

(On 'left' and 'right', see also R. Hertz, *Death and the Right Hand* (tr., L, 1960), *PRIA*, ser. ii, I (1879), 355 ff. (S. Ferguson). With regard to the warrior and his charioteer on the left and right sides, respectively, of the chariot, it may be noted that in the *Táin* Cú-Chulainn's battle-girdle and kilt are of cow-skins and ox-hides, while his charioteer wears a kirtle of buck-skin—*TBC(D)*, 187 ff. Prof. J. Weisweiler draws a distinction between a 'bull-culture' of northern Ireland and a 'deer-culture' of southern Ireland—'Vorindo-germanische Schichten der irische Heldensage'. *ZCP*, XXIV, 11 ff., 165 ff.)

CHAPTER VII THE CENTRE

1 *The Book of Rights*, ed. J. O'Donovan (D, 1847), 176–90; see *ESM*, 508.

2 *DIL*, s.v. *Fál*; *supra*, p. 29.

3 'De Síl Chonairi Móir', ed. and tr. L. Gwynn, *Ériu*, VI, 139, 142. According to the *dindšenchas* (*RC*, XV, 286), there were 'three small stones' apart from Fál, namely 'Moel to the east, Blocc to the south, and Bluicne in the north.' In 'Baile in Scáil' (*ZCP*, III, 458), these names (with *Maol* for *Moel*) are those of Conn's druids. (Cf. also *MD*, I, 18.)

4 J. Gonda, 'Ancient Indian Kingship . . ', *Numen*, III, 147, cf. IV, 149 n.

5 'Fled Dúin na nGéd', tr. M. Dillon, *CK*, 58; *BDBM*, 6.

6 'A New Version of the Battle of Mag Rath', ed. and tr. C. Marstrander, *Ériu*, V, 233 (quoted). It is noted in the text that if the high-king had been of the Southern Uí Néill the arrangement would have been slightly different. In 'The Banquet of Dún na nGéd' this difference seems to be greater: 'The custom was that when a king of the Southern Uí Néill was High King the king of Connacht should be at his right hand, and when a king of the Northern Uí Néill was High King, the king of Ulster on his right and the king of Connacht on his left.' (*CK*, 61.) One wonders whether a high-king of the Southern Uí Néill faced southwards and a high-king of the Northern Uí Neill faced northwards. With the alternation of the kings of Connacht and Ulster at the high-king's right hand, cf. 'There was a covenant between Lugaid and Ailill Aulum and between their offspring after them that whenever Aulum's offspring held the kingship, Lugaid's offspring should hold the judgeship, but when Lugaid's offspring held the kingship, Aulum's sons were to hold the judgeship. Lugaid and Ailill made this arrangement in the presence of Conn of the hundred battles over one half of Ireland. Thus the men of Leinster and Munster held kingship and judgeship.' (*Fn*, 29.)

7 *VM*, 9; cf. A. M. Hocart, 'The Four Quarters', *CJS* (G), I, 105 f. *HIF*, 425; *Celtica*, I, 388 (T. F. O'Rahilly).

8 Hocart, *KC*, 253.

9 Soothill, *HLt*, 76, 80, 135, and *passim*. Also, W. E. Geil, *The Sacred Five in China* (L, 1926). The Five *Ti* also ruled the five

seasons and were associated with the five planets. There were four seas plus a pool in the centre, while the theory was that every fifth year a sovereign should go 'to the four, or possibly five, sacred mountains'. The four peaks were in the north, south, east, and west, and 'at some period a fifth or central mountain was added'. In Ireland, the king of a tribe (or minor kingdom) was known as 'king of peaks' (*rí benn, CG,* 18, 104). Cf. 'Brega of the peaks' (*ZCP,* VIII, 265), *Brega* = 'Hills' (*IHK,* 89), 'Fir Bolg of the peaks' (*LG,* IV, 49). In India, the regalia of the king are known as 'the five summits' (*Numen,* III, 122). In China, the Four Chief Barons were known as the 'Four Peaks' (*HLt,* 104).

10 A. C. L. Brown, *The Origin of the Grail Legend* (Cb, Massachusetts, 1943), 358 f.

11 As far as we know, the first writer to draw attention to the cosmological significance of the provinces of Ireland was René Guénon in *Le Roi du Monde* (first published P, 1927; 3rd edn. 1950, p. 75). In *Celtica,* I (1950), 387, T. F. O'Rahilly noted that a fivefold conception of the world figured in the *Rig Veda* and in an Egyptian hymn of the sixth dynasty.

12 *FB,* 2 ff.

13 Soothill, *HLt,* 88, 91 f. Cf. 'from the five directions of the nine Finns', Dinneen, *IED,* 22.

14 *HLt,* 111.

15 Ibid., 36.

16 The *Arthaśāstra* of Kautilya, quoted by Hocart, *KC,* 247, and by E. M. Sturtevant, *Yale Classical Studies,* I, 219. (On the date of this work, see *SAI,* 143 ff.); *CJS* (*G*), I, 106 ff. In the Buddhist symbol of the Wheel of the Law, the eight spokes represent the Eight-fold Path to the Centre (*Anthropos,* XLI–XLIV, 845 f.).

17 Cf. L. H. Loomis, 'The Celtic Twelve', *MP,* XXV, 345 ff.

18 'The State Concept of Imerina, compared with the Theories found in certain Scandinavian and Chinese Texts'; *FL,* LXI (1950), 186–202. The Kalmucks of Siberia picture the world as being circular with a square pyramidical mountain in the centre. In the ocean in each of the four directions is a separate quarter of the world. Each quarter consists of a large island with a small island on either side, making a total of twelve lands around a central mountain (Harva, *RVAV,* 65 f.). The Kalmucks also associate a different

colour with each direction, and with this may be compared the twelve winds of different colours described in a tenth-century Irish poem and in the introduction to the *Senchas Mór* (*Saltair na Rann*, ed. W. Stokes (1883), 2; *ALI*, I, 27. Each of the four winds from the cardinal points is separated from the next by two subordinate winds.)

The pattern we are discussing also finds a close parallel in the arrangement of the Twelve Tribes of Israel in four groups of three around the tabernacle. Each group of three consisted of a dominant tribe situated at the cardinal point and two subordinate tribes. In the centre was the tabernacle, looked after by the Levites who 'were not reckoned among the Israelites' (Numbers, ii). The pattern was reproduced in microcosm on the burse which Aaron wore on his breast when he entered the Presence (Exodus, xxviii). In the burse there were twelve precious stones, arranged in four rows of three and engraved with the names of the Twelve Tribes. For a discussion of the Twelve Tribes of Israel and other twelve-tribe confederacies in the Near East, see M. Noth, *The History of Israel* (L, 1958), 87 ff. References to twelve tribe communities in ancient Italy and Greece are quoted in the same author's *Das System der zwölf Stämme Israels* (*Beiträge zur Wissenschaft vom Alten und Neuen Testament*, Vierte Folge, Heft I, (Stuttgart, 1930), 47 f.).

19 *CG*, 18, 23.
20 *CCC*, 52. Matholwch, King of Ireland, and his company come to Wales in thirteen ships (*PKM*, 29).
21 *TBD*, 5, 33.
22 *CI*, 58.
23 *LG*, V 127, 47.
24 *MU*, 2; *EIHM*, 405.
25 *MC*, II, 40 (cf. *MD*, III, 16).
26 *TLP*, II, 83.
27 *RC*, XII, 81; *ALI*, I, 27 ff.
28 Danielli, loc. cit., 191; *HLt*, 87, 92, etc.
29 *Constitution d'Athènes*, ed. G. Mathieu and B. Haussoulier (P, 1922), 75.
30 Ed. and tr. W. Stokes, *Ériu*, IV, 22 ff. On Indra, the warrior god, as lord of the New Year, see *PC*, 122 ff.; on Mars and the Year, *Trp*, 238 ff.
31 See F. R. Lewis, 'Gwerin Ffristial a Thawlbwrdd', *THSC*, 1941,

185 ff., and E. MacWhite, 'Early Irish Board Games', *Éigse*, V (1945), 25 ff.
32 *Ériu*, IV, 124.
33 Tr. E. Knott, *The Bardic Poems of Tadhg Dall Ó hUiginn*, II (L, 1926), 198. The poem belongs to the period 1200–1640.
34 *Kng*, 25, 79.
35 *ZCP*, III, 458 (ed. K. Meyer).
36 *Supra*, p. 66.
37 *FL*, III, 476; cf. *RC*, XV, 297, *MD*, II, 42.
38 Tr. E. MacNeill, *CI*, 51; cf. *CA*, 358, *MD*, IV, 278.
39 *Cm*, XXIV, 44, tr. A. W. Wade-Evans.
40 *TLP*, I, 41 f.
41 *SG*, II, 76.
42 *ALW*, I, 170, 538, 754.
43 See, for example, R. U. Sayce, 'The One-night House and its Distribution', *FL*, LIII, 161 f. In Scotland the household fire had to be extinguished before an occupier could be evicted (*FL*, LII, 304).
44 Coomaraswamy, *RVL*, 19 f.
45 *LG*, III, 4, IV, 140, V, 59, 70; M. A. Canney, 'Boats and Ships in Processions', *FL*, XLIX, 132 ff.
46 *SG*, I, 73, *ZCP*, XX, 168, *IT*, III, 198.
47 *AIM*, IV, 13. (According to another version, the fires were made by the druids 'through incantations'; *TIG*, xxxv); *FF*, II, 246.
48 *GB*, X, 147, 155, 335.
49 *HIF*, 334.
50 *De Bello Gallico*, vi, 13.
51 *ALI*, I, 78 f. In his recent study, 'The Fair of Tailtiu and the Feast of Tara' (*Ériu*, XVIII (1958), 114), Professor D. A. Binchy notes that 'in pre-Christian, perhaps in pre-Goidelic, days Uisnech, the "centre" of Ireland, seems to have been a place of religious significance, particularly associated with a fire-cult'. He also believes that the story of Mide's fire (*supra*, p. 156) shows 'that an aura of sanctity must have clung to the district even in the days of the latest pseudo-historians' (loc. cit.). Nevertheless, prompted by the absence in the annals of references to an assembly at Uisnech, he describes *mórdáil Uisnig* ('The assembly of Uisnech' referred to in medieval texts) as an invention of the pseudo-historians. Whether an assembly, was actually held at Uisnech during a particular period in Irish

history, or not, it seems incredible to us that the pre-Christian fire-cult postulated by Professor Binchy and the pre-Christian assembly the existence of which is rendered more than probable by Caesar's observations concerning the annual druidic assembly held in the central kingdom of Gaul were first forgotten and then invented again, and moreover that these spurious traditions were inserted in stories in such a way as to harmonize with evidence which can be adduced from other lands.

52 *MD*, IV, 279.

53 *Topographia Hibernie*, *PRIA*, LII (C), 159.

54 *Ériu*, IV, 151.

55 On the symbolism of the centre, see W. H. Roscher, 'Omphalos', *AKSG*, XXIX, No. 9 (1913), and other references given in *PCR*, 238, J. Loth, 'L'Omphalos chez les Celtes', *Revue des Études Anciennes*, XVII (1915), 193 ff., W. R. Lethaby, *Architecture Mysticism and Myth* (L, 1892), Ch. IV, Eliade, *PCR*, 374 ff., *MER*, 12 ff., J. G. Frazer's edition of *Pausanias's Description of Greece* (L, 1898), V, 315 ff., L. I. E. Ringbom, *Graltempel und Paradies* (Stockholm, 1951), 444 ff.

56 Plutarch, *Numa*, 11, quoted in Hocart, *KC*, 224.

57 *Rig Veda*, I, 16, 4 (35), quoted in *KC*, 222.

58 A. K. Coomaraswamy, *Elements of Buddhist Iconography* (L, 1935), 80, n. 94.

59 *Supra*, p. 120.

60 R. Patai, *Man and Temple* (L, 1947), 54 ff.; Eliade, *PCR*, 376 f.

61 R. Guénon, *The Symbolism of the Cross* (tr., L, 1958), 34, n. 1. It may be noted that Delbaeth's *five* sons leave the centre (*supra*, p. 157).

62 Harva, *RVAV*, 85 f.

63 *VB*, I, 57 (tr. K. Meyer).

64 *SG*, II, 78.

65 Ibid., 161 ff.

66 *EIHM*, 322 f; *infra*, pp. 311f.

67 See *ESM*, 508.

68 *MD*, IV, 297.

69 TKI, 23 f. According to Professor Dillon, the sentences we quote are plainly a later addition, but he adds that 'there is nothing in the language to indicate a date later than the tenth century'.

70 Carney, *SILH*, 334; *feis* means 'sleep', 'spend the night', 'feast'.

71 *LG*, IV, 179.

72 Dumézil, *RIR*, Ch. II, is a comparative study of the Indian and the Roman centres.

73 J. Abbott, *KP*, 189.

74 *KC*, 63, 93, 153, 163.

75 *FF*, II, 247 ff.

76 O'Rahilly, *EIHM*, 168; *Ériu*, XVIII, 129 (D. A. Binchy).

77 *LG*, IV, 115 f., 148.

78 *EIHM*, 168.

79 *Supra*, pp. 73f. Cf. also *HL*, 414.

80 *LG*, IV, 8, 16.

81 *CI*, 19 ff., 40.

82 *Supra*, p. 75.

83 The people of Brega are described as 'the food-providers of Cú-Chulainn' (*CI*, 19).

84 *RC*, XVI, 61; *MD*, IV, 186. Of the three sons of Simon [Magus], who begot her offspring, it is said: 'gigantic was their league of hell'.

85 T. J. Westropp, in *JRSA*, XLIX, 9.

86 *SG*, II, 375 (I, 332).

87 *SBE*, XII, 340, *KP*, 189, *RIR*, 29. This fire, the second in order of kindling, was a 'famished fire'. The fire of Vulcan, which was a safeguard against burning, has been adduced as a parallel: *Revue des Études Latines*. XXXVI (1958), 121 ff. (G. Dumézil).— The location of the three centres, Uisnech, Tara and Tlachtga, in Keating's scheme, is comparable with that prescribed for the Indian fires (which we have referred to) in a funeral rite: north-west for the original fire, south-east—'an elevated corner (of that place)' —for the orientated fire, and south-west for the defensive fire (*Āsvalāyana-Gribya-Sūtra*, *SBE*, XXIX, 238).

88 V. *supra*, note 46. In *Ériu*, V, 232, the three festivals of Ireland are those of Emain, Tara, and Cruachan.

89 Cf. *SBE*, XII, 289 f., XLIV, 347. The battle between Tuatha Dé Danann and Fir Bolg was a midsummer battle (*Ériu*, VIII, 30).

90 Cf. Sjoestedt, *GHC*, 24 ff.

91 For references to the personages mentioned in this paragraph, see the indexes to *MD* and to the prose *dindšenchas*, *RC*, XVI; also *FL*, III, 493, IV, 481, 486, 491.

92 *FD*, III, 175 ff., Lord Raglan, *Death and Rebirth* (L, 1945), 89 f.

93 *VSB*, 90; cf. Lady Wilde, *Ancient Cures, Charms and Usages of Ireland* (L, 1890), 65 f.

94 Cf. E. Ettlinger, 'The Association of Burials with Popular Assemblies, Fairs and Races in Ancient Ireland', *ÉC*, VI, 30.

95 *Ériu*, IV, 26 (tr. W. Stokes).

96 *MD*, III, 1–25. E. Gwynn's translation is quoted.

97 *TÉ*, 12. Cf. *MD*, IV, 150.

98 Cf. Mr Aneirin Talfan Davies's comparison (in a lecture) of Dylan Thomas's 'Prologue' with the *Benedicite*.

99 We have made a few verbal changes in Gwynn's translation of these verses.

100 *MD*, IV, 151.

101 *Supra*, p. 63.

102 *SG*, II, 360, cf. ibid., 88.

103 *SHI*, II, 449 f.

104 *TKI*, 25.

105 *MD*, IV, 151.

CHAPTER VIII FIVE PEAKS

1 *HRB*, 222–53.

2 *WBM*, 99, *Mb*, 93.

3 *Cm*, IX, 182 f.

4 Discussed by T. F. O'Rahilly in *ESM*, 101–10. (A division of functions between three kings, two in the North and one in the South is suggested by the story of the only three kings Colum Cille knew who would go to heaven: Cairbre, King of Oriel, on account of the gentleness he used towards the clergy; Ailill, King of Connacht, because by turning to face the victorious enemy he sacrificed himself and his death was a redemption to many, and Feradach, King of Ossory in the South, because at the approach of death he repented of his former covetousness and resigned all his treasures to his enemies —*RC*, XIII, 55.)

5 *PKM*, 48, *Mb*, 40.

6 *THSC*, Session 1948, 353, 383.

7 *Descriptio Kambriae*, I, Ch. II; *ALW*, I, 340, 405.

8 *HW*, 406 n.

9 One other commote, in south-west Wales, bears the same name.

10 According to Nennius, *HB*, 31 ff.

11 *Studies in Early British History* (Cb, 1954), 38, 27. The name of his

son, Gwerthefyr (Vortimer), originally signified 'supreme king'; *THSC*, 1946–7, 51 (Sir Ifor Williams).

12 *ID*, 17.

13 Like Partholón and Nemed, Pwyll and Teyrnon have been described as doublets (Gruffydd, *Rhn*, 99).

14 *ASt*, VIII, 71 n. (T. Gwynn Jones); *WAT*, 51.

15 *HB*, 73.

16 *BT*, 54, *WAT*, 133, *WBM*, 250 ff.; *Mb*, 130 ff.

17 *BBCS*, XII, 13.

18 Ed. and tr. V. Hull, *PMLA*, LVI, 942, 950; *CK*, 37. In Dyfed there was a district the inhabitants of which were exempted from paying chief rent because they had been the first to offer submission to a (medieval) conqueror from abroad. Remembering the attribution of *fidchell* to Munster, we are tempted to note that this district of Whitchurch in Dyfed was remarkable in that 'in auncient tyme in this parishe the meanest & simplest sort of people yea the playne plowmen were skillfull at Chesse play . . . in Welsh *Fristol Dolbarth* . . .' (George Owen, writing in 1603–4. Ed. by B. G. Charles, *Journal of the National Library of Wales*, V, 280).

19 It was not lawful for a *flaith* (*supra*, p. 111) to have swine (*ALI*, IV, 383). We have referred to the Pigs of Manannán (*supra*, p. 39); on the pigs of Balor, see *DF*, I, 30, 130. Cf. further, O'Rahilly, *EIHM*, 123 f. A sow guides Gwydion to the upland tree where Lleu's flesh is rotting after he has been slain (*PKM*, 89).

20 In an Irish story similar to the first episode in the *Mabinogi*, the person who corresponds to Pwyll is 'the Great Fool' (S. J. McHugh, '*The Lay of the Big Fool* . . . ' *MP*, XLII, 197). The impulsive conduct of Pryderi ('Care') belies his name.

   In Welsh tradition, the 'Wild man of the Woods', the prophet Myrddin, is associated with Dyfed; cf. Ch. V, n. 51.

21 In the *dindsenchas* (*RC*, XVI, 276), Manannán is described as 'a druid, a wright, and a chapman'.

22 As 'the House of Donn' occurs as a synonym of 'Munster', so too in one poem *is-dwfn* seems to be used with reference to Dyfed (*GDG*, 34).

23 *CF*, 151 ff., *PMLA*, LVI, 919.

24 *Descriptio Kambriae*, I, Ch. 2. As a pun, *Leth Moga* could mean 'Great Half' (cf. *DIL(C)*, s.v. *mog*).

25 *ALW*, I, 404. This arrangement recalls the distribution of women

between Fintan, Bith, and Ladra (*supra*, p. 114). In some texts, Ladra was given no special consort but after going south he died of excess of women..

26 I (L, 1801), 541.

27 *THSC*, 1913–14, 229 ff., 252 ff.; *BBCS*, V, 25.

28 *ALW*, II, 742.

29 See G. J. Williams, *Iolo Morganwg*, I (C, 1956), 35. A proverb runs: 'The height of good breeding in Gwynedd, the height of generosity in Glamorgan.'

30 *ALW*, I, 519.

31 *HW*, 300 n. For the Irish law in this matter see *SEIL*, 133 ff., 178. (The maximum inheritance of a daughter was equivalent to the estate of a *bó-aire*, ibid., 156.)

32 'The banshees are directly descended from these old goddesses, who were perhaps the ancestors and became the patrons of the great familes, *especially in the south of Ireland* . . .' (Hull, *FBI*, 59—our italics).

33 See *IVHB*, 120–75, 245, 251, and notes in the Appendix; *Lebor Bretnach*, ed. A. G. van Hamel (D, n.d.), 5–14, 82 ff.; Dumézil, *TS*, Ch. 16. The descent of the eponymous Cruithne is traced from Partholón; he is described as a wright (*IVHB*, xci ff., 124).

In India, some forms of marriage were peculiar to the two lower of the four main castes, and in these forms 'matrilineal elements had some importance' (Shamra, *SAI*, 203). Matrilineal succession is found in *southern* India, in particular, and especially on the Malabar coast in the south-east (*CsI*, 143).

34 The fact that one of the three Nemed groups (and also one of the four sons of Artchorp, *supra*, 381), settled abroad may indicate that the class it symbolized was regarded as being, in some sense, set apart from the ruling classes. In the mythologies of other peoples the peace-ful co-ordination of the two upper functions with the third is en-sured by the grant of wives, and temporary kingship, to the gods or people to whom the third function belongs (Dumézil, *JMQ, ITI*, 56). In Sanskrit, *Viçpati*, 'chief of the yeomanry', also means 'son-in-law' (*CJS*, G, I, 73) and the Welsh *dawf*, 'son-in-law' 'client', is probably related to the Greek δῆμος, 'people'. A number of the kings of the Cruithne are said to have ruled Ireland (*EIHM*, 345 f.). It will be recalled that Bres, the oracle on agricultural practice who became king of Ireland (*ri oc fenei, RC*, XII, 64), was the consort of

Brigit, daughter of the Dagda. Something of the role of Brigit has doubtless been inherited by her namesake, the most celebrated of the female saints of Ireland. An early story (*On the Calendar of Oengus*, (ed.) W. Stokes (D, 1880), xlvi) tells of a miraculous yield of milk given by the saint's cows—such a flood as would have filled all the vessels in Leinster. It formed Loch Lemnacht ('The Lake of New Milk'; the miraculous milk cure provided by the Cruithne is said to be commemorated in the name *Ard Lemnacht* in the same province. V. *supra*, p. 38 the manner of Bres's death). St Brigit is 'the guardian of the hearth of every Gaelic house' (*FBI*, 53) and her perpetual fire at Kildare in Leinster (*PRIA*, LII, 150) has affinities with the fire of Vesta which, on other counts, we have compared with the original fire of the clans of Nemed.

35 The main references to these various grades, in the Laws, are *ALW*, I, 32, 74, 383, 388, 660, 678. Cf. T. Gwynn Jones, 'Bardism and Romance', *THSC*, 1913–14, 207 ff.

36 According to one of the law-books (*ALW*, I, 32) the captain of the house-troop was to place a harp in the hand of the *bardd teulu* on each of the three principal feasts.

37 *Gramadegau'r Penceirddiaid*, ed. G. J. Williams and E. J. Jones (C, 1934), 17, 37. 'To gladden the company', 'to entertain' = *kyuanhedu*, from *kyuanned*, 'abode', 'dwelling'.

38 Ibid., 35. One of the chief functions of the *clerwr* was to defame.

39 *IF*.

40 *TLM*, 110, 296 ff. It is said that throughout Welsh *history* the South has been the region of innovation and enterprise and that what the South has created the North has elaborated and perfected (W. J. Gruffydd, *Owen Morgan Edwards*, I (Aberystwyth, 1937), 10). Thirty of the court poets of the twelfth and early thirteenth centuries, authors of the most abstruse poems in the language, have been tentatively assigned to the various provinces: more than half of them were from Gwynedd, eight from Powys, and only one from the South (J. Lloyd-Jones in *PBA*, XXXIV, 194 f.). On the other hand, metres which later appear as accentual song-metres seem to have found readier acceptance in South Wales (cf. W. J. Gruffydd, *Llenyddiaeth Cymru o 1450 byd 1600* (Liverpool, 1922), 67, G. J. Williams, *TLM*, Ch. IV. In what is believed to be the first eisteddfod upon record two prizes were offered, one for poets and one for instrumentalists. The former was won by a poet from the North, the

latter by a harpist from the South—*Brut y Tywysogyon*, ed. and tr.
T. Jones (C, 1955), 166). In medieval Ireland, the *filid* looked back
to three early poets of Connacht as their great exemplars, and most
learned families either traced their origin to Connacht or Meath or
were associated with patrons from those parts (Flower, *ITr*, 68, 85,
94; *IF*, 93). With the emergence of the accentual metres, 'which belonged essentially to the people' (O'Rahilly, *ID*, 255), Munster
poets came into far greater prominence.

41 *GPC*, s.v.

42 Welsh *teulu* means (1) 'family', (2) 'house-troop or war-band', and
in the dialect of Dyfed (3) 'phantom funeral', i.e. an underworld
company (*CF*, 273 f.). Similarly *cethern* means (1) 'family or kindred'
(in the dialect of Dyfed), (2) 'crew of rascals', and (3) 'fiends of hell'.
God is said to have set in Gwyn ap Nudd the spirit of the demons
of Annwfn (*Mb*, 119). In Irish tradition, Cethern son of Fintan was
Finn's teacher (*RC*, V, 202, *Fn*, 46); Irish *cethern*, 'a troop of foot-
soldiers', is glossed by *fían* (and linked with *clíar*), and an Irishman in
the sixteenth century suggested a derivation from *cith ifrinn*, 'shower of
hell' (*SG*, II, xxii n.).

43 *ALW*, I, 62 ff., 192 ff., 392.

44 *LGSG*, 275.

45 F. E. Halliday, *The Legend of the Rood* (L, 1955), 22. All the
examples are west of Truro (ibid., 24).

46 *DIL*, s.v. *oenach*, Boaistuau's *Théâtre du Monde* was translated under
the title *Gorsedd y Byd* (1615).

47 See Allcroft, *CC*, I, 88, where reference is made to the usual posi-
tions of the Homeric assembly: at the original landing-place, at the
gates of the community or at the gates of the chieftain—'at the threshold of authority'. The relation of the theatre to the cult of Dionysos
and the dedication of the circus to Consus are not without significance
in the context of our discussion.

48 *WBM*, 112; *Mb*, 158.

49 Cf. Ellis, *RH*, 105 ff.

50 We may also compare the *ystafell* which, in the medieval king's court
in Wales, was a bedroom and withdrawing room. We hear of Arthur
sitting on a couch, or mound, of fresh rushes in the middle of such a
room and sleeping while one of his knights tells of the most wondrous
thing he knew—the story of his quest and discomfiture in a land of
marvels. (*Mb*, 155. In later times, the word *ystafell* denotes the

bottom-drawer.) In the cottages of some parts of Ireland the 'west' room, a chamber to which the old folk retire to end their days, has close associations with the fairies, the past, and the dead (C. M. Arensberg, *The Irish Countryman* (L, 1937), Ch. I).

51 The first guesting house was built by Partholón's people. In Wales, the villeins were required to build a hall and other houses for the king. (Tara was built on the land of one of the Déssi; *RC*, XXV, 24.)

52 *PE*, 72 ff.

53 Cf. G. Dumézil, *Loki* (P, 1948), 258 ff. Comparison might also be made with Unferth, the honoured reviler in *Beowulf*. Like Partholón he is guilty of slaying a kinsman, if not of treason. (See references given in F. Klaeber's edition (NY, 1922), 148 f.)

54 *BBCS*, XIV, 121 f.

CHAPTER IX NUMBERS

1 Ed and tr. V. Hull, *PMLA*, LVI, 937 f.; Dillon, *CK*, 37.

2 *SG*, II, 232 f. While sitting on the stone, Finn has a vision of Heaven and Earth.

3 *LSC*, 159, 424.

4 *Contes Populaires de Basse Bretagne*, ed. F. M. Luzel (P, 1887), III, 370 ff.

5 Eliade, *MER*, 13.

6 'Lageniensis', *Irish Folklore* (L, 1870), 207.

7 *RC*, XV, 445 (*Dindšenchas*).

8 *JHS*, XIX (1899), 225 f.; Hocart, *Kng*, 179.

9 L. Frobenius, *Kulturgeschichte Africas* (Zurich, 1933), 173 ff. He compares the five-legged sacred stools of West Africa.

10 *CA*, 403.

11 W. G. Wood-Martin, *Pagan Ireland* (L, 1895), I, 303. That a cairn can be a very ephemeral cult object is shown by a custom practised by New Year guisers in Skye. To express their displeasure with households that do not give them anything, they erect outside the door a heap of stones, called *Carn nam Mollachd*, 'Cairn of the Curses', which is much feared because of the curses pronounced upon it (*BCCS*, II, 52).

12 *HIF*, 668.

13 *SEIL*, 149; *ALI*, V, 515.

14 *ALW*, I, 186.

15 *ECNE*, 152 (B. Megaw); *Proceedings of the Antiquaries of Scotland*, LXXVIII (1944), 41 ff., 50 ff., LXXXV (1953), 60 f. (A. McKerral).

16 Hocart, *KC*, 253.

17 *PRIA Irish MSS Series*, I, 200.

18 *THSC*, 1946–7, 102.

19 *MD*, III, 278, *RC*, XV, 455; *EIHM*, 121. A sixth hostel is sometimes added.

20 *ZCP*, XIX, 165; ṪKI.

21 *CGl*, 142; *CF*, 8, 418, 692.

22 *AS*, 72; *Fn*, 99.

23 *TBC(D)*, 24; cf. *supra*, p. 39.

24 *TBC(D)*, 196; cf. 325, and *TBD*, 20; H. P. L'Orange, *The Iconography of Cosmic Kingship in the Ancient World* (Oslo, 1953), 91–109.

25 *SC*, 3. In Merioneth, a 'houseful of children' was defined as five —one in each corner and one in the middle (Ex. inf. Mrs Elwyn Davies, Llanbryn-mair).

26 This system of writing is used in some 360 inscriptions (chiefly on memorial stones) of about the fifth and sixth century, mostly in Ireland and Wales, particularly the south-west of the two countries, with only a few in Scotland, the Isle of Man, and England. The signs are discussed in tracts found in late medieval manuscripts. See J. Vendryes, 'L'écriture ogamique et ses origines', *ÉC*, IV, 83–116 and references given there. On the arithmetical use of the signs see L. Gerschel, 'Origine et premier usage des caractères ogamiques', *Ogam*, IX (1959), 151–173.

27 Vendryes, loc. cit., 84; cf. *ECNE*, 213 n. (K. Jackson).

28 *Auraicept na nÉces*, ed. and tr. G. Calder (E, 1917), 71. In Indian teaching there are five kinds of breath: up-breathing, down-breathing, back-breathing, out-breathing, on-breathing. (*SBE*, XV, 50). The following quotation suggests that even this may not be un-related to our theme. 'We have in *ŚB*, xi, 8.3.6. the description of the rite by which a new-born child is endowed with five breaths. . . . There is first described the communication by the winds of the four quarters and zenith of the corresponding breaths to the victim in the horse sacrifice, by which the victim is ritually brought to life again. . . . In the case of a new-born son, the father requests five Brahmans to "breathe over" the boy in the same way; but if the

Brahmans are not available then he should "breathe over" . . . the boy himself, circumambulating him, whereby the boy attains the whole of life and lives to old age.' A. K. Coomaraswamy, 'The Sun-kiss', *JAOS*, LX, 55 ff. On the five senses as breaths, see R. B. Onians, *The Origins of European Thought* (Cb, 1951), 66–83.

29 *RC*, XIII, 269; cf. *Auraicept na nÉces*, 100; *ACL*, II, 258 (*coic*). In India, on the other hand, 'Speech has been measured out in four divisions, the Brahmans who have understanding know it. Three kept in close concealment cause no motion; the fourth . . . men speak.' *Rig Veda*, I, 164, 45.

30 *Fn*, 38.

31 *IED*, s.v.

32 *SBE*, XII, 154 f. The rite is performed in imitation of the contest between Indra, the protagonist of the Devas, and the Asuras. L. Gerschel (loc. cit., 159 n.) notes that in Roman families the children after the first four were called Quintus, Sextus, etc., and that the months, after the first four, were likewise numbered.

33 On 'five' in India, see *KP*, 295 ff.; *OS*, VIII, 247 f.; cf. *supra*, p. 107.

34 *TBDd*, 121. On 'five' in Buddhism see also Conze, *Bdd*, 14, 189 f.; *Buddhist Texts*, ed. E. Conze (O, 1954), 51 ff.

35 L. Séjourné, *Burning Water* (L, 1957), 90.

36 Deren, *DH*, 41. The equivocal nature of the fifth component appears also in the lack of correspondence between the widespread doctrine of the 'four ages of the world' and Hesiod's 'five ages', for which he has only four symbolic metals. Cf. the 'four elements' plus the 'quintessence'. On 'the swinging of the door', cf. *supra*, p. 66.

37 V.'F. Hopper, *Medieval Number Symbolism* (NY, 1938), 207.

38 *ALW*, I, 486, 292.

39 *Gwaith Guto'r Glyn*, ed. I. Williams and J. Ll. Williams (C, 1939), 133, 275.

40 *ALW*, I, 544; *LG*, V, 269.

41 *MC*, II, 143 f.

42 Ed. and tr. R. Thurneysen, *ZCP*, XIV, 16.

43 A. K. Coomaraswamy, 'The Inverted Tree', *QJMS*, XXIX (1938–9), 119 f.

44 See Loomis, *WAT*, 154 ff.

45 *MD*, II, 27.

46 *TBC(D)*, 37.

47 Joyce, *SHI*, I, 250.

48 *FB*, 7.

49 *TBC(D)*, 189.

50 Ibid., 60; *Fn*, 51. The list of the standing *fiana* includes eight Finns besides Finn mac Cumaill (AS, 182).

51 *ALW*, I, 408, 172, 311, II, 786. An Irish codex, on the other hand, has preserved the widespread myth which tells how Adam was made of eight parts—his flesh of the earth, his blood of the sea, his face of the sun, his thoughts of the clouds, his breath of the wind, his bones of the stones, his soul of the Holy Ghost, his piety of the Light of the World. (*RC*, I, 261 f.) A variant occurs in *LG*, I, 49, according to which Adam's head, breast, belly, and legs were made, respectively, of earth from different lands, and his blood, breath, heart, and soul, respectively of water, air, fire, and the breath of God. 'Thus it is that the four elements are in every man.' For a note on this myth see Stokes, *TIG*, xl.

52 *TG*, I, 414. J. Brand, *Popular Antiquities of Great Britain*[3] (L, 1849), II, 430, 432. Cf. 'Noughts and Crosses' played on a ninefold figure.

53 See *GB*, X, 294; *Antiquity*, XXIX, 132 ff. (T. Davidson); A. MacBain, *Celtic Mythology and Religion* (Stirling, 1917), 159.

54 *GB*, X, 147 f., 155, 172; G. Storms, *Anglo-Saxon Magic* (The Hague, 1948), 96 f., 195 f.

55 *PLGI*, 13 f.; *TEF*, II, 31, 272 f. There was no pestilence beyond the ninth wave (*RC*, II, 201).

56 For references to Celtic nines see *RC*, XXV (1904), 135 ff. (J. Loth).

57 *TBC*, 423. (Cf. (for 27) *SG*, I, 199, *RC*, XII, 90., XVI, 150). As for the grandson, cf. *infra*, p. 203, Pendaran Dyfed (also *HL*, 367 ff.) and *supra*, p. 199 on 'eighteen'.

58 *Infra*, p. 260.

59 *VB*, I, 16. The text states that the woman from the unknown land and Manannán mac Lir, respectively, sang 50 and 30 quatrains to Bran, but only 28 are given in each case. There were 27 years between the two Battles of Mag Tuired, and Nuadu's arm was healed in 3×9 days.

60 *SG*, II, 99, 105.

61 See references cited by Loth, *RC*, XXV, 156.

62 *DIL(C)*, s.vv. On nine days or nights in Germanic tradition, see *Trp*, 234 f.

63 Rhys, *HL*, 362 ff.; *RC*, XXV, 113 f.

64 P. Lum, *The Stars in Our Heaven* (L, n.d.), 116, 119. Cf. Dumézil, *PC*, 117 ff. on the 27 Gandharvas.

65 *TBD*, 9, 32.

66 *ALW*, I, 486, 192.

67 Ibid., 408, 224.

68 See W. H. Roscher, 'Die Sieben⸍ u. Neunzahl im Kultus u. Mythos der Greichen', *AKSG*, XXIV, No. I (1904), 'Enneadische Studien', ibid., XXVI, No. 7 (1909).

69 *LG*, II, 176, 194. In *MD*, IV, 135 ff., Dáire has seven sons, not five; cf. *supra*, p. 74. The expedition of the Fomoire in the time of Partholón is called a *secht gabáil* =? 'one of seven invasions' or 'a sham occupation' (*LG*, III, 10).

70 *IVHB*, 51 (cf. sevens in territorial divisions in Wales, *PKM*, 27, 67).

71 See S. Weinstock, 'Lunar Mansions and Early Calendars', *JHS*, LXIX (1949), 48 f.

72 *De Excidio Britanniae*, cap. 3.

73 'Táin Bó Fraích', (tr. *SILH*, 3; cf. *FB*, 69, *twelve* windows).

74 *Ériu*, II, 185, IV, 27; Rhys, *HL*, 367 f.

75 *RC*, XVI (1895), 35 f. (*dindšenchas*).

76 *MD*, IV, 22.

77 *RC*, I, 260 (tr. W. Stokes). The 'chief idol' is here called Cenn Cruaich.

78 M. Ó Duígeannáin, 'On the Medieval Sources for the Legend of Cenn Cróich', *ESM*, 296 ff.

79 J. Cuillandre, *La Droite et la Gauche* (P, 1944), 291 f. Cf. *CC*, 342 f. 350 etc. An early example of the use of twelve is provided by the numerous hollow, knobbled dodecahedrons found in Gallo⸍ Roman sites north of the Alps. These figures have been interpreted as dice representing the cosmos, and they may have been used in a game of divination of a type known from sixteenth⸍century texts. Each of the 12 sides of the figures is a pentagon. (See W. Deonna, 'Les Dodécaèdres Gallo⸍romains . . .' *Association Pro Aventico Bulletin*, XVI (1954), 17–89.)

80 *LG*, II, 271, III, 19, 123.

81 *CI*, 94 (Ailech, in the north, comprised seventeen states (or tribes), Leinster sixteen, ibid., 88, 92); *ESM*, 508.

82 *PRIA, MSS Series*, I, 24. On 4, 16 and 64 in land divisions in Britain and in India, see G. L. Gomme, *The Village Community* (L, 1890), 162–71.

83 *LG*, III, 5, V, 59, 165, 175, 297, 347, 385, etc; cf. *SG*, II, 166, 182, 186, 249.

84 *LG*, IV, 134, 162.

85 *AS*, 145 (cf. *DF*, I, 27), 72.

86 *TBC(D)*, 40—the Book of Leinster version only.

87 *VB*, I, 61.

88 *Infra*, p. 321.

89 S. Weinstock, 'Martianus Capella and the Cosmic System of the Etruscans', *JRS*, XXXVI, 101–27. On the decoration of ceremonial bowls, in Eastern Mediterranean lands, with sixteen figures radiating from a centre occupied by a serpent, the sun, or later the Christ, see *The Mysteries*, ed. J. Campbell (NY, 1955), 194 f. (H. Leisegang).

90 *SBE*, XLIV, 301 f. In the *Mahābhārata* (XIII, 15; XVI, 5, XVIII, 5), Krishna has 16,000 wives. The number 1600 occurs as that of the stars for Pliny (*JRS*, XXXVI, 127), of the women among the Fomoire who opposed Partholón (*GT*, 43), and of the army of the King of the World who attacked the Fenians in Munster (*CFt*, 19). If O'Grady's silent emendation were accepted (see *AS*, 182, 329), the standing Fiana also would number 1600, and according to Layamon's *Brut*, the same number could sit at King Arthur's Round Table (*ATC*, 66). In the Book of Revelation (XIV, 20), the measure of the river of death is 1600 furlongs, while the measure of the River of Life seems to be reckoned as 17,000 furlongs (A. Farrer, *The Rebirth of Images* (Westminster, 1949), 253 ff.).

91 *PC*, 109.

92 *TBC*, 137 (Book of Leinster version); cf. 133 n. 11.

93 *TBC(D)*, 24.

94 *JRSA*, LVII, 151 (H. Morris, quoted); P. Kennedy, *Evenings in the Duffey* (D, 1875), 84; *SnC*, II, 304.

95 *ALI*, IV, 285. The kinship system is discussed in *ALI*, IV, xlix f., MacNeill, *CI*, Ch. X, *PBA*, XXIX, 222 ff. (D. A. Binchy), L. Ó Buachalla, 'Some Researches in Ancient Irish Law', *Journal of the Cork Historical and Archaeological Society*, LII, 41, 135, LIII, 1, 75. On the Continent, the test of gentility is called the Proof of the 'Seize Quartiers'. The claimant has to show that all

his sixteen great-great grandparents were entitled to bear arms. For the very rare distinction of 'Trente-deux Quartiers' the number of armigerous ancestors is doubled. Only one family in Britain can prove 32 Quartiers (C. and A. Lynch Robinson, *Intelligible Heraldry* (1948), 178.

96 *PRIA*, LII, 160.

97 *TBC(D)*, 351.

98 *Ériu*, VIII, 44.

99 *PMLA*, LVI, 928.

100 *LG*, III, 128. In some versions he originally has 44 ships. In the verse Colloquy between Fintan and the Hawk of Achill, Míl has 32 sons before the voyage to Ireland (*AIM*, I, 32).

101 *SC*, 21 (cf. *PTWH*, III, 215); *CMT(C)*, 28 f. Cf. the evil-eyed Cailb's thirty-two names (including Badb, Samain, Sinand, etc.) which she chants with one breath while standing on one foot at the door of Da Derga's Hostel (*TBD*, 17).

102 *Cm*, XIV, 135. Mug Ruith was with Simon Magus for 33 years (*PRIA*, XXXIV, 348). 'Thirty-three' also appears as the number of the Children of Calatín (*GHC*, 78), of the Children of Fergus (*GT*, 134) and of the sons of Morna (*AS*, 71). Cathair Mór had 33 sons (*GT*, 190) or 32 sons and one daughter (*ZCP*, VIII, 263). A list of the standing Fiana includes the names of 32 individuals besides the nine Finns (*AS*, 182). The Cruithne had 33 pagan, and 33 Christian, kings (*IVHB*, 153 n.), and in some versions of the *Historia* of Nennius, Britain's cities number not 28 but 33 (*Antiquity*, XII, 44).

103 *DF*, II, 336 ff. (cf. III, 161).

104 *AS*, 71 f. Cf. the number in Finn's household, *DF*, I, 25 ff.

105 *Mb*, 80.

106 *FB*, 12.

107 G. Dumézil, *Jupiter Mars Quirinus IV* (P, 1948), 156 ff. Cf. further, the 33 enigmas in the Pehlevi version of *Gôsht-i Frýanô* (*Zeitschrift der Deutschen Morgenländischen Gesellschaft*, XXIX, 633 ff. (R. Köhler)—a reference we owe to the kindness of M. L. Gerschel; 33 parts of the body (*SBE*, XLIII, 76), the 32 marks of a great being (*Numen*, III, 145), and 'the sovereignty of 33 towns' (*SBE*, XXIV, 261). For 7, 9, 12, 16, 17 and 33 heavens in shamanism see *Chm*, 249; for 32 in Jewish mysticism, *The Jewish Encyclopaedia*, under 'Numbers in Mysticism'. Cf. Leviticus, XII, 4.

108 *SHI*, II, 392; *IED*, s.v. *mór*.

109 *EIHM*, 156, 172 n.

110 Deren, *DH*, 41.

111 They are discussed in *Llyfr Blegywryd*, ed. S. J. Williams and J. E. Powell (C, 1942), xxix ff.

112 *WTL*, I, 95.

113 Op. cit., 114 f.

114 See W. H. Roscher, 'Die Zahl 50 in Mythus, Kultus, Epos u. Taktik . . .', *AKSG*, XXXIII (1917), No. 5; also, J. Vendryes, 'L'unité en trois personnes chez les Celtes' in *Choix d'Études* (P, 1952), 233–46.

PART THREE

CHAPTER X THE STORYTELLER'S REPERTOIRE

1 *LMM*, 584 ff.; *PRIA*, I (Ser. II), 1874–5, 216; H. d'Arbois de Jubainville, *Essai d'un catalogue de la littérature épique de l'Irlande* (P, 1883), 259; *AIM*, II, 43; *ALI*, I, 46. For discussion see *IHK*, 21.

2 *LMM*, 584.

3 *Aislinge Meic Conglinne*, ed. and tr. K. Meyer (L, 1892), 110–12.

4 *HIF*, 205, 224.

5 *PBA*, XX (1934), 209 n.

6 *The Oxford Dictionary*, s.v. history.

7 *GPC*, s.vv. cyfarwydd, arwydd.

CHAPTER XI BIRTHS

1 Lord Raglan, *The Hero* (L, 1936), Chs. XVI, XVII.

2 *RC*, XII, 59.

3 *MM*, 72 ff., 65 ff.

4 *MM*, 126.

5 *RC*, XII, 60 ff.

6 *TÉ*, 10 ff.

7 *IHK*, 273 ff.; *Irish Texts*, Fasc. IV, ed. J. Fraser *et al.* (L, 1934), 8 (V. Hull); *VB*, II, 72 f.

8 *IHK*, 268 ff.

9 *CA*, 392 f.

10 *SG*, I, 253, II, 286; *CK*, 23.

11 *SG*, I, 314, II, 354; *CA*, 306.

12 *RC*, XXII, 13 ff.; *TÉ*, 56 f.; *Ériu*, VI, 138 ff.; *RC*, XII, 234 ff.

13 *VB*, I, 58, 42.

14 *HRB*, 424 (cf. *HB*, 42).

15 *HRB*, 381.

16 Keating, *FF*, III, 132 f.

17 *BL*, 62.

18 *ZCP*, XIX, 48 ff.

19 *BL*, 30. From its poetic pleading of its cause, the child was named Aí (which, according to Cormac's Glossary, means 'poem').

20 *Ériu*, III, 159.

21 *VSB*, 16.

22 *VSB*, 151, 27; *LBS*, II, 264, III, 14.

23 *LBS*, I, 331.

24 *LBS*, II, 107; *VSH*, I, cxxxv, n. 2, II, 32.

25 *VSH*, I, clviii.

26 Ibid., I, 87, 171, *LIS*, II, 44 f.

27 *The Life of Saint Columba*, tr. W. Huyshe (L, 1906), 188.

28 *CSS*, XV, 7. Cf. *VSH*, I, clviii, n. 4 (St Coemgen).

29 E.g. *LIS*, II, 11, *CSS*, III, 2, *SG*, II, 20, *VSB*, 153.

30 *VSB*, 152; *CSS*, XIII, 5; *LBS*, II, 107 f., *CSS*, III, 3.

31 *LIS*, II, 45 f. Cf. ibid., 12.

32 *LBS*, II, 108.

33 *VSH*, I, cxlii; *LBS*, II, 140.

34 For these and other examples see *LP*, I, Ch. V.

35 M. E. Noble, *Cradle Tales of Hinduism* (L, 1912), 153 ff.

36 See A. K. Coomaraswamy, *Figures of Speech or Figures of Thought?* (L, 1946), 229 ff., *BLt*, 93 ff.

37 See Westermarck, *HHM*, I, Ch. V, Briffault, *Mth*, III, 226 ff.; also *FOT*, I, 532.

38 *Ériu*, IV, 25; *CCC*, 64.

39 *HTI*, 292.

40 *OST*, I, 135 f.

41 Boswell quoted in *Ériu*, IV, 19 f.

42 E. E. Evans, *Irish Folk Ways* (L. 1957), 288; cf. *HIF*, 543.

43 *Ériu*, IV, 25; *RC*, XIII, 54, 58.

44 *SGS*, VIII (1955), 107.

45 M. Murray, *The Witch-Cult in Western Europe* (O, 1921), 175 ff.

46 See e.g. St Augustine, *De Civitate Dei*, XV, Ch. XXIII, Giraldus Cambrensis, *Itinerarium Kambriae*, Ch. V. It was alleged that 'exemplary Scottish matrons were betrayed into infidelities with him

[Satan] in the semblance of their own husbands'. See J. G. Dalyell, *The Darker Superstitions of Scotland* (Glasgow, 1835), 547, referring to the trials of Scottish witches (1660, '61). Cf. M. Summers, *History of Witchcraft and Demonology* (L, 1926), 91 ff.

47 *HRB*, 381.

48 In India, an insect called *pillai-púchchi* or 'son insect' is swallowed by women in the hope of bearing sons (E. Ś. Hartland, *Primitive Paternity*, I (L, 1909), 47).

49 *TÉ*, 25.

50 *OST*, II, 135.

51 *VB*, II, 285, ff.

52 *CT*, 3 ff.

53 *CT*, 12 ff., *BT*, 22 f., 25 f.

54 See Coomaraswamy, *BLt*, 122 ff., 126.

55 *VSB*, 153; *LBS*, IV, 184; *LIS*, I, 45. *CSS*, XV, 7.

56 *Mb*, 95; *infra*, p. 000; *RC*, XXII, 20; *ZCP*, XXIV, 38 f.; *IHK*, 581, 464, 433.

57 *Infra*, p. 327.

58 *Infra*, p. 246.

59 *OST*, III, 175 ff.

60 *Infra*, p. 250; *AKI*, I, 120 n.

61 *VSH*, I, cxlii; *LBS*, II, 140.

62 *IHK*, 269, n. 2; *FB*, 38; *RC*, III, 180; E. Hull, *Cuchulain* (L, 1911), 65 ff., 272 f. Cf. *Ogam*, VI, 81 ff. (J. Gricourt). On the *custom* of giving a child a colt which happens to be born at the same time as it, see *WFFC*, 198, *HIF*, 210.

63 *Mb*, 63 f.

64 *MS*, 89.

65 A. K. Coomaraswamy, 'The Darker Side of Dawn', *Smithsonian Miscellaneous Collections*, XCIV (i), (1935), 5.

66 *CI*, 34 f.; *EIHM*, 81 (Fiachu Fer Mara; cf. *MM*, 133); *HL*, 308, 521 ff. (Corc Duibne). The mother of the three sons who succeeded their father Éremón son of Míl was Odba daughter of Míl (*LG*, V, 57, 187). The birth of Brutus, legendary ancestor of the kings of Britain, was incestuous (*HRB*, 223).

67 *Ériu*, XI, 190, 209 f.

68 *RC*, XII, 110 f.

69 *ÉC*, VII, 96 n. 3.

70 *RC*, XII, 237.

71 *CA*, 333.

72 *FF*, II, 233.

73 *Standard Dictionary of Folklore, Mythology, and Legend*, ed. M. Leach (NY, 1950), s.v. Riddles.

74 Ex inf. Dr. Emrys Peters.

75 See *SFT*, Chs. X, XI.

76 Cf. *PP*, 58.

77 See *LP*, I, 1 ff., *GB*, X, 70 ff., *BEE*, 10 ff.

78 J. G. Frazer, *GB*, X, 97 (our italics).

79 *HRB*, 380; cf. *HB*, 41.

80 See *Mb*, 63.

81 *BL*, 30, *RC*, XVI, 38.

82 D. A. MacKenzie, *Buddhism in Pre-Christian Britain* (L, 1928), 95.

83 *SBE*, XLIX, 6.

84 *Ériu*, IV, 95.

85 *BL*, 30 f.; *HL*, 310 ff.

86 *CT*, 6.

87 *FOT*, II, 455.

88 J. S. M. Ward, *Freemasonry and the Ancient Gods*[2] (L, 1926), 28.

89 *Ériu*, XI, 98 f.

90 H. Zimmer, *Philosophies of India* (L, 1951), 157 ff. On the ambiguity of the sacred, see Caillois, *HS*, Ch. II.

91 *FOT*, Part III, Ch. I.

92 A. M. Hocart, *Social Origins* (L, 1954), 54.

93 *ERE*, s.v. Fosterage.

94 *SEIL*, 188.

95 *CCC*, 7.

96 *CT*, 7 f.

97 *BT*, 3, 23.

98 *HIF*, 211, 146.

99 *LF*, 77 ff., *HIF*, 475 ff., *TEF*, II, 14 f., *WFFC*, 68.

CHAPTER XII YOUTHFUL EXPLOITS

1 *CT*, 7.

2 *HB*, 42. For comparative material, see *RC*, XLI, 181 ff., XLIII, 124, *BEE*, 165 (A. H. Krappe).

3 *TÉ*, 12 f.

4 *SG*, I, 253, *CK*, 23.

5 *RC*, XXII, 23 ff.

6 *Ériu*, VI, 133 ff.
7 *TBC(D)*, Section VII.
8 Eliade, *NM*, Ch. V, 177.
9 G. Dumézil, *Horace et les Curiaces* (P, 1942. Cf. *MDG*, Ch. VII).
10 Eliade, *Yg*, 107, cf. 330 ff.; Dumézil, op. cit.; *NM*, 181 ff.
11 Op. cit., 40 ff.
12 Ed. and tr. K. Meyer, *RC*, V, 197, *Ériu*, I, 180.
13 In China, a wild goose and a double deerskin are the traditional marriage gifts (*ESC*, 90).
14 *Supra*, p. 64.
15 *Supra*, p. 66.
16 *CR*, II, 151. Cf. *HTI*, 277 f., *DF*, III, 140, n. 14.
17 *FOT*, II, 34 ff.
18 *GB*, XI, 240. Cf. *NM*, 81 ff.
19 *Africa*, XXV, 141 f.
20 M. Eliade, *Forgerons et Alchimistes* (P, 1956), 109.
21 *RC*, XXIV, 194.
22 M. Eliade, *Forgerons et Alchimistes*, 74 ff.
23 Ed. and tr. K. Meyer, *RC*, XI, 442.
24 Ed. and tr. W. Stokes, *RC*, XXIX, 109.
25 *PTWH*, III, 202 ff., *HTI*, 242 ff., J. MacDougall, *Folk and Hero Tales of Argyllshire* (L, 1891), 144 ff.
26 J. H. Weeks, *Among the Primitive Bakongo* (L, 1914), 158 f.
27 *NM*, 126 ff., 230, 233.
28 *RC*, XXIX, 112.
29 Ibid., 123 f.
30 Ibid., 131.
31 Ibid., 134.
32 *Supra*, p. 73.
33 *Man*, XLIX, 28.
34 See e.g. *Africa*, XXV, 138 ff., A. B. Deacon, *Malekula* (L, 1934), 253 ff., 264.
35 *CR*, II, 148.
36 *NM*, 144.
37 *Yg*, 262.

CHAPTER XIII WOOINGS

1 *CCC*, 20; *RC*, XI, 442; *CS*, 57 (ed. and tr. K. Meyer).
2 Ed. and tr. R. I. Best, *Ériu*, III, 149.

3   *WBM*, 226 ff., *Mb*, 95 ff.

4   *HTI*, 163.

5   *Mb*, 164 ff.; cf. *KCp*, 96 ff.

6   *Mb*, 183 ff., 226.

7   *CF*, 2 ff.

8   E.g. *HTI*, 163. For further references, see *SFT*, 255 ff., *OS*, VII, 213.

9   See *FESB*, 301 ff., *GL*, II, 212 ff., III, 153 f.

10   *ZCP*, XIII, 270 ff. *Infra*, 331.

11   *PTWH*, III, 36 f.

12   *ZCP*, I, 460. Cf. *DF*, III, 18 f., *CCC*, 65.

13   See *SEIL*, 81 ff., 109 ff., *WTL*, I, 393.

14   *TEF*, II, 33.

15   Quoted in *TEF*, II, 34.

16   Lady Wilde, *Ancient Legends, Mystic Charms, and Superstitions of Ireland* (L, 1887), I, 219.

17   Lord Kames, quoted in *TEF*, II, 35. Cf. *WFFC*, 190, J. C. Davies, *Folk-Lore in West and Mid-Wales* (Aberystwyth, 1911), 29 f.

18   *TEF*, II, 35.

19   *ALI*, V, 277.

20   *WFFC*, 190, *WFC*, 164 ff.

21   *Llawysgrif Richard Morris o Gerddi &c.*, ed. T. H. Parry-Williams (C, 1931), lxxxvi ff.

22   *The English and Scottish Popular Ballads*, ed. F. J. Child (Boston, 1882–98), I, 418.

23   *FD*, III, 177 f.

24   *WFC*, 131 f., *BCCS*, III, 127 ff.

25   *HTI*, 163 ff.

26   *WFFC*, 190. Cf. *TG*, I, 303 f., II, 486 ff.

27   *HHM*, II, 522.

28   *TÉ*. Cf. 'The Wooing of Becfola', *SG*, I, 85, II, 91.

29   On the Gandharva(s), see *PC*, 126, 134, 225 ff., and *passim*.

30   E.g. *LF*, 100, Lady Wilde, op. cit., I, 49 ff.

31   *HIF*, 206. M. L. Sjoestedt equated the Gandharvas with the Fiana (*ÉC*, IV, 144). On the latter as a youth group inhabiting the wild and having claims on all unmarried girls, v. *supra*, p.65.

32   *KP*, 216, *PC*, 226 f.

33   P. Sébillot, *Coutumes populaires de la Haute-Bretagne* (P, 1886), 132 f. Cf. *FOT*, I, 497 ff.

34   *SBE*, XLIV, 68 ff. (*Śatapatha Brahmana*), *OS*, II, 245.

35 Ed. and tr. E. Müller, *RC*, III, 344; *IHK*, 300 ff. On the swan as 'the Daughter of the Twelve Moons', in Gaelic tradition, see *JCS*, I, 144.

36 *SBE*, XLII, 536.

CHAPTER XIV ELOPEMENTS

1 *LMU.*

2 Ed. and tr. S. H. O'Grady in *OST*, III, 140.

3 See Schoepperle, *TI.*

4 *SILH*, Ch. VI.

5 Ed. by I. Williams, *BBCS*, V, 115.

6 A. H. Krappe (*BEE*, 154 ff.) suggests that this ending is a 'floating tale', not an essential part of the Trystan story and that originally it was a tale 'relating to a contest between the deity and the evil one'. (But. cf. n. 46 *infra*.)

7 Cf. Loomis, *ATC*, Ch. XXXI.

8 *TI*, 530.

9 Tr. T. Gwynn Jones in *ASt*, VIII, 66.

10 *SAL*, 66.

11 Cf. *ATC*, Chs. XXIX ff.

12 XIX, 2.

13 *Mb*, 128 f.

14 *Mb*, 3–17.

15 *VB*, I, 62 ff.

16 *Ériu*, II, 20.

17 *WAL*, 86

18 T. Gwynn Jones, *WFFC*, 153 f. Cf. *WAL*, 81.

19 *The Poetry from the Red Book of Hergest*, ed. J. G. Evans (Llanbedrog, 1911), 83. May is the month of the Virgin, especially in France, and May 1st is the Feast of St Phillip and St Jacob the Apostle, patrons of marriageable girls.

20 *Cywyddau Dafydd ap Gwilym a'i Gyfoeswyr,*[2] ed. I. Williams and T. Roberts (C, 1935), 6 (cf. *GDG*, clxxii).

21 Ibid., 8 (cf. *GDG*, clxxiii).

22 *GDG*, 71.

23 *GDG*, 382 ff.

24 See n. 21.

25 *FL*, XLVII, 355 (A. H. Krappe). Cf. *TEF*, I, 348 f.

26 *TEF*, I, 349.

27 *The Anatomie of Abuses* (1583), quoted in *GB*, II, 66 f.
28 C. B. Lewis, 'The Part of the Folk in the Making of Folklore', *FL*, XLVI, 37., 61 ff., 'Survivals of a Pagan Cult', *Evangelical Quarterly* VI (1934), 337.
29 *BCCS*, II, 204, E. Owen, *Welsh Folk-Lore* (Oswestry, n.d.), 341, A. R. Wright, *British Calendar Customs: England* (L, 1939-40), II. 243, 271.
30 *HDA*, s.vv. Mai, Hochzeit.
31 *ALI*, II, 391.
32 M. M. Banks, *British Calendar Customs; Orkney and Shetland* (L, 1946), 13, *BCCS*, III, 187.
33 *HIF*, 328 f. Cf. *FL*, LV, 107, 113, LXIV, 476 f., *PC*, 28.
34 *WFFC*, 163, 154.
35 See *TI*, 269 f., *DF*, III, 156 n. 2, 446, and J. J. Jones, 'March ap Meirchion', *ASt*, XII, 21.
36 *ESC*, 66, 68, 79.
37 *SBE*, VII, 108.
38 M. Granet, *Chinese Civilisation* (tr., L, 1930), 161 ff.
39 *OST*, III, 46.
40 *ZCP*, I, 460 (ed. and tr. K. Meyer).
41 *TI*, 17 ff.
42 *OST*, III, 53.
43 *RC*, XXXIII, 166, 168 (tr. J. H. Lloyd and O. J. Bergin).
44 *CS*, lv, *TI*, 11 f., *FL*, XLVII, 347.
45 See Ch. VI (n. 23).
46 *OST*, III, 294; cf. *DF*, III, xlvii n. On the Other World as a forest, see *FESB*, 122 ff., 314 ff.; as to the distinction between the fruit on the lower branches and the sweet fruit on the top of the tree (*supra*, 283) cf. *QJMS*, XXIX, 119 (A. K. Coomaraswamy). A. H. Krappe argued that in the Elopement Tales the lover is Death (*RC*, XLVIII (1931), 95 ff.).
47 *TI*, 11 f.; W. F. Otto, *The Homeric Gods* (L, n.d.), 94.
48 *SAL*, 127 f. Cf. *KCp*, 135 f.
49 *KCp*, 133.
50 *Fns*, 52.
51 *PTWH*, III, 40, 46.
52 See n. 29 *supra* and *A Miscellany of Studies . . . presented to L. E. Kastner*, ed. M. Williams and J. A. de Rothschild (Cb, 1932), 308 ff.
53 'Darmuid and Gráinne', *FL*, XLVII, 347 (cf. *DF*, III, xxxvi, n.).

54 *Yg*, 264 f.

55 *RC*, XXXIII, 55, from an eighteenth-century MS (tr. G. Schoepperle).

56 *RC*, XXXIII, 161 n. 2.

57 *TI*, 65.

58 E. Hull, *Cuchulain* (L, 1911), 240. Cf. *LSC*, 426.

CHAPTER XV ADVENTURES

1 N. K. Chadwick, *PP*, 91, 93.

2 Ed. and tr. K. Meyer, *RC*, X, 214.

3 We have omitted a section which links the tale with 'Táin Bó Regamna' and presages Táin Bó Cuailnge (see *IHK*, 311 f.).

4 *KCp*, 202 ff.

5 *MC*, III, 201.

6 'Nera and the Dead Man', *ESM*, 522 ff.

7 *KCp*, 215.

8 *Supra*, p. 83.

9 *ESM*, 532 f.

10 *SG*, II, 353.

11 *MD*, IV, 200.

12 *SG*, II, 202.

13 *SG*, II, 343 ff.

14 *LMM*, 586, n. 142.

15 See S. Leslie, *Saint Patrick's Purgatory* (L, 1932), *HWI*, 4 ff.

16 Quoted in Leslie, op. cit., 141.

17 *NM*, 126 ff., 230 ff.; B. Spencer and F. J. Gillen, *The Native Tribes of Central Australia* (L, 1899), 523; G. R. Levy, *The Gate of Horn* (L, 1948), *passim*; Knight, *CGt*, *passim*.

18 Chadwick, *PP*, 100 f.

19 *SC*; *SGS*, VI, 147, VII, 47, ed. and tr. M. Dillon; *HRI*, I, 57 (tr.).

20 Ed. and tr. K. Jackson, *Speculum*, XVII, 377.

21 *EIL*, 102.

22 *Speculum*, XVII, 384.

23 *Chm*, 79 ff., 86 ff. Cf. *infra*, p. 321.

24 Ed. and tr. W. Stokes, *IT*, Ser. 3, I, 183. (*EIL*, 110).

25 *LMM*, 387 f., *EIL*, 107.

25 For references, see A. C. L. Brown, 'Notes on Celtic Cauldrons of Plenty', [*Kittredge*] *Anniversary Papers* (Boston, 1913), 236 ff.

CHAPTER XVI VOYAGES

1 Ed. and tr. K. Meyer, *VB*, I, 2.
2 Ed. and tr. W. Stokes, *RC*, XIV, 24.
3 Ed. and tr. W. Stokes, *RC*, IX, 14.
4 See M. E. Byrne, 'On the Punishment of Sending Adrift', *Ériu*, XI, 97.
5 *ALI*, I, 205.
6 See A. F. Major, 'Ship Burials in Scandinavian Lands', *FL*, XXXV, 113; also *RH*, 16 ff., 20 ff., 39 ff., *FD*, I, 183 f.
7 Malory, XXI, Ch. 5. Cf. *HRB*, 501.
8 *TEF*, I, 315; *Béaloideas*, VIII, 126, 137 f.
9 Ed. and tr. W. Stokes, *RC*, IX, 452, X, 50.
10 In 'The Vision of Adamnán', the fourth heaven has a wall of fire (C. S. Boswell, *An Irish Precursor of Dante* (L, 1908), 37). See M. Eliade, *Myths, Rêves et Mystères*⁴ (P, 1957), 93 f. The Ancient Egyptians believed that the soul at the end of its journey was received into 'the Island of Flame' (*AER*, 115).
11 *RC*, IX, 23. Strabo says that the druids taught that 'fire and water must one day prevail'. (*Geographica*, IV, 4, c. 197, 4).
12 *RC*, XIV, 43.
13 *LIS*, II, 72.
14 *RC*, XIV, 47.
15 II, 6, 10.
16 *TBDd*, 33.

CHAPTER XVII DEATHS

1 Abridged and tr. W. Stokes in *RC*, III, 175.
2 *IHK*, 561.
3 *TBD*; ed. and tr. W. Stokes in *RC*, XXII, 9 etc. For textual analysis see *IHK*, 621.
4 *IHK*, 549, 558, 562, *GHC*, 78
5 *RC*, III, 177 ff.
6 *IHK*, 563.
7 *PKM*, 86 f., *Mb*, 70 f.
8 *SBE*, XLIV, 222 f. (*Śatapatha Brāhmana*, XII, 7). In the *Mahābhārata* (V, 9), the same story is told of Indra and the *asura* Vritra.
9 For references to 'betwixts-and-betweens' see J. de Vries, *Die Märchen von klugen Rätsellösern* (Helsinki, 1928), and *JAOS*, XXXVI, 66 ff.

For discussion, see A. K. Coomaraswamy, 'Symplegades', *HGS*, 453.

10 Ed. and tr. S. H. O'Grady, *SG*, I, 71, 72, II, 74, 76. St Ruadán had prophesied that Diarmait would be struck by the ridge-beam of the king's house in Tara (*SG*, II, 83); Béc's prophecy mentions a black man, blind in the left eye, and a black pig (*SG*, I, 80).

11 *RH*, 172

12 *Fn*, 57.

13 *DT*, 7.

14 *RC*, XV, 296

15 *DT*, 32 ff.

16 *ZCP*, I, 104.

17 *SG*, I, 314 f., 253, II, 354 f., 286.

18 *Ériu*, II, 20 ff.

19 *CR*, II, 5 ff.

20 *Fns*, 23.

21 *IHK*, 560.

22 *RC*, XXII, 58.

23 Ed. and tr. W. Stokes, in *RC*, XXIII, 396.

24 Cf. Ch. XVI, n. 11.

25 Concerning Tuathal cf. *SG*, II, 76, 514. He had long been dead.

26 *Ériu*, II, 23; *SG*, II, 375; *GHC*, 80; *RC*, XXII, 169; *ZCP*, I, 104.

27 *GB*, IV, Ch. II.

CHAPTER XVIII EPILOGUE

1 *Betha Colaim Chille*, ed. and tr. A. O'Kelleher and G. Schoepperle (Urbana, 1918), 352 ff.

2 *VB*, I, 6; tr. K. Meyer.

3 See *SFT*, Chs. VII–IX.

4 *SG*, II, 93.

5 *De Visione Dei*, Ch. IX.

6 See Ch. XIII, n. 7.

7 See Coomaraswamy, 'Symplegades', *HGS*, 453.

8 *RC*, XXVI, 9.

9 *HIF*, 481. Spirits are also banished by being set 'impossible tasks', e.g. draining the sea with a bottomless cup (ibid.).

10 *LGSG*, 327.

11 *HIF*, 339, *FBI*, 255; etc.

12 *PE*, 80 f. The part of the blind Hoðr in the story of Balder, as also the Christian tradition concerning the blind Longius, recalls the blind or one-eyed killers of the Irish kings.

13 See Knight, *CGt*, 17, 22, 59 ff. and *passim*.

14 *TEF*, I, 322.

15 *SG*, I, 75, II, 79.

16 *VB*, I, 63.

17 *RC*, XXXIII, 44 n.

18 W. R. Dawson in *FL*, XLVII, 248; R. T. R. Clark, *Myth and Symbol in Ancient Egypt* (L, 1959), 40, 43, 266.

19 Abbott, *KP*, 389, 330. On enigmatic language in Tantric texts, see *Yg*, 249 ff. Norse 'kennings' were used in magical formulas.

20 *CK*, 94 f. Cf. the contest between Néde and Ferchertne (*supra*, n. 8).

21 *GL*, II, 504 f., 584, III, 108 n. 1.

22 *ZCP*, XIII, 271 ff.

23 Cf. a riddle used in Bushong initiation rites: 'How many people are there in our village? Two, man and woman.' *Africa*, XXV (1955), 140.

24 *MS*, 44.

25 R. Caillois, *Art poétique*[5] (P, 1958), 157 f. (tr.,), following L. Renou, 'Sur la notion de bráhman', *Journal asiatique*, CCXXXVII (1949), 12 f., 17 f., 25, 38, and *passim*.

INDEX

I

II

GENERAL

Acca Larentia, 74
Adam and Eve, 95
Ādityas, 107 f.
Adonis, 295
Agni, 159, 277
aithech, 116, 127
Allthing, 151
ancient personages, 135, 136
animal connections: of hero, 43, 217, 231 f., of warriors, 248 f.; animal helpers, 264, 265
Aphrodite, 293, 295
Apollo, 143
Apsara(s), 276 ff.
Aquinas, St Thomas, 227
archetypes, 105 f., 323 f.; *see also* first
Ares, 295
Aristotle, 152, 227
Aryaman, 99, 108
assemblies, 56, 63, 143, (152), 158, 164 f., 168 ff., 171, 184, 212; *see also* Feasts
Asura(s), 41, 78, 143, 191
Athenians, 152
Aztecs, 191 f.

bachlach, 56 f., 138
Balarāma, 232
Balder, 346
Bali s. Virocana, 77 f.
baptism, 242 f.; unbaptized child, 94, 346
bard, 140 f., 145, 182
battle, 31 ff., 48, 53, 125, 160, 210, 212, 326 f., 331 ff.; in Other World, 306, 308, 343; in 'the North', 123; primeval, 41
Beds of Diarmaid and Gráinne, 288 f., 295
Beelzebub, 128
bees, 128, 136
Beltaine, *see* May
betwixts-and-betweens, 333, 349; cf. 237, 266, 294, 344 ff.

birds, supernatural, 305; *see also* Rhiannon, swans
bird-feathers: thatch of, 261, 310 f., cloaks of, 17
bird-man, 221, 227, 246, 327; bird-men, 276
births of heroes, Ch. XI; *see also* 43, 50, 211, 212, 293
bó-aire, 111 f., 125 ff., *óc-aire*, 62
boar-hunt, 71, 178, 232, 264, 283, 295
board games, 62, 154 f.; *brandub*, 154 f.; *fidchell*, 35, 143, 154, 250, 260, 274, Crimthann's, 301, 312
boat burials, 318
Book of Leinster, 17, 58, 88, 153, 208
bórama, 125
Boswell, J., 227
boundaries, 94; eliminated, 91
'boy without a father', 237, 244 f.
bráhman, 350 f., caste, 16, 112; cf. 137
brandub, *see* board-games
bridge, perilous, 254, 256, 304, 345; Brân as, 47
bull, 124; of province, 280; bull-fight, 59; bull-feast, 245 f.
buried dragons safeguard Britain, 46; cf. head, 48
burner, 66, 156
burning of house, 330, 334, 339 f.

Caesar, Julius, 85, 87, 110, 113 ff., 143, 158
caesarian birth, 237, 345, 349
cailleach, 110, 135
cairn, 188
calendar, Ch. III; Coligny, 84 ff., 93; week, 153, 194, 196; month, 86 ff., 196; black month, 84, 288; calendrical household, 153 f., society, 152; *see also* May, November Eve
Carmichael, A., 11
Carney, J., 283
castes, 112 f., 117; *see also* social system
'cattle-raids', 57 ff., 211, 212

Corrigenda

Page 56, footnote, the *bachlach*
p. 74, line 2, breadth
p. 75, l. 32, shall be
p. 126, l. 35, Munster kings
p. 148, l. 27, the four 'fifths' and the central 'fifth'
p. 183, l. 27, ever seen
p. 227, l. 3, says Jesus
p. 241, l. 8, in combat, he
p. 354, l. 34, Ó Raithbheartaigh
p. 354, l. 40, *Studies and Essays in the History of Science and Learning*
     offered in homage
p. 357, l. 2, *Centaures*
p. 357, l. 25 (also p. 392, n. 33), Sharma
p. 368, note 117, *American Journal of Philology*
p. 369, n. 4, Ch. XIV
p. 372, n. 41, the *bó-aire tánaise;*
p. 374, n. 6, *AESC*, XIII
p. 393, n. 40, only four from the South
p. 397, n. 44 (also p. 363, n. 34), *WAL*
p. 404, n. 56, *infra*, p. 247
p. 407, n. 10, *Infra*, 350
p. 409, n. 52, See n. 28
p. 422, *cyfarwydd,-yd*
p. 423, first . . . foot, 98.